A Web of Our Own Making

There no longer seems any point to criticizing the internet. We indulge in the latest doom-mongering about the evils of social media – on social media. We scroll through routine complaints about the deterioration of our attention spans. We resign ourselves to hating the internet even as we spend much of our waking lives with it. Yet our unthinking surrender to its effects – to the ways it recasts our aims and desires – is itself digital technology's most powerful achievement. A Web of Our Own Making examines how online practices are reshaping our lives outside our notice. Barba-Kay argues that digital technology is a "natural technology" – a technology so intuitive as to conceal the extent to which it transforms our attention. He shows how and why this technology is reconfiguring knowledge, culture, politics, aesthetics, and theology. The digital revolution is primarily taking place not in Silicon Valley but within each of us.

Antón Barba-Kay received a Ph.D. from the University of Chicago's Committee on Social Thought in 2013. He was Professor of Philosophy at Catholic University from 2013–22. He is now Robert B. Aird Chair of Humanities at Deep Springs College – a liberal arts college on a cattle ranch in the Eastern Sierra.

T0381725

A Web of Our Own Making

The Nature of Digital Formation

ANTÓN BARBA-KAY

Robert B. Aird Chair of Humanities, Deep Springs College

CAMBRIDGE
UNIVERSITY PRESS

CAMBRIDGE
UNIVERSITY PRESS

Shaftesbury Road, Cambridge CB2 8EA, United Kingdom

One Liberty Plaza, 20th Floor, New York, NY 10006, USA

477 Williamstown Road, Port Melbourne, VIC 3207, Australia

314–321, 3rd Floor, Plot 3, Splendor Forum, Jasola District Centre,
New Delhi – 110025, India

103 Penang Road, #05–06/07, Visioncrest Commercial, Singapore 238467

Cambridge University Press is part of Cambridge University Press & Assessment,
a department of the University of Cambridge.

We share the University's mission to contribute to society through the pursuit of
education, learning and research at the highest international levels of excellence.

www.cambridge.org
Information on this title: www.cambridge.org/9781009324793

DOI: 10.1017/9781009324786

First published 2023

A catalogue record for this publication is available from the British Library

Library of Congress Cataloging-in-Publication Data
NAMES: Barba-Kay, Antón, 1983– author.
TITLE: A web of our own making : the nature of digital formation / Antón
Barba-Kay, Robert B. Aird Chair of Humanities, Deep Springs College.
DESCRIPTION: New York : Cambridge University Press, 2023. | Includes
bibliographical references and index.
IDENTIFIERS: LCCN 2022041268 | ISBN 9781009324793 (hardback) |
ISBN 9781009324779 (paperback) | ISBN 9781009324786 (ebook)
SUBJECTS: LCSH: Internet – Social aspects. | Social change. | World Wide
Web – Philosophy. | Internet – Philosophy.
CLASSIFICATION: LCC HM851 .B3645 2023 | DDC 302.23/1–dc23/eng/20221227
LC record available at https://lccn.loc.gov/2022041268

ISBN 978-1-009-32479-3 Hardback
ISBN 978-1-009-32477-9 Paperback

For Anna

Contents

Preface and Acknowledgments

We were changed while we were not looking. Digital technology seemed at first like an unmixed boon – an extension of capacities that allowed us to do the *same* but *better*, faster, more efficiently. For people used to the post office, typewriters, and libraries, there was no obvious trade-off to moving online. Nicholas Carr's 2008 article, "Is Google Making Us Stupid?" was a polemical anomaly, during a time when Google was widely hailed as an agent of wide-spreading enlightenment. Perhaps this might have remained the general preju-dice, had there appeared no chasm between our dominant cultural institutions and the sitting president. Even so, it was clear by 2016 that piecemeal changes in how we communicated had added up to another way of doing things, such that someone who had no notion of what was going on online could no longer really understand what was going on off. Things were not just communicated differently but happening otherwise. It was then that I (like many) first took closer notice. This book is the outcome of my efforts to keep everything in mind.

My largest debt is to the thousands of informal conversations about digital technology that have informed my thinking about these changes. While these are far too many, glancing, and incidental to register, I'd like to single out those I had with Nicolas Matte, John McCarthy, Noah Chafets, Tamar Mayer, Josh Shepperd, L. M. Sacasas, Amanda Greene, Dan Silver, and Matthew Clifford. Every time you sent me a link or called attention to some new Very Online sub-trend or made a remark about how you felt your life changing, I took note and followed up; this was my research day-to-day.

I had the chance to take a first stab at these thoughts in early 2017 at the invitation of the Asociación de Filosofía y Ciencia Contemporánea; I'd like to thank those who responded to me there, in particular Alejandro Llano, José M. Torralba, and Lourdes Flamarique. I was able to formally start along these lines of thinking while a Visiting Fellow at the James Madison Program at Princeton University in 2017–18. I'm grateful for the hospitality I received there – especially to Brad Wilson (without whom this project might not have found its publisher) – as well as for the encouraging criticism I received from Charles Rubin and the other fellows. Catholic University afforded me a sabbatical (and some extra leave), which were helpful to the work. An earlier version of Chapter 3 appeared online in *The Point* and in *Eurozine* – thanks to Jon Baskin and Simon Garnett (the respective editors) for working with me on that piece. I'm deeply grateful to Leon Kass, whose friendship has lit the way for me all along. Tisse Takagi was inordinately generous with her time and editorial expertise. Sean Coomey went through the manuscript with a fine-toothed comb, supplying helpful comments at a critical juncture. My greatest debt is to my wife, Anna Feuer, the mirror companion of all these thoughts – *sine qua non*.

Introduction

This Changes Everything (So What?)

Man is his own supreme artifact.

(Louis Mumford)[1]

To be human means to oppose this reality with an emphatic "No."

(Max Scheler)[2]

It is an invention more mind-bending than the printing press, more powerful than the steam engine, more headlong than the train, or car, or jet – a second domestication of fire. Where by Prometheus's gift we once began by taming heat to hearth, we have now made light smart with meaning – cool fire of the disembodied mind. Technology has been, it's true, central to the daily disciplines that make us human ever since Adam and Eve were moved to cover their nakedness with a fig leaf. But it is something else entirely to lose ourselves to it, to be able to code ourselves into it, to become incomprehensible to ourselves without it, to disappear into our image as if into the mirror itself. There is no aspect of our life that is not yielding to it; it is such as to sweep up into itself all our standing assumptions about what we know, and what it is to be connected, and what lies before us in the shape of hopes to come. We are doing things differently. And so we are changing our mind. And so we are putting on a new self: Digital culture is becoming second nature to us. Even now, before your eyes, the world is made over and again.

Yet even as the significance of digital technology has become a front-page mainstay, it is impossible to carry on a reasonable conversation about it – I mean a discussion in which anything is at stake. Not simply because it is all taking place at an electric speed that, by falsifying anything one can put into print before the ink can dry, admits no maturity of reflection. Nor because so many different areas of experience are being so suddenly transformed, with uneven progress and to uncertain purpose. Nor because it is no longer possible for most of us to refrain from making frequent and sustained use of it in order to go about our daily business. Nor even because the stupendous promise of the digital transformation is acclaimed and denounced in terms pitched to such hysteria as to numb the mind. (And numbness is the dominant note of the age – what underlies the alternations of our hanker for stimulation and our burnt-out, overhyped fatigue.) What is remarkable is that it is no longer clear what it would even mean to come to grips with what is happening at all, what the point of criticism could even be in such circumstances. Description and evaluation have been sundered for us in such a way that we no longer know on what grounds one could stand in order to assess digital technology from outside its own terms, that is, in such a way as not to take it all for granted, as a supposition of our thought. *Does it not have many amazing applications? Does it not make life easier in countless ways? Does it not reduce human suffering? Who are you to say what's good or bad, Luddite?* Questions that should make us pause for silence have become rhetorical. Words are not working as they should.

Our discussions about digital technology are notable for their predictable pointlessness, the sense of stalemate underlying the tug of war between denunciation and defense. Almost everyone has serious misgivings about the powers of this new genie we've let loose. Almost everyone also knows that those misgivings have done and will do little to slow its development or moderate its expression. The prevailing note toward digital technology is thus by and large one of ironizing dissatisfaction. (Only about one-tenth of polled Americans think that social media is a force of social good, for instance, while two-thirds of the very people using it think it's bad.[3]) Outside a tech-topian, giddy minority, most people I have spoken to about the consequences of digital technology for their lives are at once disaffected and resigned. Just about every conversation thus consists of acknowledging that it is bad and disruptive in some ways, while being really handy and valuable in others. The bottom line remains that, regardless of how depressing or terrific its uses, it is an inescapable fact, so that it doesn't really matter what we think about it.

This state of mind is at once disorienting and demoralizing – not simply because our thinking makes no headway, but because, in consequence, it represents a loss of intelligence in action. Where our words have no weight, we cannot make sense of our experience. Where nothing's staked in thought, we're past caring about the terms in which we carry it into practice. Our words are crazed from place, our theory is jammed into being ineffective and impractical, even as our practice remains false and dissatisfying. These disparities between what we can think and say and do are the paralysis of those who have lost the way toward meaning, that is, those without a future. And it is impossible to understand what we can do nothing about, when it is all happening before we know it.

Why these disparities?

It no longer seems sensical to ask, for one, whether digital technology is a good idea. Good for what? Good for whom? (Are books a good idea? Is the alphabet?) Not only are the pros and cons incommensurable, but it is not even clear what we are to measure them against: a world without the internet?

The same internet, put to slightly different uses? A better internet? It is only possible to tally plus and minus within a well-defined framework of assessment, whereas we are in a situation in which the framework itself is moving, in which the objects of criticism are so protean as to render criticism inadequate to the task of saying something of lasting help. How can we assess the question of whether the internet is good for American democracy, for instance, when our legal and political institutions were conceived within the organizing habits, tempos, and conventions of the printed word? Similarly, questions about whether the internet is good or bad for "creativity" or "connection" or "knowledge" or "happiness" are misguided and misleading so long as we presume that what we have coming is of the same kind as what we've had. The question is not *whether* the internet is good or bad for this or that. It is how we can still care to tell the difference it makes, when the conditions for our care are themselves moving beyond our recognition of them. Is the internet good for X? It could be. But X will not stay put, when everything promises to change.

The problem of assessment is compounded by the fact that, while no single thing that we ever do online seems momentous, dire effects emerge from aggregates of our collective use. The internet is only ever other people: a permanent elsewhere. Our sense of what we each do at any given time is therefore – whether by method, design, or happenstance – disconnected and self-exempt from the knowledge that we are voting with our digits, that we contribute to what it all adds up to. To an unprecedented and dismaying extent, it really is true that no one is responsible for what is happening. (Everyone else is.) The ugliest effects in this way unfold from humdrum causes. As systems are the watchword of our age, our way of understanding aggregate responsibility for racism or ecocide or economic disparity, so clickbaiting is now the single most powerful force at work shaping the world. Its effectiveness is borne from the small habits of our banality. The more we encourage each other to "change the world," the less we can or do.

These obstacles to critique are all too visible within our practice of critique itself. One might easily draw up a bestiary of the types who have come to populate the range of stances we occupy toward digital tech, say, ye olde cranky coot; the lightheaded posthumanist; the would-be with-it; the meaning-haunted memoirist; the bravely earnest head-in-the-sander, and the glass-half-full-half-emptier, whose brow is knit with care but has some big ideas about how, with just a few tweaks and a dose of can-do-ism, we can make digital technology a force for good. This last type is of course the most common and most reasonable. It is also the most frustrating position, to my mind. I have benefited more than anyone from reading Nicholas Carr, Evgeny Morozov, and Jaron Lanier. But I have been surprised again and again at how, after a few hundred pages of incisive criticism, such authors feel compelled to conclude on a note of contrived and desperate positivity. They offer what cannot but be (in light of the magnitude of the problems they themselves have outlined) anemic and self-helpful advice about how to civilize the internet's world-rending id. As if one could tame the whirlwind by politely requesting that it shift its trajectory a little to the left.

Suggestions have their place. There are several paths before us, we should do our utmost to avoid the worst, and there are policy steps that we could take in order to correct piecemeal features of our online uses (data use and privacy laws, net neutrality, ethics pledges for software engineers, programming tweaks, the breakup of tech monopolies, and so on). But our largest problems are all problems in kind – problems intrinsic to the structure and logic of digital technology itself – not in degree. They are not such as could be set right by high-minded pleas for moderation. Policy issues like those I've named are the merest symptoms of an absolute and comprehensive social harrowing; we should take better care not to be betrayed by our own desires for reassurance. Easy hope is itself a temptation, a false meliorism that clouds our ability to take stock of what is wholesale happening. Hope that offers us five easy steps is nothing but wish-fulfillment: hope meager and for sale.

If not the hope of policy, then, what is the point of writing criticism at all? What may we hope for now from reason (even if not in reason)?

We are the last generation who (barring apocalypse) will remember what things were like without the internet. And so – though by the time these words are printed, many of the names, numbers, and references in these pages will be dated – the best way I know to keep faith with the time is still to insist on noticing just what is taking place. This is not the same as studying to remain neutral or non-partisan; while digital technology is making obvious improvements to our lives, I regard the digital revolution as a basically dehumanizing force. I know that what we have identified as "humanity" is variable and that there can be no neutral measure of what is good for us: I only assume that there is a contrast between what we happen to choose and our heart's desire, between creature comfort and the joy that makes life worth living, between customer satisfaction and leading the life we wish to lead – and that it is our capacity to care for the difference between these two kinds of choices that constitutes our dignity as human beings. Yet whether or not I happen to be right about these things, we should nonetheless continue to insist on attending to the difference between the real as it is and as it really should be. When we no longer care to explain this difference, we will have left off believing in it. I am of a mind with Max Horkheimer that the "denunciation of what is currently called reason is the greatest service reason can render"[4] – that is why it is called *criticism*. My aim here is thus not simply to think and speak, but to call things by their name in order to give voice to them. Because what is not claimed by open clarity is what dominates us. What is unthought and unsaid is what is all powerful. Such is the debt that the truth continuously exacts from our loyalty.

But while I think that making sense is intrinsically harmonizing in its demands – that what is whole, even if only in the knowledge of its absence, heals and repairs – it is also more than understanding for its own sake. Because the digital transformation is not an event occurring at a distance, but a change happening through and within each one of us. We are the subjects and the objects of this revolution; we undertake and undergo it; we find ourselves doing it, as it happens. There is, in fact, no internet outside us; that is its mirage. So we would prefer to focus on questions of legal or technical procedure than to confront the ways we've lost our minds to it, because it is easier to change policy than our own habits of self. (Nor does it ever feel like we have to.) But the impulse to confront technological problems primarily through national politics or through technological fixes is itself at once an unavoidable feature of our time and a symptom of its sickness. These are problems that cannot be addressed wholesale, so long as we continue to deny that we must change our lives. It is only by reclaiming the knowledge that we are answerable for the measure of our own lives that we can remember that our heart is the only place where the future of the world still lies buried.

The only advice I will give in these pages is therefore so simple as to be the wisdom of fools: *If you've started, stop; if you haven't, don't; and if you can't, then keep trying to think what you are doing.* At any rate, have the courage neither to talk yourself out of the problems nor to simplify them through hope for easy solutions, "for hope would be hope for the wrong thing," and the only way to answer to such problems is to first make them more complicated. This is admittedly an impractical, if not a practically absurd, position. But at a moment where words are not working as they should, it is the fate of criticism to become less encouraging the more accurate it is. And, given this choice, I would rather say something crazy true than falsely edifying. Philosophy's purpose is the opposite of technology's in this regard: What is most timely never stands a chance of being profound, much less true or right. Like Cassandra, philosophy's fate is to trade relevance for vision. Even so our hatred may prove our best hope for understanding. And even so our love of what is most alive – still untimely, yet unspent.

The thought animating this book is that digital tools represent a new stage in the history of technology: the moment at which what is understood to be the "natural" – the given and abiding conditions of our being human – and what is understood to be constructed, optional, or "artificial" are fused through our translation of the world into digital terms. The appearance of digital technology marks the moment at which our tools or media are identified with our own conception of what is true, who we are, and what is good. Or rather, not only are they identified with those things (which has in some sort always been the case), but they define them to a new extent by making our attention itself the subject of their measurement, control, and (self-)design. Whereas all previous tools and media have had effects that gradually and indirectly acted on our self-understanding, digital technology acts straightforwardly on *us*; as attention is the single most intimate expression of who and what we are, digital technology is a spiritual technology. That is, it is a technology that increases our control of the world by increasing our control over ourselves. In doing so, it achieves an aspiration that has always been implicit in modern technology itself: the mastery of human nature. Digital technology is our first natural technology.

I'd like to explain here, schematically and provisionally, what this means.

"Digital technology" refers to any electronic device programmed to recognize or produce digital (i.e., discrete) signals. An analogue signal varies continuously: The electric signal transmitting an analogue audio signal modulates over a range of possible values in a manner "analogous" to the sound wave it represents. (Picture an uninterrupted curve or wave of information.) A digital signal, in contrast, registers a specified set of values. It simplifies electric input into fixed possibilities to which the signal answers "on" or "off." (Picture a series of separate dots that, clustered together at intervals, approximate a line of information.) Audiophiles prefer analogue to digital recordings for this reason: Digital sounds clean, yet somehow aseptic; its clarity comes at the expense of the warmer, fuller ambient sound of vinyl. Yet digital audio, precisely by being simplified, compressed, and uniform, is much easier to record, store, and mass disseminate. Its standardization is its transmissibility and therefore its convenience. This trade-off marks every aspect of digital technology.

"Digital technology" and the "internet" are not interchangeable terms, though they are of course connected. What we do on our browser is the most obvious way in which we use digital technology, while the range of all digital sensors and their applications is much wider. A smart toaster, a digital camera, or a given software program is not "the internet," not as we would think of it; yet they generate digital data that may be uploaded, aggregated, analyzed, and controlled for online. By "digital technology" I, therefore mean all kinds of measurement, programming, and processing that, by issuing standardized electronic information, may be integrated and exchanged within a single, widespread network.

There is of course no such thing as "digital technology" at large, beyond our uses of it; and our uses of it are, taken singly, under our control. If I attribute a general character to something as general as "digital technology," it is not because I see in it an agent (or "noosphere") possessed of its own volition, but because I think that there are features of it from which, whatever our particular uses, emerge a general logic of pressures that shapes our responses on the whole. It is for those who make policy to determine whether the generalizations I draw are applicable in any given case. But the claim that no such generalizations are possible or useful is itself a generalization that hides its timidity under the scruples of unattainable certainty. The following five ordinary features of our uses add up to novel functional structures that bear on all we're doing in their terms.

- Digital technology conforms a network in which each node is accessible to every other. Unlike a book, the contents of which are self-enclosed between its covers, a digital device can put you in touch with every other in the world. A smart refrigerator can potentially communicate with (or be hacked by) the Dalai Lama or Kim Jong-un alike.

- The web of such nodes is possible to the extent that all input can be coded into standard signals. Electronic data renders what we say and what we do into a common code: "information." Every node in the system can therefore be in touch with every other at the speed of light.

- Moreover, the system is able to transmit data at such volume as to allow us to easily exchange highly defined sounds, images, and video. It is because of this that the internet can create a compelling alternative reality, can afford access to a space offering new identities and regions of experience.

- The nodes that make up the system are bound to no place in particular. Some version of the digital revolution would have taken place if our only access to the internet had been from our desktops. But it is because laptops, tablets, smartphones, and other smart devices have rendered the network's nodes portable and ubiquitous that digital technology has continued to colonize more areas of our life. The more we carry our devices on our persons, the more completely are our devices identified with us as persons. The more digital sensors gather all kinds of information, the more the web can claim to be really worldwide.

- Finally, our digital devices are designed to connect with and anticipate human intention; they are "smart." This feature bears as much on the way in which algorithmic data analysis can gradually "learn" to reflect and engage our preferences, as it does on how immediately engaging digital devices are for anyone who picks them up. We have in hand the first world-changing technology made for ready use – unlike the printed page, the pulley, or the wheel, it is so intuitive, straightforward, and compelling as to be child's play, fun for every age. We have only to touch and see; it is agreeable to all.

Two different themes are braided together in this list. First: Regarded as a tool, digital technology does not really *do* anything; it does not straightforwardly act on the material world. Unlike steam engines or wheels, it performs no particular physical task. Its usefulness stems rather from the fact that it can be used to measure, analyze, and reconceive all possible tasks. Its scope of action is, for this reason, completely unspecified and unrestricted.

Second: It is a social technology. Its appeal does not reside only in its instrumental means and uses, but in its power to connect us into a single global nervous system. This is in part because information technology is a technology of intentional responses. Its devices are not simply inert for us; by responding to us in terms of information and by making our responses themselves the subject of measurement, they engage us personally and in kind. It is also because our devices connect us not merely to particular others at a distance (as the telegraph did), but with everyone at once. To be connected to the network is to be everywhere in reach of everyone. To amend Marshall McLuhan: The connection is the message.

The five features above thus represent the twin promises of total effectiveness and total responsiveness; that is, digital technology is both a new *tool* for measurement and a new *medium* of being in touch with others. It is this synthesis of measurement with medium – of processing power with data, of quantitative analysis with social reality – that is most distinctive and transformative about it. But just why these two promises really belong to each other as sides of a coin needs better explanation.

Technology's issue has always been to overcome the friction of time, space, matter, and natural circumstance generally: to harness and master the elements, to monitor their use, to surmount their obstinacy to our purposes. Information technology has – in its capacity for total speed, connection, and ubiquity – achieved one version of this objective once and for all. The system as such is neither here nor there; its work is done in no time. (I mean: no human time, no time to speak of.) As nothing seems to intervene between our thinking and our doing, it is now our paradigm for what is completely handy, for usefulness itself.

We think we know that this is not really the case. Our computers and networks are made of cables, antennae, and transistors; these will keep misfiring now and then, so long as they are material. Yet it is significant that this *stuff* is usually no longer in the picture, that it never enters our mind because it never has to. That is, the conditions of interface are disembodied from the conditions of programming and transmission. The material reality of our devices is disengaged from the practical reality of how we use them and what they mean to us. I do not mean that the former is any less real than the latter, but that the illusion of their separation is unshakable for us. Their effectiveness or *handiness* rests precisely on the delusive trick by which we separate their psychic uses from their physical conditions.

Yet this new form of what is handy is also redefining our conception of its content and theme. Any tool or medium is defined by its specific hindrances, by the subject matter that, precisely by resisting our will, shapes it to its uses. A builder's skill arises through experience with the typical behavior of materials, a sculptor's art takes shape through repeated encounters with clay or marble, just as a poet finds her voice within the conventions of orality or literacy, that is, within the tropes, styles, and idiomatic resonances of speech as she finds it. Regarded in this light – as a tool for measuring and analyzing information – the most significant hindrance to digital technology now is the accidental or external one of the availability of data. As Eric Schmidt, Google's former CEO put it: "[T]echnology is not really about hardware and software anymore. It's really about the mining and use of this enormous data to make the world a better place."[5] The AI breakthroughs of the early 2010s came about because computers had become powerful enough to make use of the internet for "training data."[6] In other words, it is no longer matter or processing power that most resists us, but our capacity to gather information about human beings.

We are ourselves the subject matter of digital technology not only in the sense that it is up to us what kinds of phenomena to measure, but because we are ourselves its most important objects of measurement. More than just a means of useful data analysis, digital technology offers us for this reason the satisfaction of total *responsiveness*, the sense of having our intentions engaged, activated, met, and answered. I mean that its appeal consists, on the one hand, in its usefulness as a way of measuring any given phenomenon, and, on the other hand, its allowing us to measure ourselves in just such terms, which in turn allows us to operate, to connect with anyone, and to represent ourselves in ways that are redefining social reality. Its technical aspiration is thereby (also) a social and political aspiration. If usefulness is power, then maximum usefulness is maximum power, that is, power over ourselves – the power to measure, represent, and define ourselves and others as we will. Rather than acting on things through time and matter (as other tools do), and rather than communicating through time and matter (as other media do), digital technology acts on and communicates through the behavior, thinking, and attention of human beings as such.

The digital era thus marks the point at which our concern will be mainly the control of human nature through our control of what we are aware of and how we attend to it. I mean something analogous to our notion of the "Anthropocene." Whereas the Anthropocene refers to the age at which the natural world can no longer be understood without reference to human influence and implication, the digital age denotes the moment at which our tools will become ways of acting *into* ourselves – that is, the moment at which our tools will become coextensive with our habitual acts of consciousness – such that the kind of creature we are becomes a technological issue and choice. If the Anthropocene marked the point at which we more or less mastered the elements to human purposes, the digital era marks the point at which our own thoughts and acts will come to be defined by the uses of digital technology and by our self-interpretation in light of them. Technology will no longer be one causal force within the broader horizon of human nature and culture; it will provide the terms of the horizon itself.

To speak of a transformation in our "nature" may sound either exaggerated (since nature doesn't change) or empty (since what we mean by "nature" is itself on the move). As there is no longer wide and clear agreement about what the phrase "human nature" means, each of these charges deserves response.

In the context of discussions about our posthumanist future, "nature" is usually equated with biology. The line between technology and nature is drawn at bionics – the difference between biological enhancement and modification, say, or the point at which devices might be surgically implanted into our arm or eye or brain. Yet far from identifying the point of no technological return, these are sci-fi red herrings that miss the point. Because, if we are spending most of our waking hours on digital devices, if we reach for them upon waking and only set them down for sleeping, if this technology is our single most important means for connecting to others and understanding what we do, if it is recasting our notions of what human beings are for, then it makes no decisive difference whether the devices are physically implanted in our retina or cortex. There is more to human nature than biology: Digital technology already touches us much more deeply than it would if it were merely under the skin. If and when we start wearing Google Glasses (or Amazon Echo Frames), we will of course literally see the world as those products would like us to. But we already (and increasingly) do.

While it remains the case that we are born in given places, with given genes and to given families, our digital uses are permeating our view of everything down to and including our physical bodies. It is not only that digital modeling makes possible breakthroughs in genetic sequencing and biomedical engineering. Nor that data analysis expands medical diagnoses of disease in ways that outstrip the accuracy and experience of any human doctor. Nor even that the internet puts at our disposal scads of information about any symptom or syndrome or drug in ways that turn us each into amateur (hypochondriac) physicians. It is that our daily activities and our conception of ourselves are being progressively refigured through our awareness of their quantification. As our devices measure our sleep, our steps, our heart rate, our temperature, our Covid exposures, our locations, our routes, and so on, we are ourselves incentivized to "optimize" our practices construed in precisely such terms. The transformation of activity into data points transforms our own awareness and conception of our bodily motion in the same way that wearing a wristwatch transformed our conception of time (down to the second). Bodies are not (just) organs, but the life of what we do. Digital uses are expanding our control over our biological nature by changing the scope of what we can quantify, what we are aware of, what we think we are accountable for. Overcoming these material conditions has not made us omnipotent over them, but it has changed our orientation toward what we are constrained by and how we respond to it. Digital uses make for digital bodies; digital culture is digital nature.

To speak of a transformation of our nature may therefore also sound empty, since it has always been the case that technology has concerned itself with overcoming natural limitations and since it has of course always been the case that culture has informed our sense of nature. The definition of human nature has been drawn and redrawn by different cultural norms, which themselves change under technological pressure. Human beings are (unlike other animals) self-constituting; that is, what is "natural" to us is never simply a matter of fact, but a consequence of what we take ourselves to be. "Natural" connotes either "normal" or "whatever is external to human design" – and both of those categories are relative to our technological capacities. As Bruno Latour puts it, "the very notion of culture is an artifact created by bracketing Nature off."[7]

Technology has played no single, well-defined causal role within cultural history as such. The formative power of digital technology has arguably been much swifter and more totalizing than that of the stirrup or the phonetic alphabet, say, which were inventions of similar consequence. (I'll return to this point below.) Yet digital technology is also not simply more powerful than previous technologies, but altogether different in kind. What is transformative is the extension of quantification into our own attention, and our reinterpretation of our connections and identities into those terms. It is this quality that, as I'll explain, makes it "natural" – different in kind from previous inventions because it achieves the basic principle of technology as such: freedom through mastery.

Consider, by way of initial comparison, the way we think of mirrors as neutral depictions. We take mirrors to be different in kind from paintings, sculptures, or drawings of us. We presume that they do not show us one possible version of our appearance, but our appearance as it looks to other eyes and in itself. They offer us information that is not colored by another's perception of it. Yet by *existing at all* as instruments of objectivity, by becoming available to us as instruments of impersonal depiction, they have had all the more influence over how we see ourselves. Modern mirrors, mirrors as we know and use them, are a tool that, once invented, made neutral depiction thinkable by making it visible. By offering an impersonal view, they changed how we picture, dress, and fashion ourselves. By providing an instrument and metaphor of neutrality, they profoundly transformed early modern art, science, and philosophy. Yet it is their very transparency that makes it hard to bring their effects into view.

Digital quantification has the same character, the same power of transformative neutrality; data is the mirror that, seeming only to reflect, changes our assessment of what we see. Because, once possible, the collection of digital data becomes imperative – one can choose *not* to collect data, but one cannot unsee the possibility of collecting it (with its demonstrable benefits). We all know by now that numbers do not tell the story, that metrics are themselves conditioned if not distorted by human preferences, that there are genuine ambiguities and complexities not captured by measurement. There is nonetheless an irresistible temptation *not* to know this, and therefore to continue to quantify as possible, because data is straightforwardly actionable as the complexities of the world are not. Shall we choose not to gather data that promises a measurable improvement (that saves lives or money, that raises test scores, that makes hiring practices more impartial) for the sake of protecting the ambiguous space of human freedom? If we do choose that, we have now become accessory to the ill we have identified, accomplices to its subsistence. The desire to protect privacy (by arguing against self-driving cars, say), once quantified, amounts to a proposal to defend drunk driving. The desire to preserve human judgment (by arguing against sentencing algorithms, say), once quantified, amounts to a proposal for protecting racist judges. What we can measure simplifies our sense of what we can't, forcing the latter into view in just such terms.

Choosing not to know is, like choosing not to look in the mirror, a choice that becomes ineluctable with the possibility of measurement. As there can be no objective way to measure quantitative benefits against qualitative ones, the imperative to quantify continues to gain ground as authoritative, not to mention the fact that there are always better measurable approximations of what is opaque or intangible. Quantification may not be "neutral," but it certainly seems more neutral to us than other ways of resolving arguments about ethical goods. The point is not that data leaves no room for argument, but that it conceals it under the seeming neutrality of quantification. By seeming to offer a transparent view of our own thinking and doing, it thereby disappears into our image of ourselves.

This is the first of three senses in which it is a "natural technology": As a technology of measurement and quantification, it proposes a choice that seems no choice. In implicitly selecting for more information over less, it is also (in a second sense) the formative expression of a new system of norms, a new way of understanding what is true (what is objective, say, compared to what is "biased") and what is good (what is equitable or optimized, say, compared to what is racist or inefficient) through precise, aggregated measurements.

I do not mean that the imperative for digital quantification is the expression of a particular theory of what is valuable; it would be misleading to think of it as defining a new culture (one more, alongside the Hittite and Incan, or alongside oral culture and print culture). It is rather a new kind of attitude toward culture and value altogether, a new vantage from which to monitor how we behave, how we see ourselves, and what we strive to become. Digital technology is a natural technology to the extent that its seeming neutrality becomes our highest arbiter of reason and therefore the highest measure of our own self-understanding; its authority is the greater precisely by virtue of *seeming* to set itself beyond human decision or preference. Just as noting that a particular conception is "politically motivated" or "culturally constructed" has become a stock way discrediting it (since what is constructed is contingent by being one possibility of many), digital technology provides the standard by which all particular human judgments may be seen to be partial and therefore arbitrary and therefore flawed. It is the means by which scientific efficiency – neutrality – becomes the good that, without seeming to, is giving ethical content and contour to human practices.

Digital technology is therefore in this second sense a natural technology because we are ourselves the medium of its uses; because, in using it, we seem to gain a window onto how human beings "really" are, and therefore how we should be. The quantification of human behavior is by no means new. Statistics as we know it – literally: "the science of the state" – arose in eighteenth-century Europe as the means of bureaucratic control, the rationalized management of industrializing populations. And choice architecture – the engineering of human preference through "nudges" in design – has long been a feature of public spaces and buildings, of commerce and advertising, of military campaigns, and of any undertaking in which an imperative to maximize aggregate outcomes has driven the use of measurement. What is different about digital technology is the ease and refinement with which the data can be gathered. What is measurable can be controlled for; and our data points now extend (in principle) to all activities of waking life.

Contrary to our most common way of expressing our worries about digital meddling and control, such power is not simply exercised on us from the top down, by corporate data-mining, predatory algorithms, authoritarian surveillance, or malicious disinformation campaigns. These remain all too convenient bugbears to the extent that they place responsibility at a distance from us. No one in particular controls the attentional incentives of the whole system; its design is (at the most general level) of our self-design. I mean that choice architecture only influences us to the degree that we identify who we are and what we do with the logic of digital exchange. The design of human behavior is possible because we have already internalized the conditions for it as transparently useful, convenient, or necessary. Control through quantification is effective only to the extent that we have already opted in and fitted ourselves to its terms. Even as we claim to find surveillance abhorrent, we long to go viral – to be seen is to be valuable.

Digital information does not therefore simply register what would be the case anyhow, but (like mirrors) it creates new objects of attention, inquiry, and interpretation by making it possible to notice and respond to data in new ways. More than offering a new way to value neutrality or a new way of depicting human acts through their quantification, it is a functional medium of consciousness itself and a new way of imagining ourselves in connection to others. Its role as a social medium is not simply to help us transact social relations but to refigure them. The friction inherent to the medium is, as I've said, not just processing speed but the checks that others' intentions place on mine. Its matter is what we and others think, mind without end. Like any other medium, it shapes its contents in definite directions. But unlike any other medium, it puts our attention immediately in contact with that of others, without seeming intermediary. This side of it – the third sense in which I take it to be a natural technology – requires particular explanation.

Attention has always been in demand; it tends to translate into influence, because whoever has your ear is on the tip of your tongue. But our proxies for attention had been only very approximate ones (sales, votes, subscriptions). No one gave much thought to attention as such before the end of the nineteenth century for that reason; nor had there ever been a way to measure and track the sum total of mentions or references to something in casual exchange. Digital technology is a technology of attention not only in that it makes it possible to quantify attention itself in an immediate and unambiguous way (clicks, likes, downloads, views), but in that it becomes our way for measuring and understanding social value. "Likes" are no longer understood as a proxy for attention; they mark our conception of attention itself as a "resource." Just as being diagnosed with a particular psychological disorder at once helps us identify our symptoms and allows us to start thinking of ourselves in certain ways, attentional quantification both diagnoses a new category of good and allows us to begin to regard ourselves as defined by it. As quantitative information tends to defeat qualitative knowledge, it is because we *can* quantify likes that we are tempted to identify them with social standing and value itself.

Attention is an impalpable good; it does not necessarily amount to anything else (as Facebook, Uber, and many other start-ups initially find). Yet as a medium of attention, exchange, and participation, another mark of digital technology is that it is *ideal* or virtual – its objects are images; ideas; words; and other specific, encoded acts of attention. It is a form of exchange in which minds seem to act directly on each other, without the friction of temporal or material intermediary. Thoughts have always acted on thoughts in speech or writing. But speaking has a restricted scope; books have always been defined by the tempo of printed matter; and not everyone could participate in publishing, radio, or television. Objects of culture have been material; and what is material separates and binds people precisely because, by having an independent existence outside them, we can gather to it in common. Ideas have, in contrast, never pressed and repercussed so directly on each other as they do online, without any apparent intermediary through which to relate to others. Digital ideas are as images in a mirror – the harder to see by virtue of their immediate presence in response. There is nothing in this world but other people's minds.

More than its attentional and ideal character, however, digital technology is transformative because it affords us a basis for universal comparison. Cultures have always been orders of comparison; it is because I distinguish or equate myself to others and the norm that I can aspire to act and think in my own way. But digital technology makes the possibility of comparison, the conception of it, universal; it replaces the function of particular cultures in this sense. It is, in other words, not simply a repository of our social identities, but the master metaphor that allows them all to be translated into the same terms.

The clearest expression of the social significance of digital technology is the platform. A *platform* is, etymologically, a ground-plan, a "flat form." In digital terms, platforms are the level playing fields that set the terms within which we can contrast ourselves to others. It is to the extent that the input of each is expressed in standard kinds of information that all our identities can be counted up, aggregated, and related to each other within the form. Just as the compass transformed our conception of navigation by allowing us to venture into the unknown – creating a new total map, because every destination could be geospatially located and charted in advance – so does the platform provide a basis for total human comparison.

The two basic elements of any platform are photographs (or footage) and categorical input. Pictures are (like numbers) themselves specular, mirror-like: They propose themselves to us as objective data, quantifiable objects of attention. By "categorical input" I mean the fixed ways in which the platform solicits information about us, as well as the tags, handles, emojis, and standard terms, which, ready-made for aggregation, make up our self-expressive vocabulary. Our platform identity thus emerges from an amalgam of typified, voluntary input in terms that can be measurably contrasted in specified ways to all others. It is only by becoming known quantities that we know how we count with others.

That expressing ourselves within the terms of a platform changes how we think of our own identity and our own connection to others is obvious. There is no question that our virtual identities raise our control over how we come across and who we are to a higher power. The growing political salience of identity as such is partly owing to our new scope of virtual self-representation. As platforms are commercial services, there is an underlying incentive to develop our identity precisely within the terms they offer. And the quantification of identity undoubtedly affords us new ways of precisely measuring diversity, equality, and privilege.

Yet these new powers of digital self-representation rest on the extent to which we flatten ourselves to conform to the platform's terms. It is by becoming a number that we can more freely define ourselves: The popularity of platforms demonstrates that we desire standardized comparison more than some other form of incomparable authenticity. I do not mean that there are not enough boxes in the menu to cover our individuality, but that the platform disambiguates and standardizes the menu of boxes that are there to be checked at all. It is not that we are all becoming the same; it is that we are distinguishing each other by making use of the same system of operative contrasts, and therefore that our differences are becoming the same in kind. Nor is it the case that mass typification gravitates toward harmony or agreement (it's the opposite, if anything); it is that platforms create the encompassing conditions for imagining all social relations as parts of the same normal whole. The platform is a great panoptic mirror in which, by regarding each other, we see ourselves. It is the world we have in common.

The overwhelming attractions of widespread social comparison have concentrated an unprecedented degree of attention in a few places. No single source of print or television ever reached as many people as the most popular platforms routinely do now. And, just as large cities have always been at the cutting edge of world culture, the concentration of digital attention, the sheer speed and scope of exchange within its global cosmopolis, has acted as a catalyst for widespread cultural change. As comparison is relation, relation is communication, which is, in turn, a stimulant to innovation and social transformation. As Montesquieu puts it: "The more communicative peoples are, the more easily they change their manners, because each man is more a spectacle for another; one sees the singularities of individuals better."[8]

Never has such change been struck so fast. The printing press and firearms were technological watersheds with world-historical implications, but they took decades or centuries to assimilate. Digital technology has, by contrast, so changed human life within a couple of decades that teens are today growing up in an altogether new cultural environment – with different expectations, habits, and standard points of orientation from their parents'. There is now arguably a greater chasm between someone age twelve and someone age fifty (or forty, or thirty) than there ever was between people separated by a millennium of pharaonic rule in ancient Egypt. The fact that we must make a concerted effort to remember how we did things "before" digital technology bespeaks the abrupt and thorough extent to which it has captivated our imagination of the ordinary.

The runaway success of digital technology as a natural technology in the three senses I've outlined – as an instrument of quantification, as a mirror of aggregated human behavior, and as a cardinal mode of social relation – consists, in sum, not simply in its efficiency, but in its becoming our shared, working metaphor for what is universal. One might gloss over the five features I've started with above as implying the possibilities of total connection, total speed, total experience, total ubiquity, and total attention. These are not simply measurable tasks, but aspirations resting on the imaginary appeal of what is "global," what is maximally shared and true. Data analysis has eclipsed human judgment as our shared conception of what is most authoritative. The quantification of attention has become our central medium for thinking about the policies of human behavior and about the exercise of our own self-determination. And platforms are replacing nations as our most important social imaginaries.

It might be said that I am overestimating the real significance of digital technology, that the circumstances of our life offline go on basically the same, even as our hypertrophic imagination and our capacity for virtual delusion grow by leaps and bounds. One of the strangest features of our time is precisely the disparity between technological exhilaration and our sense of social, political, and cultural exhaustion – retrenchment, logjam, frustrated variations on old themes, and scant headway on longstanding problems. There is genuine uncertainty about whether digital technology represents a transformation or whether it is no big deal really, a parallel universe in which our imagination finds itself at frictionless play. Yet what is "imaginary" is no less real than the physical – our bodies, families, laws, and nations are not (just) brute facts; they draw their meaning from rapports that, though invisible and intangible, bind us to others through our being committed to picture them in certain terms. The world as a whole only ever exists in the act of our imagining the connections that sustain it. Digital technology is a new act of the imagination: a new figure of the world.

It is nonetheless very telling that we continue to want to oppose the real to the virtual, that the contrast between them remains intelligible and compelling to us. Part of what is strange and new about the construction of our virtual social imaginary is that it is, as I've mentioned, apparently unconstrained from material conditions, such that it is changing our sense of what counts as a condition at all. Our thinking and imagination have never been so starkly disconnected from (what we have come to call) "reality." Any new medium of communication demands a retranslation of thought into its terms. But translation into digital terms is specifically untethered from material circumstance, in ways that both amplify our sense of autonomy and make autonomy harder to situate with respect to offline reality. The transposition of our values into the digital realm represents a sort of bargain: We enlarge our freedom only so long as we continue to identify it with dematerialized digital activity, which in turn reinforces the need to keep doing so, regardless of whether other aspects of offline reality are in keeping with it. As our attention to words, ideologies, and virtual racket intensifies, our practical possibilities are bleached and diminished.

But this formulation suggests, falsely, that our practice is not itself coming to be established in digital terms, whereas it is one of the themes of this book to show how thoroughly the digital revolution encompasses all aspects of human life, how the internet does not keep online. The contrast between the virtual and the real is itself a virtual one. Yet the digital world also establishes the priority of what is virtual as the site and origin of what matters to us. Hannah Arendt writes that the project of modern technical man is "a rebellion against human existence as it has been given, a free gift from nowhere (secularly speaking), which he wishes to exchange, as it were, for something he has made himself."[9] Science fiction had long pictured this exchange as corporeal: We would come to fabricate and program every aspect of our bodies, our food, our dwellings, and our climate, severing our natal dependence on nature once and for all. We have now achieved the same dream of self-determination not by transforming our bodily existence, but by translating our vision of what is valuable into online terms, terms in which our will has greater latitude. That is, as we have not so easily succeeded at mastering our given natural and historical circumstances, we now have found out and adopted the means to change our way of thinking – about them and each other.

A modern, secular person reflecting on medieval Christianity's view of the afterlife sees in it a kind of alienated projection of human longing, or an instrument of clerical control, or a mythic consolation for suffering and injustice on earth. But as heaven and hell were as real as any other motives actuating all who lived in view of them, the digital world (even if it possesses no physical reality) is real because we actively make it so, because we transpose and sublimate our terrestrial desires into its excarnate, virtualized understanding of them in ways that seem to make us more powerful. The difference between the afterlife and the virtual imaginary is that the former rests on faith, "the evidence of things unseen," while the latter rests on the evidence of things enumerated by principles of quantification that are self-evident to us. Faith is belief in personal forces; technology is control of impersonal ones. Yet the imperative to interpret what *cannot* be measured in terms that *can* be is not itself a datum of scientific knowledge. And that imperative or desire arises from the fact that what is given can coincide with what is wrought in just such terms. So that, if there is an abiding difference between what is "really" up to us and what "seems" to be up to us (in online terms), we will continue to want to simulate the difference away. The digital age will therefore be marked by our continued effort to completely identify offline reality with online experience and by agonizing frustrations at their insurmountable, residual differences.

Our unease toward digital technology is therefore borne from the fact that we are sensitive to its costs, to its destabilizing all familiar patterns of life. It will reform every last cultural practice into its terms. Yet "digital culture" is not analogous to older senses of the word: "culture" suggests "cultivation" – the gradual growth of human intention into forms that exceed anyone's design. Forms of culture are forms of time. As nothing takes time online, there can be no lasting, stable culture from it. There are trends or brainstorms of the hive mind, but they do not accumulate. Online trends differ from culture as a random throng differs from a body of people. The internet is not so much a solid form as a liquid, or an ether; it is a solvent of other forms. As McLuhan says: "[A]t the speed of light, there is nothing but violence possible, and violence wipes out every boundary"[10] – not because communication in these terms must be hostile or mean, but because, by freeing us from time, it supposes permanent disruption and upheaval. If settled norms, practices, laws, and places are our roots, digital culture is uprooted and uprooting.

At the same time, we continue to express allegiance to it because digital technology has become our clearest metaphor for universality as such, for humanity, for the global village, for what is always everywhere the case – for what is maximally true about everyone regardless of their place, for what is impersonally so beyond belief. By giving us access to new kinds of self-determination, identity, and voluntary power, it is our most vivid instrument of freedom. It offers an experience of time that, by dissolving ties to place and history, allows us to begin again. It is the most powerful instrument of equality there has ever been; it allows us to compare human beings in ever more minute and thorough ways. Data is a new form of control and self-control. Above all, it is our way of figuring neutrality as the highest form of objectivity – as the way we value what outstrips particular values.

It is this conflict between social turmoil and the goods we must now pursue in digital terms that makes for our anxiety, for the uncertainty of our response, such that our thinking and our doing – our criticisms of digital technology in theory and our uses of it in practice – have been dissociated. The effects of digital technology are hard to see not just because it is hard to see the mirror itself for what it is, but because we cannot yet fully fathom the depth of our own commitments to it, that is, to our new vision of ourselves.

There is only one other invention that bears comparable imaginative significance and that therefore has a fundamental relationship to digital technology: I mean the bomb. (One might add the rockets used for the Apollo space missions; but they were in fact extensions of nuclear of technology and its uses. The rocket is the bomb pointed outward into space.) Arendt pointed out that the development of nuclear weapons made available a new, existential sense of shared humanity, since everyone on earth found themselves equally vulnerable to the same threat.[11] The internet was invented by military researchers precisely as a way of diluting the threat of the bomb: If a nuclear weapon destroyed one particular hub of communication, the other nodes could continue speaking to each other. So that, whereas the bomb was conceived as a potentially localized event – an event with a specific radius or horizon – the internet was invented to decentralize and dislocate communication. The system as a whole cannot be pinned down because it occupies no one place.

The bomb made outright war between world powers suicidal; in its guarantee of mutual destruction, it thereby weaponized every *other* conflict and turned everything *else* into a proxy for war, especially information, ideology, and propaganda. The internet is now that everything else; it is war waged otherwise and elsewhere without end. Hacks and cyberattacks, (dis)information campaigns, meme- and info-wars are the continuation of war by other means, now that all-out war has been displaced from reality.

The bomb and the internet are also ultimate technologies: inventions that express the finality and totality of human connection in terms that make it impossible to imagine anything beyond them. They are universal possibilities, totalizing systems of relation. One of them represents the brute fact of physical destruction, the other is the ideal one of "merely" virtual exchange. But both of them express the possibility that everything could happen to everyone at once: the singularity at which everyone is instantaneously in touch. Both of them are the metaphors by which we imagine ourselves unified into a simultaneous reality and a single humanity; they have magnetized and reconfigured everything else outside them into their terms. Both of them have been zealously promoted as instruments of world peace; both of them are expressions of our permanent readiness for total war – or rather, they make nonsense of the very difference between peace and war. Both are forms of maximum shared connection, of common destiny, purpose, or fate; they are the doomsday ends of our secular eschatology. The global village is manifest in bomb and internet: the bomb is the internet in body, the internet is the bomb in spirit. Both of them offer the attraction of total knowledge and control, the pinnacle of technical achievement that puts an end to time as we knew it. Both therefore make it impossible to imagine the future. One of them represents oblivion; the other memorializes every human thought. The one is heat to incinerate suns; the other is light containing the world in thought. They are, taken together, the omega answering the alpha of creation. Both are machines for killing time, no wonder.

The work that follows focuses on four connected themes. To summarize them: I first explain how we should understand our digital shift alongside other momentous shifts in the history of media – from oral cultures to written ones, from written to printed, and from printed to digital. As each of these prior changes involved momentous consequences to our conceptions of knowledge and time, the digital does too. This rehearsal of media begins from zero, so some of these themes will be elementary to savvy readers. But beyond my greed for putting the big picture into my own words, I am arguing that digital technology is also something more than just another member in the historical sequence of media shifts by pointing to the unprecedented ways in which it integrates medium with tool, and therefore knowledge with its uses.

Second, I consider more generally what technology is and what it means – the sense in which it has always been part of what's human and the sense in which it has qualitatively changed within the past few hundred years. My focus here is on our chronic ambivalence toward modern technology – on why it is that we anxiously regard it as having a runaway mind of its own, even as we continue to identify our own aspirations more and more closely with it. I'll suggest how these two apparently incompatible principles arise as concomitants of the same dynamic. Modern technology revolutionizes our social ideals and expectations by supplying us with the material conditions for new forms of freedom and equality, even as it also promises to destabilize any given social arrangement.

I show, third, how it is that, in transforming our means of relating to each other, the internet is reshaping our basic notions of what counts as society or politics at all. Our new way of communicating is reconfiguring our senses of community and of ourselves as members who conform it. These changes are in turn redefining our larger-scale "social imaginaries" – our perception of what it means to be citizens of a democracy and of a nation – in typically polarizing ways.

Finally, I look at the ways in which digital technology bears on our aesthetic sense of our own experience of reality. I look at three central ideals driving the commercialization of experience, the rise of AI, and the many ways in which we are increasingly reinterpreting ourselves in terms of our machines – aspirations that motivate our continued participation in digital services. I call them "the ideal of frictionlessness," "the ideal of obedience," and "the ideal of perfection." In pursuing these ideals, we are thereby reshaping the notion of what is valuable about human beings. I do not think that we "worship" digital technology as a new god. But to the extent that we continue to identify the progress of our culture with technological progress, to the extent that we see ourselves and our goals in its terms, and to the extent that our conception of perfection is intrinsically connected to our conception of the divine, digital technology will continue to occupy a role undeniably analogous to that of religion in other ages. It provides us with our clearest collective allegory of what is objectively highest and good.

These shifts in norms, institutions, and aspirations have not taken place all at once or once and for all – as parts of a wholesale civilizational quest, they are each open-ended, uneven, and ongoing. Our ideal of digital connection or perfection is, like all ideals, incompletely achievable. I am proposing, rather, that we can say something about the new *kind* of goods that we increasingly aspire to and about how those goods are making a decisive change to our conception of who we are. Nor is this whole trajectory necessary: Technology does not "do" or "want" anything of its own, even if it nonetheless contains a logic that unfolds in spite of you and me, whatever our intentions for it happen to be. Nor, much less, do I mean to claim that this trajectory is good. Whatever boons it offers – and those are untold and undeniable – we are, in my view, continuing to trade away the richest possibilities of human vision, the kinds of ideals that justify our very existence, for the lesser comforts of safe and predictable rule by data. Nor, finally, am I preaching for the return to the not-so-good old analogue stone age. Some things are better and some are worse in every era, and the situation preceding digital technology was beset with its own problems, which, while no less than totally important, have now faded from urgency. It may well be that all we can accomplish is to see more clearly what was always there but could not be brought to light except by being lost, in hindsight. This is nonetheless our time to live; beyond defense or denunciation, it remains the role of criticism to insist on what is specifically at hazard at each juncture as our way of keeping awake to it.

If the present technological age has a lasting gift for us, it is to urge as decisive the question of what human beings are *for*, what the point of us is at all. There is no straightforward answer to this, except insofar as our hopes are expressed in our attachment of thinking to doing. The world can be neither understood nor helped, unless we realize ourselves responsible to it. And there is no other demonstration of responsibility than the common miracles of life, work, and devotion. We can be lucid in theory only because we are bound to practice; it is our capacity to build and love in deed that creates the world anew by rendering it intelligible. It falls to us to mind and to respond. Now and even now, before our eyes – that is only ever where we find ourselves.

Left to Our Own Devices

Just as water, gas, and electricity are brought into our houses from far off to satisfy our needs in response to a minimal effort, so we shall be supplied with visual or auditory images, which will appear and disappear at a simple movement of the hand, hardly more than a sign.

(Paul Valéry)[1]

A child whose natural hardware is not so different from that of every child ever born picks up a smartphone and is mesmerized in no time. Children want to make the adult world their own, they imitate and try things on for size, but they are met with steep obstacles everywhere. Eating with a fork, tying one's laces, and playing with a ball (let alone driving a car or baking a pie) require disciplined acculturation. Anyone who desires to practice those things requires standing, gradually acquired habits of patience and dexterity. Children need coaxing, suggestion, and correction to sustain efforts whose fruits they are not yet in the position to believe in. They cannot at first see how drudgery can be redeemed by excellence and art. But no such barrier presents itself in the case of the phone or computer. They are devices that grant immediate satisfaction; to use them is to enjoy them. How long must we be asked to practice reading or an instrument before we are sustained by our own delight in them? Most parents, in contrast, soon find themselves placing terms on how long and often their children may enjoy their time before the screen. I have seen my young niece, barely old enough to toddle and to prate, fully pacified by a game that consisted in nothing other than popping animated bubbles on a screen at her touch. When the time was up, she wept bitterly and every time. Screen time is, like sucking your thumb, an activity that needs little introduction. It recommends itself.

"Interfacing" – the way in which we engage digital devices like the smartphone, tablet, and computer – is fun because it so easily answers to your own capacities. It meets you where you are and confirms your ability for it. You need just eyes and fingers for starters. Data bolts through fiber-optic cables in staccato trains of thought – information pulsed out into light. Just so, interface is a medium you work out in terms of pressure, motion, and location within a defined "window" of vision. One or two fingers are required, but no great coordination. Accuracy is not so important, since mistakes are as easily made as (auto)corrected. Only two basic acts are required for interface: directing and pressing, pointing and clicking – all these are versions of the instructions "here" and "elsewhere." These acts express two directions of logical motion: further *in* to a menu or program, or *out* toward a beginning screen, a fixed place to which all options are subordinate. (That is your "home," the settled place from which every project gets its start.) Where the printed page is arranged sequentially, from horizontal A to Z laid out before you, the digital window is a medium we press to *enter* into or *escape* from. (And to "enter" is also to "return.") Once this twofold character of responses is grasped, the content makes itself available to your inspection. There is little or nothing else to pick up, where all is there at hand.

There has never been any other mechanism like it, any other that is so ready, mobile, and "friendly" to use. It is, in this sense, a natural technology, a tool that is effective by being compelling in its own right. The basic satisfaction of using digital devices is, in other words, something more primal than reading and writing, perhaps even more than walking and speaking (which inhere in us, but are cultural achievements nonetheless). Interface is, as its designers claim, in some deep way, *intuitive*: self-evident. (I have been in several households where it was the young children who were the ones able to help their parents figure out technical glitches on their devices – is there any other tool for which that has been the case?) Like the postulates of Euclidean geometry or "I think, therefore I am," it seems to follow from our familiar sense of how things already are. It used to be that film and television were the most captivating talkers in a room. It's rare now to attend a play or to watch TV without someone taking a peek at his phone. We have discovered that sitting through a movie is a slog.

To call them something "natural" is not to call such devices good. But it would be a mistake not to notice the remarkable and unique intimacy with which digital media, of all media and tools ever devised, lay claim to our attention. So long as we miss the causes and character of this transparency, the ease and simplicity by means of which we fall into it, we overlook the fact that its power is all derived from its kinship and access to the workings of our conscious mind. It is because it is becoming so closely matched to us that we increasingly see through it, that we are unable to distinguish our world from the digital. So in asking what is digital, I am also asking who we are becoming (and what becomes of us).

1.1   THE DIGITAL IS A NEW MEDIUM, THAT IS, A NEW FORM OF THOUGHT AND TIME

The term "medium" has a baggy range of meanings – architecture and sculpture are media, in one sense, as are smoke signals and Morse code. All of these are shapes that bear our meanings. But there are hierarchies of media, media within media. Some media are world-shaping and culture-defining as others are not: Painting and basket-weaving have been more or less important at different times, but they have probably never been the single most important means through which a culture figured itself. The digital, on the other hand, takes its place alongside other transformations of media's centers of gravity; it represents a "break in continuity" (as Henry Adams called modern industry[2]) of which there have been but very few: from silence to speaking (a special case), from speaking to writing, from writing to printing, from printing to computing.

The digital belongs in this sequence and does not. It belongs because it is now our predominant means of conveying meaning. Like other media, it is thereby also a kind of environment, an atmosphere of resonances and operative assumptions, a state of mind – a lens as inconspicuous as water is to fish. It does not belong, however, because it is as much a medium (a way of communicating) as it is a tool (a way of doing). Nor is it just one tool. Its versatility of purposes is so astounding as to make it a master tool. That is, it does not help us to perform just one specific task better (which is what most tools do), but it is the means by which any number of tasks are transacted – buying and selling, reading and messaging, travel and logistics, photographing and recording, working and gaming, dating and friending. Aristotle called the hand the "tool of tools" (meaning: the tool by means of which all tools can come to be of service).[3] But the hand is now getting a run for its money.

The relation between media and tools is not straightforward. The mindset of the printed page was perhaps exhibited as well by industrial assembly lines and government bureaucracies as by the methodical discipline of classroom ABC's. But the medium and the tool have never coincided before as they do in digital technology: Neither television nor the printed page can *do* half so much so well themselves. It is, accordingly, the innovation of digital technology to fuse medium into tool. The computer is a new kind of technology altogether because it integrates our way of communicating into our way of doing – our work is information.

To show why this fusion of medium into tool is what is most significant about digital technology requires describing each separately. The first question is therefore what media are, what difference they make.

There is no getting around media. It is a profound fact about us that we cannot know or say anything, except by proferring a token (a word, a symbol, a sign), which renders thought public and discursive. We are forced to work through some medium other than thought in order to work out what we think; it is only so, through some roundabout common measure, that we can mean the world to others. All speech is in translation. Medieval philosophers contrasted this form of knowing to that of angels, who apprehend what is true as immediately evident: a telepathic meeting of minds. For us, unlike for angels, *logos* means both "thought" and "word"; it expresses the shared reality of reason and speech. Like the soul and the body, they need each other to *be*, but are not the same. Thinking is more than a matter of words, and yet without words no (human) thinking could take place.

There is a creative relationship between what we mean to say and the material reality by means of which we say it. On the one hand, it is a peculiarity of all our speaking knowledge to be aware of its own inadequacy, to be able to mean more than we can say. That is why great works of literature, philosophy, and theology can strike familiar chords in us, as if giving voice to our own experience better than we ourselves could do. On the other, we are not ordinarily aware of the fact that we are speaking a particular language, that we must use words shaped by accident and history. We see things through words as through a transparent pane of glass, as if our terms for things had an uncomplicated connection to the things themselves. But speech – and all media to which we commit it – also has a material reality with ponderable tendencies. Even if language does not determine all there is to say, it is not an empty conveyance for its meaning. The pane of glass has a bent, an inclination, a sort of mind of its very own.

There are different conclusions one might draw from this. For one, the scope and depth of what we mean must be commensurable with the means at our disposal. A toddler cannot even mean to write a sonnet. (It is both a matter of vocabulary, and a matter of the fact that his desires do not yet live up to the form.) Nor could a lover write a sonnet that expressed utmost human passion in a language that consisted only of "zero" and "one," no matter how sincerely meant – the medium would not be adequate to the richness of the thought. No one can be a virtuoso prior to existence of the instrument.

It may be, furthermore, that languages, as a consequence of culture and geography, have their special genius for particular zones of our experience (as some have elaborate and refined nomenclatures for horses, snow, clouds, kinds of kinship, or shades of courtesy, where others have one or none). Nietzsche wrote that "certain languages cannot even *want* what Horace is able to accomplish."[4] Charles V is supposed to have said (in a widely recycled anecdote) that he would pray in Spanish, socialize in Italian, woo in French, and admonish in German.[5] These differences are hard to pin down, though anyone with some experience of them will attest that languages each have their emphases, moods, and textures.

Yet there is, finally, the difference that the medium makes to its content. It is not impossible to imagine Tolstoy writing *War and Peace* as a series of tweets. Yet if your messages are limited to 280 characters, you will be pressed to favor quip over narrative. It is not impossible to imagine e.e. cummings as a bard in Homeric times. Yet his works, as we have them, are inseparable from the conventions of modern typography. While no medium causes its contents, each medium nonetheless contains an implicit logic of preferences and affinities that set the tone for our speaking just this way. One may always defy this logic – but then choosing to swim upstream will nonetheless exert a formative pressure (just as choosing an anachronism carries a meaning different from the anachronism's original expression). Every medium of communication embodies a theory of what should be said to the extent that we must commit to saying it in certain terms. The study of a medium is the study of the rhetoric internal to that form – the consideration of how the *is* shapes the *ought* of speech. This rhetoric is then what gathers a community into speaking coherence with itself; it gives shape to the aspirations of a culture as a whole.

There is a longstanding dispute about whether technological changes are inevitable. One side speaks as if technology had agency of its own ("It will occur no matter what"), the other insists that every technological change is the consequence of human decision and so a change like any other ("It is always up to us"). A parallel dispute occurs between those who assert that certain technologies are in themselves good or bad, and those who assert that technologies are neutral to their uses. While I will revisit these issues, I want to begin by noting that all four of these positions miss the character of media as media. The progress of technology is not autonomous: It is as embedded in choice and circumstance as any other historical pressure. But nor is it the case that technology is neutral to our purposes. Rather, the character of our tools and media inclines to certain uses; they have a penchant that, if you would avoid it, you must consciously work to defeat. They possess you to say what you say by bearing on how you say it. Picture saying: Television doesn't stupefy people, people stupefy people. Or again: Imagine writing an epic poem over text message or making a classical sculpture out of breadcrumbs. It is not impossible, but when was the last time it was on the cards? The thing you are working with shapes your work by informing your thinking. In other words, media cannot be strictly neutral because they are latent with specific possibilities and because our perception of those possibilities is always to the purpose: What suggests itself as merely possible is always operative on our envisioning of how to proceed. What *can* be *must* figure into our understanding of what to do about it. Lines of sight are lines of thought, and mindlines are guidelines: lines of action.

The master relay of media, the history of its history as a whole, runs, as I have said: from silence to speaking, from speaking to writing, from writing to printing, from printing to digital computing. The elements of this sequence don't obviously belong together. (After all, isn't writing just writing, wherever it is? And don't we still have talking and printing today?) Each step looks less consequential than the last (which is itself a measure of what we take for granted in ourselves). And the suggestion that our predominant techniques of communication entail their own psychologies, epistemologies, aesthetics, and theologies is incomplete: In stringing these together, I am of course abstracting from the full account of these changes. The mere presence of writing or printing is not enough to explain cultural history. Their effects have been uneven, variable, halting, and hybrid. Writing was long in use in the West before one could speak of a culture of literacy, while printing was long in use in East Asia without the momentous consequences that we attribute to Gutenberg. Still, each of these social transformations required a specific kind of information technology to take place – or rather each required the other in order to transform our experience – so that by attending to the single thread of information technology, it's possible to see the logic of a trajectory directed by well-defined tendencies, affinities, and principles.

Language gave birth to human beings. It could not have been a conscious invention because its birth is the emergence of what's human from what's not. It made an appearance out of nothing – Athena spirited full-formed from Zeus's brow. Even if preceded by other happenings, time out of mind, there was a new beginning in the word. It is the word that first expresses distance between ourselves and the world; it is the word that made it possible to hold things at arm's length, to see them (nominally) in a different light, and to tell a lie by casting them in shadow. It is through the word that sight became in-seeing. As Adam named the animals, to have the power to name is to declare the world speakable in common. When the significance of language dawns on the deaf-blind it is the revelation of a lifetime, the revelation that everything has a name, that words make spirit visible. Helen Keller writes: "I knew then that 'w-a-t-e-r' meant the wonderful cool something that was flowing over my hand. That living word awakened my soul, gave it light, hope, joy, set it free!"[6] It is our nature to live by the word, and many die for it. Word calls world into being.

Oral cultures have been by far the longest-standing human norm; whereas *Homo sapiens* have existed for one or two hundred thousand years, the first extant scripts are only five or six thousand years old. Of the thousands of languages ever spoken, only about a hundred have ever been committed to writing so as to have something like a literature. This great disparity remains true for languages spoken today.[7] Literacy is the historical exception.

Yet a community of words not written down is incalculably far from our own habits of mind. Oral poetry, to take up one example, is governed by an economy of demands that are irrelevant to writing. It was for the ear, it was recited to illiterate audiences and sung to the accompaniment of music. The Homeric epics were composed to be remembered. Their strict rhythm is mnemonic; there are formulaic repetitions of epithet and structure that orient the teller along the way. (In other languages rhyming or alliteration did the trick.) Some words or phrases cannot fit the metrical scheme at all – those must be excluded. The epics are episodic: They were not recited in one evening, from start to finish (as we would read a book) – that would have taken all night – rather, rhapsodes would pick up somewhere *in medias res*. Nor did Homer read or write himself; the figure of the bard is represented by tradition as being blind. "Homer" is itself, furthermore, a name that we attach to two great epics because it is hard for us, as book-people, to take seriously the thought that such masterpieces as the *Iliad* and *Odyssey* could have been worked out through word of mouth, gradually improvised and elaborated by generations of story-tellers speaking to and coming from audiences all around the Aegean Sea. (A *rhapsodos* is someone who stitches songs together.) Whether Homer was one man or woman or a whole line of rhapsodes working out what they knew by heart, we cannot know. It is very likely that each new telling of the poems was a little different from the last until they were finally written down, centuries after their original appearance – as a fly in amber is fixed beyond change.

But writing does more than arrest its contents: By being written down, episodes of the *Iliad* that might have been recited as self-standing wholes had to be rationalized, put within one sequence and in causal relation to every other episode. While the spoken word necessarily fleets and evanesces, the written word transcends its immediate context; its magic is to make speech timeless. Writing enumerates, codifies, systematizes, sequentializes, schedules, classifies, and abstracts. It thereby magnifies the power to keep track by the numbers: to list, to tax, to own, to owe, and to conscript – it is the controlling germ of cities and of empires.[8] It standardizes time and maps space; you can get the whole story straight. Writing teaches a new conception of being bound by contract and so of having rights. ("Can I have that in writing?," "Show me where it says that," "Read it and weep!") It also teaches a new conception of evidence, blame, and culpability: Latin *culpa* (fault) and *scribere* (write) share the same root, which means "to scratch" or "scrape." Both the rules of conduct and the record of our deeds can now be on the books.

Writing is a new memory and therefore a new conception of what connects us to others and to God. Oral culture is heroic and legendary. (Or rather, this is what it became once writing was in the picture, since "legend" means "what's read.") But literate culture makes history – an awareness of our own place determined within the fixed continuum of time.[9] It gives us a past. The subject of our discussion may endure for everyone and no one. Writing thus contains the aspiration to make its subject permanent, and so becomes the archive and repository of a new culture. It creates a new sense of permanent identity; one's own name and achievement in letters may now become immortal. In doing so, it also makes possible a new sense of belief. Oral people do not "believe" in their gods – they know them within their collective observances – whereas the Abrahamic religions ask that you willingly consent to bear witness that a Book is God's own spelled-out revelation. (Jesus enjoins his disciples to "rejoice, because your names are written in heaven," God's plan is "as it is written ..." and to die is to be translated.[10]) Only with literacy can belief be a matter of conscience – something you take upon yourself to subscribe to, whether others around you do or not. It is by transporting the context of belief outside our immediate circle that writing creates the conception of the miraculous. It is, further, because there are many other books in circulation that new authors can take a page from them, that there can be a body of work, a republic of letters, a literature, a continuous conversation by which past and present sit together at table, world without end. Writing makes "humanity" thinkable, a new way of laying claim to the universal and of knowing ourselves responsible to it.

What was known and knowable was once as much as someone's mind could hold. But as writing vastly expands our stock of common knowledge, it disables the powers of recall of each. (Those who are illiterate or dyslexic have more to remember, and they are usually able to remember a great deal more.)

As you loosen the context of accountability, you widen the gate of possible misunderstanding. The spoken word is personal: It temporarily addresses itself to some group in particular, demanding that we heed the speaker and that we speak in turn. Writing widens the circle of listeners – consider that oratorical speeches delivered by Greek and Roman generals had to be repeated several times to reach everyone in earshot. (Only the most incompetent orators of antiquity read from prepared remarks.[11]) In contrast, the only way to permanently silence a book is to burn it.

Writing transferred the weight of utterance from the unlettered ear to the bookish eye. When I cannot understand an unfamiliar word in speech, I ask the speaker to spell it out – I hear it by first "seeing" it written on the blank page of my mind. I see what you mean; your word no longer disappears into remembered time, but stands still before my eyes as a new object. Karen Blixen observed this in the Kikuyu natives' first encounters with writing. When she writes a man's name on a piece of paper, he keeps it wrapped around his neck, like an amulet, a fetish: "He could not afford to lose it, for his soul was in it, and it was the proof of his existence. Here was something which Jogona Kanyagga had performed, and which would preserve his name for ever: the flesh was made word and dwelt among us full of grace and truth."[12] Does this seem backward? It is only a slightly exaggerated version of a writer's love for his creatures or of our standard practice of certifying our identity at the bank. (The illiterate must scrawl X so that their existence is not written off.) The written word becomes the signature of our identity; and, once written, it becomes hypostasized, a reality of cares in its own right. It puts you – literally – in two places at once.

Writing also has the tendency to freeze thinking into mere words. As Plato warned (at the dawn of the literate age), it is because words are written that we are then at risk of taking things too literally, of mistaking the letter of the law for its spirit, of acting by the book, of going through the scripted motions, of writing things in stone, of identifying a wider reality with what looks plausible on paper. It is only once you write that you can have a book with your name on it. Virgil's poetry, in contrast to Homer's, belongs to a particular man whose name has been preserved: His poems are measured by an authoritative version ("author" and "authority" now have meanings that converge). Nor must literate poets begin, like Homer, by invoking Memory as a divine Muse, since what is written down is no longer so miraculous as the act of bringing speech up from the psyche's hidden insight. While to the oral poet all memory is present, the literate one will scoff at time – "No, Time, thou shalt not boast that I do change …" Only in a literate age would it occur to us to be proud about keeping our word, precisely because we don't have to.

For over two thousand years, reading remained the work of specialists. Books were copied by hand at great trouble and expense. If you can only write in stone, then you will tend only to write what should never be forgotten (Holy Writ, laws, the names of the illustrious dead). If it is extremely costly and laborious to produce books – as it was until the fifteenth century – then only certain kinds of books will tend to be written and copied: those deemed indispensable, for whatever reason, by the aristocracy and learned clergy. Most ancient writings did not pass this test consistently enough to survive the interval. No naughty kid was passing notes in class in the twelfth century. (He was not taking notes at all – paper was too dear.) Nor were books widely available as private, portable objects. It was only in the thirteenth century that a Bible was bundled into a single book: an enormous object weighing around ten pounds.[13]

Up through early modernity, the written word retained vivid connection to the spoken. Augustine's surprise at finding Ambrose reading *sotto voce*, rather than out loud, shows that silent reading was once considered a feat;[14] monks mumbled or mouthed the words on the page up through the twelfth century.[15] Scribes gradually developed the literate practice of separating words with spaces, distinguishing between upper- and lower-case letters, and adding punctuation, in order to facilitate reading to yourself. The central practice of medieval education remained the *disputation* (the vestige of which today is the graduate oral exam); the text was regarded as a summary or a reminder of the chief points of an argument, rather than the express reenactment of the argument itself.

Literacy meant something else again, when it migrated from papyrus scroll or vellum parchment to the printed book. Printing cheapened, at a stroke, the dissemination of the word: The press's style is much more prolix than that of chisel, stylus, brush, or quill. It multiplied the audience that could join in the conversation, and in doing so changed that conversation, made it faster and widespreading. The printing press is the emblem of enlightened modernity. *Sapere aude* – or: "You be the judge!" – is a watchword that can only apply to a people who all read, and so have (potentially) all the same facts before them. And where all have access to the same books, everyone can have a distinct point of view. As printing decontextualizes speech, turning one's auditory "audience" into an imaginary "readership," literacy invented the notion of the individual perspective, lens, or worldview. The originality of "genius" became prized.

Printed writing is pregnant with a new awareness of privacy: the inner parliament, the court of conscience. Paintings of people reading – from late medieval depictions of Mary to Gerhard Richter's *Lesende* – are depictions of their interior space of silence. Protestantism's *sola scriptura* thus accords divine authority to introspected truth. Stillness becomes audible (and speaks volumes). Dispensing with theological learning and precedents, the word of God is yours to know in your own language, by your own light, to the best of your inklings. And a new relationship to God means new ways of reading the self as good or evil. The early modern myth of Faust relies on the suspicion that forbidden books spell trouble. One of the best-selling books of early modern Europe was the *Malleus Maleficarum*, a treatise that allowed readers to catalogue (and therefore fix on) the marks of witchcraft. Burning witches in the sixteenth and seventeenth centuries could become all the rage because a new reading population had learned how to do it themselves.

Nations imagined themselves as wholes on the basis of language for the first time – a shared literature, a shared vernacular, made it possible to conceive of a nation as a shared project and aspiration, beyond allegiance to particular monarchs.[16] (The difference between a dialect and a language is that the latter has an army and a navy, as the Yiddish witticism has it.) No country could be governed by a written constitution prior to the printing press. Only if the law is widely read and known can it take the place of unwritten custom and tradition. And the printing press is (in this broadest sense) democratic: Where everyone can have a voice, everyone has a say. It respects no authority other than what can be shown to everyone's satisfaction, all to a man.

It was only with the printed page that spelling and type were standardized. Habits of reading finally severed the spoken from the written word. Poetry and song remained closely connected in the poetry of troubadours through the late Middle Ages, while the rise of literacy coincided with the appearance of opera (the song now fully cut off from the poem). Much modern literature calls attention both to the act of writing itself and to the way writing is encountered specifically on the page – from Herbert's "Easter Wings" to T. S. Eliot's footnotes, from Sterne's black pages in *Tristram Shandy* to Dos Passos's fictional press releases and Joyce's prose *glissandos* – it is not written with the ear in mind, but for the silent eye. The folktales and epic songs of oral ages have given way to the novel. Novels are not written to be memorized and recited – they are for enjoying one's own solitude, heightening the scrutiny of clandestine motives in sympathy with others' distinct points of view.[17]

It is easy to see that where the audience is most everyone, and everyone is to judge, then only what is accessible to many will find an audience at all. Shakespeare was a crowd-pleaser, Paine's *Common Sense* is a raw meat screed, and Lincoln's speeches were written to move and to persuade – we marvel, for that reason, at their audiences' average literacy in contrast to our own. But widening literacy and the availability of the printed word carries with it assumptions about what reason itself is: Literate reason must draw a brighter line between what is true and what is mere opinion (since opinions are a dime a dozen), and so it must convince a non-specialist audience with arguments that stand relatively on their own merits. Appeals to authority and tradition are weaker, since the very worth of tradition must be now established by reason (why should I take your word for it?). Scientific arguments are thereby promoted: The accuracy of printed diagrams afforded a new way of widely sharing and standardizing visual observations, without which modern science might not have gotten rolling. Modernity starts out, that is, by widening the difference between given facts and values. Alongside the intensified privacy of our subjectivity, new criteria of neutrality, skepticism, impartiality, and objectivity emerge. Alongside modern individualism, mathematics and natural science become paradigms of reason. What is true must be clear to all, beyond a doubt the printed word.

The trend is clear enough. Information of all kinds is very hard to come by on your own, from scratch; any group that can make the sharing of it easier will have an edge to expand and innovate. As the means of communicating have cheapened (considering that oral culture places a steep tax on memory), so the audience has grown, so the amount of available information has multiplied, so the amount anyone needs to carry around in their head has diminished, so the ease of accessing and adding to the pool of information has increased. The digital pushes this logic to its limit: The gap between a notion popping into someone's head and the transmission of it for all the world to see has narrowed to the barest exertion. The distinction between audience and author has blurred or vanished.

This has consequences for the kinds of conversations available to us. It means that information – ideas or pressing news that are readily grasped as relevant to everyone – can spread faster than ever before. (There is no particular radius of action since it mostly doesn't matter where you are; and the time for response is always *now*.) It means that units of meaningful information have shrunk, and so their context thinned. It means that we are less likely to pay attention to anything in particular, since there is so much else competing for it. (The more information is available to us, the less likely we are to follow up on it: We always *can* and so we *don't*.) It means that the quality of the information must suit a lower denominator, on the whole. "The more wonderful the means of communication, the more trivial, tawdry, or depressing its contents"[18] – such is the price of speed and ease.

That the digital is an entirely distinct medium from the printed word (rather than just the printed word sped up) is the subject of the rest of this book. But consider, for starters, the expectations implicit in printed matter. Books and newspapers and magazines take time and cost money to write, to produce, to buy and read. That cost is much lower than it was in the medieval scriptorium, but it is still the case that everyone involved must pay a price to take part in the life of a printed page. That a book is "self-published" does not usually recommend it. There are many silly books, but a book on the shelf means that a press has been willing to pledge its name and profit on the writer's authority and expertise. Once printed, their words cannot be revoked; they must hold up without the author. Printed writing thus fixes thought into a longstanding span of time – even hot button books should have a shelf-life of several months. The formality of print derives from our awareness of the longevity intrinsic to it.

Books speak at length, furthermore. A reader must put in the time to know them and to be in the position to criticize them with authority. They are wholes – they self-contain their contexts. If someone misconstrues a sentence, you can correct him by pointing, chapter and verse, to a different passage, or by clarifying the frame of reference. The presumption is that authors ought to sustain a coherent, sequential argument throughout, and that the reader has an obligation to pin down all parts within that whole. To read a book well is to read between the lines with this principle in mind, to note discrepancies, raise questions, and reconcile the parts as possible. "Even Homer nods" is an accusation that could only be made by the literate, who, godlike, have the whole text before them at any time, and for whom consistency is therefore paramount. When an author refers to other sources, those sources should (in principle) be open to all, documented and indexed like scientific evidence. "Hearsay" and unrecorded testimony are suspect kinds of evidence within the written form. Literate attention engages all of these facts.

I need hardly say how inapplicable they all are to our reading online. Not because we treat all websites as equally credible, but because the very fact of being online tells you nothing about the value of what you are reading. If "I read it in a book" carries the authority of the written word, "I read it on the internet" carries no more intrinsic weight than word of mouth. What we can access requires little investment on our part, and the cacophony of views is such that the burden is no longer to gather information *in*, but to select it *out*: You notice what you choose and choose what you notice. Or websites offer to do this on our behalf (such that the verb "curate" has roared into fashion). When information has become an overwhelming flood, when our awareness is constantly drawn to and involved in everything occurring to the world's nervous system, the only way to get by is to skim the surface: to surf or browse or post on it (mice scurry, and "cursor" is Latin for "running messenger"). Our reading tends to be promiscuous and casual. Attention becomes scarce (and therefore valuable), since we cover a wider area. Successful online writing must be good at hooking you and stringing you along. The information environment as a whole incentivizes what packs a pithy punch, what's pushy, catchy, hyperbolic, or eye-popping. The content of our "feed" should be "snackable." When I sit down to grab a quick bite, I want to watch something juicy and undemanding on YouTube: The two acts of consumption are analogous.

Consistency and coherence are strong presumptions of the printed page, where A and not-A cannot flagrantly exist side by side within one system of thought, simultaneous and co-present. For a text to be a whole means that each part is ideally aware of and responsive to every other: what Plato called logographic necessity. You cannot argue with someone from an oral culture by pointing to a contradiction in the text – precedent and collective memory have more prestige for oral peoples than systematic consistency. Just so, the digital medium does not reward the presentation of a coherent, contextual whole. The form of printed patience is to gradually pull you in; but you must bring yourself to read for that to happen. Digital attention forms into discrete bursts that scatter and cascade – it baits you in spite of yourself with "thumb-stopping" content. And where there is always more than we can read, where the news comes to us in morsels and fragments, the gotcha accusation of inconsistency matters less since it is soon buried in the midden. The medium values candor, shock, and authenticity over sustained coherence, decorum, or erudition. "What's on your mind?" Facebook asks you to type; or "how is your current mood?" "Say something," the YouTube chat box commands.

So what if what I say today is not what I said six weeks ago, who cares? The mood has changed. Or rather, *it had better*: Why would anyone follow you on a regular basis if you did not regularly change, supplying food for browsing? You need to make a stir to create an impression.

We are now astride these two worlds – our norms of literacy are still more or less keyed to the printed page, even as the digital becomes our central medium. People are still more likely to lie over email than when asked to put pen to paper; we take ink more seriously.[19] Yet the digital does not keep to itself; our online habits of mind follow us onto the printed page. Not only do we find it more difficult to sit still and read at patient length, which in turn makes it more difficult to care about the practice of writing good prose. (Literate concerns like proper spelling, nice handwriting, or scrupulous documentation of sources seem quaint and bookish to average digital natives, who are learning literacy as a second language.) But the printed page is also coming to look more like the digital one. Where else are most printed pages first written? The East Asian cell-phone novel (a novel written in text-message-sized installments) is an extreme example: Five out of the ten best-selling novels in Japan in 2007 belonged to the genre.[20] Rupi Kaur (a Canadian poet whose *Milk and Honey* spent 189 weeks on the *New York Times* bestseller list) started sharing her work on Tumblr and Instagram: Her published poems follow the lower-case conventions and informality of online writing. *Milk and Vine* – a parody of *Milk and Honey* that borrows from well-known "Vines" (the short loopy videos of a discontinued app) – has also been a smash.

The practice of fiction is being reshaped as a whole. Internet novels, for one, are no longer, as before, the province of sci-fi and cyber-punk; they are now about our ordinary interface with the uncanny online (Joshua Cohen's *Book of Numbers*, Patricia Lockwood's *No One Is Talking about This*, Lauren Oyler's *Fake Accounts*). As life online becomes identified with life full stop, memoirs will increasingly take digital experience itself as their theme (Olivia Laing's *Lonely City*, Maël Renouard's *Fragments of an Infinite Memory*). To generalize further in the gross: Authors (like Rachel Cusk, Annie Ernaux, Emmanuel Carrère, or Karl Ove Knausgaard) who fuddle the bounds between reality and (auto)fiction compel our imagination as never before. It is as if we are already so glutted on fantasy by being online that the authority of real experience has become the more valuable. Where the point is to "feel something," then the most entertaining escape is based on an incredible true story. Along similar lines, contemporary novelists are also expected to be more politically committed, because we understand their work as expressive of their identity (and therefore as representing ours or failing to). We are relentlessly aware as never before of their personal convictions, and so we cannot but read their narratives through those convictions – artists are now an inescapable part of their art. (Note the asterisks that attach to the work of Peter Handke or David Foster Wallace – the obligatory rehearsal of their misdeeds that must preface any commendation of them.) They prefer addressing their narratives to current social issues than to "universal" or "human" themes. Fiction is less interested in the exploration of altogether new kinds of perspectives (one of the tasks of modernism) and more in "relevance" to the promotion of existing marginalized voices. Our intensified awareness of real stories and events everywhere overwhelms our interest in art for art's sake.

The point of this tour of media history is to emphasize that each medium tends to favor certain attitudes and conceptions of what is most worth saying, of what counts as a virtue of thought, and of how to prosecute an argument at all. This is the meaning of McLuhan's famous saw that "the medium is the message," and of Neil Postman's refinement of it, "the medium is the metaphor"[21] (though the point that each artistic medium has its own specific excellence goes further back, to Herder, Lessing, and German Romanticism). In other words: What started as a means has a way of recoiling on the kinds of ends you tend to choose. The movie is not as good as the book – not because the movie could have been better, but because you shouldn't judge it by the book at all.

Each medium thus embodies a standard of rhetorical authority. It proposes itself to you in terms that shape your habits of mind according to the tacit measure of an "ideal" audience member (as listener, reader, or user). And in shaping our responses to meaning, it thereby constitutes us as members of some larger community – as people encoded into a specific network of others. The medium does not determine what is said, but it is in its terms that we relate the parts of our experience into some larger order, and therefore give a definition to our conception of both: A medium is a figure of speech. The conformations of media are also the metaphors through which we know the world as a whole. They translate us in to their way of thinking – into their implicit forms of attention, knowledge, time, community, culture, memory, self-identity, and silence; they figure out our gods. We make good with them; they talk sense into us.

More specifically, each medium expresses a particular relation between knowledge and time. As transmission of information is faster and its volume grows so far beyond the size of what any one person could track or keep in mind, the contents of culture themselves lead shorter lives; the buzzwords for what's timely mutate faster. Where printed culture aspired to be momentous, online culture aspires to have the moment's notice. Digital objects are for the time being; instant classics are not supposed to last. Where the printed word is cumulative and progressive, intending to stand the test of time, there is no such thing as an online canon. Online writing does not reward attention – nor is it meant to, since its claim to attention is precisely that it is happening now. Following what's going on at the moment serves as the main criterion of what merits notice. What is easily accessed is what is easily disposed of; what is ephemeral is trivial. Under what circumstances would you consider buying a printed book consisting of someone's social media posts or emails? Under what circumstances would you take the trouble to learn a blog entry by heart?

The internet is therefore a new kind of collective memory, selecting for what is disposable while preserving it indefinitely – it is a machine for producing what is forgettable by rendering it unforgettable. As a shorter-term memory, it is also a shorter-term identity – that is, by severing our bonds to past and future, we are created into a new form of digital self. The longstanding, fixed identity of the printed word gives way to an identity loosened up to the expansive possibilities of role playing and self-representation. Where your identity was once "your papers," it is now your data. Where the audience is the author, to be online is to participate; and so speech becomes performative – your way of playing out your identity for others as you construct it. In other words: Saying blurs into doing, medium into tool.

1.2   THE DIGITAL FUSES MEDIUM WITH TOOL THROUGH DATA

I've so far not been careful to specify the difference between tool and medium. The logic of each has long diverged from the other. Roughly: The one effects, the other speaks in signs. An ordinary tool – a hammer, a match, a washing machine – extends our power by performing a part of one activity, and so by breaking that activity up into smaller tasks. (A prehistoric axe could do a dozen things – pounding, cutting, hunting, starting fires. A modern hammer does just one of those very well.) The more efficient our tools, the greater the fragmentation of activity, the more they call for other tools and gadgets to do the job: The industrial assembly line is a perfect picture of this Swiss Army process. The dominant media of words, on the other hand – speech, writing, printing – have shaped the world by giving us some more or less unified setting within which to say what we know. Information could not "do" much on its own – book learning is not street smarts – though of course print proved the means of creating literate populations. The point is that where tools are fragmenting, media are engrossing and encompassing. Ordinary tools and symbolic codes have tended in different directions.

Yet this may be the sort of distinction that only literate people would be tempted to make. That is, within oral cultures words are functionally identical to other tools (as spells or calls or invocations, say), so that it is only the written page that severs speaking from acting, forcing each out of touch with the other and into rarefied specialization. Oral references are operational, known in practice, rather than conceptual.[22] Hebrew *dabar* (e.g.) means both "word" and "event." That there should be such things as "speech acts" counts as a philosophical insight only for literate people, who have learned to think that speaking is not a mode of action. Digital technology constitutes a return to this conflation; it is a backlash response to the longstanding divergence of saying from doing. Where the printed word fragments and specializes theory from practice, it is the mark of the digital to overcome the difference between tool and medium, unifying attention and undermining claims to specialized expertise. To be online is to be both a passive witness (as one takes in a book) and an effective agent (as one takes up a hammer). Communication and action are joined into one and the same means. Online, to know is to do.

We have long paid lip service to the principle that knowledge is powerful; but Bacon's maxim had never been so simply true. The digital will never be able to replace certain kinds of work altogether, but it is important that the "information economy" is no longer functionally distinct from hands-on labor, as it was when it only described the work of bureaucrats, journalists, accountants, and other mandarins. Where work was once on paper, paperwork is now network – work of (almost) all kinds is now online. The global financial system is fully digital, as are the logistics of commercial supply chains. With the "internet of things" – the increasing digitalization of embedded devices – agriculture and industry are digital too.[23] Not to mention all the gadgets that increasingly integrate routine activities into Wi-fi "functionality." From your toaster to your fork, from your pet to your pacemaker, from your alarm clock to your refrigerator, baby-monitor, car, and umbrella – what works best is to be connected.

The operative principle in all its applications – the bridge between theory and practice – is quantification. To "compute" is to reckon or to count. Data is information that is measurable, knowledge crunched into numbers and therefore rendered actionable to use. (What is the first thing to do, if you are hoping to lose weight? Buy a scale to count the pounds each day.) Quantification and measurement are themselves acts of interpretation; you must choose which aspects of a phenomenon are significant (so that "engagement" is measured in clicks, say, just as we have used the IQ test as a shorthand for intelligence or the polygraph for truth). And this will mean that if you can count some things and not others, you will have an incentive to count on the former.

The medium of data-gathering has a way of shaping our understanding of how things work by allowing us to analyze them into homogenous, discrete steps – the dividing is the conquering. (French for "computer" is *ordinateur*: What's digital is made to order.) In other words, data allows us to focus our view of an activity in such a way that we can objectively reckon with it. If something can be systematically measured, it can be digitalized; and you can in turn take action to improve your metrics. To digitalize is to be able to respond in kind to numbering. Digital facts act, that is, only insofar as quantification tunes out qualitative understanding of other unmeasurable aspects. Data translates knowledge into significant numbers. If you can count it, you can write a program to make it count. "What we measure is what we strive for."[24]

The digital's foremost excellence is therefore efficiency: the indefinite optimization of the outputs we have singled out to quantify. All digital computing is nothing other than receiving, transmitting, and analyzing strings of binary code: sequences of 1's and 0's. (A byte is a unit of eight binary digits, "bits," a gigabyte is a billion bytes.) Any online task – whether sending a text or paying for parking – must be coded into such terms to be possible. It is because this translation is so fast and widespread that the digital is the most effective means of gathering, coordinating, collating, analyzing, aggregating, and disseminating information ever devised. The digital makes every aspect of reality easily commensurable. By programming it all into the same quantitative medium, it projects it all onto the same qualitative plane.

The commensurability of information is efficiency in practice. An earthquake shook central Mexico in September 2017, on the anniversary of a previous one that resulted in the death of thousands in 1985. Whereas responses to the earlier one were sluggish, chaotic, and inept, this time resources were quickly and seamlessly allocated. Rescuers spread out where they were most needed, ambulances did not overwhelm particular hospitals, blood was donated where it was called for, supply centers listed on social media the precise number of blankets and of bottles of water that they required, and abuses were widely broadcast. Such a massive operation could be fluidly coordinated only because every agent was interpreting his own efforts in light of the big online picture at any given time; many lives were saved. When it comes to such complex, self-organizing operations, the digital is the marvel of the modern world, the emergence of a spontaneously ordered web from autonomous intentions: The "wisdom of the crowd" is our invisible hand. Just so, Uber owns no cars: It is car choreography. YouTube makes no videos: It is a means of labeling and organizing footage. Facebook provides no friends: It is a place to assemble and keep tabs on your own. Stalin's quip about the Pope's lack of armed divisions no longer applies. The digital is, at its best, the harnessing of parts into a whole group effort.

For such efforts to become whole, however, the group's data must be concentrated in certain platforms or websites, which, as the necessary facilitators of commensurability, have thereby acquired enormous clout. Most kinds of knowledge are not power, not straightforwardly. But data is, and more of it is more. Every action we perform online is potentially computable by the site's analytics into patterns of use and consumption – how long we spend on each site, how well we respond to this or that variation, what we are likely to prefer. Every keyed response counts and is counted. ("Impact" is measured in the number of reiterations everywhere online: "Follow us on Instagram!") Google has tinkered with every aspect of its home page "look," experimenting with forty-one shades of the color blue: The company claimed in 2014 that that change of shade alone brought in an extra $200 million.[25] In other words, even as the digital works for us, we are working for it. Even while we count on digital technology to make our life more efficient, we ourselves are objects of quantification that are reckoned on.

Digital analysis is becoming better at giving us what we think we want by micro-analyzing our attention. This is partly because of the commercial incentives intrinsic to the medium (to which I'll return). But it is also because the more we make use of it, the better we are teaching it to anticipate our uses. It is through our input that we are perfecting the internet (for us, for others, and for companies) – it is the data from our ordinary browsing that irons out the kinks and bugs. The obstacle in many industries is thus not how fast to process, but how to obtain enough data to train programs accurately. Amazon's Mechanical Turk is the most notorious example of commercial crowdsourcing: The website pays online workers pennies to perform discrete "human intelligence tasks." This data then serves as grist to programs that will eventually automate some (lucrative) application of those tasks on a vast scale. Workers tag pictures that train up face-recognition programs, say, or the programs driving driverless cars. China has (for parallel reasons) gained a massive edge from its digital protectionism; as the world's most populous country, it is able to keep its citizens' data in-house for use by Chinese companies. Where existing data is not to the purpose, China has set up "digital towns" or "AI villages," where workers clock in for eight hours a day to generate data for particular projects: a new form of work that harvests bare acts of attention and intention.[26] At least these workers are getting paid – most of us are content to inadvertently generate scads of the same data for free any time we go online: useful idiots. And the political demand that we be paid for this goes under the undignified name of "data dignity." But the whole internet is one big Mechanical Turk operation, a system tagging, aggregating, and optimizing new responses – it has unlocked new strength from sheer numbers. "We value your feedback!" The automated message really means it. Data is digital currency: human experience codified and accumulated for profitable exchange.

Data collection is also necessarily a form of surveillance; there is no intrinsically private input so long as you are online. Total privacy is total tracking: The more secure your input, the more information you must give up to protect your identity (at *some* stage or another of "authentication"). Total convenience is also total tracking: The more transparent digital services are to us, the more transparent we are to them. Each time a smartphone pings a Wi-fi network, it creates a data point that can then be sold, on aggregate, to location data companies, who in turn sell their data to third-party advertisers. While the ping does not disclose any other information, it is not difficult to connect the dots, if one should care to.[27] The collection of meta-data is still largely unregulated in the United States, even as the possibility of total surveillance comes clearly into view. If data is power, then complete data is absolute power, which corrupts absolutely.[28] Whereas in the United States we have so far shown Panglossian confidence in private companies' assurances that they will keep our data private, it's clear that the medium seamlessly lends itself to much more intrusive forms of total scrutiny. China (to which I'll return) is even now implementing massive initiatives of digital surveillance, including the Social Credit System. Based on what each person buys, whom they associate with, and what they post online, they are assigned a "citizen score," which is in turn used as a means of flagging suspect behavior or of assigning privileges (like traveling or taking out a loan). "Transparency" here means: We know where you go and what you think. To the extent that our browsing history becomes our life history, such analyses will become more accurate. The screen is a *monitor*.

Even if no such dystopian outcome is in store for us, the practical character of our online "presence" – its pervasive involvement in our ways of doing things, its character as a unified medium – gives basic shape to the way we speak, write, and think. To communicate in the digital world we have to speak its code. Handwriting and speaking are also codes, but they are richer in shade and ambiguity (in other words: less easily quantifiable and captured into data). A letter (like hearing someone speak) offers you qualitative knowledge that the author is not in a position to control. You can tell someone's education (spelling), neatness (smudges, staying between the lines), and perhaps something of their style and personality. Handwriting was, until recently, treated as something very difficult to fake, a unique expression of our selves. The mail travels slowly, and so a letter has to begin by addressing its reader, recounting its matter at length, and then signing off with valediction; literate prose must develop its thought and expects a measure of attention in return for its trouble. It would be crude to refer to a personal letter as a "transmission" or as a "text" – like referring to a friend as an "individual" or an evening together as an "interaction."

A text message, like all electronic input, makes it possible to be in instant touch; it cancels space and time. The price paid for speed is that the digital code is narrower, simpler and more explicit, than handwriting (which is in turn less supple and more standardized than the living voice). A text becomes data only by tuning out certain kinds of formal ambiguities. We exercise correspondingly more control over how we come across. You will still know something of someone's personality over text, but probably not their spelling or neatness. (You have a type; and to "type" means to make typical.) Autocorrect depends on our sticking to a smallish list of words; there is an added "tax" to expressing yourself in ways the software doesn't recognize (since you must take the additional trouble to correct it), and so it tends to shrink and conventionalize vocabulary. You can kiss salutation and valediction goodbye ("hey"). Nor does the text message lend itself to expansive speculation. It is better to chop up a train of thought (to send three short texts, rather than one long one), to be pragmatic and strategic about what you say. Writing is word processing; speech is chat.

It is because texting is a medium of spontaneous communication abstracted from voice or body that it requires a new slang of self-narrated gesture and response: SMH, BRB, ROFL, and so on. It is because text-messages' code is emotionally flat and inexpressive that there has been a corresponding inflation in the use of exclamation marks and all caps in the digital age. And it is because speech becomes text online that the emoji or emoticon was invented to go with it. My father-in-law never uses exclamations or emojis; my wife and I are, despite our better knowledge of him, often perplexed by the tone of his texts, which read like deadpan and severe communiqués. ("Great news. Congratulations on the baby.")

But adding emojis does not make texting as expressive as writing had been, since "emotion" has become one more data point through this process, one more disambiguated mark. Three quarters or so of all emojis exchanged are emotional signals of some kind.[29] Emojis (like hashtags, handles, and all digital conventions) are coded responses, the nature of which forces you to pigeon-hole your speech in certain terms. Clickbait makes aggressive use of this code by frontloading the emotional form to frame the informational content: "10 reasons why celebrities LOVE this product" or "You won't believe how well these dogs dance!" (President Trump's tweets offer a master-class on this. He often punctuates his comments with an emotional instruction: "bad!" "Sad!" "WITCH HUNT!") Whereas in a hand-written letter content and affect were woven together within the context of the prose itself, digital communication pries "logic" and "feeling" apart. Referring to articles and videos as "content" is the fitting lingo of the digital age. The phrase "Shall I draw you a picture?" was an accusation of stupidity for people disciplined to print, but pictures become necessary online to earmark logical response. Speech must come captioned to make full sense ☺.

The binary and encoded character of the medium means that our mode of encountering its content is also fundamentally either/or: on/off, like/dislike, accept/reject, agree/disagree, swipe right/left, thumbs up/down, positive/negative feedback. Input is meant to be unequivocal. Characters are either typed or deleted – there is no smudge or trace of ambivalent erasure, there is much less involuntary input than in person, where our body, face, posture, tone, cadence, and rhythm betray more meaning than we know. To communicate online is thus an experience consisting in discrete, voluntary responses; it is a place of greater safety, or at any rate invulnerability. When we choose to share our image, we can do so on our own terms: Our online identity is self-fashioned, because we are each behind the scenes and don't need to come across.

Just as we have greater control over what and how we share, sites and platforms have greater control over what they share with us. They aim to please and we are teaching them how to. Their power of customization means that our preferences become more valuable. The digital does not exactly offer common content like the book (every copy of which looks the same), nor is it an environment in which there is a large stock of common reference (i.e. where most users can be expected to have seen and read most of the same things). While the internet is in theory universally accessible, in practice our experience of the medium is fully personal – not just in what we choose to visit, but in what we're likely to see once we get there. Its services are getting better at showing you what suits you: Search-engine results, advertising, and recommendations are trained to your IP address and preferences. When you look for what you want to find, you find what you are looking for. You may even install browser extensions to see the words you want to see (e.g., instead of "Republican" or "Democrat," you can read "Devil" or whatever) – though this is of course unnecessary so long as we stick to our favorite websites, which perform the same trick in subtler ways. Google is getting to know you better every click of the way; it means to become all things to all people.

Finally, the data-driven character of the medium is such as to translate larger human questions about how to live into technical puzzles that may be "problem-solved" – "life hacks," "fixes," shortcuts, tricks, "cheat codes," ways of "unlocking" or "accessing" contentment, "processing" issues, improving the outcome-based analytics of your "performance:" the so-called gamification of the ordinary.[30] Health is "wellness," sanity is "mental health," and happiness is engineered into "humanomics" or "smart living." In one company's telling: "Humaning is a unique, consumer-centric approach to marketing that creates real, human connections with purpose, moving [our company] beyond cautious, data-driven tactics, and uncovering what unites us all."[31] If this sounds like it has been written by a robot, it is because it represents the ultimate extension of the modern division of facts from values, in which values themselves become assessed as quantifiable facts. Data has been so effective in so many domains that truth and reason are increasingly identified with quantification per se. Just so, algorithms and artificial intelligence are used to supplant human judgment in all sorts of areas: They predict and diagnose illness, uncover racist linguistic patterns, hire employees meritocratically, determine penal sentences, and pledge more unbiased outcomes across the board. Such analyses promise to get it right more often on the whole. Whether they really do – and I'll return to their limitations in Chapter 4 – the point is that data is the form of online thinking, its basic, tacitly agreed-upon intellectual currency. The paradigmatic form of evidence in online speech is therefore statistics of just about any pedigree or origin – bullet-pointed, portable facts and figures, requiring little context, justification, or interpretation. As we improve our predictions of *what* is happening, we are correspondingly less able to understand *why*, to ask whether and how it is good. It's the thought that counts – you don't even know.

1.3   THE DIGITAL IS A MEDIUM OF PALPABLE IMAGES

The internet is a place of sights and sounds, graphics and video. Some statistics to impress you: As of 2020 (during quarantine), about 63 million Netflix users in the United States were streaming an average of 3.2 hours of video each day (or a total of 6 billion hours per month).[32] YouTube users worldwide (over 2.6 billion of them) watch another billion hours of video every day.[33] Instagram has had 2 billion active monthly users – several millions of whom are professional influencers.[34] In 2022, advertisers are set to spend $50 billion on digital video – the figure was about $4 billion in 2013.[35] And Americans have been, as a whole, spending over 10 hours on devices (including TV and radio) per day, half of which are screen time (though the number doubled during the pandemic).[36] All this requires a genealogical description via another screen I have hardly mentioned so far.

One might say that the digital was begotten from the coupling of print with television, of the word with the image. Television belongs to another family line of mass media: photography, film, radio, television, cable television, and video games. This line is different in kind from (and runs slant to) my earlier media history; it is a line of broadcast sensory experience, rather than of discursively coded information. Whereas the printed page needs educated deciphering, broadcast media proposes itself (as if) to your unmediated ken. We came to rely on television for the news and entertainment; it occupied the center stage of our culture. Yet it is not a medium that can serve most workaday purposes of communication, nor has it ever predominated as our main means of exchanging words. The digital, in turn, has overcome this handicap by consolidating the transmissive value of print with the aesthetic sensorium of broadcast experience. Regarding this latter aspect, the trend from the daguerreotype to the internet has been consistent: to make sights and sounds progressively more portable, more vividly animate, more responsive to individual preference and control. It is within the context of this trend (to which I now turn) that television has had transformative effects on our habits of mind. Its framing of information has been continuously preparing us for what the digital is and does to all appearances.

Our attention has been glued to the tube for the past half-century. The practice is dying out: Americans over 50 still watch it for about six hours a day, while teens average only one.[37] But television undoubtedly changed the way we look at things. The tipping point in this regard – the first episode of national significance in which the image captured the word – is often said to be the 1960 Nixon–Kennedy presidential debate. A majority of the radio audience picked Nixon for the winner, while those watching thought that Kennedy did best. Nixon was not wearing makeup (whatever else, he was no looker). But Kennedy also understood that the point of being on TV was not to debate exactly, not to enter into nice distinctions, but to hold forth for the eyes of the nation.[38]

It is clear that the appearance of things has since figured much more importantly in politics than it had. The image, the skin-deep optics of a person or situation, is as important as the substance. Or more precisely: "Coverage" of the surface makes up the substance itself, which must now have high production value, must play to the camera, and must be picture-perfect posturing to succeed. Television tends to promote actors and celebrities in popular opinion (and therefore in politics), those with name- and face-recognition, the studio-bronzed, telegenic characters we all already know. Most ordinary Americans in 1860 could not have known Lincoln from Adam, would not have recognized him on the street. If he were running for president now, it is doubtful that he would be able to overcome the handicap of his peculiar appearance, that "Hoosier Michelangelo – [his face] so awful ugly it becomes beautiful," as Whitman wrote.[39] The same would be true of obese Taft and wheel-chaired Roosevelt. Successful contemporary politicians, on the other hand, must be "good television," dazzling personalities made right for TV.

To think in images is altogether different from reasoning in words. Photographs and footage, by virtue of their realism – by virtue, that is, of the presumption that the camera lens is a transparent window to another place – simplify the need for accompanying description. They seem to need little introduction, to lack a history; you don't need to *believe* them to be true, their self-evidence meets you more than half-way. If an image looks flattering or incriminating, the *prima facie* supposition is that it can just skip the proverbial thousand words, that it can speak for itself by abrogating the work of justifying its context.[40] At best, TV images (like photographs) arrest attention as words may only rarely do – TV footage feels like raw sense data to us, as if it is an episode we ourselves are "there" to witness in person. ("Tele-vision" is mongrel Greek/Latin for seeing-at-a-distance.) These images may stir us to act on behalf of causes that, being out of sight, have been kept out of mind. At worst, the rhetoric of images and music is persuasive to the extent that it insists on saying precisely nothing by "framing" its content. Images manifest connections that, not making explicit truth claims, cannot be fully debunked in words. Most ads, for instance, are neither true nor false; they offer us a fantastic picture of ourselves made happier by a product. Their picture is therefore outside refutation. What's on TV are "shows," so that discursive reasoning must become "talk show." Description on the page becomes the arbitrary "spin" of "talking heads" on the screen: Opinion there is, like footage, a matter of hot "takes," "angles," "viewpoints." You can see what you think.

Where images play a central role in the rhetoric of information, as they do on TV, three things follow, which have prepared us for the digital. First, information tends to become fragmented, since continuity and sustained attention are not essential to reasoning in images. Programs may be shorter and disconnected where pictures carry the idea. The implicit "ideal" viewer must be able to tune in at any point and, with no prior knowledge, be roped into the plot. A newscast likewise consists of sound bites, talking "points," atomic "segments" disjointed, inchoate, and self-contained. What is presented must be immediately comprehensible and epitomizing. Programming must render viewers inattentive – and is therefore stupefying – since information cannot be expected to accumulate into demanding trains of expository thought.[41] Programs are thus brief, decontextualized, and discontinuous; anything must be able to succeed anything else in a given timeslot. (You are everywhere offered a jumping-off point, and so are forced to jump to conclusions.) Nor can they provide us with content of such a sort that we are not left wanting or needing more of it tomorrow: They must generate demand for information that only they are able to continually resupply. TV is (like all media, in different senses) self-referring and self-justifying; TV is mostly about what's on TV. Daniel Boorstin famously argued that mass media create the "pseudo-event," a new kind of occurrence contrived into being in order to satisfy our expectation that something newsworthy must always be happening.[42] He is right – not (as he implies) because there were no such pseudo-events before mass media, but because our conception of what qualifies as an "event" at all is medium-specific. There were no press conferences, celebrity sightings, or big-name interviews before newspapers, radio, and TV enlarged demand for novel content.

Second, as we are flooded with a crush of incoherent images, as images jockey with other images for our attention, those images must grow more sensational in order to stand out. ("Newsflash!") What is splashy, what is bells and whistles, what is lurid and loud and otherwise titillating for its enormity, must always attract more viewers than reporting in intelligent depth. TV is in the business of shocking you because that is how it scares up business. Such electric jolts are the most important way in which the medium establishes the intrinsic discontinuity of its contents (so that the news is always "breaking" from the past – it is always the event OF THE CENTURY! – and to succeed is to be "stunning," "smashing," or a "hit"). It is a pleasure to be wonderfully surprised. TV is therefore a medium that inherently promotes sex and violence; it is not an accident that that's what's on. Love and death are the two subjects that most interest us, and sex and violence are their most uncomplicated correlates. One has only to put them on the screen to catch the eye. A book of prose filled with sex and violence, no matter how smutty, must nonetheless take the trouble to unravel them, must develop in time what the screen can show at once, graphically, leaving nothing to the imagination. It's only because you can air them without further ado that violence may become "senseless" and sex "gratuitous." And as we grow inured to what we see, their depictions must escalate to keep their edge within the competition for new sensations. For that reason, what makes news is bad news, and always trending worse.

Finally, television has educated us in the presumption that information should be a commodity, a form of massively entertaining, broadcast fun. The goal of every non-subsidized television program is not to educate, but to increase ratings, to keep your attention by constantly diverting you. Educational programming then must be jazzed up to resemble a TED Talk or pale by comparison. ("Don't go away! It's all coming up after the break!") It can only do so to the extent that it leads our attention on, while making few demands on patience. Watching television is not at all like sitting through a theater play: The camera switches frame every few seconds, arresting our sight through a steady montage of viewpoints. We are ordinarily not even aware of the relentless intensity of this succession. But just try watching extended footage shot from a stationary camera – it is more boring than paint drying (which is why other people's home videos are so dull). No book, no matter how gripping and fast-paced, can compete with this tempo. Information becomes a commercial product on TV, events become "stories" on demand. Facts become fun facts – trivia factoids that are tasty piecemeal, out of context. Longstanding, run-of-the-mill problems are often neglected in favor of those that feature extravagant spectacle within the media "circus." If something does not grab you, you can surf to channel another scenario, a different "human interest" or show of compassion. No sweat; you take it easy.

As TV accustomed us to thinking in images, it soaked into our ordinary idioms and practices. Consider the colloquial use of the word "like" (as in: "And then he was like: yes! And then I was like: ugh!"), which television helped usher in. The word grates on the ears of grammar sticklers because it is not meant for the ear at all. It belongs to the forms of predication of a visual medium – the conversation of people who understand themselves in clips, pantomimes, and tableaux – rather than in words alone. "Like" strikes a pose for dramatic effect, it is a visual (or mimetic) quotation that enacts a response rather than articulating it – it is, in this regard, the predecessor of memes, GIFs, selfies, emojis, hashtags, and other flashes of posterized meaning favored by the digital. (Epic fail! For the win! That Feeling When ...! Or a repurposed image of "Me: [... doing something]" in juxtaposition to "Me: [... doing another].") It was once considered unmannered to move your hands and to gesticulate while speaking: the impropriety of a literate age.

But even as the remote made it easier to change the channel quickly, and even as cable multiplied and specialized our niches, TV still leaves us in a passive position, subject to the spectacle of moving pictures. The digital's accomplishment, on the other hand, was to make that spectacle subject to us, by making us participants. The decisive conceptual bridge from TV to the digital was therefore videogames, which were the first medium to put us onscreen with virtual agency and identity. It's videogames that first gave us a widespread way of touching the screen, allowing us to call the shots. The digital's decisive innovation was then to expand this possibility so as to make all screened actions interactive; words and images became not just something to look at, but something to manipulate, something you could put your finger on. ("Digital" means finger-ish.) It achieved this feat by welding sight into virtual touch; the cursor is what lends your sight a pointer, allowing you to see yourself getting in on a piece of the action. So if literate culture moved the word from the ear to the eye, digital culture is moving it once again, from a contemplative eye to a tangent one that, unmoved, moves as far as I can see.

Interface is the aesthetic experience of the fusion of tool with medium. Sight and touch – the primary senses of the digital – happen to be the senses by means of which we can make the crispest distinctions, our most precise feelers of what's out there. Interface is therefore designed to have a certain "look" and "feel" ("haptics"). But while interface requires fingers, it asks very little by way of fine-grained tact. Digital surfaces are polished and clean, without texture, edge, or bite. The feel is frictionless; it is not supposed to call palpable attention to itself. The point of the cursor is therefore not to be in touch, but rather to translate touch all into sight, writing you into a space where to see is to point out, and to point out is to do. It is sometimes explicitly shaped like a hand, sometimes only implicitly so (since an arrow is another way of saying "finger"). Look here; it's as good as done.

What's remarkable about this is that sight is (unlike touch) our most aloof and theoretical sense.[43] Sight takes in the world all at once; the speed of sight is the speed of thought. It has, as such, the quickest and most direct commerce with the mind. Many of our terms for thinking – evidence, clarity, idea, insight – have a visual pedigree. Seeing and thinking go together – "I see" means "I understand." We consider something "in light" of something else, we bring our thoughts before "the mind's eye," the "inner eye," and so forth (the mind doesn't have an "ear" or a "tongue"). But sight's knowledge usually comes at the price of direct involvement – you can see much more than you can immediately act on – so that it is only heroes and gods who can bring their vision into awesome being: "I came, I saw, I overcame" or "Let there be light!" The power to act on sight through digital interface is therefore akin to the power to put theory into immediate practice. That is, whereas sight is usually the most passive sense, when activated it approaches omnipotence (as we say the camera "shoots" and lover's glances "slay" – the basilisk ability to kill on sight). Interface is like that; within the context of the screen, it renders sight and therefore *thought* effective. "He seemed to become each thing he saw" (a description of cyberspace in Gibson's *Neuromancer*).[44] Interface abbreviates the significance of the hand and body, investing sight with will and thought with the capacity to do. Before the screen, we command the view. It has never been so easy to do so much, to flatter the straightforward experience of our will, where sight and touch go hand in hand.

The visualization of touch online implies new dispositions toward what's on the screen vis-à-vis the page. Printed words are signs existing within the material reality of the page, to be figured out and construed. You may underline and annotate, but there is little else to do with them except to take them in. They only come awake because you work to breathe life into them; your attention is the energy that makes them come to light. The direction of attention's light is reversed online, where words shine out toward you, trying to arrest your attention's flight to elsewhere. They stand within an altogether different web of possibilities: They may be copied, pasted, linked, shared, retweeted, enlarged, scrolled away, flipped through, swiped at – they are made iconic, transformed into pictograms of speech. Whereas reading, writing, and acting on what you've learned are sharply separate activities in a world of print, to be online is necessarily to be involved in all three: to move by clicks, to find ourselves "engaged," as we input, comment, react, and navigate. We picture words as action items.

While the words may be literally the same, the aesthetic context within which we encounter them online shapes our reading habits. The balance of power shifts decisively toward the user; where you can change the content as soon as notice it, the objects of attention have less authority of presence or substance of their own. Online words have no self-standing, material reality; they are mutable, there is no intrinsic pressure to ponder or to weigh them. Whereas printed words are not primarily meant to appeal to the eye, online words are both themselves screened and are only ever set within an environment of images that is putting on a show. "Visuals" are our readiest measure of quality. We judge the credibility of websites (surveys show) not by their discursive content but by their optic style, the background and setting of what's said. Words themselves must have the right look, they must jump out at you, they must be styled to be credited online. Text-based websites are an outrage to the eye of our online mind, or, like Craigslist, they look seamy. (The Drudge Report is an interesting exception that proves the rule: Its cheap look is its way of signaling its claim to offer the unvarnished, non-mainstream truth.) The screen makes it easy to move through images quickly, but it's a strain to read a whole book on it. The web is not a library, so much as a bulletin board.[45] Amazon could easily sell books by simply listing titles; but it has understood that, when situated online, the book will only sell by the cover. Web users need not be fully literate: Part of the success of WhatsApp in some parts of the world has been to make it easy for people to exchange recorded messages in place of texts.[46] Where print (at best) was food for patient thought, online content aspires to the condition of eye-candy for the social media feed.

Nor is it only words that are transformed. The online fusion of theory and practice also means that, to the extent that the digital allows us to put an image of ourselves on screen in social media, it is a theatricalizing medium – the inherent demand for greater agency turns us into actors. We are pushed to participate in some way, so that what's on the screen is all in play. I mean that as my identity becomes (more) a matter of preference, it becomes an exercise in controlled self-representation. And when all eyes are on you, there is no information you could share about yourself that is not for show – to share an image of oneself is to send a message; to post is to make a statement. It is a form of self-description that is itself self-promoting; online speech is a speech act. Just so, when our engagement with others becomes a matter of exposure, part of our own identity is constructed through expressing explicit approval or disapproval, liking or disliking the identities of others in public ways. You may follow or unfollow – to "cancel" someone is to kill them off, as in a play or a game. Video games, the original form of online navigation and once a byword for antisocial behavior, are becoming (for digital natives) a chief medium of spending time with friends in real time, a convenient way of keeping safe and contained while attending to the same world as others.[47] Even when you know those you are gaming with, you are role-playing – sending a message, making a scene.

1.4   WHAT'S DIGITAL IS IMMATERIAL

I've described the digital as the fusion of tool with medium through data (conceptually) and through palpable images (aesthetically). As the digital joins up the sequence of communicative media with the sequence of broadcast experience, it also joins both of these up with an additional sequence: that of transportation. The digital constitutes, in this respect, the fusion of the TV with the car. It is a medium of moving without moving, of transportation without locomotion, and therefore of discorporate and excarnate space and time.

When novels, films, and cartoons from earlier decades tried to imagine the technology of the future, they got a few things right – Kubrick's *2001* features phone-televisions (Skype); the *Jetsons* dreams of the mechanization of household chores (Roomba); and many of our current biomedical possibilities were anticipated by Francis Bacon, Aldous Huxley, and Philip K. Dick. But, with a few exceptions (like Forster's *The Machine Stops*), they went badly wrong in one respect. They pictured great innovations in transportation: ships zooming through the cosmos at time-warping speeds, car-planes flying to work, or bodies being tele-transported to different locations on command ("Beam me up!"). We have not in fact made much headway with moving our bodies around. Our transportation networks now look much as they did in the 1960s – boats, planes, trains, and automobiles – while our space program has basically stood still. (If anything, mass transportation slowed down a bit with the discontinuation of Concorde flights.) Instead, we have the internet, a medium for transporting stupendous amounts of data at the speed of light.[48] The sci-fi mistake remains a telling one, however: The internet was difficult to imagine in advance, because its success lies in its very translucence, its incorporeality. We couldn't see it coming because there's nothing there to see.

The digital makes possible an unprecedented separation between material and its uses. Where is the internet? What is it? How does data travel and where is it stored? What is a computer? A microprocessor? How does it all work? If you know the answer to any one of these questions, you are a rarity. The digital is so effective in its own right that these questions almost never come up; one need not think of them at all in order to work the medium with thorough competence. Our words to describe the basis of computing reaffirm this sense of unreality. Data is stored in the (Google) Cloud or the (Microsoft) Azure and transmitted "wirelessly" through the "ether" (just as you're "on air" on TV); to be online is to be "up"; and the internet is the everywhere medium – it is wherever with you. The phrase "I broke the internet" is a joke, because it's not clear what's there to break. The internet has no landmarks or monuments. As Leonard Kleinrock, one of the inventors of the net, put it: "It's like oxygen. People don't ask where oxygen comes from."[49] It's all up in the air.

Look at this progression. Before cars and paved roads made a casual road trip possible, we needed a hand-drawn map, or first-hand knowledge of the terrain, or frequent verbal directions, in order to travel any great length from home. Our conception of the territory was the map. Printed maps then made navigation easier by handing us a ready-made key to travel by means of established road markers. Such maps free you from the need to know where you are going; they make it possible for strangers to find their way around. In many modern cities, the map's view was then built into the layout. Streets built on a grid (like Chicago's, Washington DC's, or uptown Manhattan's) or numbered (or lettered) in straightforward ways offer a readily legible mapscape to the mind. You need not pay close attention to any particular place, once houses and streets are regularly spaced out and labeled (just as we do not pay close attention when someone else is driving). Such an order enlarges your room to maneuver by lightening the burden of what you are responsible for noticing while you make your way.

Such maps are maps of agency too; latter-day maps presuppose the presence of cars, which themselves have transformed the physical and psychic landscape. Since you can commute faster and farther with them, cars sprawl cities out even as they concentrate activity into urban nodes. They standardize roads, they create the need for vast parking lots, they make some areas inhospitable, they pollute. They also bring into being new modes and icons of all-American individuality. Jack Kerouac, James Dean, Thelma and Louise, Dom Toretto, the Hell's Angels: the creations of self through style, the romances of the open road. An "auto-mobile" means a "self-mover," and so a car is a "freedom machine," an autonomous cell with no fixed place and free from scrutiny, where you are both in full control and on the edge of losing it. The experience of acceleration is the fantasy of total self and self-surrender: You feel yourself ecstatically alive at insolent speeds. (We are the more aware of this as we rage and fume in traffic.) The car has therefore been the vehicle by which we have marked the mythical difference between childhood and adulthood since the mid-twentieth century – the means by which you are handed the keys to sex and death: a dream come true.

But car maps have built-in limitations – they cannot indicate that "you are here." If you get lost, you must find yourself again by matching paper to surroundings. GPS navigation eases this burden of knowledge one step more: Not only does it locate you, it accounts for circumstances that you cannot see (weather, traffic, construction), and reroutes you by itself in real time. If once you're lost, again you're found and up to speed by satellite. As long as you can drive a car or follow a blue dot on a screen, you may remain otherwise oblivious, it makes no difference. To ask for directions is to inconvenience a stranger: It is to make yourself vulnerable by advertising the fact that you are not a local. We do not always speak the same language; nor are all verbal directions comprehensible or accurate. GPS lubricates our motion through the world by sidestepping these bothers altogether.

A driverless car – a vehicle steered by digital controls – would represent one more degree of frictionlessness. It is a new map of agency: We give up the trouble of being on familiar terms with a few places, of learning a handful of routes like the back of our hand, in exchange for getting around everywhere without our knowing it. Human drivers must each come by our experience slowly and riskily, taking note of our failures. In contrast, when a self-driving car makes an error on the road, all the other self-driving cars then "learn" not to repeat it – they operate with one memory. Such navigation makes my radius of action larger yet again (in theory, measureless) – it facilitates mobility and frees up hours of commuting time. The means at our disposal make it both easier than ever before to forget that they exist, and harder than ever before to do without them. Travel still takes place by moving bodies around in cars, but the process of traveling becomes more inconspicuous. One need no longer look out the window, if one would rather nap or watch TV. As the digital streamlines our activities and goals in this way, it is more difficult to keep that transformation meaningfully in view: Its immateriality, its usefulness, and our dependence on it are all closely related. That is the net effect.

The digital fuses the car with the TV in two different senses. Cars, televisions, and digital devices all may be described as concentrating our attention on a window of vision. Whereas a driver takes her life in her hands, a TV viewer has nothing much at stake in watching. A digital window resembles the driver's in that it empowers us by abstracting us from direct contact with what we see; while, unlike the driver and like the viewer, the digital user can direct his motion through the medium while remaining invulnerable. But this invulnerability obviously comes from the division of the body's experience from the mind's, the real from the virtual. A driverless car expresses this division perfectly not only because the rider becomes once more a programmed spectator of what's out of the window – both in control and (relatively) invulnerable. But because, once we no longer need to keep our hands on the steering wheel, we are likely to be spending that time interacting with another kind of window entirely – our body and mind all out of touch.

The digital also integrates transportation with spectatorship in a new way. Up until the 1830s, there were fixed limits to speed: We could only travel as fast as water, wind, or horse could draw us. Up until the 1830s, there were also natural limits to communicating human sensory experience: The only way to know what happened in other places and times was from written account or from taking someone's word for it. The railroad and the photograph by coincidence appeared within a few years of each other in that decade, dissolving those natural limits. They are correlative inventions, complementary aspects of the touted annihilation of space and time. It is the achievement of both to eliminate the need to attend to the interval between us and the objects of possible experience. As the railroad made it possible for people to travel comfortably and to see the sights, the photograph made it possible to capture the unfamiliar into souvenir. As the railroad scattered and blurred possible experience, the photograph froze it into focused place. As the railroad shortened time by gaining speed, the photograph memorialized experience by claiming instants from time's flow.

The trend in transportation has been to pick up speed, even as the trend in broadcast sensoria has been, as I've said, to involve us more closely in the real-time action. The digital overcomes the difference between these two sequences, not only by transforming transportation, but by transporting experience in "real time" at the speed of light. It combines the car's sense of agency with the TV's sense of invulnerable spectatorship. It does not propel you into world, it propels the world into you; the road becomes the information superhighway. It is what we have instead of zooming spaceship travel – it brings us into contact with distant people and things not by taking us there bodily, but by canceling the friction of what's in between. While we still need to move bodies in space, and while virtual experience in some ways enhances the value of what's real (a theme to which I'll return in Chapter 4), the digital offers a new interpretation of time and space in which one is only ever everywhere and everywhen at once.

Space and time have always been the most significant obstacles to technological innovation. It is no accident that many of the greatest achievements of civilization have taken place in cities, where dense groups could work in proximity to each other. The sign that we have annihilated these obstacles is that we now regard them as inconveniences – a residual "lag" in our expectation of the supply chain, an annoying delay in the order. (It isn't likely that anyone would have conceived of what's between origin and destination as an "interval" at all before the use of electricity – the faster the speed, the sharper our awareness of what's in the way as mere impediment.) As far as speed is concerned, we have already reached the point at which the amount of data we can exchange online is limited not by the available processing power, but by the internet's infrastructure itself – the thickness and quantity of the 800,000 miles of fiber-optic cables that tunnel and web the world.[50] News travels as fast as we can make it, so that we mostly no longer experience speed online at all when things are up and running by split seconds. Time is not of its essence.

The very need for a shared place of work, for all manner of sheer physical proximity, is diminishing. Prior to the pandemic, companies and governments still took the trouble to do some of their business in person – for summits, team building, and sealing important deals. It was a tacit acknowledgment of the subtle checks that online communication places on attention, candor, and intimacy: A Zoom call, even among friends, retains the sense of being a transmission. But many of those face-to-face meetings will prove increasingly difficult to justify, as the pandemic has habituated us to the principle that all work that *can* be done online *will* be done online. It is safer, more convenient, more efficient, less polluting. More and more of the action will take place remotely, offering flexibility and mobility, while cutting costs on rent.

What cannot take place online has been thereby pushed into cruel prominence: the education of the very young, the care of the very old, the final visitation – all acts that ask us to make contact. So too the blue-collar work of those without a choice, which we have labeled "essential" (in other words: what we need that's not online; in other words: what cannot meaningfully take place out of touch). In the early days of the pandemic, there was an irrational rush on toilet paper. It was a panicked avowal of the limits of our online self-sufficiency – such are the clownish ingressions of the body into our virtual isolation.

The absence of spatial and temporal constraints carries over into our experience with digital devices themselves; the digital has no material presence. So smooth and seamless is our aesthetic encounter with it that our perception of what is material about it must be artificially induced: Just as a word processor's icons are mostly borrowed from the physical world (the paper file for "open," the paint brush for "format," and the floppy disk for "save"), the smartphone's clicks and whirs are simulations of concrete, mechanical effects used to orient us in our doing without mattering. As the digital is composed of surface images, it can never be said to be fully "there" – what we access is through or despite its physical substance, but not in or by way of it. Better said, while its body is there, it is (like ours) disconnected from the interest of its mind, a disembodied cerebration.

Immateriality is the condition of the screen's awesome pluripotency. The screen can bring you every image precisely because images have no material presence. It is therefore banalizing. Where everything is interchangeable with everything else, images need not be *committed* to matter. The Nuremberg Trials were not televised so as not to degrade the dignity of the defendants. The Supreme Court remains off limits for cameras to protect the gravity of its proceedings. Queen Elizabeth II's coronation was televised despite controversy, but the transmission was tightly controlled. Could it occur to anyone to pray to an image onscreen? To go on an online pilgrimage? It is merely a sign of something elsewhere; there is nothing to it. The screen is an empty vessel, less a presence than an absence. It cannot admit of solemnity or sanctity because it cannot place events, cannot set them apart from the rest of our activities. It is not only that it is possible for any image to succeed any other (which implicitly equalizes them), but that you may be watching in any attitude or context – standing in awe or slouched in pajamas, it's no matter. Coverage is exposure. The internet is a vast machine for replication: Any time you access, refresh, or save a page, a copy is made of it and stored on your device or on the server. But even "copy" is the wrong word, since there is no fundamental distinction between original and image: The principle is facsimile, cliché, repurposing, proliferation, and transmission of digital images of all content.[51] (Which is why, in turn, so much online content is a remix, mash up, and recombination of things found elsewhere.) Does it seem mad that some may once have thought that cameras could steal the soul in pictures? They were not wrong to the extent that images put you into easy circulation, render you into a token presence, encourage you to pose.

This lack of material presence, this identity between original and image, also applies to other media in the age of mechanical reproduction (e.g., photography and film). It has long been asked, along these lines, whether photography should be properly regarded as a fine art just like painting and sculpture.[52] The question is more than idle snobbery; it is not about, say, whether photographs are beautiful or should be allowed in museums. It concerns, rather, the relation between art and its material disciplines. Pre-modern art was, after all, defined by material limitations, by conquering what is recalcitrant in stone and wood, in pigment, in metal, and in voice. It is only gravity that teaches the ballet dancer to leap, it is only because stone bulks mute and brutal that we admire the triumph of sculpture or the Gothic cathedral spilling and uprisen into air. Creative form had always been this victory, this grace reclaimed from matter's heft.[53]

But if photography already seemed to make it too "easy," too close to automatic to come up with the finished product – making it impossible to distinguish the photographs of artists from the haphazard shots of amateurs, thereby scrambling older canons of evaluation – the digital makes it easier still. Pictures do not have to be developed, reels do not have to be spliced, you need no clunky specialized equipment to record. Old-school photography now seems downright artisanal by comparison. More than just about images and footage, something similar happens to digital words: No matter how muddled the prose, online words *look* perfect on the screen – bright ideas flawless and glowing on the page, they obscure the need for biding time to craft. Not to mention the fact that the medium demands new content as fast as we can pitch it, even as great writing remains – like good wine – a labor that must always begin from nothing to come to full expression through spans of vacant, fallow years. Art should slow to bear the weight of total scrutiny, the patience of the breath of life's creation. Whereas to "move fast" has always been to "break things," not to make them; and it is harder to slow down when the imperative is faster.

This is not to say that the digital cannot sustain art. Novels are being written on word processors, films are being shot on iPhones, video games and virtual reality will open up new aesthetic possibilities.[54] (Installation art is now often made with a view to the way in which its audience will "participate" and "interact" with it by means of their phone; the selfie is part of the attraction.[55]) The point is that these new possibilities are distinct from the old insofar as the new ones are disembodied. Online images are *ideas* rather than *things*. There is nothing in the digital to resist you, to force you to work a medium that is intractable and obstinate to your ready-made intentions. Nothing in the digital gives you pause: The use of it is highly cerebral, rather than material for hands-on craftsmanship. Its there-ness is no object; it doesn't mean a thing. And these new possibilities are correspondingly transforming our aesthetic canons and criteria. The question that usually concerns us is no longer (as in the eighteenth century) "Is it beautiful?" or even (as in the twentieth century) "Is it art?" – which everything and nothing is online – but "Is it real or fake?" That is, is it too good to be true? And can you tell the difference? And does that even matter?

Beyond aesthetics, the invisibility of the medium – its weightless mastery of space and time – conforms our experience of everything we do by means of it. Even as we shop, or write, or search, we are spared the friction of tangible encounters that would have otherwise marked such tasks (standing in line at a store, putting pen to paper, flipping through a book). The medium makes things easier for us by reducing our perception of the concrete people or circumstances that intervene to deliver for us. (I check the weather online, rather than taking the trouble to stick my hand out of the door.) Even when we "know" that shopping online has implications for brick-and-mortar retail business, it is hard to feel that virtual shopping means a thing, that buying by clicks is as real as forking over actual greenbacks to someone in a store. Consider the kind of scrutiny that Walmart's labor practices have been under over the years, compared to the relative pass that Amazon's warehouse practices long received (until relatively recently): One we see, the other we don't. Or consider how much news coverage is devoted to air pollution from car and plane exhaust, compared to the environmental costs of digital technology. The gold needed to make one cell phone (one of many minerals involved) results in more than 220 pounds of waste; small electronics result in carbon emissions that match the whole pre-Covid airline industry's – the International Energy Agency projects that digital devices will use up 45 percent of residential electricity by 2030; and the production of microprocessors requires dozens of toxic chemicals (so companies outsource the task to countries with lower environmental standards and laxer labor laws).[56] We do not (yet) have to *face* these consequences. Their costs are hidden in plain sight, since the very convenience of the digital makes them easier not to think about. The more useful something is, the harder it is to bear in mind: The digital's trick is thus to show us everything we wish while erasing its own tangible presence and effects.

The dematerialization of the digital is thereby also the dematerialization of our identity. Chances are that much of your most valuable information – the marks you make, your moveable effects – are stored digitally now: your finances, your pictures, your music, your emails, your contacts, your daily dealings, your life's work. How many of these do you have on "hard" copy? And wouldn't it be strangely wasteful for you to print it all out? The great domestic cluttering of the twentieth century (consequent on the development of plastics and the mass accessibility of cheap goods) is being met by the great decluttering of the twenty-first: Digital files do not get scuffed or wear out or gather dust or take up closet room. Digitalization frees us up to move. But if your data suddenly and inexplicably went up in a cloud, would you know what to do with yourself? Paper is flammable, but it does not go away without a trace; paper is still opaque, obtrusive, stubborn stuff. So long as there is paper, printers will continue to jam up[57] – you cannot get rid of it all at once. It is because totalitarian regimes could not burn their files in time that we have any written documentation of their doings. Where does our digital identity leave us? We are safer from local accidents, but more vulnerable to globalizing Ragnarok. It is harder to weigh the likelihood of each, when what matters isn't matter.

As the automobile has long been our most vivid way of imagining our autonomy – our rebellion, our mid-life crisis, our ego's project – the digital is making us a new one. The car's gambit is to increase your power of choice by restricting your bodily motion. It is because you consent to the terms of a small metallic cloister that you can then direct the sounds, the temperature, the direction, and the velocity at which you hurl yourself into space. It magnifies speed by intensifying privacy. The self-driving car – as a figure for digital agency more generally – widens this contrast once again: It enhances your power to move by diminishing your responsibility for steering it. You surrender your immediate power of agency for safety's sake and ease. (Google's prototype for a driverless car has no steering wheel; Teslas have nothing a driver could access under the hood.) Whereas older cars could not relieve you of the burden of looking out the window, self-driving cars do: As there is no need to face forward all the time, they will likely be configured more like lounges, bedrooms for leisure. You are freed up as a subject the more you are subject to it. Our autonomy takes the form of being a passenger, our life and limb in digital hands. It is the car's "self" that does the self-driving.

Technology in the *Jetsons* is meant to replace drudgery, freeing us up to lead the best lives of which we are capable. But what will we be doing while our self-driving car propels us along? (What are we doing in our free time already?) The digital's final disappearing act as an immaterial medium is not into thin air, but into us: As it frees up time, it takes up more of it, or all. The integration of the TV with the car takes place not only, maybe not even primarily, through devices or autonomous vehicles, but through the biometric and attentional quantification of all we do and how we roll. The digital's form of agency is, in sum, instrumental: to use and be of use. You need no longer steer the wheel so that you will have more time to make use of digital devices. We are ourselves now on the map, no longer measuring the territory but measured as the vehicle and territory in play. It is the car that's now in the driver's seat; we take a back seat as consumers.

1.5   WHAT'S DIGITAL IS COMMERCIAL

In 2016 the United Nations resolved that access to the internet be reckoned as a basic human right.[58] This sounds batty at first, since human rights (like shelter, food, education, medical care, and freedom from torture) sound like perennial needs for leading a decent life. Whatever one may think about that, the resolution highlighted the point that those without access to the internet are more and more living in a world divided from what is politically, economically, and socially current. The point was not that someone could not flourish without the internet (just as one might do so without formal education, which the United Nations also deems a right). But that the price would be a rustic isolation; one could not participate in the modern economy and its conventions without it. As Twitter's motto accurately puts it: "it's what's happening." And so it is extraordinary that unlike any other such medium of exchange, the digital is fundamentally a market venture – the lion's share of its hardware, software, and platforms are controlled by outsize companies.

Media and tools have never been evenly distributed. Literacy was once the privilege of a small class; it is still (in global terms) a relatively elite skill. Electricity and telecom companies have also gravitated toward few hands for obvious reasons; they are services designed to integrate widespread nodes into networks. But in no case had the primary medium of communication – our foremost way of conducting ourselves and our affairs, shared by about 5 billion people as of 2022[59] – been so centralized. To participate in this way of doing things is to stand in need of commercial infrastructure: access to electricity and the web (the cables or towers of which are owned by a telecom), a phone or a computer (a device with its licensed software), as well as a web browser (or a domain), email and social media and whatever else. TV is similar (though airwaves are public in some places). But nothing like this applies to the printed word, since the means of printing are relatively cheap, and words may be handed out on the street, or dropped from airplanes, or scribbled on the wall. To use the net you must buy into it – there is no digital samizdat. Even where cities or airports have started giving it away for free, they are not making it themselves, but paying for networks that are privately controlled. There are a few "public" sites (like Wikipedia), but there is no public internet as such, no equivalent to public roads or transportation. The recent defeat of "net neutrality" in the United States has made this clearer than ever: Online information will be easier to disseminate for those willing to pay for it. To have truck with the printed word, one is a reader or a writer. To be online, on the other hand, is perforce to be a customer, a user. The internet is, unlike printed media, a "service."

That the various aspects of this service happen to have coalesced into few hands is in obvious contrast to the digital's libertarian and democratic self-image. On the one hand, all can join in to innovate – there are fewer middlemen, watchdogs, gatekeepers, or barriers to entry. "Competition is one click away" (Google). During its jubilant first decades, it seemed to many that the internet would be an equalizing economic force: As an open-access technology, it would allow competition to flourish for the good of producers and consumers alike – a free market dream, entirely governed by the laws of creative destruction. But the result has been, on the other hand, just the opposite: oligopoly and consolidation. The four biggest publicly traded companies in the world by market capitalization are (as of the first quarter of 2022) you-know-who: Apple, Microsoft, Alphabet (Google's parent), and Amazon. (Facebook's Meta has recently dropped to an ignoble tenth.)[60] The market value of the top five companies of Silicon Valley has fluctuated somewhere between $5 and $7 trillion.[61] Apple sold about 230 million iPhones in 2021; there are 1.4 billion devices running Microsoft's Windows 10 and 11; Google handles something like 8.5 billion searches a day; Amazon has accounted for over half of all online commerce in the United States; Facebook has just under 3 billion daily active users.[62] These Brobdingnagian numbers – so large as to be practically meaningless and ticking up even as you read – bespeak the most staggering concentration of consumer attention and wealth that the world has ever seen.

It is true that anyone without online access or literacy is now at gross economic disadvantage. Those who cannot or will not enter into the system find themselves in a position analogous to those who would continue to barter after the invention of ready currency. But it is likewise true that the internet has taken away with one invisible hand what it had first proffered with the other. The digital economy undoubtedly created new kinds of goods and resources that disrupted existing commercial empires. Once established and widely accepted, however, these new resources have themselves become stratified into new hierarchies of wealth and status: Yesterday's anti-corporate counter-culture rebels are now the silicon Man.[63] Is the internet a decentralized, democratic medium? Only in theory, only in the sense that "neutrality," the leveling of the field, the loosening of structure, sounds as if it *should* promote equality. In fact, it doesn't.

Commercialization and centralization go hand in hand here, because oligopolies serve platform users best. The usefulness of Facebook, Yelp, eBay, Instagram, or (arguably) Amazon does not derive from any particular content they provide, but from the fact that they concentrate the attention of an immense number of users in one place (the "network effect"). They are valuable to the extent that I can presume to share them with people or companies I haven't yet met; they broker and facilitate links. And once we have learned to use a particular platform, it's a drag to switch to something marginally better, just as there is a disincentive to changing your phone number: You lose connections. Facebook's user base has continued to grow even while beset by scandals and criticism (#DeleteFacebook). Under what conditions would you switch your email to a different provider? (Or to a different operating system?) Websites savvy to this ask you to create wish lists or profiles that, by generating customized recommendations, act as a hook to keep you coming back on the basis of data you have already given out. If to be online is to be burdened with the onrush of information, what is simplest is to stick, in any case, more or less to sites we know. It is not just platforms that benefit from the network effect, but news media, gaming, video streaming, and any service that gains from becoming a stock reference. "Foundation models" for AI research require enormous amounts of data and processing power, such that only the largest companies can afford them.[64] Online services are not (just) selling products, but popularity (with ads that then benefit from it); or, like Apple or Google on the hardware side, a cluster of services (YouTube, email, Android, and so forth).[65] There tend to be few shows in town, because it's more convenient that few winners take most or all.

The immateriality of the medium – its volatilization into data and images – goes hand in hand with its commercial character too. Whereas cash money can get lost, requires the taking and giving of change, and deteriorates in circulation, digital currency is "contactless," without a trace: One can buy at will, without getting one's hands dirty. Amazon has, as usual, shown the way of future shopping: Its site offers one-click purchasing, its (now discontinued) Dash buttons allowed one to order household products at a push, its Alexa will order something for you on vocal demand, and its grocery store offers "Just Walk Out Shopping" – you don't have to bother with waiting in line or putting your hand in your wallet. The point is to abbreviate all intervening material obstacles between attention and consumption, so that any impulse may become an impulse buy. There's a push for companies to bundle different kinds of services together – from food delivery, to gaming, to social media, to credit cards – so as to integrate all kinds of online activities into a general atmosphere that mingles attention with acquisition.[66] (And what else is the Metaverse?) So long as attention is to someone's credit, profit is in the air. There is no better illustration of the notion of "liquid modernity," that is, of the ways in which – relatively unconstrained from the coherence of established roles, projects, and institutions – the exercise of our will may be modular, flexible, and therefore fragmented, such that, as Marx put it, "all that is solid melts into air."[67] (A Verizon slogan: "Rule the air.")

But the trend toward immaterial transaction is only one aspect of the general fact that the currency of the internet is attention measurably captured. Its most reliable means of centralizing attention is to personalize its content, to get to know you better so you can better know what to get. Google does not answer your questions willy-nilly: It ranks results according to an algorithm that takes into consideration many factors, one of which is the interests of its advertisers. Google Maps orients you to business locations that have paid for explicit mention. Gmail tailors its ads to what it happens to find in your inbox. Amazon too makes much of its profit by recommending things to your attention. Facebook and Instagram have their own algorithms, which customize ads to suit us. Whether one is using a "free" service or paying for an adless version of it, to be online is directly to someone's profit. Whereas in print or on the airwaves, the time is divided between content and "a word from our sponsors," the digital has (like infomercials) blurred this distinction altogether – between intimacy and product placement, between using and buying, between using and being used. We call it "clickbait" when the headline is more enticing than the substance of what's clicked on; but all online content screams out for styles of attention and advertises itself to notice. Companies no longer sell just their product, take it or leave it, they sell consumer "experiences" – not just a service, but the feeling of satisfaction that attends the process of buying it. And where our every online move is tracked, counted, and measured, they can, as I've said, deliver on their promise with increasing accuracy. As Tim Cook, Apple's CEO, put it: "when an online service is free, you're not the customer. You're the product."[68] "Free" services are paid for by selling ads; in this sense, they separate the role of customer from the role of user. But even when such services are not free, it's the same; Tim Cook's widely quoted zinger is itself part of Apple's branding campaign, as some tech companies now scramble to sell us privacy from data collection.[69] Whether in privacy or publicity, however, every online action is a transaction of human capital. That's the deal, the business of living now that you're a hot commodity.

There is, along these lines, no sharp distinction between the maintenance of digital hardware and its commercial character. When my phone warns me that it doesn't have enough room to back up its data, it is not a guileless notification, but an advertisement encouraging me to buy more storage. Companies stop "supporting" older models, stop providing updates for them, and even deliberately slow them down, in order to phase them out, to nudge customers to upgrade. No digital device is built to last more than five years – they are "designed for the dump" and "made to break."[70] It is increasingly the case that we are licensed as mere users of digital devices, not as full owners: The warranty is no good if you tinker with your device's hardware or install some kinds of software owned by a competing company. We do not "own" such devices in the same sense that we own other kinds of property; there is arguably a new sense of ownership at work here, in which we pay for experience rather than tangible acquisition.[71] Tesla has placed restrictions on the use of their electric vehicles for Uber and other ride-hailing apps, for instance. Google Translate is the legal proprietor of whatever words you input. Likewise, the trend in online entertainment is toward "hosting" content; that is, not selling it for keeps, but selling access to content that you continue to subscribe to once you rely on it (as with Netflix, Spotify, Audible, Amazon Prime). There is nothing to walk away with.

The awesome powers at our fingertips are in this way paid for at the cost of an unprecedented dependence on the companies that design them: The gap between the simplicity of our user interface and the technical complexity of the devices themselves – between users and designers – is chasmic and is growing wider all the time. Children once used to take mechanical contraptions apart, in order, by tinkering, to learn to work them. We played at being inventors in this way – the crazy complexity of a Rube Goldberg machine is charming because it makes the ingenuity of a process explicit to the naked eye. To know was (practically) to make. This is no longer possible or true: Digital devices are unforgiving; there is no room to maneuver, no workaround, they cannot be pounded, kick-started, or jury-rigged to work. The hardware's nuts and bolts are too intricate to be touched by most engineers, let alone the layman. This is the case not only for digital devices, but for all services and appliances that run on computerized circuitry. There is less and less for independent mechanics and repairmen to do: Breakdowns must be left to specialized technicians at the dealer. What is "intuitive" and streamlined for us is all Surface (the name of Microsoft's touchscreen devices); it is highly fragmented, specialized, and microscopic "under the hood," or "behind the curtain." Increasing transparency in interface is increasing opacity in underlying function.

Our power and our powerlessness go together online. On the one hand, to be a user is to be effective, to see your will be done. On the other hand, if anything goes wrong, if any bug gums up the works, if your device crashes, then you are in the helpless dark, there is nothing then to do. Most of us have precisely one course of action when facing digital malfunction: *try restarting it*. It is a mark of the fact that we do not engage our devices as comprehensible, such that our only path to rectifying error is to eject ourselves from the process altogether, to start up again and hope for a better outcome – as when we hang up on an incompetent customer representative and call the same number again praying to talk to someone else. What I will is divided off from what I cannot help. The experience of being a digital user reinforces our sense that knowledge is freely chosen or strictly enforced, entirely subjective or objective.

Tech is thus the purest expression of a service industry, in which customer and expert are the two most important roles. Unlike buying a book, the experience of being online is not separable from the experience of consumption: I mean that being a reader is notionally distinct from being a consumer as being a user is not. This is partly entailed by all advanced technology. The progress of technology can itself be described as the process by which we can all become more powerful as we each become more haplessly dependent. But over the past century our appliances and tools have come to outsmart us to a new degree, they pass our understanding such that the role of user becomes indistinguishable from that of consumer, at the mercy of the technicians who know how things work. We are cast into this role not simply because we are paying customers, but because we cannot account for the difference between our experience of the world and the systems that make our experience possible. The technical processes are the more hidden to the extent that our experience of interface is so fluid as not to call attention to itself. We don't learn about them by doing, because the technological conditions underlying use have nothing to do with the experience of use itself; that's just the way it is and by design.

More than a matter of our complacency or of perverse commercial incentive, however, to be online is to be a customer because one finds oneself involved in the quest for simplification. The theory of digital technology is the promise to make life easier, to liberate us from mechanical or mindless tasks. The practice of it is in fact to multiply such tasks: The speed of transmission, as I've said, puts us in contact with more information than we could ever know what to do with. No one can reasonably keep up with all the things that demand our online attention – from email, to news, to social media, to TV, to all kinds of notifications. Whereas printed literacy places the burden on the reader to tune in to the page, online use places the burden on the user to tune out and narrow down what can be attended to. To be a user is therefore to desire to be disburdened, to be involved in the search for hacks, cheat codes, walkthroughs, multitasking shortcuts, abbreviated instruction manuals, frictionless ease, and "friendly" services. ("Make Google do it.") But the imperative of simplification, in turn, means surrendering degrees of knowledge and freedom for convenience. When was the last time we read through all the fine print of the contracted terms of service, before clicking "I agree"? Would it make any difference if we found something to object to? And who has the patience? To simplify is itself to outsource the terms of our agency to make things easier. The digital thus both complicates life and then sells us simplicity as its own remedy; it awakens in us a new taste for convenient speed while also involving us in a cycle of entanglement and disentanglement that only ever deepens our dependence.

To be an online agent is to live in a world of magic effect and technique – to be caught up in a way of doing things that we don't understand because we don't need to, since understanding is itself a hassle of which we've been relieved. As Clarke's third law has it, any sufficiently advanced technology is indistinguishable from magic (at any rate, to most of us). That the help features of many software packages are called "wizards," or that background programs are called "daemons," or that analytics and software firms are baptized with preternatural names like "Oracle," "Prophet," "Delphi," "Palantir," "Halcyon," is no accident. So too names like "Unreal" (a popular video game engine) or "Magic Leap" (a company making augmented reality glasses) or terms like "angel investments" or "unicorn" companies – all fabulous. To fix an issue, we can head over to the Genius Bar, a name which bears witness to a world of magic ruled by programming whizzes, web ninjas, and alpha geeks.

This is obviously not the magic of other ages; we are supposed to know that the principles governing digital technology are impersonal. Nor do our devices delight in burnt offerings or in the blood of bullocks. But our life and death reliance on technical processes of which we have no informed conception is such as to resemble a condition of conviction or belief rather than understanding (a point to which I'll return). We believe because it works; it would be silly not to. But what is objectively the case for us is practically incomprehensible; the more advanced the technology, the more we are at the mercy of unforeseen and inscrutable disruption. The real basis of belief is itself so opaque to our responsibility for it that it is, in this sense, morally regressive; the theater of slogan, repetition, incantatory assertion, association, and juxtaposed images that marks the logic of advertising is also, by extension and in different senses, the logic of digital justification. It is not what is true that is effective, but what makes a special effect that becomes true.

Digital devices, as I've mentioned, eliminate tangible friction to make interface a matter of sights and sounds. Still, it would be wrong to overlook how extraordinarily compelling the tactile aesthetics of digital devices are – liquid, dark, and glistening with crystalline perfection. Their design exhibits physical products without a history: fallen from the sky full formed, without flaw or seam or crease, like the alien monolith that bewilders the apes at the beginning of Kubrick's *2001: A Space Odyssey*. One cannot but wonder at how thin these devices are, how weightless out of all proportion to the weight of what they can do. The trend to create objects without buttons (so that the screen is the site of interface) reinforces the sense that they are metamorphic and impregnable, that they have no umbilical connection to an origin beyond themselves. Apple in particular has attended to this, emphasizing their devices' lack of "hard corners," in imitation of organic shapes and to escape the sharp edges of mass-produced industrial design.[72] The minimalism of their devices is also indebted to the simplicity of traditional Japanese aesthetics. But the overall effect is not so much organic or spare as uncanny. As Jonathan Ive, Apple's erstwhile chief design officer, put his version of Clarke's third law: "when something exceeds your ability to understand how it works, it sort of becomes magical. That's exactly what the iPad is."[73] All but weightless: iPad Air. They are artless artifices, miracles of touch and go.[74]

A world of magical agency and effect is, at bottom, a world that prizes novelty as its highest good. This is the deepest reason why the digital must be commercial, why there is no such thing as a socialist or state-run internet. It is not simply that market innovation, disruption, and revolution are the best means by which to generate new products, it is that innovation is itself a (commercial) goal, a satisfaction that's its own reward, a purpose of our novelizing habit of mind. There is a clear imperative to always be launching new versions, new operating systems, new suites and devices on a schedule that is independent of qualitative progress. All major digital platforms are busy tinkering not just with what they offer, but with how they look; they often make changes in layout and feel that are but marginal differences in function. (You can then switch back to the older version, if you wish, which suddenly becomes "classic.") The contrivance of variety, the pseudo-speciation involved in repackaging and rebranding measures, sells because it keeps asking us to take another look. It is our desire for what's new that keeps us posting, refreshing, checking email, and reaching for our phone after a text notification, no matter how low our avowed expectations. It is also part of the reason why fake or outrageous news is shared faster and more widely. What is "new," the "latest," replaces what is "good" as the guiding social norm; what's big is the next big thing, what's not updated is stagnant and irrelevant.[75] "Think different," as the Apple ad put it. (Not "Think differently.") It is a hope for surprise – that something new will show up and take place again and again to change the face of things. It is a form of attention that is after more and moreish wonder. Addicted to what's new in effect, it keeps us coming back for more of the same, just this once.

1.6   THE DIGITAL IS A NATURAL TECHNOLOGY OF ATTENTION

I have been working up to the point that the digital is a "natural" technology, that is, a technology so useful as to serve as a paradigm for usefulness itself, a technology that achieves the goal implicit in technology as such. It does so because, in monopolizing how we think and work, in occupying our field of vision as no previous tool or medium has done, it thereby lays bare the underlying connection between our attention and our intentions; that is, it singles out attention, the intimate exercise of our care, for quantifiable scrutiny as nothing else could or has. Perfect usefulness is to capture our attention by allowing us to act on it. By seeming *merely* to facilitate that act, it changes us all the more.

Attention is not neutral. It is the act by which we confer meaning on things and by which we discover that they are meaningful, the act through which we bind facts into cares. It is therefore the medium of our lives, the way we work out what matters to us, how you do what you think and think what you do. What is worthy of attention, what we are in the habit of remarking, what we dignify with response, what we think should be brought to attention, is the definition of what is valuable, its origin and root. If something is to have any meaning to you, you must first give it some thought. To attend is to tend, to mind is to love – to learn is to have by heart. And while this has always been so in every context, there had never been a technology that called attention so nakedly, as such, to this basic context of our lives. It is because the technology is itself so frictionless to the constraints of time and matter and space, that who we are emerges new before us virtually revealed, as in a mirror.

So far, I've presented what I take to be the basic features of digital technology. They are mirror-like features that have themselves been instrumental to its widespread success, its record-time absorption of all areas of our life, and that have made it all the harder to keep the magnitude of this transformation in view. To recapitulate: Digital technology has so readily become the predominant medium of our thinking and our timing because it enhances our powers as effective agents (blurring knowing into doing), because it allows us to make sense through images and chat (lowering constraints of educated thought), because it is immaterial (rendering transparent our interface with the world), and because it is commercial (activating preference to profit as never before). We might, in general sum, say that the more digital technology is capable of anticipating and accommodating our desires, the harder it is to keep it in view, the greater its formative power, the more it looks just natural or intuitive to us. What's "natural" is, in this sense, the highest achievement of contrivance. Just as mirrors are themselves invisible, digital technology sinks in by covering its own tracks.

But this analogy between mirrors and digital technology is perhaps more than an analogy; it runs deeper still in ways that bear exploring. People in antiquity could see themselves only in still water or on polished surfaces of bronze. St. Paul's statement that "now we see through a glass, darkly" implies that mirrors adumbrated images only very dimly.[76] The older word for a mirror reflection is "shadow" – a synonym that would never occur to us today. Modern mirrors, mirrors offering crystal-clear images as we know them, are an invention of the Italian Renaissance. An ordinary tool suddenly magnified our consciousness of our public appearance and transformed our self-regard by training us to see (and think) of ourselves from an external point of view. It became arguably the dominant metaphor of early modern thinking, facilitating sea changes in painting and in the fine arts (the development of perspective), the sciences (the objective view from nowhere), and philosophy (the "mirror of nature"[77]). It exemplified the program of the new humanism, a new preoccupation with things as they "really" are, not as they ideally ought to be.

Mirrors thus made three connected differences. First, they provided us with a medium for thinking about objectivity as such, about the world as it looks, undistorted and impartial. I do not say of my mirror-image: "That's just one version, one of many ways of seeing myself" (as when I see a drawing of myself or cringe to hear my voice on tape). I say: "That's me, that's what I look like."

We *seem* to see a neutral image as it truly is, what's there for all to see. I don't mean to imply that the mirror lies (it can't), but that it is a technology that affords us a new kind of opportunity for visualizing the truth.

Because of its objectivity, moreover, the mirror is also a new medium of self-love. We have learned to see ourselves in these terms – when people from remote tribes are shown their picture, they don't recognize the image as their own. Yet, having learned to take this view, our own spectacular good looks flatter us, because we cannot but invest our self-image with our self-conception: When you see what you love, you tend to love what you see. The Florentine friar Savonarola demanded mirrors be burned (along with books, art, dresses, and cosmetics) in his 1497 bonfire of the vanities; if the suggestion now sounds prudish, it is because we no longer can imagine ourselves outside the induce-ments to fashion, apparel, cosmetics, and presentability we take for granted, all of which suppose the existence of a mirror (or a photograph, which is the mirror-image made permanent). Mirrors gave our vanity a new history, self-respect became self-regard.

Finally, it is their transparent effectiveness for picturing the world that, by fusing objectivity with vanity, allowed mirrors to transform our way of looking at things altogether. Mirrors are, like digital technology, a tool that, precisely by and in being invisible, changes how we picture everything else. You can see yourself "just as you are," but that way of looking is itself a technological construction. So the more invisible these technologies are, the more we see the world through them, the harder it is to think the world and ourselves without them, since they are themselves identified with the world as we know it. That is, we are committed to seeing the world in its terms, even as its neutrality makes it impossible to get that commitment into focus; it flatters our sense that there is no commitment there at all beyond objectivity.

These similarities – the way the digital mirror is the more powerful the more it seems to simply register what data and images are "really" out there – will recur in different versions throughout this book. What I mean to emphasize here is that there is a mutually reinforcing relationship between our sense of what's objective and what's in fact most transforming us, that our sense of the digital impersonal ("data") is quickly becoming identified with our sense of what's most authoritative, and that it is by drawing us into its invisible mélange of impersonal and personal that digital technology is so compelling. A mirror on the wall is like an eye – the only object it cannot depict is itself. So too the digital black mirror shows you only what you want to see by itself escaping notice. And by captivating our attention, it is cre-ating a new form of it. Who is the most beautiful of them all? Both mirrors answer you all the same.

All media are undoubtedly technologies of attention; to be literate is not simply a skill, but a frame of mind, a way of organizing the world into of coherence. Still, reading is unnatural in a way that speech and attention are not – it is not an absolute condition of human being. There has never been any medium or tool or informational environment so answerable to intention as the digital, no other medium for which immediate responsiveness to attention is itself what's supremely valued as important. Such sensitivity to intelligent response has only previously been present in our dealings with gods or other human beings. But others tend to have a mind of their own; we cannot make them respond as we like on demand. Whereas digital responsiveness is such as to do just what you want; it is a mirror of your intention. The better to serve you, the better to see yourself in it.

The primary goal of all online services is to reflect your preference; the constructive feedback between what you see and what you get is the order of the day. Google's first name was "Backrub." Your searches or feeds are ordered, censored, and sifted by your past activity (in other words, your "history"). The search engine's aim is to put your own words in your mouth, before you've had to go to the trouble of completing the thought. The perfect one is "something that understands exactly what you mean and gives you back exactly what you want" (Google's Larry Page).[78] Google has also said that it aims to build tools and apps that "should work so well you don't have to consider how they might have been designed differently."[79] Ive has said that Apple's goal is to make their products such that you would not notice their design or complexity; the products we use should know us well enough to seem "strangely familiar."[80] And tech companies are increasingly sanguine of their success on these fronts. As Eric Schmidt put it: "we know where you are. We know where you've been. We can more or less know what you're thinking about."[81] Zhang Chen, the chief technology officer for JD – a Chinese e-trade company that partners with China's biggest search engine – promises that "we will know you as well as you know yourself."[82] Facebook notoriously tracks enough data points to be able to demonstrably mobilize the crowd: In the 2010 congressional elections, it claimed to turn out 340 thousand extra voters on the strength of a single message.[83] Data is "an X-ray of the soul."[84] Our mind's their own business.

These tumid claims are evidently plausible only to the extent that we are busy making them so; that is, to the extent that we continue to reify our thinking into online terms and to integrate digital acts into the time of our lives. Digital services are constructive only to the degree that they are reflective. As AI researcher Stuart Russell puts it, content-selection algorithms do not work simply by learning what we like to click on, but by reinforcing our preferences in such a way that they become easier to predict.[85] That is, such services suit us only because we are actively remaking our preferences to suit their image: a picture of ultimate convenience. They give us what they make us feel we want.

But it is also clear that the attraction is not simply a commercial contrivance, but a consequence of the fact that digital technology arrests our attention by always having something to offer us, by always giving us something to play with, to think about, to figure out. Our mind is primed to pay attention. Taking note is pleasant in its own right; it is painful to be sense-deprived (to be locked up in solitary confinement, say, is one of the worst long-term punishments we have envisioned). We are also primed to take effect. When children discover a light switch on the wall: on and off and on and off it goes (though part of the fun is to see how long it takes to activate a parent). And so each time we click and something happens as a consequence – each time we receive the spicy buzz of a notification, each time we take action or are nudged to good effect – we are rewarded with a sizzle of dopamine, a stimulus of achievement, a Pavlovian prompt that we then seek in its own right. Sean Parker, Facebook's founding president, has acknowledged that their service works by "exploiting a vulnerability in human psychology."[86] Justin Rosenstein, the inventor of Facebook's "like" button, has compared Snapchat to heroin.[87] And there is some evidence that this takes place at the physiological level, that our brains undergo "rewiring" to keep up online.[88] As "Narcissus" is etymologically connected to Greek *narke* (meaning "numbness" – hence "narcotic"), so to gaze into the digital mirror is vivid brain-candy, a mind-numbing enticement.

The neurochemical rewards are not a cause, however, but a consequence of the fact that digital technology constitutes a new and therefore unique form of attention whereby you can act on what you think. The digital, as I have said, abridges the usual span between willing and effective doing – *gedacht getan*, as the German phrase has it (what's thought's as good as done, meaning: Your wish is my command). This simulacrum of omnipotence is basic to the structure and experience of digital affordances themselves.

Any digital task – from ordering food to clearing out our spam folder – grants us the satisfaction of surveying a well-defined menu of tabulated options. Even when the implications of the options are not in themselves clear, even when I am communicating with others, digital activity itself is seamlessly straightforward: I take charge, the task is limited and self-contained, I tick the box, and there's the closure of an unambiguous effect. The software is unobtrusive, obedient to our beck; I am in the best position to judge. It is the satisfaction of unlocking, of solving, of overcoming clear-cut obstacles unlike most other problems in the human world, which admit of no clean fix. Children are not born knowing how to operate buttons or digital devices. But, as tools whose whole work consists in binary responses to keyed input, digital media feel like an accurate reflection of our attention because, by facilitating response to our intention, they effectively empower and therefore practically transform our self-regard. As they have designs on our attention, our attention is by design. Our will be done (or what have you).

Digital responsiveness to attention constitutes, moreover, a self-contained and distinctive experience of speed. Attentional speed is our implicit expectation about the coursing of events: It is not simply the impersonal rate at which things measurably happen, but the pace at which we feel we should keep up to stay on top of things, the rate of optimal attention to what is relevant to us. City dwellers often remark on the slow pace of the countryside – of "sleepy" backwaters – because they are used to things being done on a busier schedule. Just so, when a book or a film moves too fast or too slow for us to follow (or when it does not speak us – droning on about a subject we don't care about, say, or in a foreign language), we grow drowsy. Monotony is soporific because when our attention is not clicking, the world's colors blear together. The effect is deliberately induced in lullabies or bedtime stories like *Goodnight Moon*, with their dissociation of the ordinary trains of thought that comprise a stable world. Waking consciousness is itself a habit of temporal coherence; every tool, medium, and environment implies a time zone of effects. The more we are tasked with, the tempo of our thinking must then speed up to match.

The digital changes what feels right on time: Offline must be "downtime." I have lost my access to electricity and running water a few times, have had my share of car breakdowns – none of them were as frustrating as the experience of losing access to the internet. It is like holding one's breath under water – not just to slow down, but not to be able to have and be and do what one is used to. Surveys claim we are checking our phones about once every six minutes. Most of us keep them next to us while we sleep. Half of us are checking our email during the night. Young adults are sending about 110 text messages a day. About half of all smartphone users describe their device as something they could not live without.[89] Digital media enthral us because there is always something going on in them, and because, deprived of them, there is no context for those same habits of gratification, response, and engagement. Without them, I can no longer pay attention as best I know, as fast.

What is striking about these digital satisfactions is of course how at odds they are with what goes against the grain of momentary preference. Attention is dear, something we "pay" or "give," because it is the activity through which we allocate our limited energies to value, through which our time accrues to care. All worthwhile practices must be worked out to be mastered in time. Learning a language, a sport, or an art, focusing on some single task or skill, repays continuous study, but we only learn the hard way: by enduring temptation and discomfort, by falling on our face, by holding our immediate whims in abeyance in the service of a lasting vision. Our education is only slowly wrested from greater and greater forms of failure. Habitual attention is a form of humility. You hold yourself in readiness for what you do not know you do not know. But while the finest feats are still as difficult as ever, while there is no mastery without risk, the cheapest things have never been so convenient, so accessible, and so fun. No medieval author complains about the attention spans of the young. We still need to attend, but no longer have to (just now). Offline life can't keep up, must always bore by comparison, and so we turn back, jonesing for impulse to response. The word "hype" originally meant "drug user" (as in "hypodermic needle") – and then "to cheat," "to short-change." And that's addiction's trick: gambling on short-term kicks at the expense of wider view.

But while it is commonplace to speak of digital media as an addictive drug – while we undergo "withdrawal"[90] from it and while it is clear that a few people are so disabled by their attentional habits as to require clinical rehabilitation – our unseriousness about treating our high as genuinely pathological reveals that this is but a figure of speech. It is a sensational way of expressing our new attentional acceleration and our new anxiety about the ways in which we can no longer do without it. The difference between doing speed and speeding through the web is that our dependence on the latter is no longer self-contained to one practice. As an order of attentional time, it styles our perception of what's possible, and therefore of what's necessary, and therefore of what we can reasonably expect, and therefore of what we may imagine or hope for. The default device at arm's length – the means by which we make ourselves useful, what's convenient in acceptance – is only ever our devising of the world. Digital technology is no longer just a product, but our turn of mind – the configuration of our needs, our novel attention to the world's uses.

The core of our dependence is, as I've also said, different in kind from that of our dependence on other tools and media; it is totalizing to use and ready to respond as nothing else. It is "me" reflected back as if from another "you," my attention captivated by a simulated other and so attention immediately expressing a preference for its own reiteration, whatever else. (Mirrors have been not just sites of vanity but fitting metaphors for incest and autoeroticism generally.) That is, it is not simply that digital technology makes it harder to attend, or to heed, or to exercise the control of "negative capability" (as Keats called it); it is that it makes it plain that, given the choice, we would *prefer not* to – that we would rather be online than sustain attention to anyone or anything. It is a principle of many religious traditions, conversely, that contemplative attention or prayer raises awareness to a higher place: joy in conscious presence. ("Be still, and know that I am God."[91]) What comes naturally to us, however, what is relaxing and effortless, is in fact the desire for absence – the desire to be on the move, the desire for attention to be forever elsewhere. The digital forces us, as no other technology, to face the unquenchable lust of the mind to be diverted nowhere to no end. It is an experience as familiar and squalid as what is called in German *Neugier* – greed for novelty – or as what might be called sin: the commonplace seductions of what we know to be smaller satisfactions. Have it your way, you're on your own.

The paradox is that our experience of digital absence is in fact a simulation of an experience of total commitment, of utmost concentration, such as we all want to want. When we are at one with what we are doing, fully intent on best activity, we seem outside of time: We are transported with delight, elated, rapt like a child at play. What's best is what attention finds self-sustaining. This looks like what the digital gives us too; we seem to be wired, engrossed, plugged in, glued, hooked up, and lost in thought.[92] But these experiences are two poles asunder. The former always opens us to wider possibilities of being, even as the latter wraps us up further in ourselves. Zombies are images of mindless alienation for us, but also of their admirable opposite: unswerving, single-minded dedication. Just so, engagement and doomscrolling, boredom and fascination, are always two sides of a coin. The digital thus evokes the experience of total attention while tending to empty it of substance beyond the moment; the satisfaction of being connected overwhelms the significance of its contents. The more we are rewarded, the less we are fulfilled. If undivided attention is a discipline, if attention is the blessing of our care, then the digital teaches us that we are always pulled away from it into the fragments of an absent-minded void.

The thirst for speed is only ever partially slaked by acceleration – the desire to be transformed, to skip ahead, to scroll down to the apocalyptic end of time itself. But the demand for acceleration is itself a sign of displaced satisfaction, unrequited longing. Each time I reach for my phone, I'm only ever waiting for it to be you. Each time, it's only ever me again, self-consuming and consumed by the device.

We are called to know ourselves by becoming other. To do your will and see it done: It is the deepest human desire. There is no joy in being idle, in mere wanting without doing; it makes no difference in the world. Some of the oldest extant cave paintings are stenciled human hands – proto-selfies – just as people still scrawl on bathroom stalls or score their names into monuments and trees. We take a childlike delight in flinging stones into a becalmed pool. We want to create a stir, to make an impression in our own image, to see ourselves writ otherwise and translate. The iconic images of our first visit to the moon are not of the moon herself, but of Neil Armstrong's footprint and the planted flag. It is as if to say to others "Here I was, therefore we are" or "Look at me, we share the world." I make my mark, I have done, and I am in effect. It is in othering myself that I know the pleasure of being.

But Narcissus found a shortcut. He did not fall in love with himself (as is sometimes said), he fell in love with the transparent image of that self, and so with another that was not wholly other – a reflex of attention surfacing. Just so, everywhere you look into the digital, you cannot escape you: Self-love's spell, unrequited, is to be insatiable, clear to distraction. You will keep finding yourself. You will keep missing yourself.

2

Led by Our Own Lights

Generations appear to flower, flourish, and wither at the speed of light. I don't think that this is merely the inevitable reflection of middle age: I suspect that there really has been some radical alteration in the structure, the nature, of time. One may say that there are no clear images; everything seems superimposed on, and at war with something else.

(James Baldwin)[1]

We have a tendency to speak of technology as if it were a factor external to ourselves – *Is it inevitable? Is it neutral or does it have preferences, wants? What does it cause us to do? What are its effects on culture and history?* These formulations are wrongheaded: Not only do they attribute independent agency to technology, but they keep it at an artificial distance from what we care about and how. Technology (and perhaps especially digital technology) is not an independent force, but a framework of practical possibilities by means of which what is needless becomes useful, and by means of which what is useful then becomes necessary for leading a good life. It thereby gives shape to what we care about. It is, as I've indicated, a language of expression: not a language in which the world is described, but a language in terms of which the world is enacted – a language in which we read parameters of action, opportunities at hand, what's choosable and choiceworthy, what's a matter of convenience, what looks like a good idea at the time, what's normal, and therefore what's right.

Yet our penchant for considering it as something other than ourselves is itself worth noting. It indicates an anxious interval between who we are and how we do that is peculiar to modernity. The brief evocations in this chapter speak to this gap generally, reprising these themes from the last chapter in a higher key. I want to suggest that technology is not external to most intimate cares, even as we also continue to sense that it has a life of its own. It is the dissonance between these two aspects of our experience that shapes our ambivalence toward digital technology in particular. Yet in order to bring this into focus, it's important to raise the prior question of what technology is at all and how it comes to matter. So here goes my brief theory of technology, from the top. (If you've no patience for these questions and would like to keep reading about digital technology as such, by all means leaf ahead to the next Chapter.)

Our nature is a question mark; instinct does not settle us. We are born more helpless, pliant, and unformed than any other animal: We are the only creatures in need of education to finish who we are. Our teeth and digestion are both carnivorous and vegetarian. Our singular upright stance frees up our arms to lend an idle hand or grasp a thought. We are no longer led by the nose (snout-first), because our gaze is up and running, parallel to the horizon and visionary beyond what's obvious before our feet. Our anatomy opens up this space within our reach, as far as eye can see.

Yet we must also work to make room for this space to come into view. We stand on our feet by nature, but you must always be on your toes. It is the work of a lifetime to become an upright human being. Without cultivation and the law we would not know what to do with ourselves. (Or we would know too well.) This cultivation consists, among other things, in our labor and in its instruments: tools or weapons picked up and handed down.

But our oldest stories about technology are of overstepping. Prometheus thieves fire from the gods and is punished for it – his liver pecked out by buzzards every day afresh. Ancient Greek and Roman poets refer to agriculture, to the mining of metal, and to the building of ships to scour the sea as the devices of a fallen age. Milton, like Cervantes and Rousseau, echoes these, writing that men were instructed by Mammon when they first

> ransacked the center, and with impious hands
> rifled the bowels of their mother earth
> for treasures better hid. [...] Let none admire
> that riches grow in hell; that soil may best
> deserve the precious bane.[2]

The spirits of Coyote and Raven are, in Native American stories, responsible for stealing fire and inventing lies. Adam and Eve are not punished for invention, but the invention of clothes to hide their shame is the first sign of their fallen state (in which they must toil to eke out survival). Trickster cunning generally, the wit that finds an edge to beat brute brawn, goes hand in hand with mischief everywhere. Tools help us do our work – but no one has imagined paradise as a place in which we must sweat to eat. We cannot do without tools. Yet we hold them suspect.

Every new tool specializes some aspect of activity; it magnifies and concentrates some task, replacing a deed once performed without its help. Every tool therefore requires surrendering capacity in one way, by making us more capable in another. As glasses make it easier to see, they weaken our eyes. As cars make it easier to ride, our knowledge of the region is more tenuous. As weapons make it easier to kill, the skill and force needed to wield them diminishes, from beep to bang in no time. (Conversely too, the blind develop a sharper sense of touch, the deaf become adept at reading lips and motion – those who lose some tool or some skill then compensate by souping up another.) The more useful and able our tools, the dimmer our awareness of how all the elements of our experience are related to each other. Tools are a crutch; and yet we become more powerful by leaning on them.

As our tools change, we change with them. What is at first convenient – from the fig leaf to electricity – becomes worked into our way of doing things, and over time transforms our nature by giving it new expression. We are not simply Adam and Eve *plus* clothes and books and indoor plumbing: We are creatures who can see things differently; that is, creatures of habit; that is, creatures who can have a change of heart. A bird or a lizard that picks up a stone is only ever that: a bird or a lizard with a stone. "A man of the cloth" or a "woman of letters," a virtuoso pianist or a knight in shining armor, are something more again: They are types of human beings that cannot exist without certain tools. Tools grow on us and into us, as we grow into them; they are our invention and the invention of us. We cannot figure ourselves without them.

"I would be just who I am without hammers and smartphones." King Lear's words in response:

> O, reason not the need! Our basest beggars
> Are in the poorest thing superfluous;
> Allow not nature more than nature needs,
> Man's life is cheap as beast's.[3]

We do not need houses, fire, or language for bare survival; but we would not recognize ourselves in the "bare, forked animal"[4] without them. Because our cultures are not rightly measured by the standard of survival, but by that of living well. We are our ordinary selves only when we are got up and accoutred: What is superfluous is necessary for us to do our thing. There is a distinction between nature and culture, but it is not as that between night and day. It is rather like the difference between matter and form – between stuff and structure – each of which do not exist in separation from the other. Living well is as much the work of hands as of the imagination that gives shape to what we do.

"The Sorcerer's Apprentice" is the story of all our tools – we create them to serve us and then we recreate ourselves to serve them – with one difference: Unlike the frightened apprentice, we quickly cease to marvel at the magic that we made them what they are. Tools soon blend in; they vanish into plain view and out of sight, woven, notched, textured, stylized, typified, hammered, and seamlessly inscribed into our way of thinking things have always been. Tools disappear into our metaphors for action, which in turn then govern our intelligence of what's doable, and then what's practical, and then who we are at work ("the rudder of the organization," say, or "a cog in the machine"). Culture is the process by which a stick becomes an arm.

We have never been prone to notice how deeply we are shaped by and identified with our tools. What is useful has a way of vanishing from view. Tools help us build up patterns of uses and functions that come to seem given over time, and each generation takes its bearings as to how the world is by how it works and how we work on it. As a Korean proverb puts it: "knows his way, stops seeing." The mother of invention is not comfort, but need, obstacle, and limitation – the edges of desire sharpened into cunning. We need reminding to "stay hungry," and the history of technology is the history of one of our hungers.

Culture is possible because we can familiarize it, because we are able to take the world we inherit as the settled basis for creative action. We have it in us to take up culture for our natural environment, for the given background of our lives – in other words, we have the capacity for taking it for granted, for believing in what surrounds us and in what we are told about it, as if it were a matter of fact. Everyone supposes him- or herself at square one, no matter what's around. (The only sure means to avoid this disappearing act is to refuse a name or an image to something: the Jewish reverence toward God.) To forget what's new and to remember what's missing are our most uncanny powers.

We have no straightforward way of assessing whether it would be good to adopt a new tool, because its adoption will itself change the terms in which we assess it. All technology gives us an edge, helps us spare some time, saves some effort; few inventions lend themselves solely to wicked uses. The material goal of civilization is to get comfortable, to take it easy. Suddenly, with a new tool in widespread use, the issue changes from "This is what we do" to "What would you prefer, the easier way or the harder one?" (A choice that is no choice.) Each new such choice thus casts all available possibilities in a new light, reforming their practical significance. The heroic few will always choose the uphill struggle. But all our conscious attention, as creatures, is organized toward corner-cutting and energy-saving: It aims at sedentary ease, at finding out the resting point.

Nor is a technology's significance available in advance, affording us the means to measure it against the hypothetical alternative of not choosing it. A tool's meaning only comes to light by using it; and it takes time for innovation to sink in, for us to internalize and realize its uses. (The inventor of the automobile could not have foreseen the suburbs.) The implications of a new way of doing business are not fully worked out until the new means pervade the old ends, transforming them. And it is precisely a medium or tool's unanticipated uses – possibilities at first entailed yet unexplored, untold, unthought – that gradually emerge from the periphery to make a decisive difference. We can't formulate the most important questions about them until it is too late.

All tools, as culture's means, are signs and symbols of the social theory that brings them into being. Any technology encapsulates and manifests a way in which its user relates to other people (who helped making it, who have a use for its fruits, who will acknowledge it as significant). A tool – from the axe to the Xerox machine – is more than a detached and movable thing, it is a part of the world of uses that sees a place for it in common. We take a tool up to the best of our knowledge; we make it our business on a certain understanding.

As tools are specialized, so is work. As work is specialized, so grows the division of labor. As the division of labor grows, so does our dependence on others, who are trained to different kinds of tasks. And beyond a certain order of complexity, it becomes difficult to reckon ourselves in the picture, to understand our own place in the concatenated scheme of things (in "the economy," or "public opinion," or "society" at large, say). Modernity is marked by increasing specialization into compartments, checked and balanced "spheres." The notion of a "Renaissance man" – someone who could contribute to many branches of the tree of learning, is out of reach for us today. We therefore long for a simpler life. Natural man in Montaigne's and Rousseau's writings – the noble savage sufficient unto himself – is a poetic image of autonomy, of a self-sufficing life, transparent to its needs and satisfactions. To be at one, to be of a piece with the natural: This is the desire that drove the Romantics to the wilderness and Wendell Berry back to the land (like Virgil in his day). This is also a favorite subject for apocalyptic and reality TV: *The Walking Dead*, *Naked and Afraid*, *Fat Guys in the Woods*, *Survivor* – we imagine, in the midst of our affluence, what it would be like to take matters into our own hands, to be whole.

Most of us are nonetheless content to watch these contestants struggle from the comfort of our couch. Telegraph, telephone, television, cyberspace: Our recent tools are tools increasing action-at-a-safe-distance, remote controls. No one wants to feel the pressure of necessity for its own sake – or rather, we may desire to desire the pressure of adamant duress, the decisive and unequivocal demand that would make up our minds for us, but we cannot really choose it. You can chain yourself to the mast for a short amount of time or embed yourself with a jungle guerrilla. But if you can take it or leave it in the long run, it is not necessary. Once your dysentery gets too bad, you will call for an airlift if you can (and would be very silly not to).

There are almost no examples of cultures that have voluntarily given up a tool more effective than what they already had, a technology that would have made a decisive difference to their survival, their comfort, or their standing with their enemies. Some Greek cities avoided the use of arrows, regarding them as cowardly (compared to fighting face to face). The Japanese acquired, mastered, and then gave up guns until the nineteenth century.[5] The ancient Chinese invented gunpowder but did not mechanize it as artillery. But in all these cases, the innovation was at odds with a more powerful principle within those societies – honor was more important than effectiveness, say. And the preference proved temporary. A culture must be in some measure receptive to innovation; those that are not so disposed have been sidelined to dependence or wiped out. Would we choose to forfeit life-saving medical treatment for the bubonic plague, if we had the choice to return to the Middle Ages? We have (so far) refrained from nuclear war – from using a weapon so powerful that its greatest use consists in lying idle – but would we trust our enemies to give up their nuclear capacity along with us? As there are no atheists in foxholes, there are no techno-skeptics in matters of practical necessity, in matters that are (often) a dire matter of survival. It is with us, in those cases, as with people who have resorted to cannibalism to keep alive on castaway rafts – we may commend someone who refrains, but can you blame someone for trying? We do what we can, and we are what we can do – always with an eye on our neighbors.

There is a difference between using a new tool within an old way of doing things, and the change that the tool gradually works on the whole environment itself. At first, cars (for instance) saved time: They accomplished the same purpose as horses, but faster, better. Then two things happened. Cars created cities on a new scale; networks of roads spread us out farther than we ever had been – allowing us to make previously inconceivable commutes (and to be stuck in traffic). They transformed our perception of feasible distances. They thereby created a new default, a new normal. If you ride in a car to work (instead of walking or riding your horse), it soon becomes just "what is done" – no one continues to sing hosannas for a shortcut once established. But if you *then* choose to walk to work instead (in a world with cars), you must choose the hard way, with cussed stoicism, every day once more again, again, again. You can always hold out, but it is hard to row upstream when the effort seems arbitrary, when it's just up to you, when there's no shame in giving up, when the temptation to do otherwise accompanies each and every time. In other words: Once a particular technical capacity is optional, it is *more* difficult to stay the course without it than when, originally, there was no choice at all. If you go your own way, your faith in it must be stronger than was once required. Technology progresses according to the logic of Duns Scotus's argument for the existence of God: In a pinch (or a pandemic), what is technically *possible* shows itself to be absolutely *necessary* – and we are always in a pinch. Once friction becomes optional, it is no longer a living option. It is unbearable for human beings to feel that our effort is unnecessary, that our pains sustain no greater meaning.

There is a patience by which innovation is digested into speech and practice, a gradual action conforming culture into nature over time. "It would be interesting to know how we shall ennoble our new media as we have already ennobled and made significant our old – candle-light, fire-light, Cups, Wands and Swords, to choose at random."[6] Here is a test: Can you picture a classic poem – a poem to be anthologized alongside Chaucer's words and Wordsworth's – that uses hashtags or includes the word "modem" or "Instagram"? I can't, not seriously. And yet, looking back and back: There are such poems about bread and ships and books, perhaps even about airplanes and bicycles and typewriters and the radio. Time makes all the difference, and time makes the difference constant: As we come to depend on our tools for living well, they are woven into the aspect of the world. Myth "transforms history into nature."[7] We bless our tools with our attention, we work to make them real and they become working reality. It is not that I look down on Twitter as an unworthy subject of poetry, it is that I doubt that it – or any particular digital object – can matter long enough to make a timeless dent.

What is new is treated with suspicion. Our words "innovation" and "revolution" – like Greek *neos* and Latin *novus* – indicated upheaval, tumult, social disorder, up through early modernity. What is newfangled is untoward, strange, and probably immoral: The word "uncouth" first meant "unknown." Oral cultures innovate, but they do so by presenting the innovation as continuous with ancestral ways, rather than by touting the value of what's new as such.[8] The printed word looks to progress, by contrast; it makes the accumulation of new knowledge within the span of one's lifetime so patent that it feels like we are gradually getting somewhere (good). Even so, inventions that we would now regard as quaint – the written word, the steam engine, the telegraph – were first met with scorn. "Modern," what is without precedent, was not always a good thing; and even now (when "new" and "modern" are default terms of commendation) we do not trust what we don't already think we recognize or know. This is not a failure, but a necessary attitude. Culture is alive, and any living form needs antibodies to keep itself.

There is history because we are given to find ourselves in time. But there is modern history because of rapid changes in science, industry, and technology. Marx's thesis – that changes in the means of economic production are history's causal motor – would never have seemed plausible before widespread industrialization; but it is becoming *truer* than it once was. Telescope, microscope, steam engine, photograph, internal combustion, telegraph, automobile, airplane, the bomb, the internet: modernity in nutshell.

That is, there is no reason to assume a fixed causal relationship between technological invention and cultural formation – there is no reason to assume that technology has occupied some fixed role within the creation of mores, conventions, and traditions. The stirrup was perhaps one of the most momentous discoveries ever made; it has been argued that it allowed mounted warfare to be effective and that it therefore made feudalism possible.[9] But the stirrup's use is well-defined and limited, and – assuming it was a mainspring of feudal life – it played little or no explicit part in the religious and political views of the Middle Ages. Even if it was present as a powerful formative cause, it was a cause that was different in character from its effects, a cause that was only gradually and indirectly stabilized into the morals, imagination, and metaphysics of the peoples using it. Digital technology, in contrast, is not one tool among others – it is increasingly the medium, means, and meaning of culture itself. It so accelerates differences in degree that it marks a difference in kind. "Stirrup culture" doesn't make sense – "internet culture" or "digital native" does.

Over the last two hundred years, as steam and electricity have sped labor up beyond the natural limits set by our bodies and the elements, we have also added new technology more quickly than we have known what to do with, than we have been able incorporate. Changes that were once incremental must be swallowed whole without much chewing. And so it is only recently that we have come to think of the tool as alien to nature, that we have so sharply opposed "natural" to "human" or "man-made" at all. ("Nature" now means the raw wilderness.) Likewise, there were no Luddites before the nineteenth century, no talk of "dark Satanic Mills," no rage against machines: All these are symptoms of cultural indigestion. The difference between the shape of our ordinary life and that of someone born one or two hundred years ago is the greatest it has ever been. Modern conservatism (like religious fundamentalism) came into being and is intelligible only in response to industrialized, globalizing progress. Our consternation comes from the fact that our practices – the acts that make up the shape of daily life – have had to accommodate technology again and again, and so have been subject to bewildering and continuous social readjustment, faster and faster with each new revolution. We cannot be sure where we stand. Since the rates of readjustment are variable for different groups, professions, and classes, modern technology therefore entails permanent culture shock and culture war (i.e., social conflicts about the common ground beneath our feet). The social contexts that shape our deepest convictions are on a faster schedule than shifts in our convictions themselves, which soon find themselves out of place and out of sync with what goes on.

In general: There is a span of time in which new tools can be assimilated into the heart of human aims and practices, the time it takes for changes in culture to become canonized as the perennial norm. There is, on the other hand, the span of time it takes to make revolutionary discoveries in technology. The first time, moral time or "normal" time, has perhaps never changed much, while the second time has drastically been speeding up. Our sense of what is right now lags behind our power to effect; progress is disruptive and uneven. It is our fate to count on this disparity between our capacities and our knowledge, between the certainty of change and our uncertainty as to its implications, between what we can figure on and what we can figure out. This is the abiding signature of our age.

New tools prepare the way for new convictions; more than anything else, modern technology makes room for social and political equality. We tend to think of human rights in terms of essences: inalienable, God-given qualities possessed by each and all of us at birth. And it's right for us to think so. But if this were the whole story, it becomes impossible to understand why anyone would have thought otherwise, how anyone could fail to notice this fact, and what it is that underpins our possession of these rights even now. Pre-modern inequality was not (only) a matter of ruthless, cynical exploitation. It relied on the widespread perception that a community could not take up the work of culture and self-government unless some other group took up the needs of productive menial labor, and on the corollary thought that different people were capable of and needed for different tasks. Slaves were spoils of war in antiquity – no one existed beyond this possibility. And slavery was keyed to patterns of activity rather than to identity, racial or otherwise: Who you were depended on what you could be expected to do; your place was your given role.

Technology is the means by which we have loosed ourselves from our given roles within these patterns. Consider the following sketch of a trajectory.

Virtually no one questioned the fact of slavery, virtually no one maintained that it was categorically wrong, until early modernity. Aristotle had some reservations about it, distinguishing "natural" slavery from slavery that rests on duress alone – and he said that if tools could do work on their own, there would be no need for slaves.[10] But the question had no practical traction until the eighteenth century or so. Christianity, which became central to the message of abolitionist movements, is not itself incompatible with slavery: Christian masters were enjoined to be gentle to their slaves, but not to free them. ("Servants, be obedient to them that are your masters according to the flesh," writes St. Paul.[11]) The thinking of most all pre-modern agricultural states is that some people must be forced to do harsh, backbreaking work, so that others might be free to think, to pray, to make war, and to govern. Were they wrong to think so? There was no visible reason available to think that things could be otherwise, that those activities could be anything but a privilege open to a few. Division of physical labor was also a division of ethical and spiritual labor. Even Marx agrees that neither capitalism nor communism would be possible without machines to supersede feudal forms of work.

The perception that slaves are "naturally" suited to their work is, of course, a self-reinforcing and self-perpetuating one. If a class of oppressed people grow up unlettered and unlearned, chances are they will really not be well suited to certain kinds of work, if suddenly given the chance: The chains of history and culture are severed only with terrible trouble. Conversely, the claim to superiority of ancient and medieval aristocracies was rooted in their superiority for waging war, which itself depended on their control of certain weapons and tools that amplified their force. Horses, swords, armor, and the training to use them skillfully were expensive and hard to come by; those who could possess them and had the time for them were better able to wield the force of arms. ("To be mounted is already to be a master, a knight ... Honor begins with a man and a horse."[12]) The justification of their nobility rested on this real practical difference. Their status was, in turn, understood to entail its own God-given prerogatives and responsibilities. Differences in practical capacity were inscribed into lineage; birth was destiny.

Technological and economic changes in early modernity meant that Europeans could for the first time glimpse a vision of a flourishing society from which slavery might be excluded. (While it no longer seems like it, the refusal to enslave others who look like you was a world-historical achievement.) This was partly because the burden of manual labor and material extraction were put out of sight by being shifted onto the shoulders of the New World. But a number of new inventions served to erode the sense that class differences were natural or permanent. Cheapening firearms made it easier to kill at a distance; they helped destroy the aristocracy's claim to superiority in war. An emerging bourgeois class amassed and traded wealth more widely than before, and the accumulation of capital, as a new mark of status, slowly dissolved the bonds between political power and land; it allowed groups previously marginal to vie for emancipation. The printing press and Protestantism severed the connection between knowledge and traditional authority: Modern arts and sciences are more meritocratic (and therefore more accommodating to parvenus) than feudal politics. The steam engine then began to relieve at least some forms of backbreaking work (not rendering work less *strenuous* necessarily, but more mechanical, less reliant on individual strength, and so more accessible, as wage-labor, to women and children). The practical differences that had underpinned the perception of natural differences were canceled out by these new possibilities in context.

Technology equalizes access to the same tasks, neutralizes differences that had once seemed decisive to the grammar of our roles. The apparently necessary division of labor underpinning slavery no longer had clear grounds. And what counts as absolute right or wrong is always relative to what is felt to be an untenable or intolerable way to live.

Thus the 54th Massachusetts Infantry Regiment was a living argument for the equality of all African Americans during the Civil War. For if black men could wield the same weapons and die as courageously as whites, how could one justify the thought of fundamental difference? Thus the racial segregation of the Tuskegee Airmen was all the more outrageous. For if black men could pilot planes as well as whites, why were they treated as a group apart? Thus the modern civil rights movement followed from the Great Migration to northern cities. It was the conditions of industrial labor, the shortage of which created opportunities for African Americans during the World Wars – in steel mills, meat packing plants, and automobile factories – that called attention to blatant disparities in law and treatment throughout the country. Thus when Jackie

Robinson could play the game of baseball, he proved in deed that there was no practical difference on which to base the different treatment of the races.

Modern racism in America first shows up when whites could no longer point to some practice or institution that could vindicate their natural superiority, and so began to actively fear that blacks could displace and replace them – as formulated by the crude threat that one of "them" might marry your daughter. Racism is, in this sense, an effect of heightened equality, of the dissolution of social barriers.[13] (One might say something analogous about sexism.) The absence of a practical difference serves as the occasion for a retreat into identity: Since we could no longer point to a difference in what we could *do*, we began to appeal to what we supposedly just *were* in essence. (Malcolm X and Frantz Fanon therefore emphasized that meaningful equality could not be bestowed from without but had to be violently wrested, if the oppressed hoped for true emancipation.) The notion of racial essence may then outlive the practical difference that once seemed to justify it, as its metaphysical ghost. This may also suggest that "normal time" has not yet caught up to technological time – though, as I've said, it never does catch up in modernity, and stories about other races also serve psychological needs that outlast their practical significance.

If the first consequence of industrialization was to relieve us of the sense that a class of people were needed to labor, a second was to cancel out the sense that physical force was a source of meaningful difference between men and women. Again, this essential difference was once grounded in the perception of a practical one; if men were better suited for manual labor and for war, then they could lay claim to a different set of privileges and tasks. The success of women's suffrage movements in the late nineteenth century coincided (non-coincidentally) with the development of electrification. As work becomes rather more a matter of pushing buttons and operating machines, brute strength means less. The advent of a new form of technological war demanded women's participation as never before – the "total war" of World War I required the transformation and collaboration of every aspect of the economy; women were no longer on the sidelines of conflict. Peoples and armies became coextensive. Or in Churchill's words: "the wholehearted concurrence of scores of millions of men and women ... is the only foundation upon which the trial and tribulation of modern war can be endured and surmounted."[14] It was substantially through the recognition of this fact that women gained the right to vote in an avalanche of countries immediately following the First War. (That was when Churchill came around to the idea too.) Further technological transformations – the growth of bureaucracy and white-collar work as a proportion of the economy, the increasing specialization and mechanization of agriculture and military, and the development of reliable birth control – have eliminated the sense that the sexual difference between men and women could justify any political difference. The armed forces, one of the last institutional holdouts, will soon abolish all legal differences between men and women by making the draft gender-blind.[15] And so "the wife economy is as obsolete as the slave economy."[16]

Whatever residual markers of sexual specialization still exist in practice are further dissolved by the impersonal character of online speech. The genius of Tinder is that it equalizes consent in dating: One gender need no longer be tasked with the presumptive burden of approaching the other. As transgender and nonbinary people give birth to children, pressure will continue to build not to identify pregnancy with women in particular.[17] If and when we mechanize gestation and birth, there will at last be no relevant difference left. It is household cares (mainly women's) that both allow technological society to be viable and constitute the final area of resistance to its customization, mechanization, innovation, and consumption.

Given any assertion of political difference in kind between people, the question is always: What needs doing and what can these do that those cannot? The force of modern technology is to undermine the sense that there could be anything at practical stake here, since more or less everyone is able to do more or less everything. As Marx says: "All bounds of morals and nature, age and sex, day and night, were broken down [by modern industry]."[18] It is no accident that the single most consequential political fault line in the United States has been and remains that between urban–industrialized and rural–agricultural populations, separated as they are by the widest differences in practice. As Marx well knew, landed populations everywhere are more hierarchical and conservative, and industrial and post-industrial populations are more fragmented and progressive: The work of farms and ranches places limits on how fast and far social relations can be reshaped.

The emancipation of African Americans and women does not mark an end-point, not simply because their emancipation is ongoing, but because where there is no decisive practical difference between men and women, there is no political case against gay marriage. Where aspects of one's identity become voluntary online, it becomes easier to construct and communicate new, nonbinary forms of gender. ("Gender is over.") Where there is a more fluid perception of global borders, the mass movement of populations is on the rise in all senses (immigrants and refugees, as well as tourists). If and when self-driving cars become the norm, there will be one fewer rite of passage that sets off youth from adulthood. Where automation continues to displace the need for human labor, calls for universal basic income will become more compelling. I do not say that all these distinctions are on all fours with the others. But the shape of them is consistent: In changing our sense of what people can do, technology must also change our sense of who we are, and of what's at stake in our identity.

What should we conclude? That our notions of equality are just a matter of our tools? That if we did not have this technology, we would think otherwise? (There is a sci-fi series in which people suddenly lose access to electricity and firearms: They soon revert to a basically feudal mode of life.[19]) Or is it that technology allows us to reveal (or "unlock") something that was true all along? Allows us to realize something true in practice?

Neither, exactly. It is like asking whether the categories "cis-gender" or "person of color" are inventions or discoveries: In a sense they have always existed, but in another sense they have not *as such*, not in just those terms and in contrast to such and such others, not as express and self-conscious options. And when it comes to our status as social creatures – our rights, our identities, our sense of fairness – what we take ourselves to be makes all the difference to who we really are. It is because I take myself to think and act and feel in light of the terms available to me ("American citizen," "Latino," "proud parent," or whatever) that I can be identified with these roles, and it is only because these categories are options that I can inhabit them and thereby be transformed by them. That these roles are not permanently fixed – that as new roles open up, others go out of business – is what it means for us to be people of our time.

So while it flatters us to think that we have discovered that people have always been equal, equality is also an insight achieved, and it is achieved in part by the history of our forms of labor and communication. The point is not that equality is arbitrary, but that it is sustained by our perception of underlying practical patterns – by our sense of what our work is, and of what we are capable of. This is counterintuitive, as I've said, to how we ordinarily speak about equality: as something true by virtue of who we *are* – as basic to our identity – rather than as a consequence of what we can *do*. Evidently, there is no equality so long as it remains a matter of words that have no life in practice. But respect and dignity are missing something if they are simply bestowed for the bare fact of existence; the only basis for a non-religious conception of equality is the perception that we participate equally in the same tasks and endeavors. In this sense, we need to be able to find more ways to (meaningfully) judge each other, not fewer; it is practical standards that afford us the basis for regard. It is to the extent that we can all play the same game of baseball that we can respect each other for being more or less excellent at it, that we can have some cooperative sense of the work that, binding us, makes us valuable to each other. We should, for this reason, insist on the solidarity of people in their working capacities and roles rather than on the essential identity of races.

Digital technology's equalizing role is paradoxical. It smooths our encounters with others – at once allowing more and more people to share the same practices and diluting the significance of individual agency. It intensifies our perception of identity, while also neutralizing its practical demonstrations. It thereby makes it easier to see equality in theory, and harder to realize in practice. This is our political tragedy: that we pay for equality with the frictionlessness of mutual isolation – that the circumstance that allows us to feel more equal is the same that deprives us of the contexts in which we would have to come to grips with others: the hard work of recognition, acknowledgment, and love in practice.

Modern technology enhances our equality and autonomy because it undercuts and uproots established traditions, norms, and roles – it expresses the underlying logic of capitalism, which is to make workers interchangeable and to increase the scope of the economy to everyone. But traditions, norms, and roles are, more than relations of dependence between people, relations between the past, present, and future. Digital technology's speeding up, the relentless succession of its content and vehicles, constitutes not just a feature, but a new stance and attitude toward time.

Media and technology bespeak forms of time, not just because they measure it, but because they help define a rhythmic pattern between daily needs and cosmic demands. Media have their tenses, their characteristic time signatures, their shapes of organized culture; they are the means by which we pace ourselves. Many traditional (oral) societies have had cyclical cosmologies, operating on the assumption that the future would resemble the past. Ancestral lore was worth studying because it contained the keys to all possible experience. Christianity introduced a (literate) linear narrative: Time was read as "before" or "after" God's irruption into history and as bounded in the future by the Second Coming. Karl Löwith argued that modernity secularized this view.[20] Modern societies no longer expected the end of the world as a religious event, but we began to look forward (in print) to an earthly utopia, ushered in by scientific enlightenment. The idea of progress assumes the best is yet to come: the discovery of the idea of the future.

Digital technology narrows our experience of what matters to the punctual *now*; it aims to free us from the constraints of space and time altogether. Memory binds us, memory haunts and stains; but memory also gives us meaning and coherence to extended time. In contrast, the logic of relentless speeding up, refreshing, and updating – all the ways we are held rapt by the immediacy of internet experience – frees us up to an unprecedented degree to create the terms of our own life by magnifying our sense of what we will in the present or short-term. The past has little to say to us because there has never been anything like this; nothing is time-honored – what's past is past. The complexity of literate history is flattened into the mythology of ready-made use. And so our time is episodic and in brief.

The consequence of this speeding up of time is most visible in the new antagonism between the ages; constant change means that the young cannot see themselves in the old, or vice versa. Childhood as we knew it (as an age of carefree innocence devoted to play and schoolwork) is itself a modern form: Whereas in traditional, agricultural societies, children grow up quickly because they can join in the work as soon as they can toddle and can stand on their own as soon as they reach puberty, industrial society requires years of rote education just to catch up to square one. This is shifting again. The young are growing up in a world apart; they are perhaps for the first time identifying as a natural bloc unto themselves.[21] ("Ok, boomer.") Where everyone communicates from behind a screen, and where every issue is relentlessly politicized, children and teenagers have a more conspicuous platform in politics – it is easier for them to be taken seriously, to have the sense of being full participants. The case against lowering the voting age will accordingly grow harder to sustain.[22] It is impossible to imagine Greta Thunberg and the Sunrise Movement at any other period in history. And climate change is itself a problem of our attitude toward time: It pits those who have long lived in a world of now against those who fear there may soon be no world for them to inhabit.

The old, on the other hand, have lost their source of natural authority, their claim to respect, since much of their acquired life-wisdom feels irrelevant to new kinds of problems that they barely comprehend. (Think of our new aware-ness of "ageism" or of Mark Zuckerberg's smug testimony before discombob-ulated U.S. senators.) Other, more radical forms of temporal discontinuity are evident in groups whose interpretation of the future is a form of apocalyptic giddiness or gloom: accelerationists, who are gunning for the destruction of capitalism,[23] or anti-natalists, who think that we should refrain from having children for environmental reasons.[24] To be unable to imagine tomorrow is to be tempted to despair.

When technology forces cultural changes faster than culture can accommo-date them, it is destructive to the possibility of culture itself – since nothing in practice is allowed the time to coalesce, to take shape and adapt. What is meant by "human nature" was a matter of time revealed and preserved: the way things were, have been, and should remain. But where there is no time, there can be no abiding sense of normal – the new now is the normal. Without time, no nature can emerge, no history, no web of relations. The Inuit called people from European civilization "the people who change nature."[25] Rachel Carson wrote, "Given time – time not in years but in millennia – life adjusts, and a balance has been reached. For time is the essential ingredient; but in the modern world there is no time."[26] Time is what we most need and least have: time to stop.

Climate change and digital technology are temporal opposites. Whereas our experience of being online is focused on the fragmented and overwhelming experience of *now*, the problem of climate change stems from our inability to act coherently in connection with the distant future. Long-term solutions are not within the scope of digital technology, the point of which is innovation and upheaval. The long term is precisely what has no digital place. So long as new is normal, no sustained vision can accumulate into settled practice. We are freer for the time being. But this freedom blinkers us from acknowledging our obligations to past and future. The future is no longer a given; we can only hope to have one. If yesterday carries no weight, if we cannot see how we belong to the future, then we don't have a prayer. We have a history together; what's now is still to come. But we go to a lot of trouble not to know this. Or rather: We don't know how to know it any longer.

"If present trends continue ..." – so presages every prophet of despair. This is the Malthusian ominous: the grim indulgence of wanting to assume the worst just because we can project it. Our greed for predicting the future (and our futures' covert resemblances to the halcyon past) is itself a sign of our inability to think the present. There have always been prophets of gloom, who have claimed to be standing at edge of a great watershed of disaster, absolving us from our responsibility for the solutions. But as some things fall apart, other compensations, hitherto invisible, tend to come to light. The practices of decent people are leavened with more adaptive resilience than meets the eye. Our tendency to catastrophize, to announce the total revolution of everything, has long been part of our modern disorientation as to where we stand, and is itself a symptom now of our digital desire for oversimplification, stimulation, and acceleration. (Novelty is what sells, and the greatest novelty imaginable is the end of all things.) I do not mean that it is not true, but that we hasten the end of the world by believing in it.

Is the progress of technology inevitable? It is inevitable that human beings will continue to seek the imaginable good, as we collectively find it; it is not inevitable that we should imagine it in just these terms. Technology is not an independent force; it is, as I've suggested, the mode in which we encounter practical possibility and necessity. What confuses our sense of agency is the fact that while we *each* feel like we use a tool by our autonomous volition, the tool is itself a way in which we are fastened into dependence on a wider social order. And so long as we continue to picture our best selves – our freedom, equality, and identity – as dependent on digital or technological terms, then of course technology will continue to develop. The history of technology is and will continue to be the history of our collective quest for the good and right life.

Ought we therefore to embrace everything that comes our way in permissive laissez-fair? No. To reason that "my parents were opposed to something because it was new and strange to them; they were wrong; therefore I will embrace what is new and strange to me" is lazy and culpable. To oppose what is unfamiliar on grounds of being unfamiliar is bigotry, that's true. But to advocate what is novel just because it is novel is no less negligent. Both positions amount to the same: They would, unthinking, surrender the judgment and vigilance that we must always exercise at every point to lead our lives well. Both positions would settle in advance that which is always at hazard within what faces you today. In the long run, we are all dead – but that doesn't mean we ought to hasten the day. The good is only ever at stake here and now in living presence. Our decisions must be concrete to be responsible; we only ever do good here in particular.

To express the necessary friction between the present and the future – this is the stewardship of the world, the task of every life in every generation. We must struggle to clarify what most matters within new circumstances, to press the new to prove itself, to count the costs, to argue over what is gained, to give our best thinking to the question of how to accommodate the new within the highest purposes that make sense of our life. The only ethical lesson of technology's neutrality of averages is that it is too easy not to think about it, that indifference and lethargy of spirit are the greatest threats of all, that the name of evil is "whatever," and that our vision of what's right only takes place where we can make it happen. More technological capacities are on the way, but how they will take shape is always in our hands. This time, it is different. This time, this time and time again, we are called to make it good.

3

The Sound of Our Own Voice

> How can we bring before our minds, with sufficient distinctness, the consequence of a universal interchange of thought by the speediest method? The world, it has been said, will be made a great whispering-gallery; I would rather say, a great assembly, where everyone will see and hear everyone else ... The most remarkable effect, if I may judge from my own narrow thought, will be the approach to a practical unity of the human race; of which we have never yet had a foreshadowing, except in the gospel of Christ.
>
> (Ezra Gannett, preaching a sermon about the transatlantic telegraph, 1858)[1]

If to be modern is to continually identify new technical means with new possibilities of human freedom and equality, it remains to be said more specifically how digital technology bears on the shape of our political life now. The internet is a social medium; its foremost attentional attraction is that it involves us immediately with an indefinite number of others. This is its decisive edge over television and the printed word: its participatory character – what is "inter" in the net. As I've said above: The connection is the message; its central theme and subject is other people. It thereby has exceptional political resonance. Because if politics (broadly) consists in the practices through which we govern ourselves as parts of a given whole, the internet is now the form of politics itself.

But our online dealings are marked by a series of bewildering contradictions.

- The internet is a medium of the moment, of evanescent, confessional intimacy, such that speaking our mind, updating our status, and over-sharing the minutiae of our breakfast is the fun of it. Yet every online act is recorded, archived, and searchable – indiscretions or outrages are more public than had ever been conceivable. They are (in theory) more indelible than if they had been etched in stone.
- The internet is "open access." It affords us all we could ever need to educate ourselves to the highest standard; it grants us the means of exchanging

reasons with others on an equal, neutral footing; it makes it easier than ever to be savvy and canny in the scrutiny of public claims. Yet it seems in fact to promote to our attention what is already familiar, to make us less curious and more ignorant, to narrow the range of views we encounter, to generate the most corrosive skepticism alongside the most naïve credulity, and to degrade public conversations into mud-slung ad hominem calumny.

- The internet engages our sense of being unique individuals: Our preferences are customized ("just for you"), our feedback and "voice" are constantly solicited, our idiosyncrasies and preferences noted, validated, and indulged. ("Your opinion matters!") Yet the medium standardizes the terms in which we express those preferences, while indexing quality to quantitative hits. Aggregated "storms" of "views" or "likes" where the collective hive mind is buzzing viral sift "influencers" from "followers."

- The internet is a medium in which I may see, speak, and do anonymously. It is sometimes difficult to tell whether we are dealing with other human beings at all, or with automated software. It renders us private and opaque to others. Yet it makes it easier and more desirable than ever to be on permanent display, to court widespread notoriety and celebrity, to perform one's "brand." We surrender scads of private data about our affairs in exchange for access to online services. Companies have a greater window into our waking psyche than ever before. "Transparency" is routinely touted as a self-evident good.

- The internet has from the beginning been labeled "democratic." It is an astonishingly effective means of mobilizing collective participation; fund-raising; circumventing information barriers; and, through easy whistleblowing, keeping institutions honest. It has promised to be an effective means of organizing movements of, for, and by the people. And yet it is at the same time making possible the most invasive forms of panopticon surveillance that have ever existed; it has never been so easy to scrutinize, track, censor, and control the information available to and generated by hundreds of millions of people.

The recurring property of these contrasts is their all-or-nothing opposition: the sense that what goes online is at once everywhere and nowhere, that it is not governed by the boundaries that have shaped political communities and their speech, that it has no appropriate radius or circumscription. One might say that our online meanings are either private (what only I or a voluntary few can see) or universal (what everyone can) – but not held in common, not resulting from the defined in-betweens of family, neighborhood, municipal, regional, or citizen life. As most of these commons had been constituted by and through shared forms of readership or viewership for much of American history, online communication ruptures our shared perception that, like it or not, we find ourselves in a particular setting in which our differences are to be reasoned and worked out, that we cannot avoid confronting and settling something at shared stake. There is no definite "we" to the everyone medium, no boundary at which it necessarily must stop short of reaching all at once. The people implied in our sense of what's "public" online are not "we, the people" but digital humanity at large: to be a digital user is to be conscious of the fact that all contemporary digital acts are (in theory) simultaneously available to one's inspection. Online information has no intrinsic political form. It is thereby at variance with politics as such.

Political life takes place in bonds and bounds. All of us are vulnerable and some are dangerous: Our desire for justice arises from the finitude of our bodies and resources, from the permanent temptation to cross the line, and from our need for each other to govern the common promise of what is owed to each. Political life therefore lays down and upholds the principles by which my body, bodies of citizens, a body of laws, and the body politic relate to other bodies in kind. It is the art of drawing and sustaining borders, limits, and bottom lines between the irreducible plurality of needs and interests. Such bounds constrain us even as they enable us to be connected to and in communication with others in practice. Without this definition of extents, without this relation to possible action, our aspirations can have no particular meaning or location. Our vision of freedom and justice is bodied forth between the lines.

Yet laws, bodies, and borders are, by being material and historical, always in a sense contingent – there can be no purely rational deduction for why some people are born there and others here, for why the line should be drawn exactly thus. The meaning of such borders may be manipulated into the service of xenophobia and worse. But such limitations are likewise a condition for whatever nobility politics is capable of. It is only because we can claim something in particular – because I am this body and not another, because we belong to this country and not another – that we can then be claimed by the aspiration to extend it to others. Like our bodies, therefore, political boundaries take on more than just material significance. The law's authority rests not on force alone (unless it is merely coercive); it sustains and is sustained by the bonds of imagination – our loyalties, our habits, our particular patterns of care informed by what's been achieved for us and what remains for us to still achieve. Our form of government, the law of the land, takes shape in and through each of us.

The internet, in contrast, is at basic odds with the attachments of bounded political life. It is a medium of the mind or the unsettled imagination (which may suppose itself everywhere at once), rather than of the body or of what ancient Greek philosophers called *thumos,* the heartcords – the human capacity to form attachments to people, things, and places. All media are of the mind in one way or another; but the strange schizophrenia of our digital condition is that even as our bodies remain fleshed – bound by law, inherited by family, and shaped by history – our minds are now outlandish, unfixed from the formative shapes of given place. Our perception of bounds as merely irrational or arbitrary is all the greater when one is always seamlessly in touch with any number of alternatives: Bounds are categorically maligned as intrinsically divisive, as marking an invidious distinction between "us" and "them" that entails antagonism and ethnocentric exclusion. It is rather what is beyond borders, what transcends national distinction, that is supposed to be best and truest.[2] This goes for nationalism too, which has, paradoxically, itself become a global movement united by a common cosmopolitan adversary. But a completely global or "inclusive politics" is a contradiction in terms – a notion that can only make sense of itself in opposition to those who see politics as a practice bound to limit (just as "all lives matter" is either a tautology that goes without saying or a slogan pointed at one implicit target).

We are refiguring the real into the virtual in ways that aim to expand our powers of self-determination: The internet offers us the possibility of enlarging the scope of voluntary choices by diminishing the significance of given bounds. And yet the political future of that ambition remains uncertain and hazardous. Not because online associations, friendships, allegiances, or identities must be less satisfying than those in terms of other media (certainly they are no less defining). But because digital relations cannot offer a full-bodied political alternative to the given bounds they undermine. More precisely, the medium, by virtue of shaping our political imagination in certain ways, poses a problem for the definition or integrity of political form as such – that is, for the notion that a nation or any kind of political entity, insofar as it hopes to remain a unity, must be one among (and defined in contrast to) others. The medium occludes the imagination of national politics as a context unto itself. That is, our political practice as a nation remains bound to realities that cannot fully be translated into the voluntary terms in which we transact as global citizens on the digital plane. The implicit demand that politics become "rational" (i.e., reduced to rights self-evident and applicable to everyone everywhere) is, in this way, permanently disruptive, disorienting, and destructive to political life as such. This is the political version of my thesis that digital technology is a natural technology: The medium is a form of authority that implies not just a new way of conducting politics, but the project of transcending politics altogether by establishing a neutral, mirror-like system of legitimate assessment.

I don't say that there is not a great deal to like about this system – there *is* (that's just the problem). But whatever its fate, I'd like to present in this chapter some of the ways our new medium is reforming life together. Because to the extent that it becomes the primary means of dealing with others, it will continue to exert formative pressures on how we conceive of associations, how we exchange reasons, and how we see ourselves. All three of these, I think, will then tend to shape our imagination of national politics, prying apart certain kinds of extremes that are emerging as typical of our age: cosmopolitanism and ethnic nativism, open borders and xenophobia, the politics of technical rationality and Know Nothing politics.

The internet is by no means the only cause of our coming unstuck.[3] Nor can The Internet as such ever provide a sufficient explanation for any social phenomenon. My position is, rather, that no major political phenomenon is now entirely legible without it. Digital relations do not cause events; they figure them.[4] Versions of the point I am making have been made before, moreover, about different media. ("For most people there are only two places in the world. Where they live and their TV set."[5]) The internet is continuous with these older trends, while precipitating them to mark a difference in kind. It is not simply that the telegraph or the internet reach more or fewer people, or are in more or fewer hands, or disseminate better or worse information. What is different is the way in which each of them implies a specific conception of the public sphere and of how we each take part in it – the way, that is, in which the medium weds our individual imaginations to a conception of the political whole. Whereas the radio and TV were primarily national concerns, online speech is trans-political; it is inherent to the medium to not seem to belong to any specific domain. It has no "pride of place," it does not come with the territory; there is no local or national web, only a worldwide one. Even if this is not the case in fact, the illusion that the net is untethered from place makes it more powerful by continually tempting us to imagine ourselves as transcending the bounds that render us political creatures at all. Digital relations are therefore not just a threat to liberal politics – to the ideals of unrestricted speech, impartial law, free competition, and the marketplace of ideas – but to politics as such: to the practices of personal authority embodying a vision of bounded life in common. Where there is nowhere between here and everywhere, political speech cannot take place.

I concentrate on the United States here not only because it is the case closest to home for me, but because, as the United States is not exactly a "nation" – an ethnic or linguistic whole whose roots are lost to history – the imagination of the union is central to American politics in an especially pressing way. When contrasting the tendencies of online political life with some previous sense of politics, however, I would not imply that there has ever been a time when our country was one pristine and harmonious unit, living in benevolent solidarity. It was never just so; who exactly "we" are has been one of the most vehement questions of American history all along, one that admits of no permanent or easy resolution. Our reliance on the printed word did not prevent the Civil War. It may even be that print made it much likelier than it would have been, had television or the internet already been on hand as organs of a fully national press. Still, in comparing online tendencies to printed ones, we can make out several differences in kind, one of which is the erosion of the sense that there are questions on which we *cannot but* come to terms, that common measure is a matter of necessity, that we need each other to work out our differences within some particular setting. If print allowed us to imagine modern forms of political unity in the first place, the internet – even as it in some ways widens the scope of political participation – renders the very thought of "us" suspect or unworkable.

3.1   EVERYWHERE ASSOCIATIONS: COMMUNITY AND LONELINESS

> A real community, as distinct from social life, is only possible between persons whose idea of themselves and others is real, not fantastic.
>
> (W. H. Auden)[6]

Most talking points of digital rhetoric come couched in terms of connection and small-town community. Thus Facebook calls itself a social utility that gives people "the power to build community and bring the world closer together."[7] Twitter has a "Communities" feature, "created to give people a dedicated place to connect, share, and get closer to the discussions they care about most."[8] Its former CEO asked us to think of it as "the global town square."[9] One of the founders of Flickr likens it to a "land trust," of which his colleagues are "custodians."[10] Wikipedia has a "commons" and a "village pump" (where users discuss technical issues). Jimmy Wales (its founder) suggests that we think of it as having the status of "a library or a public park."[11] YouTube's mission statement: "We believe that everyone deserves to have a voice, and that the world is a better place when we listen, share and build community through our stories."[12] Apple also calls its flagship stores "town squares,"[13] while its App Store has a page to help you "find your community."[14] Firefox is "more than a browser ..." (yes, you've guessed it). Every platform has a defined list of "community standards." Most online platforms likewise go out of their way to advertise connectivity, dialogue, a culture of collaboration, engagement, the fostering of meaningful connections, participation, feedback, teamwork, sharing, and discussion as goods that are demonstrably available through their services. The very activity of being online is one of being "linked" or "connected" to the network. Stretching the notion *ad absurdum*, Facebook refers to its 2.1 billion users as a "community."[15] (Which is a bit like saying that everyone who has walked into the same mall is joined in brotherhood.) The term commands affective (and unthinking) enthusiasm from all quarters.

Yet we are conscious of the fact that if the internet makes it easier to keep in touch with our community, it also makes it easier to move away, to do without them, and to isolate ourselves in ways that would have otherwise not been possible. Rather than providing a novel solution to the predicaments that attend an age marked by increasing mobility, urbanization, and anomie, there is evidence that the internet's various versions of community-building are not only not working, but are making us lonelier and more socially distressed than ever. If the testimony of our own experience were not enough, many studies have by now connected spending time online (as little as ten minutes per day) with higher rates of suicide, depression, obsession, stress, overeating, anxiety, FOMO, and sleeping disorders. One study found an increase in Facebook use correlated with a decrease in the quality of mental health. In another, 63 percent of Instagram users reported feeling miserable about it.[16] This comes at a time in which (for various reasons) 60 million Americans, about 20 percent of the population, report being unhappy with their lives on account of loneliness (or "perceived social isolation," as social scientists call it). The percentage is higher for older adults – about 35 percent of people over forty-five.[17] From 1985 to 2004, the average size of Americans' social network (defined as "number of confidants") diminished by about a third.[18] And so a version of the all-or-nothing paradox I've noted above obtains here too: As the internet helps us be more and more connected to others, we are also conscious that it somehow keeps us isolated from them. However promiscuous and haphazard our use of the term "community," there is no question that the notion hits a nerve, that it speaks to a deep-seated need in us, as never before. No one living in pre-modern tribes was singing the dewy-eyed praises of "community." It takes a (global) village. How so?

Modern politics has been marked by a relative transition from a political life defined by local, hierarchical, situated relations to larger units of stranger sociability: Our relations to each other are now mediated by a framework of rights, duties, and norms, abstracted from our specific identities. Or conversely: The way in which we conceive of those identities is less a matter of hearth and kin and more a matter of categorical affiliation – American or Chilean, Christian or Muslim, Democrat or Republican, and so on.[19] And whereas feudal politics required trust in particular people, modern politics shifts social trust primarily to laws and institutions (which are supposed to function regardless of whether anyone within them is trustworthy). This also means that instead of understanding our lives primarily in personal service to this or that potentate, or as members of this family or tribe, we must now see ourselves as members of a whole of which we can have no direct or comprehensive experience. It is a "social imaginary" that is borne of a new kind of political conception: We represent ourselves as incorporated into a collective unit governed by professional politicians whose legitimacy consists in shielding us from the burdens of political engagement while remaining responsive and accountable to our interests.

This refiguration of home and belonging is itself enabled by media and their imaginative forms. As Benedict Anderson argued, the printing press was decisive to the creation of modern states. It was by virtue of circulating the printed word in the vernacular that a hodgepodge of loosely connected (in some cases, antagonistic) groups were able to begin to imagine themselves as a unified *nation*, one people with shared concerns in the present, bound together by birth, tradition, and distinctive destiny – an actor in history with a working narrative of what it is about. Whereas medieval kingdoms were comprised of overlapping bonds of face-to-face fealty and obedience, the nation state's foundation rests relatively more on a rational picture of what we have in common; so far from being a natural given, we are primarily bound by an *idea* of who "we" are and ought to be. The Tomb of the Unknown Soldier – as a distinctive kind of national monument without precedent in pre-national states – bears stirring witness to this living, yet nameless, common sacrifice.[20]

The press is in this sense essential to the identity of modern states, supplying the context of common reference that replaced first-hand experience or hearsay in pre-modern forms of government. The size of an ancient Greek polis – on the order of ten thousand voting citizens – was about the limit for how many people could squeeze inside an amphitheater to assess the merits of particular candidates and to vote. Modern representative democracy multiplies the size of the citizen body manifold at the cost of direct personal acquaintance. And so it was (originally) the printing press – by way of tracts, pamphlets, books, newspapers – that allowed the citizens of modern nation states to conceive of themselves and to proceed as members of an (otherwise abstract and fragmented) whole. Political communities are forms of communication. Whereas violence is speechless, political legitimacy is grounded in our capacity for having speech in common and in our modes of participation in the media that convoke us.

More than a question of nationhood, however, the printed word soon became the foremost means of identifying and pursuing common interests in modern societies – it is how someone could reach out to others outside of their immediate circle. This is because, as Tocqueville observed, political influence is distributed so much more widely in modern democracies than in pre-modern aristocratic regimes, which means that any one citizen, taken singly, is correspondingly less politically able: "[I]n a democracy an association cannot be powerful unless it is numerous." The printed word supplied the common resource by which citizens could communicate and organize around shared concerns:

[I]n democratic countries it often happens that a great many men who both want and need to get together cannot do so, for all being very small and lost in the crowd, they do not see one another at all and do not know where to find one another ... The newspaper brought them together and continues to be necessary to hold them together.[21]

The printed word is, in this sense, both the meeting place and the starch that allows citizens to cohere into groups or factions: It is the condition of their association and the form in which they conceive of it, from a starting position of individual helplessness.

The internet evidently occupies the analogous place for us now, supplying the means by which a highly fragmented and mobile society can keep track of itself. In contrast to the abundance of newspapers and pamphlets in Tocqueville's day (which had to be acquired and read piecemeal), the internet provides one common mode of access, a single "portal" opening onto all kinds of transaction and communication. The unification of the internet into a single medium is, in this way, an exact counterpart to the atomized dispersal that marks our modern social situation. It is our common place, as the Supreme

Court has now repeatedly acknowledged and codified it.²² (I note in connection with this that, along with the language of "community," the language of "place" is a defining feature of online rhetoric: sites, forums, chat rooms, boxes, spaces for ideas, and "home.") In its combining the functions of public and private communication, it has become perhaps even more important to our understanding of community than print ever was, since the internet affords us the sense of being in direct, sustained, and immediate contact with others, in a way that print could never match. Speaking of a "community of print" is an imaginative stretch – one can gather only fitful and desultory news about the invisible gathering of others sharing one's position before the page. It was much more difficult than it is now for authors to hear from their readers or to understand the reception of their own work (reviewers were correspondingly more important). An "internet community," on the other hand, seems closer to a patent reality, when one can chime in and quantify the response of others in real time.

And yet something about this way of relating to others is nonetheless shot through with loneliness and asociality. "Community" and our nostalgic terms of online approbation suggest that some aspect of connection is missing within this form of "connectivity." To the extent that we can express unqualified approbation of any "community" (as a marketing or lifestyle adjective), it is also a sign that we don't inhabit a real one. In order to describe why, it will be useful to mark out two contrasting ideals of communal setting, two polar notions that are more or less realized in actual communities.²³

Many of us, if asked, would perhaps name the family as a paradigm community, the closest to ideal in our experience. This is itself a recent development. Aristotle argued that a household is not yet a community, because its members are bound by natural and affective ties, rather than by principles of political justice.²⁴ Nor did the inhabitants of medieval kingdoms define themselves (even figuratively) as families: The political meaning of blood kinship was too obvious to bear out the comparison. Yet the family has undoubtedly been essential to the political rhetoric of the past two hundred years – partly as a consequence of the reconfiguration of fiefs into peoples and states, partly as a consequence of the development of market economics, which has implicated our interests with those of others in new ways. ("Economics" is, etymologically, the science of household management: Our household is now the national and world market.) Family has therefore played a conspicuous part in the rhetoric of fascism and communism. If in the United States we have been warier of speaking about motherland or fatherland (mom and apple pie notwithstanding), it is not uncommon to hear American companies, or organizations, or groups of friends enjoying the sound of referring to themselves as "families." It is this principle, the claims of family, that rivets us to *Breaking Bad*, to *Big Love*, and to any number of films and shows about the mob. The announcement that "we're family" will reliably melt any American's heart. While our families do not have the longstanding existence that they did when many generations remained tied to a single landed property, the nuclear family's ties are nonetheless the most abiding that many of us are likely to have. It is a community of compelling authority. Come what may, we're in the same boat: We stick together.

A contrasting ideal of modern association, by contrast, is one closer to the social imaginary that (in theory) governs modern liberal states, one primarily based on equal, free, and voluntary participation. You are joined to others not through personal authority, but through reiterated consent to the legitimacy of impersonal procedures, laws, and norms. One's commitment to such a community would be understood to be based primarily on mutual benefit, and, in this sense, on claims appealing to voluntary affinity or rational self-interest alone: If the basic principles are denied or infringed, you are entitled to opt out from the proceedings. You are the one best able to identify your interests, and your participation is in some sense provisional and conditional. Affection and loyalty are possible – you may set up a family of choice (in contrast to a family of origin) – but if push comes to shove you may always take it or leave it all. ("When in the course of human events …") It is a community of controlled autonomy: It's up to you.

Each of these extremes – the ideal of the family and the ideal of voluntary reason – corresponds to the ideal of the *nation* and the *state*, respectively. The nation state is an amphibious form that is supposed to include the best of each. Both ideals offer deeply satisfying yet incompatible forms of freedom: to be bound and to be unbound.

The ideal of familial community is one of unconditional "belonging," shared commitments, and legitimate authority. The bonds of family transcend self-interest; its hierarchy is gentle, fair, and natural. Its claims are based on love; its roots are indissoluble and unconditionally acknowledged by all members, who are supposed to have each other's best interests at heart. Its members have strong reciprocal (though not necessarily symmetrical) claims on each other based on a tie that exceeds their willing of it – they need each other, they understand themselves as parts of the whole to which they necessarily belong. The whole is prior to its parts, and the parts are more or less permanently differentiated into their roles. Its drawbacks are that the demands of families can be vexing and difficult, that conflicts are often most violently intense among those who are very close, that there are definite limits to its membership and to how equal its members can become, that personal authority may be abusive, and that the claims of love are not (ultimately) a matter of justice.

The ideal of impersonal association is, in turn, one of autonomy, convenience, equality, and individuality – you lead your own life; you hold the reins. It is (again, in theory) impartial to the specific identity of its members. The rules are fair and fairly applied so as to render each agent unconstrained within a certain sphere; there is a strong identification of freedom with privacy, with being left alone to pursue one's designs; no one is beholden to anyone else; the whole is for the sake of the parts, and everyone should be able to perform any function he or she is qualified for. Its drawbacks are that social bonds are only as strong as your will (since the rule of law always stands over them and is in a position to arbitrate); that there is no strong need to push for compromise when you discover you don't need or want to; and that this independence may result in alienation from others: "Such ... might be called a completely abstract or depersonalized society."²⁵ Whereas familiar tightness usually places restrictions on who we are and what we do, voluntary equality spaces us out.

The logic of online communities is evidently more like the latter than the former; they are associations exhibiting the ideal principles that underpin modern states more than actual states do or can. (States are shaped by history, precedent, and circumstance. Nor is it so simple for anyone living in them, no matter how fortunately placed, to "opt out" by, say, moving to Canada.) As a form of disembodied relation, as a means of dealing mind-to-mind, online communication places us (or seems to, or feels as if it ought to and can) on a more equal footing: An online community is governed by the promise of immediate autonomy. Insofar as we think of it as a communal setting or medium of relation, it offers us a version of purely voluntary citizenship. The promise of total transparency – of "mutually assured surveillance" – is to replace *trust* in public institutions with direct citizen oversight of them.²⁶ But so great is the ease of this kind of association that it emphasizes all the more what's missing in such terms. That such associations should then seek to mimic or simulate the experience of rooted belonging, that we should wax rosy about "community" as an unadulterated good, and that the language of online networking should be rife with folksy, small-town descriptions, are all symptoms of the sentimentalization of the freedom to be bound that we specifically lack online. It is the self-indulgent evocation of a good that we are not committed to in practice, but which we enjoy longing for all the same. The more we realize the workings of impersonal association, the more we are haunted by the evocation of being bound by a small, familiar community.

This description is of course too simple. Most of our friendships and ties are not simply face-to-face or online but some hybrid of the two. The PTA, the local council, the parish, and state government are all institutions to which we belong by virtue of where we find ourselves, and with which we also keep up online. If you stop responding to your family's or your boss's emails, it will be attended by very different consequences than if you leave off responding to a random person online; you cannot opt out without consequences. Nor do I want to deny the ways in which online services facilitate offline bonds; I realize that many have found their lost childhood friends online, that Skype and Zoom make it possible to keep up with one's grandchildren, that discovering likeminded others who share one's hobbies or interests is uplifting, that an increasing number now meet their match online (about 40 percent of heterosexual couples in the United States²⁷), and that online resources may help one find out about family roots or local history. America has, furthermore, always been the country of free association: From the time of Roger Williams and Anne

Hutchinson, Americans have been able to move when sectarian disagreement grew too fierce – to go west, to escape to the big city, to make a new start, to seek out others like me. We are a country of loose national allegiances, and we have long quested for "intentional" community in the face of that fact.[28]

But online communication does more than facilitate more-of-the-same. First, because there is an unstable distinction between the internet used as a supplement to offline relationships and the internet used as a substitute for them: There is an easy slope tending from the former toward the latter. Reconnecting with an old friend, say, or speaking to grandchildren on Skype are extensions of existing relationships that are not primarily situated online. But even in such cases it is clear that, by allowing us to be in frequent contact at a distance, online associations make it easier to move away, to live at a distance from friends and family, to keep our neighbors at arm's length, to work from home, and to spend more time entertained alone. That is, while we are piecemeal in better touch, the comprehensive effect of easy online communication is to undermine the sharpest need for sustained face-to-face relationships – while also tending to recast them within a pattern of discrete, autonomous, voluntary exchanges, since just how often and by what means we are in touch becomes a matter of choice. (Are we in better touch with friends on Facebook or worse? It is like asking whether we are better spellers with auto-correct.) The internet is, in this respect, a social lubricant, and therefore a social solvent. It allows us to take up opportunities that would not otherwise be available, to widen our scope of action, and to spend less time at the office or in traffic. Online teaching promises to broaden access to education (to prisoners, say, or to those who have day jobs), while telecommuting promises to equalize employees by allowing parents to continue to work while looking after young children. But as the net becomes the master link, it tends to cast our relationships further into the second kind of communal pattern I noted above – empowering us as autonomous individuals – which entails the thinning out or dissolution of communities bound by place and time. Participation becomes a matter of input; time spent face to face becomes FaceTime.

Beyond our immediate circle of family, friends, and coworkers, it is also obvious that the medium transforms and supplants many offline practices. The convenience of doing business online is taking over the humdrum experience of going to the mall, the bank, the travel agency, or the bookstore. The trend in all service industries is to eliminate human contact in the pursuit of "speed, efficiency, cost, and stress reduction."[29] The ease with which we have our way online shortens our patience for suffering fools and standing in line for very long. (Standing in line to exercise the franchise can call us to a sense of civic solidarity: One stands side by side with fellow citizens one is not likely to otherwise encounter. But is that worth the trouble of waiting in line for an hour or two? And what if online voting managed to increase the number of participants in any given election?[30]) The convenience of online dating, in particular, makes it less likely that people will take a chance offline: A growing number of people have never asked anyone out in person, just as about half of breakups take place over email.[31] Asking someone out in person may lead to the embarrassment of finding out they don't like you, or that they are already taken. The embarrassment is buffered online where everyone on the site is explicitly looking, and where, if you are turned down, there are more fish just clicks away. (About 45 million Americans now use online dating services; up to 70 percent of same-sex relationships start online.[32]) Yu Wang, chief executive of one of China's largest dating apps, claims that online dating is already the social norm there: "If you approach someone you don't know and start flirting, you're a scoundrel," whereas on the app "you don't expose yourself, there's no danger of getting rejected, you cannot lose face."[33]

If it is more convenient to deal with others online, it is because we encounter them in clearly defined transactional terms – whether shopping for a used coffee table or for a spouse, others show up primarily as instruments of our purposes. I do not mean to exaggerate the compassionate humanity with which we deal with servers, tellers, clerks, and potential dates in person. We are perfectly capable of objectifying them too or, worse, not giving them a second thought. Not to mention the fact that automated business is quicker and (almost always) more efficient than dealing in person. The efficiency of online transactions is nonetheless directly connected to the fact that we don't have to worry about others or what they think of us. They amplify the sense that my preferences are foremost in my dealings, because my aesthetic "experience" is part of the service provided by the site or platform – I am more autonomous as a user, but I am only a user because I am a customer.

As they become our generalized instrument for sharing information and finding communities of like-minded others, digital relations affect our understanding of community and sociability in well-known ways. By prioritizing efficiency, the internet allows us to identify, speak to, and transact with others who already share our views and preferences – that is, to treat association as a voluntary good that we enjoy through platforms. We thereby undermine the formative character of sustained communal associations. Associations of all sorts are means by which we may further our concerns, but they are also – ideally – places in which those concerns come to be shaped and acquire some content larger than our whims. In other words, it is an online mistake to think of human communities as platforms for furthering our readymade desires, since it is precisely within families, friendships, neighborhoods, congregations, clubs, and other organizations that our desires come to have shared, recognizable, and higher aspirations in the first place. Political deliberation is intrinsically "inefficient," not because it is corrupt, but because efficiency is altogether the wrong standard by which to judge it. Efficiency measures a relation between industrial input and output, whereas the end of politics is not a "product" distinct from the activity of discerning through conflict and debate the ends of life in common; unlike industrial processes, the good of politics must include deliberation about the very goods to which it aims. There is no other *essential* reason to object to technocracy or government by algorithm.

Our political education forms us only to the extent that we come to be shaped by social pressures we do not ourselves choose – efficiency is the opposite of politics in this sense too. All standing associations make for tedious work: They involve constant negotiation; inconvenient attention to others; thwarted projects; inefficient use of time; and awkward, jury-rigged compromises. None of these things seem choice-worthy in their own right; no one in his right mind would go out of his way to prefer the carping, tattling, jostling intrusions of deadbeat relatives and nosy neighbors to the seamlessness of cyberspace. And when digital communities are known to be within reach, the preference becomes all the *harder* to imagine sustaining, for the reasons I've stated. Not to mention the fact that people who do not fit into close communities because they fall outside its codes or because they cannot accede to its forms of recognition will undeniably find life oppressive there and will report leaving their small town with relief. As I write this, I myself have been living in an isolated, rural community of about forty inhabitants. It is wonderful to belong, but it is terrible to feel at every moment under the scrutiny of knowing eyes. The real blessings of community are only paid for in real thorns in one's side – in daily headaches and in rage.

To put it starkly, therefore, an abiding or "familiar" community is in a position to shape us to the extent that our membership in it is to some extent difficult to eschew – because of where we are born, or where we live, or whom we are promised to, or what we owe to particular others. A community in this stronger sense is *not* primarily a community of shared values and voluntary identities (this is our online fallacy), but a setting in which we must inescapably work out our differences about shared concerns. It forces us to come to grips with those we think disagreeable or dead wrong, with those whom we are tempted to despise; it consists in an often brute, thankless, and fierce reality that is overlooked by our sloppy sentimentalization of it. "Dialogue" sounds like a terrific thing, until you realize that real negotiation means having your nose constantly rubbed in others' short-sightedness, meanness, and incapacity to recognize your own fine qualities. "Empathy" (as we cursorily use the term) is the bittersweet imagination of others' pain at a distance: The closer you really are to people, the harder it is to help or bear them. So too "community," as a buzzword, is nothing but a friendly synonym for "group" – it is "category" with a smiley face. In actual fact, the "tighter" or more "close-knit" the community, the more opportunities there are for friction. And friction is chafing and abrasive.

But friction is also what forms and holds together in a pinch, what gives you traction with others; all of the inconveniences of life in common may (also) prove ethical disciplines of the will that, by forcing us to depend on others and forcing others to depend on us, teach us to deepen our capacity for neighborhood. The online ideal is a "smooth experience," in contrast: a mode of relation as frictionless and slick as the design of the devices that are the portals to its "streaming." To the extent that I associate with others in the online mode, I am in a position from which I may retreat, refrain, abstract myself at any point. There are no (or few) strings attached, the setting puts little pressure on the shape of my own desires. This is just what convenience *is*, what endows our online experience with such a compelling sense of our own empowered individuality. And it is what is good about voluntary autonomy: You can sign up for whatever speaks to you, and you're off the hook for what doesn't.

The frictionless pursuit of self-interest does not rule out the fact that any one of these interests may be worthy and rewarding. Very many people find genuine solace, for instance, in the realization that there are others "like me" online, that they are not alone in having this or that interest, condition, or predicament. Seeking out others like me can also mean becoming radicalized toward violence, hatred, and aberrance (by ISIS, say); but these are conspicuous exceptions in a much larger web of connections whereby, say, parents of children with rare disabilities can experience the relief of being able to find others in the same situation – such cases can be multiplied indefinitely.[34] As an instrument for coordinating and "harnessing" the efforts of large numbers of scattered people and resources, furthermore, the internet has no parallel or precedent: It is an astoundingly effective means of "crowdfunding" a cause through many small contributions, and of recruiting people to pitch in to achieve concrete, limited ends. (Such capacities for social logistics have lessened concerns about the warping influence of money in political advertising, for instance.) Getting many people involved in the service of short-term goals and cutting out the middleman is what the net does best. Within a social situation such as our own, where transient and circumstantial acquaintances are the norm, we need the internet. And if we did not have it, we should have to invent it.

Even as the content of our online interests may be commendable in any given case, however, the assumptions implicit in the form itself undermine part of what we feel we mean when we make claims about "community." The internet works to connect us with others by encouraging us to think of ourselves as independent agents; it dislocates us from the sense that common ground is at stake, from situations in which we experience the unavoidable pressure of others' concerns on our own life. As we become better able to customize and fine-tune whom we deal with and how and why, the contexts in which I must come to terms with what I do not already think or want necessarily diminish. The nostalgic endorsement of "tight-knit community" online thus stems from the fact that while some part of us misses the benefits of a different kind of close, longstanding ties – common solicitudes and trust, continuity of memory, support and solidarity in trouble, and so on – we are also busy forfeiting those very benefits insofar as we expand our online involvement with others. Where I am less obliged to others, others are less obliged to me. The more connected we are online, the easier it is to keep others at arm's length. The ideal of autonomy expands our power of choice, and in this specific sense makes us freer – but floating free we're also lonelier, just a click or two away from opting out like Bartleby or from "ghosting" out of the picture.

I signed up a couple of years ago for a service called Nextdoor – a "private social network" for city neighborhoods. The promotional material hits all the right notes: "these days people don't know their neighbors, or how to contact them," "we believe connecting with others is a universal human need," "we can cultivate a kinder world where everyone has a neighbhorhood they can rely on."[35] As far as the site is concerned, however, "community" means keeping abreast of local events, posting requests for babysitters or notices of runaway pets, sharing safety information, and selling stuff. One is invited to set up one's profile by selecting from fifty-seven distinct categories of "interests," "so there's something for everyone. Which will you choose?"[36] Community here means an aggregate of individual convenience with respect to physical proximity – a "private social network" in full oxymoron – rather than anything like sustained attention to the same things: Where the people involved do not know each other personally, it is not even possible to gossip or swap stories.

"Nextdoor is where you connect to the neighborhoods that matter to *you* so you can belong."[37] The service simulates a certain kind of belonging that we long for. We can thus *feel* more connected within terms that only ratify the self-centered independence of each agent involved. The service may prove the occasion to meet the neighbors, but overall it makes it easier not to deal with anyone I'd rather not; the pressures of face-to-face contact become all the *more* unbearable, the more readily we can dispense with them. We are put in the position not of neighbors, but of consumers, restricting our involvement to our own terms and conditions. Not to mention the fact that there will always be something paradoxical in the thought that you can altogether *choose* your own community, your neighborhood, your family: We may sign up for these (in different senses), but we cannot well reckon their ultimate meaning to us simply in terms of what we choose, since we must be chosen in turn by them, and we are in for more than we bargain for. Mark Zuckerberg testified to Congress that "it's not enough just to connect people; we have to make sure that those connections are positive."[38] To the extent that it is possible to ensure this, we are no longer speaking about human connections, but of their wishful affirmation by technical means.

Nextdoor, We Work, WeLive (#wecommunity), Fabric, and all manner of new digital community platforms are, for all these reasons, not simply simulating offline communities, but helping dissolve them – and then selling the narcotic self-indulgence of "belonging" back to their users. The same point holds for our analogous enthusiasm for what is local, artisanal, hand-crafted, "cottagecore," or traditional: We admire and consume them in terms that destroy the conditions for their nourishment. They are evocations of an intimacy in which we have little or no stake. When community or roots have become a "lifestyle," it is a sign that their politics is so void of substance as to have become aesthetics.

One last wrinkle. Against the claim that the internet is a medium of individualism, one sometimes meets the contrary worry that the tech industry's "community" rhetoric entails a more sinister vision of political collectivism (the dystopian worry dramatized in, say, James Ponsoldt's 2017 film, *The Circle*). Thus Franklin Foer:

> When it comes to the most central tenet of individualism—free will—the tech companies have a different way. They hope to automate choices ... Once we cross certain thresholds—once we transform the values of institutions, once we abandon privacy—there's no turning back, no restoring our lost individuality.[39]

And this worry – about whether the internet emphasizes collective conformity or individual choice – closely ties in to more general disputes about whether the internet is clustering us into likeminded "bubbles" and "tribes" or disjoining us into monads.[40]

But these poles are mutually facilitating correlatives of a single phenomenon. Just as online automation and conformism are a direct consequence of the ways in which online services successfully flatter our sense of uniqueness (so that the automation of choice and the perception of customized free will go hand in hand), tribalization, mobbing, and atomism are corollaries of the lack of sustained care in offline common. All such extremes stem from the fundamental fact that online socialization is a matter of individual preference rather than of situated, necessarily cooperative concern. Just as a "tribe" in any pre-digital sense must designate something very different from groups aggregated by specific preferences or positions, what Foer calls "our lost individuality" is a fiction so long as it is understood solely in terms of abstract "choice" and "free will."

Mass and individual are the longstanding extremes into which the social fabric resolves itself in the absence of intermediate, local institutions by means of which citizens are shaped to political action. More than just assemblies of people, masses are a consequence of industrialized, urbanized, egalitarian states in which citizens have no abiding, life-long commitments to each other or to where they live: A "mass" (as the word suggests) has no form or structure because its parts have no fixed relation to each other. As Arendt puts it, "The truth is that the masses grew out of the fragments of a highly atomized society whose competitive structure and concomitant loneliness of the individual had been held in check only through membership in a class."[41] The commonplace that one is never so alone as in a crowd expresses this exactly – even as one may find oneself acting in concert with a large body of people, one is fundamentally alone when all are joined only by their own immediate interests and preferences. And as McLuhan observed, the mass is also a consequence of how technology allows us to relate to others and shapes the ways in which we picture our place within some communal whole: "[P]rint technology created the public. Electric technology created the mass."[42] This is precisely and increasingly our situation. Insofar as digital technology mediates our relationships, we tend toward complete homogeneity *and* complete individualism: Both of these are rejections of the need for politics. We find ourselves either an integer or a number: It's all for one, and every man for himself.

3.2   EVERYWHERE REASONS: CONTEXTS AND INFORMATION

> It used to be that, when you communicated with someone, the person you were communicating with was as important as the information. Now, on the internet, the person is unimportant at all. In fact, [the internet] was developed so that scientists could communicate ... without knowing where the other person was or even who the other person was ... In the future, you won't know if you're communicating with dogs, or robots, or people, and it won't matter.
>
> (Lawrence Krauss)[43]

Communication is a community's most important activity: What we can expect to say to each other defines and sustains our perception of the whole of which we are parts. Our form of community is in this sense embodied in a certain kind of running conversation and a certain conception of reason itself. Who we think we are will shape what kinds of arguments are likely to gain public purchase, what ideas will widely resonate, what we think is most worth saying, and what is regarded as unspeakable. Making sense is an act of common faith. The internet seems to widen the scope of what is sharable, in this sense, to humanity at large; it would seem to free us from merely local conventions of speech, from being judged only by a few who may or may not happen to understand us. It promises, on the face of it, to transcend the linguistic and political divisions that had marked prior media on the way toward a purely human community.

Yet wider scope also complicates our sense of what we can get across and where others are coming from. And as online communication makes it easier to broaden and multiply the audience – as it moves us into a space of autonomous minds – it also abstracts us from a body of considerations governing the rhetoric and substance of other media: Who is speaking and why? Who is being addressed? What conventions and expectations are being adhered to or defied? What is the manner and likely tone? We speak online in the relative absence of circumstances that shape our understanding of words on a page or spoken.

Most problems with and criticisms of online communication, most apologies for misunderstanding or defenses of past remarks, make their way back to the problem of context, to the problem of how to take someone's words. In one way it's obvious why this should be so. As ready access to all manner of views and sources has increased – and as information is so readily copied and repurposed online – some of it is bound to be misconstrued. Yet the need for context is not (just) a need for more information, since context is what goes without saying when you are able to get across what you mean. Information is a matter of factual content, while context is what informs our sense of how we should respond to it. Words rarely speak for themselves. We are aware that they may not mean what they mean to us in particular: In any offline situation, we implicitly measure them by the speaker's authority, capacity, and likely intentions. But such judgments are themselves social; they are woven into the principles and practices of our political form.

"Context" means how things hang together. It relies on a background common sense to which we appeal when we ask someone to "put things in perspective" or to accord them "due weight" or to see them "in proportion." These expressions invoke a set of considerations about what ranks highest in "our" esteem, an underlying agreement that throws into relief the features most relevant to form a fair estimate of someone's words or deeds as "rightly understood." We will always argue about how to weigh the relative importance of these assumptions – what should count as an ameliorating or exculpatory circumstance, for instance – nor has there ever been a time when such arguments were straightforward. But disagreements about the application of principles within a framework can be fierce without calling the existence of the framework into question.[44] And as no medium is completely self-referring and self-enclosed – as disputes about what's true in writing cannot simply be resolved by pointing to other written pages, absent other shared judgments about just which ones count as authoritative – there must be such a framework in order not only to resolve disputes, but in order to formulate and elaborate rival sets of reasons *as* disputes at all.

What is unprecedented about our own situation online is the relative absence of just such a framework, as a consequence of the net's reach. What is "appropriate," "mainstream," and "normal"? What is "offensive," "weird," "extreme," "disturbing"? Who exactly is a "fascist" or a "communist"? Where is the "pale"? What is a "safe assumption" or a disagreement in "good faith"? What is the difference between good judgment and a "slippery slope"? None of these questions can be settled conclusively and in general; they are not self-evident. It is no coincidence that it is debate about just such issues that makes up much controversy online, where we cannot reliably measure what someone says by who they are or what they take themselves to mean.

The contextual opacity of words on the screen makes certain kinds of questions about identity, tone, and intent undecipherable. In 2005, someone set up a website threatening to kill and eat a rabbit ("Toby") unless fifty thousand dollars in donations were made by a certain deadline – it was probably (?) a prank, but the creator managed to raise over twenty thousand dollars for it all the same. Several high-profile characters have turned out not to be "real" people at all: "Edoardo Martins" (a celebrity photographer who was cobbled together from other identities), Lennay Kekua (the hoax girlfriend of football player Manti Te'o), and "lonelygirl15," a popular early video diarist (who turned out to be a paid actress). When a "Union of White NYU Students" appeared on Facebook in late 2015, advertising itself as a "safe space" for white students to celebrate the "pioneering will and greatness of our unique and virtuous people" in obnoxious terms, it proved impossible for NYU administrators to determine whether they were dealing with the work of sincere white nationalist students, anti-racist satirists, or external or internal saboteurs.[45]

These are extreme examples of a more ordinary fact about public online communication sometimes called "Poe's law:" Without some explicit indication, it is impossible to create a parody that someone, somewhere won't mistake for an earnest position. Without knowing something about the author's purport, words cannot be secured to one sense. Our perspective on their meaning is necessarily flattened and foreshortened; online words are to reason what cubism is to art.

This flattening shows up as a problem with assessing humor in particular. "Trolling" is a phenomenon that is only possible to the extent that there can be permanent ambiguity about whether someone is hostile, snarky, clueless, captious, or "just messing with you." The term covers a varied range of online provocations that are intrinsically unfathomable because their success depends on their not being *seen* to be provocations at all – a successful troll must appear to be artlessly in earnest and can always retreat into plausible denials. In contrast to Socratic irony, irony that is in principle decidable (if only we knew what the speaker thought), trolling may be undecided and undecidable; as he will never be forced to "really" explain himself, the troll may not even be sure what he himself means. Indeed, the troll will likely not even think of himself as a troll at all. The troll's own intentions are a black box; the term exists mainly as a pejorative description of anonymous others who harass, heckle, or annoy us.

The closest analogue version of trolling is the "bull session" – a noncommittal mode of speaking in which we develop what we mean by trying out opinions among friends. The digital troll must not only commit his views to writing, but he finds himself in a very different sense "among friends." The troll looks to elicit an emotional, knee-jerk reaction from an unsuspecting victim, who is made into a public spectacle; trolls score off expectations of some particular online group, so that when someone takes the bait to justify what "we" think, those views can be ridiculed by another putative "we" looking on. Much (if not all) humor depends on our perception of another's intentions. Trolling is therefore specifically possible because there is no way to distinguish irony from sincerity outside of some context of foregrounding practices and assumptions about them. To know what's funny, we say you have to "be there" – but there is no "there" online.

The absence of context – the prying apart of practical circumstances from information – exemplifies another version of the general all-or-nothing polarity I've noted above: the problem of the missing middles, missing forms of shared action that provide some common measure. Without these to supply the background of context, the conversations available to us online tend to extreme standards of personalization or depersonalization, as I'll argue here. In other words: There is pressure for reasons to be either neutral or to be justified by and pinned to the speaker's identity. A new emphasis on "facts" or data as the paradigmatic form of reason and a new emphasis on *who* gets to say what – on particular "voices" and identities – are each parallel ways of trying to solve online ambiguity.

"Public opinion" was, like the modern nation state, first envisioned on and through the printed page. The consciousness of a unified public opinion or national conversation only dawned on eighteenth century Europe and America insofar as this common space of exchange could be represented as the ongoing relationship between print media and their readership, and therefore as an instrument of deliberation.[46] But "public opinion" is as much a fact of our political situation as it is a constituting ideal of it: It is how the nation thinks out loud. It supplies the implied common measure of a pluralistic society, a setting in which the merits of different principles and proposals may be aired, weighed, contested, and adopted or rejected. Like the "marketplace of ideas," the free exchange of critical opinion is governed by the assumptions that (on the whole and in the long term) the public is capable of identifying its best interests, that the public is responsive to better arguments, that the stronger argument can prevail against the weaker, and that therefore the goal of reason is persuasion. With the centralization of press outlets during much of the twentieth century, the limitations of this procedure became more apparent: a few private companies held a disproportionate amount of sway. But the underlying expectation about the aims and meaning of public debate as the nation's means of deliberation nonetheless stood (at least until the arrival of cable television) and in some form continues to stand (or totter).

The notion of public opinion could only emerge in early modernity, furthermore, alongside a recalibrated understanding of "reason" – both in itself and as embodied in certain institutions. It has been the longstanding task of modern thinking to determine the extent to which all truths may be decided from a point of view outside or beyond the context of any particular culture, tradition, or authority – as it were, from "nowhere."[47] "I think, therefore I am" is the case regardless of who I happen to be. The sense in which we use the word "fact" – as denoting a state of affairs independent of our judgment of it – came into being in the seventeenth century for the purpose of facilitating this new form of impartial discussion. (*Nullius in verba*, as the motto of the Royal Society puts it, "Take nobody's word for it.") It has been the genius of modern liberal societies to reflect this shift, loosening the connection between our understanding of reason as such and any particular conception of the moral good or the confessional truth, thereby sharpening our emphasis on context-independent justifications.[48] Public opinion and modern reason belong to each other.

But this separation of reason from authority has nonetheless always relied on the legitimacy of secular institutions for adjudicating disputes. The political pamphleteering that followed the introduction of the press in some ways resembled our current trouble with fake news – it spread conspiracy theories; stoked social divisions; and freely disseminated inflammatory and scurrilous matter, for which there has always been a broader market than for the sober truth.[49] Nor were these kinds of sources ever entirely done away with. Yet their worst effects were ameliorated by increased state censorship, by the emergence of widely authoritative scientific institutions (like the Royal Society or the Académie française), and, much later, by the widening acceptance of the distinction between respectable newspapers (which might profit from the presumption of credibly working in the public interest) and tabloid journalism. The transition from one medium to another, in other words, required new norms of reading and of trust in authority. The view from nowhere starts somewhere.

Just what will be regarded as a "settled fact" or a debatable "opinion" has varied widely. To call something a "fact" is to appeal to common sense, and the composition of that sense changes: What makes sense is not necessarily what is most rational. But the importance of the distinction between knowledge and opinion does not rest on some specific content being counted as factual – that is, as the settled basis on which an argument may be advanced – but on being committed to some shared set of practices by which disagreement can be worked out, whether or not I happen to agree with the outcomes. Neither public opinion nor our understanding of reason have ever floated simply free from their social location.

Both have been volatilized by being moved online. Concepts like "public sphere" and "national conversation" have been expanded and transformed to a degree that has rendered them only very dubiously useful. In contrast to a situation in which a limited number of news outlets competed for the scoop on the public's behalf, our attention is diffused over an apparently unlimited number of easily available sources.[50] At any rate this seemed the promise that attended the internet in the early 2000s: that an open-ended multitude of bloggers would at once diversify the news and crowd out the standard juggernauts, that an international troop of pajama-wearing geeks would do for fun what the news networks and newspapers had made their exclusive business.[51] The prevailing attitude embodied the fallacious assumption that the news would be the same in kind, but more of it and better.

The reality has been more troubling. There are, on the one hand, many more choices available to us online, when it comes to taking in the news; there are both more views available and more people with platforms to make news. But the availability of choices – the fundamental fact that we can always look elsewhere, so that the burden of attention switches from what we can tune into to what we can tune out of – renders the news rather more into a commodity, content for consumption filtered by my preferences. Nearly all Americans now get the news digitally; about half rely on social media, about a quarter on podcasts, and about two thirds on apps or websites.[52] All of this intake is of course dictated by commercial algorithms: You are shown what you are likely to like, that is, what is likely to keep you coming back to the site. The polarization of American political life is, as is well known, a direct consequence of the way in which our preferences play a greater role than before in shaping our encounter with what happens.

On the other hand, in contrast to this dispersal of attention stands the fact that, when it comes to major news outlets, our collective attention seems *in fact* to be as or more centralized than ever. So far from being abolished, the "mainstream" has consolidated itself in new ways. The winner-take-all pattern of the network effect prevails in the news too. A few sites absorb the lion's share of public attention, with, after a sharp drop-off, an indefinite number of smaller niches trailing behind.[53] Yet this situation is by no means equivalent to the centralization of media that prevailed for most of the twentieth century. The dominant websites must compete for attention within a medium of ready choice; they cannot afford to carry on as if they were still only in print. The online effect on mainstays like the *Washington Post*, the *Wall Street Journal*, and the *New York Times* is clear to anyone comparing their website now to a daily edition from thirty years ago: Sensationally headlined articles have increased (since websites must be updated many times a day, to reward repeated views), the border distinguishing editorializing from reporting (once regarded as the church–state distinction of journalism) has blurred, and all have become more flagrantly partisan. The old sources have succeeded only to the extent that they have been able to remake themselves to suit the requirements of their new commercial environment; they sell subscriptions to a political narrative (rather than ads, as before). There are, in this sense, perhaps as few mainstream views as ever, but each has abandoned the presumption of relative neutrality in favor of naked partisanship. Fox News has changed its motto from "fair and balanced" to "Most watched. Most trusted" and "America's watching." The change is remarkable not only because the network no longer sees fit even to pay lip service to "balance," but because of the implicit equation of attention with credibility. One America News Network takes it one step further with "your nation, your news."

The initial jolt of polarization in the news dates back to the 1987 revocation of the Federal Communications Commission's fairness doctrine (which required broadcasters to present contrasting views of controversial issues in the public interest) and to the Telecom Act of 1996, by which Congress deregulated communication technology. That Rush Limbaugh was nationally syndicated in 1988 and that Fox News was launched in 1996 is no coincidence. Their immediate success also indicates that there was enormous pent-up appetite for news and commentary in a downright conservative cast – that is, that the news of the major networks under the fairness doctrine was not received by millions of viewers as fair. More than just opening the gates to a different kind of news, however, the rise of factional news was attended by the discoveries that opining is cheaper than reporting, that there was no commercial incentive to measure political content by the bipartisan center, and that the point of public opinion is not so much deliberation and persuasion as the extreme affirmation of the opinions one already happens to hold. The rant became the unit of political communication long before Instagram or Twitter. To the extent that the news is now made by ranting (or by ranting about other people's ranting), there are fewer and fewer professional reporters needed to do the job: One America reached 35 million homes in 2019 with a total staff of only about 150.[54]

The dominant networks that preceded this situation – ABC, NBC, CBS, PBS – had been a coherent force. Undoubtedly they were partial expressions of a dominant class and ideology (is it better or worse that they were not unabashedly so?). One might say that their moderation was paid for in hypocrisy. Nor can it be denied that any notion of representation entails the exclusion of some, and that fewer views are excluded now than they sometimes were. But where I may always speak for myself, the indefinite multiplication of views blunts the sense that any one in particular speaks for me, along with the presumption that ideas are in some sense being tested against each other and that there is something staked on that outcome. The notion that one exchanges views for the purpose of deliberation – that they are public for the sake of a conversation that makes up the fabric of our common horizon – has lost all credibility. Public reason has become (mere) freedom of expression.[55]

What is missing from public opinion online is not attention to the same things, but rather the sense that those things arise for us in contexts that we cannot avoid. Our current sense that the news is partisan derives in fact from the overwhelming importance of choice, from the fact that we are not limited to any determinate set of options for informing ourselves. What is missing is, again, the middle: There are fewer media that occupy some intermediate place between what most everyone is reading and what some few are, which in turn stems from the fact that the connection between medium and place has been definitively severed. This matters both because of the role that such a connection once played in developing regional and national identities, and because it was arguably just such intermediate settings that allowed public opinion to be representative. To the extent that it makes public discussion fully open and direct access, the internet (and the migration of public opinion to social media in particular) represents a public sphere in which everyone can speak and in which no one in particular must be heard.

Along with this fraying of context comes a recalibration of what counts as reason at all. It is telling that the internet was first conceived as a means of efficiently sharing scientific information; in a sense, this remains the case. It is a consequence of the digital medium, as I argued in Chapter 1, to promote the sense that data, quantitative information, is what is most reasonable, since it purports to be neutral or beyond mere opinion. Within such a media environment, questions that would otherwise be ethical or moral are now routinely framed or supported in empirical terms ("studies show that …"). Human flourishing becomes the "science of well-being," measured according to bodily health and to how feelings of contentment are reported in surveys. It is the presumed bracketing of human judgment that makes these expressions of quantification most appealing, the sense that they stand above interpretation. Even if the facts never speak for themselves, it is undeniably an important feature of what we want to mean by "facts" that they *seem* to, and that they are therefore supposed to dispense with the need for context. And if it was once precisely the criteria of what were to count as "facts" that made up public context, "fact" has gradually come to mean that which can dispense with social context altogether. Yet it is precisely as political or social information undergoes this fragmentation into "facts" – precisely as all such information is evaluated by the standard of objective neutrality that scientific facts are supposed to embody – that it becomes more partisan and polarizing. As Maya Angelou put it, "The facts sometimes obscure the truth."[56]

Every fact is the result of a judgment about a standard of evaluation and admissibility. There is more or less balanced and sober reporting, but there can be no such thing as objective or neutral reporting, reporting without any interest, perspective, or view. The implicit demand for unbiased news is incoherent. (Because it cannot fail to be true in some respect, it is an all too easy accusation to level at other people's news.) So that where the very characterization of what is newsworthy becomes optional for us online, where our sources of information are so varied as to be tailored and commodified to suit me, it cannot be surprising if this variety serves the cause of polarization rather than of centrist consensus. After all, there is no pressing reason to distinguish my notion of "bias" from your notion of "substantive objection." The sheer diversity of points of view, so far from making us more conciliative and tolerant, in this way retrenches us in our own position, makes it easier to corroborate our preferences. More is said, less is heard.

What is remarkable is that this retrenchment is nonetheless carried out in terms that continue to subscribe to the ideal of neutral scientific expertise. Those who most prominently oppose carbon caps and other environmental restrictions resort to claims that human-caused global warming is false on scientific (or para-scientific) grounds, rather than countering with political or prudential arguments that other considerations should be prioritized over environmental ones on this or that question. In other words, this polemic – with the suggestion that I may have "my" science and you may have "yours" – still takes place under the presumption that empirical claims are indeed the decisive ones. Various other moral positions have routinely presented empirical studies to back their case, *pro* or *contra*, whereas it is not even clear whether and how such questions could be answered in empirical terms at all without begging all of the crucial questions (when "life" begins or what "marriage" is, say). Such is the compliment that preference pays to objectivity, and, while there has always been pseudo-science, the internet allows it to proliferate side by side with academic research, as if they represented independent and plausible alternatives to each other. Every position is accessible and defensible to those who seek it out; when everything is projected onto the same screen, any set of dots can be connected. (Even the most outrageous online conspiracy theories about the moon landing or September 11 closely mimic the language and methods of empirical science to make their case: The vaguer they are, the harder to disprove.) The constantly outraged rediscovery of the fact that scientific institutions are political – I mean that they operate as a body and on the basis of shared consensus, that they are founded in order to prioritize some kinds of aims and not others, that they are made up of human beings who are socialized into particular interests[57] – is itself frequently used as a cudgel with which to wholesale impugn the merits of their findings. It is sometimes said (euphemistically) that there is a "consensus gap" between expert opinion and online media on certain issues: But such a gap is necessary so long as information is optional.[58] So far from being able to mitigate or negotiate disagreements, therefore, the prestige of neutral "facts" online is entirely compatible with their political abuses. Our commitment to neutral reasons and our partisanship continually reinforce each other.

Disagreements that might once have been about values and relative goods are therefore now about the profession of facts themselves, about matters true or false in principle. It is no longer a question of whom you should vote for or whom you should be persuaded by, but of who can be said to have won the election at all or of whether a vaccine is effective – in sum, of what information you are willing to consent to. Such differences about facts (rather than values) are more emotionally satisfying because they have the guise of empirical objectivity, because they feel more stable than disagreements about the good (which may not admit of conclusive resolution), and because most of us are not in the position to resolve them and are therefore not even accountable for them. Different worlds of facts, different outlets and sources, take the place of culture in the absence of other shared experience. Everyone has heard that values are just "subjective," so there's no point in arguing about them. But facts are our new values; allegiance to facts is coming to define our collective identity more than the nation itself. Differences of opinion thereby become unintelligible to each other, since it is more exciting to think that the other side is engaged in a conspiracy of factual lies than it is to think that they see things otherwise; not only do we not speak the same language, we do not even speak about the same things. It is easier to bond with others when the enemy is demonized on factual grounds – when he is made out to be a Russian sleeper agent, or when she is alleged to be running a child-pornography ring in a local pizza parlor, say. The abundance of actual lies only makes the reality of this analysis more powerful.

Both these tendencies – the sense that I may indulge my own preferences and the sense that what is true is what is objective beyond any given preference – bespeak the missing middle context I've been calling attention to here. Why this absence should manifest itself most sharply for us in political and moral questions is obvious: Politics is the one domain from which we cannot escape, the one domain in which our differences must be weighed against each other with practical consequences. It is the political that, in this sense, obliges our different experiences and ideals to communicate within the terms of a single form. But such a form is a practical achievement; it is only sustained by how we figure it, how we imagine ourselves as parts of the whole, and how we respond to common reasons. Far from constituting our sense of public reason, online media offer no unifying means by which we can and should and must conduct discussion with others.

This absence of common sense online then makes it very difficult, and sometimes impossible, to settle questions about the propriety or sincerity of others in that setting. Approbation and reprobation are, as I've said, social standards – consequences of how "we" see things, judgments embodied in our offline habits and practices. Everyone agrees in principle that some arguments should be beyond the pale of reasonable conversation. But just which and who are you to say so? Any concrete answer must be made against the contours of situated propriety; the question cannot be answered in the abstract. Online speech takes place precisely in the abstract, however; and it is this basic moral incoherence of information that then tends to resolve into the two all-or-nothing responses I noted above: the leaning to seek out others who already entirely share my preferences (the "personalization" of reasons), and the contrasting tendency to judge others on the basis of words alone (their "depersonalization"). I mean that within a medium in which we cannot necessarily tell who speaks, who hears, and how others respond, a medium in which the objects of our attention are voluntary and wildly divergent, we will naturally gravitate on the one hand toward customized groups in which we feel "heard," validated, and at home, even as we will also tend to judge others rather more by their words, or on the strength of their words alone (since that is all we can know about them), on the other hand. Where context is equivocal, our reasons bend either toward emphasizing those truths which we already believe in or toward evidence that can be unequivocally assessed. Let me pick up each of these sides in turn.

The online tendency toward bubbles is, as is widely known now, a consequence of the greater scope of my choices about whom to listen and relate to online. I no longer choose between the three or five or ten main newspapers or channels, but have the perception that I may tailor discussions to suit me. It is a consequence of a more general sociological phenomenon whereby homogeneous groups tend to drift further from moderation: Homogeneity of conviction magnifies marginal preferences such that the more left or right the center of gravity of the group, the more extreme the tone will tend be.[59] Extreme

views are likely to be more straightforward; the certainty of zealots is appealing to the moderate. And scandalous falsehoods and mischaracterizations are
more newsworthy, juicier, and more likely to be disseminated on social media
than their retraction or rebuttal, say. There is an immediate incentive to repost
lurid information under such circumstances (namely, claiming others' immediate attention and frenzied response) and none to refrain – nor is one likely
to suffer any consequences for adding one more echo to the chamber. What's
more, it turns out that from the point of view of algorithmic analysis, the most
predictable users are those with the most extreme or distinctive views. In other
words, the more extreme our own views become, the more tractable and transparent we are to the commercial uses of our own data.[60]

The drift toward homogeneity is not merely the result of the sociology of partisanship, but rather belongs to the absence of a context or a frame of reference
outside words alone. Conversations about politically sensitive issues on Reddit,
for instance, are frequently "raided" or trolled by other groups, whose intent is
to disrupt the ability of the original participants to communicate.[61] The solution
to these abuses would seem simple: to monitor the participants in the discussion.
But this is easier said than done, since it is often impossible to tell an imperson-
ator from someone in earnest online, and since the discussion's administrator will
then have to make distinctions between who has principled reasons for arguing
and who is "just saying things." Such distinctions cannot but then intrinsically
tend toward bubbles of gerrymandered homogeneity, which, in turn, increase
our sensitivity to what we see as "bias" in other such groups. ("Bias" comes to
mean just that: I have access to sources that say otherwise.) Polarization proceeds not just by exaggerating the truth in one direction, but by focusing on the
most egregious cases of exaggeration on the other side. By becoming the way in
which we share politics with others, ideological conformity becomes a substitute for shared practices. The unit of political participation becomes the "shit
storm": the short-term, ritual exercise of aggression toward someone who has
offended against us and who thereby constitutes us as a community.[62]

Online speech is therefore "tribalized" precisely to the extent that it is "personalized." It is not only that we have access to sources that corroborate our
views, it is that we may move around in an information environment in which
we need encounter nothing to qualify them. Not just because there are fewer
contexts in which we encounter views we find objectionable, but because it is
not even clear that the stakes of such differences (however perfervid our experience of them) need be anything more than virtual. In such circumstances,
it cannot be surprising if we revise our view of just what counts as "abhorrent" or "offensive" or "beyond the pale" accordingly, moving it closer to
where we already find ourselves.[63] The presumption that being "safe" or
"inclusive" should be a condition of rational discussion, even where it seeks
remedy for genuine intimidation, likewise follows from this online logic, since
we have fewer resources for distinguishing hatred from disagreement, or my
discomfort from your error. If there is such a thing as the center, on the other

hand – if the center, however fictional, is the ideal measure that puts divergent reasons in contact with each other and thereby renders them intelligible and legitimate to each other – then it must always be an uncomfortable, unstable, and unpleasant position to be in. No one in particular wants the center, it is not a choice-worthy position in its own right. That is why it matters that we continue to try to have one.

Along with this personalization of political reasons there has been a parallel attempt to depersonalize words, to treat them as sufficient and self-contained indicators of meaning, regardless of the motivations underlying them. This is continuous with older policies of political correctness. If we are aiming to create a public sphere that is at once civil and impartial to the identities of its participants, then the only tokens we can monitor with certainty are words themselves, since we cannot police the feelings or intentions of the agents. Words undoubtedly are (also) political, and "I didn't mean anything by it" cannot be an automatic get-out-of-jail free card for every egregious occasion. Context is, in this sense, the very thing that political correctness was meant to surmount. But wholesale, categorical pillorying has therefore been a constant feature of online controversy, since words themselves are taken to be clear-cut, unequivocal tokens of error or discrimination. Careers and reputations are ruined because someone has said the wrong thing in passing and public shaming is increasingly understood as the most effective way of bringing public pressure to bear. Publicity functions as our threat, our weapon.[64] Language (and images) function in these situations not as one circumstance within a complex situation, but as the only salient one – because it is the only one that we can treat as incontrovertible. I may not know for certain how you feel or how far you are to blame for systematic societal ills, but I have a screen shot of what you wrote. Our overwhelming emphasis on the politics of language and communication stems from this incentive to pretend that basic problems – longstanding differences in poverty, segregation, education, and opportunity – can be addressed by focusing on the words we use, which are only the very tip of the epiphenomenal iceberg. When our main way of knowing each other is a matter of words alone, we are thus driven to use words as an unambiguous index of culpability, to judge them beyond a shadow of a doubt at the expense of possible nuance.

The hybrid character of the medium matters here more than anywhere. Digital words are, as I've argued, altogether different from printed writing: By reaching us at once, they are generated and responded to in what is always (potentially) the heat of the moment. In their pressing immediacy, in their overwhelming irruption into our window of attention, their temperature of address is rather more like that of oral speech. But unlike oral speech, it has no necessary location or relation to its audience. Oral words are just one way in which I know you as an agent in the world; your digital words, unsettled from any other way of knowing you, are asked to bear the total burden of your identity. Who you are is what you talk about. What you say (and how you label yourself) is therefore how you perform your identity into being.

Even as digital writing gives us greater power over our modes of self-definition and even as it gives us an objective way of judging others, the decontextual-ization of information about others for the same reasons leads to novel and irresolvable kinds of misunderstandings. The widespread insistence on the sani-tized language of political correctness has been evidently resented by those who, unregenerate, are forced to use it, and the aggressive repudiation of it has been a feature of conflicts about free speech. Politically correct language mutates much quicker than what I've called "normal" or cultural time above allows; the trib-alization of speech has meant an acceleration of refined identitarian nomencla-ture, and some such nomenclature has been developed in and through the argot of academic activists, who justify their work partly through such linguist inno-vations. The defense of free speech has itself then often enough taken the form of deliberate provocation and envelope-pushing – what can you *make* me not say? But even where the threat of public shaming serves as a deterrent against voicing certain views, it has not served to bring about a wholesale change of mind. Nor do we have any widely accepted social convention as to the proper limits of free speech. The galvanized opposition to political correctness has, in turn, intensified efforts to make public speech and spaces "safe." Which has then contributed to a situation in which everyone is unsafe: Where it is words as such that are at issue, everyone becomes a possible vigilante and a possible target of vigilantes, since any one of us may say the wrong thing or be misunderstood at any time. Most of us are not afraid of Big Brother, but are terrified of all the little brothers who follow us and are keen to tell as soon as we trip up.[65] (And we are all little brothers.) In the absence of any other kind of consideration, our words impact on and react to each other, recoiling apart toward extremes.

The conflict between personalization and depersonalization recurs all the way down. (How could it not, when there's nothing to go on but words or footage?) On the one hand the desire to stigmatize speech per se is predicated on the assumption that offenders should be treated as representatives of a cer-tain offense. It is not only X who should be castigated, since we may not know much else about them, but X as a representative of an oppressive bloc. (A "Karen," e.g.) On the other hand, it makes such accusations deeply per-sonal by emphasizing the categorical minutiae of the participants: When it comes to accusations of racism or cultural appropriation, judgments about who gets to say what are based on just who is speaking. As the new term "posi-tionality" implies: What matters is not what you're saying, but where you're coming from. The *New York Times* online shows you, adjacent to the title of each opinion column, a small headshot of the author – you can "see" whose perspective you're getting – while Black Reddit requires a race-verification pic-ture in order to participate in the conversation. When speech's most important function is understood as the empowerment of its users, then power necessarily occupies a higher position than truth. By detaching words from speakers in all these ways, the internet has therefore tended to make ferocious policies of "zero tolerance" at once necessary and impossible.

But there is no one of us whose every word could bear permanent and total public scrutiny, nor is it at all desirable that they should: We do not always mean what we say, and we need opportunities to venture thoughts for which we will not be held accountable (how else could we find our best voice?). Where more of our private communication takes place in public, however, where digital words are a quasi-oral performative medium, and where we are constantly engaged in making a permanent public record for ourselves, then such a record must be unforgiving, since any part of it may be presented as proof positive of the objective unforgivable (if we should have the misfortune of falling within the glare of the public eye). Even if you take yourself to be communicating with some, you are always liable to all. But unlike spoken words, or yellowing pages, the impact of such a record is not softened as it recedes from us in time. Words, stock apologies or "thoughts and prayers" offered on Twitter, come as cheap as the offense.[66] High-profile apologies now include public actions to atone – to donate to charity, say – which is just fine. But repentance cannot be judged in the abstract; we cannot know if someone has had a change of heart when apologies become a matter of words or of public performance. The digital medium makes public offense easy and forgiveness either performative or impossible. Forgiveness, when it can be proffered, marks a personal bond. Yet the medium, by being impersonal, is also rancorous and inhumane, since we are each capable of being offended – and indeed we partly create our identity and group memberships in relation to what we take offense to – but there is no corresponding observance through which we might collectively forgive. And it really is harder to forgive and forget offenses that remain indelible, offenses to which we are always able to return, if we wish, as if for the first time. The medium is itself offensive and traumatogenic. If trauma may be described as psychic pain that we cannot contextualize or assimilate into the narrative framework of our lives, it's no wonder that our accepted uses of the word "trauma" have upsurged. It's no wonder that a medium of decontextualized psychic intimacy should bear on our notion of what counts as "harm."[67]

The personalizing and depersonalizing tendencies of online speech are two necessary consequences of speaking at large, of exchanging words ungoverned by convention or context, which in turn must refer to considerations of practice. Communication entails a shared responsibility; speech as such cannot create the conditions for communication or community. Information is atomic and discrete – it is, if anything, destructive to communal coherence, which is only ever the stories we tell about what we mean in common. Wiki-thinking, listicle-thinking, is made up of lists of pros and cons; how you choose to add them up is totally up to you. Our choices play a greater role in shaping what we think, even as our common sense about how to judge the words of others is thereby thinned out. The power of speech is subordinated to the hype of preference.

At the outer limits of this problem, there is the general question of what it could mean for public claims to be true or false at all, when claims are a matter of words. When the Cambridge Analytica scandal was reported early in 2018 – revealing how the company had improperly culled information from about 87 million Facebook users to target voters with inflammatory and false political ads in the 2016 elections – coverage dwelt on how unwitting Americans were led astray, "influenced," or "manipulated." The same analysis was applied to the thousands of Facebook ads paid for by Russian-sponsored actors during the election.[68] It is undoubtedly true that propaganda wars take this shape, that misinformation is an instrument of political control. It is the aim of such propaganda to undermine public trust, to muddy the information environment in which we form our political judgments. But is "deceit" an appropriate designation for circumstances in which there is no presumption that the truth be told?

"Deceit" suggests that the deceiver is in the position to lay credible claim to authority, that someone is duped under circumstances in which it would have been reasonable or appropriate to presume that what is said is true. Even a quack *promises* that his product is salvific (or your money back). But a banner ad that simply makes calumnious assertions online – assertions that no one is answerable for – does no such thing. Disinformation campaigns do not work by telling us lies, so much as by offering us opportunities to make-believe the kinds of half-truths we already wish to credit (as commercial advertising does). The truth of the matter is more frightening than the Russians: that when we see what we want to believe online, we don't make an active effort to make sure we are not misled; that we prefer to disseminate the juicy to the true; that we would always prefer to have confirmation for what we already think; and that we now have unprecedented options to do so. Talk of "disinformation," "meddling," and "interference" appeals to categories that are not adequate to the phenomenon they are being used to explain. It is impossible to isolate and quantify the effects of disinformation, precisely because it cannot be said to come from "outside" anyone's avowed personal convictions. The trouble with urging people to pause and think for themselves, that is, is that we all already think we are doing just fine in that department. It takes a Socrates to think otherwise.

3.3   EVERYWHERE PEOPLE: FACING AND DEFACING

> A life spent entirely in public, in the presence of others, becomes, as we would say, shallow.
>
> (Arendt)[69]

I have been aiming to show that as the internet becomes the main setting for our exchanges, we lose sight of what we have in common with others within a definite setting of action, and that this bears on our conception of community and of reason as such in specific ways. I think it may also be asked, by extension, what type of human being comes to be under the influence of such a medium, how our conception of ourselves may be shaped when our thinking and relating take place online.

To ask this question of a medium of communication, rather than of a political form, might seem wrongheaded, since the very fact of using the internet does not seem to commit us to any content or to any definite view of the good. But what is remarkable about digital media as our chief means of exchange is just *that*, its apparently apolitical character, its promise of transcending the connections between words, people, and places that had previously defined politics. This has implications for something more than policy controversies and elections, since the political defines not only the explicit goods of the public sphere, but likewise the cast of our ambitions, how we draw the lines between private and public, and how we define ourselves in contrast to others. The net provides us with the most vivid, powerful, and constant experience of autonomy available to us, and – where such an experience plays a greater and greater part in our ordinary practices – it will play a greater role in shaping each of us in its image. How we see and speak to others necessarily changes how we see and what we tell ourselves.

The crucial psychological fact of online experience in this connection is that our public appearance is not where our corporeal presence is: that the face we show is up to us, while our online presence has no geographical location. The scope of what I may do and see outside of public scrutiny is wider. The severing of my public appearance from my real, offline one entails another all-or-nothing contrast, along the lines of the previous ones I've touched on. In an obvious sense, it allows us to enjoy guilty pleasures we would not be caught dead indulging. The relationship between appearance and accountability is a question that has long interested philosophy and fiction – as in Plato's Ring of Gyges, Wilde's *The Picture of Dorian Grey*, Wells's *Invisible Man*, and Teshigahara's *Face of Another*. Such stories make plain the fact that if you cannot lose face, then you have no skin in the game and are free to do whatever impulse dictates. Even in modern super-hero stories (where facelessness is used for good), invisibility is a power: To act unseen is to be able to act beyond the scope of law. Online anonymity affords us something like this voluptuous irresponsibility, at any rate within the bounds of what can be seen and said and done virtually.

There is a growing pool of data, for instance, that shows disparities between how Americans report our own attitudes toward various social questions, compared to the terms of our online searches – the latter betraying a much viler picture than anything we say about ourselves in surveys, even anonymous ones. The conclusion is supposed to be that the uglier results provide a more accurate picture of what Americans think. "Google is a digital truth serum," as Seth Stephens-Davidowitz puts it; it is supposed to show us as we truly are.[70] Yet the point cannot only be that we are meaner in private than we are in public, that we are nothing but a nation of hypocrites. Even if this were supposed to represent a new discovery, the point must also be that online searches give us license by which to indulge our perennial nastiness with something like impunity, and that the occasion for its indulgence actually amplifies and feeds what is worst in us.

Yet anonymity is only half the story. Social media is in fact motivated by the opposite principle: the desire to appear to others and to have others respond to that appearance. It affords us the pleasure of making a spectacle of ourselves, even as it is clear that this sense of publicity bears little relation to the ordinary one of being seen and known by the eyes of others. Our images take on their own personality online – they give us the possibility of self-consciously representing (or "curating") ourselves in ideal terms, even as we surrender the ability to see who sees us and under which conditions. The intensified narcissism of the former circumstance is attended by the necessary voyeurism of the latter. Our faces thus take on a sort of life of their own, involving us in a new kind of social reality that is to be cared for in its own right: the mirror image unstuck from its original.

In this way too then our online identity represents a retreat from shared life with others within the bounds of place and time – sharpening at once our desire for privacy (as the means of escaping all scrutiny) and for publicity or transparency (as a means of creating an image there for all the world to see).[71] The all-or-nothing polarization of our national politics is enacted within our very own online selves.

The irreducible human difference between seeming and being has become more pronounced in modernity, with changes to our socialization. Whereas fewer than 5 percent of the world's population lived in cities in 1800, the proportion is over 50 percent now (and over 80 percent in the United States).[72] This demographic change placed our relations to others on the novel footing of stranger sociality, as I've already mentioned: We have had to create forms of collective agency based on shared laws and categorical identifications (on the basis of nation, or language, or creed, say), rather than on personal allegiances. The market economy, to take one example, places us into relations of mutual benefit and dependence that far exceed our knowledge of the particular people involved: the awesome powers of the modern market directly stem from the fact that I can learn and benefit from others without needing to know or understand them.[73] The genius of modern politics, economics, and science has been to widen our involvement with networks and supply chains of people we need never know and therefore must learn to figure and imagine.

Megalopolises (like Paris or London) transformed the meaning of one's appearance, raising it to a higher power. Where it becomes the norm to move among multitudes of strangers – where we can reinvent ourselves, or melt into the crowd, or potentially encounter new intimates whom we might never have met but for a fluke – how we come off becomes a larger, self-conscious part of our public identity. More than a mark of rank or status, it becomes a means of expressing my aesthetic preferences, my taste, my self. Alongside the growing sense of bourgeois privacy, the seventeenth and eighteenth centuries thus saw the rise of commercial fashion, of drawing room ostentation, and of public spaces like the theater and the opera – venues where one could flirt, show off, and see and be seen.[74] It was the outset of the society of spectacle.

Alongside this new kind of social consciousness emerges a corresponding worry about the superficiality, hypocrisy, affectation, and shallowness of civil society. One finds already in Montaigne, Pascal, La Rochefoucauld, and Rousseau examples of modernity's corresponding stress on what is "inside" – authenticity, sincerity, and the heart – in contrast to what is skin-deep or fake. One also finds a new emphasis on the importance of showing one's face in public as an act of political significance. Tocqueville insists on the point that associations allow citizens not just to know but to *witness* each other – "there men see each other, active measures are planned, and opinions are expressed with that force and heat which the written word can never attain"[75] – adding that this visibility binds private interests into public ones, within a situation where the temptation to withdraw into private life prevails. The connection between politics and public appearance has remained a basic guarantee of political life in Europe (the ban on face coverings in France being the most conspicuous example) as in the United States, where the right to assemble and petition – to show our face in public – is essential to the definition of citizen implicit in the First Amendment. Where fewer know us personally, our face becomes our single most important public marker. (One might conjecture that this norm would weaken during a time when face masks were required in public. But even as we were expected to mask up in public, we were also expected to unmask on Zoom – our new public space – and the face remains both the most important target of biometric surveillance and the means by which we humanize victims of crimes.) There is, finally, a new worry about the psychic stress that city life places on us – about the fact that if one tried to relate to everyone around in a large city, it would be overwhelming, a shock that one could not process. The social theorist Georg Simmel, for instance, analyzed the blasé, standoffish attitudes we associate with urban life as the defensive effort by which urbanites keep their fellows at bay, precisely as a strategy of keeping oneself sane in the face of overwhelming numbers of strangers.[76]

The divergence between seeming and being that marks our modern social experience then reaches its peak expression online, where we are both in contact with multitudes that dwarf the size of any city and where how we appear to others is relatively up to us. This fact alone constitutes one of the greatest attractions of our digital experience – the sense of invulnerability, of not having to show ourselves in ways we do not control, of having more power over how we come across to others. We thus increasingly prefer to text or to email rather than to meet someone in person or to call them on the phone.

We feel an ineradicable disquiet or thrill about entering into the presence of others; we unconsciously bear ourselves differently when alone in a room than when sharing it with anyone else. Most of us learn to manage, but such social anxieties have a deeper significance. The fact remains that face-to-face (or *viva voce*) communication may always betray more of ourselves than we mean to – that how we come across is not simply up to us (that's what makes it "real" time). Our body, our voice, our gestures, and our attitudes are not simply transparent expressions of our will, and so we are always susceptible to looking foolish or clumsy, or to revealing more than we would prefer to show. To be seen is to make some portion of our mortal history available; to show our face is to consent to having a public reality. We enter a social domain in which the praise and blame of others may not match up to our own assessment of ourselves, and in which our own reality is in this sense at stake and in play. Even if there is always more to us than meets the eye, we need others to recognize us as a coherent reality, so that we ourselves may come to recognize and realize it. It is precisely this constructive relationship between who we are and who others take us to be that makes us political animals.

But as our identity becomes unmoored from some more or less particular audience, from the common settings that have always defined us, it becomes more difficult to imagine ourselves as primarily answerable to and formed by some fixed group or community. The expression "internet famous" (in contrast to old-fashioned notoriety) captures this exactly: that someone's face may be known to tens or hundreds of thousands of people, and yet still be someone no one has heard of, since all those in the know may be so scattered as never to have met each other. It is not that we are in danger of forgetting that we have parents, neighbors, or classmates in the real world – these are still the most vivid and patent markers of who we are. But to the extent that online forms of sociality become more important to us, to the extent that our self-understanding is shaped by those forms, it is because we are bound to be always tempted to a place where we may avoid the inevitable frictions of offline relationships.[77] Our online lives unfold, in contrast, within a safe space to and from which we may always retreat to do our will.

The disparity between virtual anonymity and publicity is well captured by the senses of "shame" in online contexts. The internet is – as a faceless medium, as a medium of seeing without being seen – an essentially *shameless* medium. Shame is an experience of seeing others seeing us; it is also a corporeal affect (we blush, cover our face, or hang our head). Both these conditions are absent online where we are removed from presence and on permanent display: We offer up instead a face that cannot blush. The fact that we may gawk at each other without being aware of it is captured by our use of the phrase "I stalked you" simply to mean "I looked you up" (implying, i.e., that I saw you without your knowing it). And yet – precisely because the internet does concentrate public visibility and attention – shame is also by far the most important term of opprobrium of internet accusation (more than guilt, say), the defining accusation of its politics. It is the means by which we summon visibility to our aid when we take to the internet for redress. Internet "shaming" comes in a variety of forms – from posting compromising details for the purposes of private revenge ("doxing"), to writing insulting and politically motivated reviews of companies, to government broadcasting (in some countries) of the faces of offenders who cannot easily be brought to justice. Common to all of these forms is the fact that our intimate details may be readily exposed to mass visibility, that the ease with which this may be done is out of proportion to the harm that it may do, and that it is therefore subject to the abuses that attend to any form of mob justice.[78]

The separation of public shame from private shamelessness then marks out what are arguably the two most intense kinds of online satisfaction: pornography and outrage.

A tame estimate suggests that somewhere around 10 to 15 percent of all worldwide internet use is pornography related; that a large majority of children are exposed to pornography online before the age of eighteen; and that tens of millions of American adults regularly watch online pornography.[79] ("The internet is for porn," chirps a recent musical.) The ratio of pornographic web traffic to traffic that is directed to political news sites is, according to one count, about 100:1.[80] Just how all this carries over into offline relationships remains a controversial subject – as in the case of violent video games, there is no straightforward causal relationship between sexual violence and pornography use.[81] But regardless of the character of this link, pornography is a banner example of the subterranean regions of a medium that we may explore with impunity, indulging appetites that may shade into and create new demand for the downright criminal: In 2018 tech companies flagged 45 million photos and videos of children being sexually abused.[82] Where there is no shame in onlooking – where we can lurk as under a spell of invisibility – the medium offers a means of indulging private desires that are outside the bounds of social accountability. Online browsing tempts us to a twilit, oneiric realm in which our fantasies take on manifest forms outside our minds. And yet – even as international estimates suggest that up to 99 percent of men and up to 86 percent of women "consume" porn[83] – this "outside" has no acknowledged public reality.

The poles of shame and shamelessness, of collective privacy and private publicity, are likewise a condition of the outrage industry, the ecstasy of grievance that so forcefully claims our public life.[84] This is partly a consequence of a surfeit of information: The news must be sensational to clamor for our interest, and this widens the market for teacup storms. But the participatory character of the net means that we may often deal with others whom we will never have to face up to, and that this intrinsic shamelessness affects how we are likely to respond to them. Social media is not a place for discussion – mostly you just put yourself out there and sort of hope that something happens. But anyone who has tried to carry on a discussion with online interlocutors knows how easy it is to be roped into name-calling and moral slam-dunkism, no holds barred. We are prompted to immediate and spontaneous response, and since we are not likely to be held to what we say, the terms of our disagreement can quickly get out of hand. Not to mention the fact that we are only ever performing for the home team: The goal is not to convince others, but to score a sick burn for the regard of those who already see things our way. Where reasons are a matter of words with little possible relation to offline life, there is nothing preventing us from losing our heads entirely. Godwin's "law": The longer an online discussion goes on, the likelier it is that someone will reach for Hitler or Nazis to make a point.

If many online bigots and loudmouths turn out to be perfectly pleasant in person, we can hardly be surprised – just as there are plenty of friendly dogs who bark viciously from behind a fence, and plenty of nice people who are transformed into irate bullies when they find themselves behind the wheel of a car. That's not to say that many others won't or don't carry out perfectly reasonable and courteous discussions online, but that they hold themselves there by exercising their own self-restraint rather than by the demands intrinsic to the medium. The internet makes civility and persuasiveness optional, like everything else, by allowing us to separate our political convictions from our social offline selves – to privatize, in this sense, what is public.

It is not just that internet communication makes it easier to insult others, however; it is that it does so while expanding the bounds of what we feel we ought to take into our own hands. The personalization and depersonalization of online speech renders our reasons at once more categorical and intimate. Everyone has the means to police offenses against this or that group or cause, and since we can immediately weigh in – since it feels, that is, as if what is on the screen is in some sense immediate to and part of our direct experience – we are each liable to become an open nerve of anger. It is this combination of engorged accountability and relative impunity that makes online speech so eager to aggress or take offense. Hence the "crybully." Godwin's law is the flipside of the fact that you may punctuate any discussion with a bland "disagree": It is because our punches can't connect that we may pack them with all the raw force we can muster. Has anyone *ever* won an online argument? (Has there ever been one?) As words matter more (because they are the main way others encounter us), they also matter less (because there is finally nothing doing or at stake). We pretend to discussion, performing outrage while secure behind the screen, just as dogs bark more fiercely because they are protected by the fence.

Even so, facelessness is only one side of our online experience. Widespread access to the internet in the 1990s was on the whole faceless, giving rise to the fear that chatrooms and dating sites would remain packed with creeps and predators. Yet the advent of social media in the early 2000s was in fact made possible by the discovery of the opposite possibility: that, so far from wanting to remain invisible and anonymous online, we *wanted* others to see our face, to be judged on the basis of appearances.

Facebook started out as a means of allowing Harvard undergraduates to rank each other's looks (hot or not?). The site's subsequent success has turned on its ability to translate the ambiguities of social life into data points: both as a matter of self-description (the categories under which we represent ourselves) and as a way of quantifying popularity in terms of instant gratification (as "friend requests," "shares," "pokes," or "likes"). It was this quantification – along with the ability to keep in touch without effort – that has allowed Facebook and social media to become, more than just a tool of the offline world, a new kind of social reality with a logic of its own.

As Mark Zuckerberg put it in 2009:

> Think about what people are doing on Facebook today. They're keeping up with their friends and family, but they're also building an image and identity for themselves, which in a sense is their brand. They're connecting with the audience they want to connect to. It's almost a disadvantage if you're not on it now.[85]

This personal "brand," this public identity with a life of its own, has no parallel within prior media. Unlike our written work, a profile is an ongoing production of the self – an autobiography in real time – rather than a narrative expression of our vision or thought. Unlike earlier uses of photography or footage, I am just as much the subject as the object of the work: I show you not just myself caught on camera, but the representation of myself as I would like you to see it. Your online self is not just broadcast or exchanged, but continuously "there," an omni-you available to the public at all times. Thousands of others may encounter us only in this persona, which makes it an object of distinct care for us: It begins to seem like that persona *is* you, stands for you in a way that requires constant management, response, and upkeep.

When such calibrated self-representations acquire primary weight, what we say and show must bear the whole burden for who we "are." For the purposes of social media, we are what we post, how we let others see us; our choices are performative because the actor and role are projected onto a single plane. To post is to make a statement. This theater of self then accounts for new genres of norms and gestures like the Facebook "relationship status" (which has become a romantic milestone in its own right), the self-conscious ostentation of one's food or shopping or travel, as well as "virtue signaling" (the perception that lip-service to political causes online itself counts as a form of social activism). Retweets *are* endorsements for this reason: Inasmuch as you choose *not* to delete your post at any moment, it becomes an expressive act, rather than the speech of a noncommittal medium. Communication through social media inherently consists of such "signals" – the exchange of affected attitudes and simulated identities only ambiguously related to what we may know about our friends offline. Like all theater, our social media "presence" is acted out on the platform.

The theatricalized self promotes specific kinds of aesthetic judgments ("fake" or "real"?), along with an underlying theory of what most matters. What is valuable about you is what makes you remarkably different – the association of identity with "brand" points to the fact that your specific difference is what is valuable to others and so what is (potentially) marketable to them. The commercial purpose of social media is, accordingly, to give us a standardized setting within which we may communicate our uniqueness. To do so, we insist on our most idiosyncratic differences: the terms "weird," "quirky," "nerdy," "nutty," and "crazy" recur again and again, no longer as disparagements for social pariahs, but as laying proud claim to difference. Normal is what other people are (or, at best, it is itself a clever way of expressing your difference from the mass), though it is not good to seem like you're desperately trying to avoid it. You soon discover that it requires the ability of a fiction writer not to put yourself forward in clichés; where voluntary self-definition is the source of identity, it can be no surprise that everyone's brand starts sounding more or less alike. What makes you special? Scroll down to choose an option from the menu. Where difference is what we all have most in common, difference is in-different (i.e., to be expected). Trivial difference is the new normal; there is no social media counterculture for this reason.

That this socially mediated view of ourselves is estranging – that our profiles are not our "real" selves – is a familiar enough point. Just as the invention of modern mirrors changed our self-regard, social media opens up the temptation to craft one's offline self with an eye to what will improve the online one – to hit the most epic selfie spots, say, to do it for the meme, or to cultivate some form of commercial exhibitionism (in which, by appearing with certain products, one might be paid by companies as an influencer). The ease with which we may "share" invites an alienated view of reality, a seeing of what is private through the public's likely eyes, and with a view to their permanent and reiterated approval for what's shared. What is more striking is how hard it is to keep in mind just how tenuous this relationship between real and mediated selves is as, surveying the beautiful lives of others, we nonetheless feel our own to be inadequate by comparison. The hypnotic quality of the medium is such as to cause us to continually overlook the fact that we invest social media accounts with a significance they don't have, that we are enamored with crafting appearances, even as we are also conscious of their being simulacra. Where surfaces are the basis for all judgment, where my friends are my followers, we are by turns vain and envious, self-aggrandizing and hobbled by self-doubt. I am not supposed to "judge" (and who are you to?), but am nonetheless on display as an object of universal scrutiny and comparison. Likewise, where photographic editing makes it easy to look good, when everyone's gorgeous life is rubbed in our face all the time, it is easy to become fatigued both at our own humdrum imperfection and at the cheap aesthetics of edited perfection. The superficiality of glamor is obviously nothing new. What is new is the degree to which the private can be exposed to the public on social media, and the degree to which the confusion of both withers the substantial reality of each.

This collective performance of identity is a great leveler, our shared enactment of egalitarian rise and fall sped up into hourly episodes of fortune. The permanent availability of everyone to everyone's scrutiny means there can be no heroes or aristocrats on social media, people towering over the rest of us because they are qualitatively better – how could there be, in these terms? – only those with more or fewer followers. The Pope's Twitter account necessarily sounds as self-helpful as any other quote of the day. No one can be all that interesting all the time; to the extent that it demands this of us, the medium cuts us down to its size. Images of heroism and achievement are in demand, but the fact remains that the medium is saturated with poignant and inspiring stories, and that, where it is always optional to take one or flip to the next, they are there for our benefit. Our violent emphasis on the cosmetic differences that make up our identities thus takes place within the terms of a setting in which nothing essential is at stake – belittled within a medium of my preferences, their very exposure marks their petty unreality.[86] No one is a hero to his servant, as the saying goes. The same may be said of our followers, not only because we offer ourselves to their judgment, but because we are busy recreating ourselves for the likes of you. Our thrill at the daily viral churn is thus also propelled by the sense that social media offers the spectacle of fate's lottery and of the crowd's final judgment of it: Any follower may become a leader at any time, but when it comes your turn to rise, we will try to put you in your place once more by our side. The light contempt with which we treat our social media presence suggests, in part, our unease with this fact. But the recurring demonstration that the mightiest are as flawed as we are is one of our highest egalitarian satisfactions: the ritual destruction of others' claims to superiority.

While it is easy and common to write off the online self, the self of "digital natives," as mere snowflakery, it is nonetheless important to underscore the conditions that continue to shape it. The online self is, in sum, a self in control over what it seems, a magnified reflection of our will. Its setting is one in which all are alternately invisible and on display, shameless and shaming, private and transparent, safe from scrutiny and completely exposed to it: These are, in sum, the two poles forced apart when identities are abstracted from the abiding concerns of shared and accumulated experience in place. This self is weaker and enervated when it comes to the practice of offline confrontation; it has no thick skin because it has fewer occasions in which it is called to thicken it. But, conversely, as its online experience and experience of digital relations becomes primary to it, it is more immediately identified with what happens onscreen – more vulnerable to taking online speech personally, more sensitive to aggression and bullying, easier to take offense, and altogether less inclined to judge that online shit storms blow things out of all proportion, when there is little or no other context for public speech. To be an online self is to be porous to the overwhelming and totalizing sense that what happens on the screen is happening to me and inside me; it is to be by turns engrossed and dulled by the whole world's invasions of our privacy – at once saturated with our possibilities of connection and participation and voided of any contact with them. In a medium where nothing touches us, everything comes flooding in to hurt us. And so our pain, hurt, anger, and resentment – as being untransferable and non-fungible – become more significant to how we lay claim to our identities. They emerge as what's most real in the virtual world: the feeling proof that I am.

It is therefore telling that whereas it is easy to stumble on footage of sex online, footage of people killed or dying remains (along with child pornography) the ultimate taboo, the one event we have widely agreed to keep out of sight. The transgression is manifest in our horror at killings broadcast or televised live: beheadings by ISIS, the on-air murder of journalists Alison Parker and Adam Ward or of Ambassador Andrei Karlov, as well as the real-time streaming of the Christchurch massacre by the killer himself. Death is the one event that must outstrip our desire for public prestige – the one event that, being of the body, cannot be fully "mediated" away into the mind's eye. If our time online is always lived in the view of others, we each die alone and once. It is the one fact we cannot share, the one act we cannot really simulate or act out. To die is to become a body, a body that can be acknowledged only by being touched; and physical touch is the one sense we cannot reach online. To die is the opposite of being online. But the taboo also suggests that we are uneasy not only at the thought that children may encounter the video (why exactly, given everything else they may watch?), but at the fact that we know there is something trivializing in the way in which we encounter online footage: The taboo bespeaks both our own desire to watch, our sense that death is the greatest spectacle, and our discomfort with erasing the last line that distinguishes reality programming from reality.

3.4   EVERYWHERE POLITICS: EQUALITY AND AUTHORITY

> In all very numerous assemblies, of whatever characters composed, passion never fails to wrest the sceptre from reason. Had every Athenian citizen been a Socrates; every Athenian assembly would still have been a mob.
>
> (Madison)[87]

All three of the subjects I've addressed here – the implicit conditions of online community, of exchanging reasons in the absence of context, and of our performative identities – are already political subjects, since they define and are defined by the ways in which we picture life with others. Contexts of action are contexts of vision: The ordinary uses of time govern our imagination of what is good in practice and of the shapes into which we project our hopes for a better life, country, and world. Our uses of the internet in this sense also suggest or imply a metaphor of political community, along the lines I've suggested: one fulfilling the aspirations of the modern social contract. Devised as a neutral medium of rational scientific exchange, the internet is an impersonal, unified, unbiased, equalizing setting. It is so to the extent that it remains ideal, a place of fluid mentation and projected fantasy dispensing with corporeal friction. It is for that very reason a perfect "space of reasons" that places us behind a "veil of ignorance." I can deliberate with others in a setting in which my body (in theory) makes no difference, nor does my background, nor does the immediate possibility of intimidation or force. The individual is understood to be logically prior to any social situation. Rather, I enter this realm as an autonomous, voluntary agent, unconstrained by accidents of birth and free to represent the self I would like to be.

This vision is on bombastic display in John Perry Barlowe's "Declaration of the Independence of Cyberspace," a widely circulated proclamation protesting the passing of the 1996 Telecom Act:

Governments of the Industrial World, you weary giants of flesh and steel, I come from Cyberspace, the new home of Mind. On behalf of the future, I ask you of the past to leave us alone ... Cyberspace does not lie within your borders ... It is an act of nature and it grows itself through our collective actions ... We are creating a world that all may enter without privilege or prejudice accorded by race, economic power, military force, or station of birth. We are creating a world where anyone, anywhere may express his or her beliefs, no matter how singular, without fear of being coerced into silence or conformity. Your legal concepts of property, expression, identity, movement, and context do not apply to us ... Our identities have no bodies, so, unlike you, we cannot obtain order by physical coercion ... [the Telecommunications Reform Act] repudiates your own Constitution and insults the dreams of Jefferson, Washington, Mill, Madison, De Tocqueville, and Brandeis. These dreams must now be born anew in us ... We will create a civilization of the Mind in Cyberspace. May it be more humane and fair than the world your governments have made before.[88]

The document exhibits a whole nest of contradictions – perhaps the richest of which is that Barlowe concludes by placing and dating it: "Davos, Switzerland; 2/8/1996." Over two decades later, we are of course less ebullient about the internet's utopian possibilities, but the proclamation nonetheless clearly spells out what are still some of the medium's deepest attractions: that our online selves inhabit a "space" or reality distinct from the physical one around us, that such a space can neutralize some of the abiding constraints of offline political reality, and that that neutrality is continuous with the autonomy that modern liberal thought has worked to approximate. Disembodiment is a condition for our progressive empowerment: Digital data is intrinsic to no place, while our bodies (and their histories) are the single greatest obstacle to the open-ended expansion of our self-determination.

In thinking about the social implications of this picture, however, the fact remains that politics has an essential connection to what is tangible – to the allocation of resources, to the scope of my agency as it comes into contact with that of others, to the tractability of our inherited opacities – and that the practical and personal circumstances of what is tangible are precisely what our online view refuses us, what cannot come into focus there. The presumption of online neutrality is therefore troubling not only to the extent that it masks new forms of inequality, nor only to the extent that "neutrality" usually entails a particular set of political commitments, but because the medium itself cannot acknowledge its own debts to place, history, and the concrete forms through which alone freedom is expressed. That is, the issue is not that digital media contain unstated assumptions, preferences, and organizing principles (as does every medium); it is that those they contain are at unprecedented odds with the conditions of political life as such. To the degree that it allows us to imagine ourselves as agents beyond the body, the medium is therefore trans-political: It promises liberation from the constraints on our bounded offline selves, even as it remains the case that it is only within the bounds of these conditions that our vision of the good takes root.

The consummate value of our online experience is frictionless *immediacy* – the perception that I have direct access to everyone, that I can skip the line, that I can circumvent tedious or fruitless offline procedures, that I can always get a hearing, that I can exercise my will. And it is this very immediacy and directness of participation that we have in mind when we refer to the internet as "democratic": Its promise is to obviate the gatekeepers of knowledge and power. Yet the two most penetrating observers of modern mass states identified immediacy not only as an expression of our desire for equality but also (paradoxically) as the greatest threat to our political freedom. Tocqueville calls attention throughout his work to the inherently homogenizing, leveling, and centralizing penchants of modern democracy – tendencies that streamline government efficiency, on the one hand, while increasing state control to a degree that ultimately debouches into an impersonal bureaucratic despotism (all in the service of equality). Arendt analyzed the phenomenon of twentieth-century totalitarianism as stemming from the impulse to give the political will of the people immediate and effective form – as an attempt, in other words, to render the popular will omnipotent.[89]

Here is her defense of the alternative:

Positive laws in constitutional government are designed to erect boundaries and establish channels of communication between men whose community is continually endangered by the new men born into it ... the boundaries are for the political existence of man what memory is for his historical existence: they guarantee the pre-existence of a common world, the reality of some continuity which transcends the individual life span of each generation ... To abolish the fences of laws between men—as tyranny does—means to take away man's liberties and destroy freedom as a living political reality; for the space between men, as it is hedged in by laws, is the living space of freedom.[90]

The reality of the law – so far from being simply "neutral" or "impersonal" in some objective, universal sense – is inseparable from its concrete foothold within the boundaries, forms, norms, customs, and finite limits of particular nations. It is not *only* that. But, as the memory of generations, its truth does not stand outside them; it is only known in and through a people's political experience. Such boundaries are (like our own bodies) not irrational constraints on political truth, but its concrete expression – its life in time. The extreme of political immediacy, in contrast, converges with total tyranny, because some group can claim to represent the pure will of the people, regardless of preexisting boundaries and forms.

If the nation state was borne from the imagination of the printed page, we might conjecture that a different kind of political form will belong to the internet. Maybe. But whatever its political destiny, it's also clear that it works against the grain of the historical differences within which positive law is located and sustained. By abstracting and displacing us from concrete attachment to what is common, it devalues the meaning of political difference as such – the legitimacy of the plurality of people and views that renders politics meaningful. To the extent that we connect online, as I've argued, our judgments are less keyed to contexts of conduct and more to our self-represented, voluntary identities.[91] Where there are infinite differences available to our immediate inspection – a cosmopsis of available places and meanings – it becomes more difficult to imagine that localized difference should be able to claim deepest sense and legitimacy. If, therefore, certain features of the internet as a medium complicate, disfigure, and bewilder older political facts, it is less because the internet's specific conception of the political is at odds with our national one, and more because it finds itself at odds with the basic meaning of the political as such. Given how much of our online involvement is motivated by politics, this may sound like a counterintuitive suggestion. I do not mean that the internet makes us apolitical, but that the way in which it engages us politically represents an ideological intensification that – as in our expressions of performative outrage – comes at the expense of legislative or political change. The amplification of online activism and criticism is fully compatible with political stagnation. By making it easier to participate for the moment, the internet makes it harder to act in long-term concert. It prevents the conditions of lasting political legitimacy or coherence to emerge, even as it eats away at the existing ones.

The untethering of the medium from place emphasizes, furthermore, two extreme poles that are emerging to stake out the dominant political conflict of our age, in the United States and throughout the world. I mean the conflict between a transnational, globally minded liberalism for which national differences must be made subordinate to humanitarian ones, and a reactive nationalism for which racial or native identity is the decisive marker of what is common. The internet is not the only cause of this. These are longstanding possibilities that inhere in the modern nation state, which is itself founded on mass, egalitarian principles. These extremes reached their terrible maximum in the totalitarian regimes of the twentieth century: the scientific universalism of the Soviet regime – the USSR was the first nation to erase any reference to history or place from its very name – and Nazi Germany's "blood and soil." Likewise, in the second half of the twentieth century the spread of worldwide commerce and networks, the development of supra-national organizations, and the emergence of global environmental problems have long raised questions about the meaning of our national allegiances. My contention is, rather, that the way in which we imagine politics online facilitates and exacerbates these extremes in a new way. Each represents a failure of the imagination of what national life should be; each attempts to refigure what is common in the face of the specific pressures that follow from making the web worldwide and dominant. A medium of missing middles works against the very conditions of stable political form: Its political consequences are extremism, convulsion, and fractious upheaval.

Let me back up to make a better leap. The prior question to investigate is about the internet's relationship to regimes or political forms – particularly whether and in what sense it can be said to be "democratic." Political forms are imaginative forms, as I've said – they rest on the way in which we see ourselves as parts depending on, participating in, and identifying with some greater whole, on the pride and allegiance that we have to it, and on what each generation is willing to sacrifice of itself to keep that whole alive beyond its day. By calling these forms imaginative I do not mean that they are not real. Ideas, opinions, and motives are as real as can be; they are the bones and sinews of human conduct. The United States is one such imaginative form, an idea of political life – if a critical mass of citizens ceased to be committed to maintaining it, it would cease to exist. It is in this way as tenuous as the causes of freedom, justice, and equality themselves. But the conception of any such form crucially rests on our habitual and familiar way of encountering it, and therefore on the media through which we figure it.

   It would be wrongheaded to insist on seeing fixed one-to-one correspondences between political forms and media.[92] Just as there have continued to be monarchs after the appearance of the printing press, it is clear that the internet is not incompatible with every order of government now extant. It is nonetheless hard to dismiss the suggestion that there are elective affinities here. An oral culture – a culture in which information is not widely available and in which social trust accordingly depends on pledges of honor, on taking others' word to be their bond, and on authoritative pronouncements – will favor aristocratic, tradition-bound, and hierarchical forms of political life, say. It is likewise impossible to conceive of the United States (with all the legal and deliberative institutions that are direct consequences of our written constitution) without the pervasive uses of the printed word.[93] Tyrannical or authoritarian regimes have, furthermore, always tried to centralize, suppress, and control the information available to their citizens. Faced with any given political form, one may therefore raise the question of the ideal relationship between its citizens and the communication or knowledge necessary for the healthy life of its laws – and, by extension, the question of whether any given medium confirms or contradicts the habits of thought and reason most appropriate to that form.

   What accounts for the commonplace that the internet is "democratic"? What makes it feel like it should be? It is undoubtedly a participatory medium, where information is widely shared and opinions freely available; it gives voice (and therefore power) to more people; it makes it straightforward to call attention to abuse; and it makes it easier to coordinate public efforts, logistics, and campaigns. "Democratic" means, in such cases, that everyone gets to weigh in and be counted. Yet participation as such is neither a political act nor does it spell democracy, as is clear from the endless surveys, polls, and quizzes that flatter us in exchange for the data that improves our platforms. The solicitation of our two cents is, as I've argued, both a mode in which we are roped into participation and the way in which the medium engages our preferences for its commercial purposes. For participation to be democratic in any real sense, what is decisive is not the fact *that* we participate, but the kind of issue that calls forth and formulates our occasion for participation. Just as it would be silly to call the people's choice of Pepsi or Coke an expression of democracy, retweets or likes are pseudo-choices in which, unlike (political) votes, nothing is at stake except our shadow selves.

The full case that the internet is good for democracy as such would require spelling out what is meant by democracy, identifying the optimal social conditions for it, and saying why the presence of the internet facilitates and shores up those conditions more than other media. And all of these issues are contentious.[94] Perhaps we might minimally agree that the ideal liberal democratic citizenry is one that has reliable access to authoritative sources of information (information that is not only authoritative in its own right but widely acknowledged to be so), that the citizenry's interests should be pervious to reasoning with that information, that the merits of those interests should be publicly deliberated with a view to testing them and persuading others, and that each individual citizen should then be in a position to make up his or her own mind as to how to proceed on the conviction that emerges from such deliberation. Holding it up to this ideal pattern, it is unlikely that the internet improves on any of these conditions with respect to older media. It has undoubtedly eliminated controls over information that, by virtue of the need for selection, necessarily limited the availability and preferred the dissemination of some views over others in the print and pre-cable age. But this problem was solved by creating another one: an information environment of such vast proportions that we may choose whom we want to listen to, with no social cost for doing otherwise.[95] As Matthew Hindman has argued, the internet has eliminated the exclusivity of the *production* of political information, while reproducing it within the process by which each person chooses and filters it.[96] As it is easier to speak in public, it is in fact more difficult to be heard, to have one's view noticed and represented. The internet is therefore democratic in the sense that you always feel as if you can weigh in, not in the sense that your weighing in carries more weight.

Not all participation is democratic, because the content of our views is only meaningful when exercised through democratic institutions and forms. To draw a somewhat fussy analogy to national politics, the United States is not supposed to be a direct democracy, but a republic – in other words, a government in which the popular will is carried out indirectly, through the mediating office of institutions and their representatives. This design is more than a matter of convenience and the division of labor. One of the dangers that the Constitution is supposed to check and balance against – one of its primary targets – is precisely the possibility of the "immediate" exercise of the popular will through impromptu popular assemblies. Some of the objections put forth by the authors of the *Federalist Papers* are what we would now call elitist – they were skeptical that the voting population could reliably identify their own will and best interests, especially on technical subjects (like international treaties or banking). The stipulations that U.S. Senators be elected by state legislatures (as they were until 1914) and that the President be chosen not by popular vote but by the Electoral College – in other words, that the most important Federal positions be decided at one remove from popular opinion – were partly conceived as means of ensuring that candidates of distinction would stand a better chance at being elected.[97]

But if these presumptions have lost credibility for us, there is another set of considerations, advanced by Madison in particular, that should still give us pause when we implicitly measure our form of government by the ideal of immediate participation. He writes that

The people can never err more than in supposing that by multiplying their representatives, beyond a certain limit, they strengthen the barrier against the government of a few ... The countenance of the government may become more democratic; but the soul that animates it will be more oligarchic. The machine will be enlarged, but the fewer, and often the more secret, will be the springs by which its motions are directed.[98]

There are two principles here that are helpful for thinking about the internet. First, a situation of direct democratic participation favors the centralization of power. In the absence of mediating procedure, some will amass more control – those who can successfully pass themselves off as speaking for most or all (which is, of course, the mark of authoritarian government). While representative and mediating institutions seem to dilute the people's immediate self-determination, the procedural friction of these institutions also checks, displaces, and retards what power can accumulate to any one in particular. Second, democratic institutions do not just constrain power, but bring it into being by providing the language through which the people can have a "voice" at all. The "will of the people" is not a given; it has no independent existence in our minds such that questionnaires could be "snapshots" of it. Rather, it is collectively created by and expressed specifically through an electoral process. When we go to the polls, we are voting both for our candidate and for the practice of voting itself as a method of decision. It is in this sense that Madison distinguishes between the unrestrained exercise of political passions and the popular will, purified into constitutional legitimacy.

Democracy is not just the act of equal participation, in other words, but our commitment to the coherent form through which we exercise our views in such a way that they can be translated and put into communication with each other.

The space of freedom possible in such a form only emerges alongside its frictions and inefficiencies. If we were given access to direct or immediate voting – a situation in which every decision of national interest were decided by popular referenda expressed via app or platform, say – the government would not thereby become more "democratic" – not because our votes would not count, but because those posing the questions would become all the more powerful, because any given result would be correspondingly less binding, and because the outcomes would not obviously serve the best version of our interests. Such a situation would, furthermore, make the designers and owners of the platform unduly powerful even while, as Madison warns, rendering their influence invisible. The platform, privately controlled and illegitimate, would define the form of government. Greater convenience is (in this instance) directly at odds with the exercise of democratic freedom.

Proposals for direct participation or e-government remain rare so far. And if we are accustomed to identifying the greatest threats to American government as those stemming from the undue influence of lobbyists or the "deep state," it is for very plausible reasons – that those in office will mainly seek to benefit themselves, that representatives will not represent. But my point is that there is nothing specifically democratic about platform egalitarianism. To conflate immediate participation with democracy (as if the more the better) represents the danger described by Madison, Tocqueville, and Arendt that direct democracy tends toward authoritarianism or soft despotism. Both are similarly motivated to action without intermediaries. The impulse for representation at the cost of mediating forms and procedure generates the same all-or-nothing paradox that we run across again and again when thinking about the internet: that a more informal, egalitarian, and streamlining medium, so far from better representing the interests of more people, actually lends itself to the consolidation of power into fewer hands. The most significant experiment with it – a voting platform started by Italy's 5Stars party called "Rousseau" – came apart at the seams because of disagreements between the private company that owns the platform and the leaders of the party itself.[99] It is a telling example of the latent political role that the commercial proprietors of platforms cannot but play, when they control the medium through which democratic choice is exercised.

Yet surely some kinds of online participation – by virtue of no longer being at the mercy of the priorities of the major news networks, say, or by virtue of giving everyone a means to voice their views – are at least democratic in inspiration? What I've said so far doesn't yet touch the basic intuition that the internet is democratic inasmuch as it puts just about all human knowledge at anyone's fingertips – a capacity that, without aspiring to be a form of government, nonetheless brings tremendous pressure to bear on our routine experience of all kinds of public authority. The internet is a fathomless resource for doing-it-yourself: flogging, fixing, figuring out, sleuthing, researching, fact-checking, diagnosing, sharing, and swapping just about anything one can imagine. To engage in any of these activities online is to have to depend less on other people, to forego recourse to the experts we would otherwise need, to be relatively more autonomous, to make up your own mind on the basis of what seems like impersonal access to the bare facts themselves. If the internet has anything to do with politics, then it does so by establishing new relations between information and what is authoritative as such. In particular: it is in creating a new view of facts based on the expectation of neutrality or unbiased "objectivity" that it continues to shape our thinking about politics.

Yet one could scarcely conceive of a more destructive political principle than neutrality – I mean one destructive of the very possibility of common and legitimate authority itself. Wikipedia offers a microcosmic exhibition of the destabilizing relationships between objectivity, immediacy, and authority online. Much has been written about Wikipedia's successes as a globally sourced website that works for the public interest. Its limitations are also familiar ones: that it is more valuable as a source for matters of fact than as a way of placing facts in context, that it offers information that is merely good enough, that it is written in colorless prose, and so on. Even so, YouTube uses Wikipedia to flag conspiracy-theory videos, Facebook has information buttons that link to it in order to substantiate news articles, and Alexa and Siri rely on it to answer factual questions.[100] It is perhaps our single most authoritative source of common sense and information arbitration – or, as Wikipedia itself puts it, our "guardian of truth."

Guardianship is a political act. What are the conditions of Wikipedia's? The site is committed to the two principles I've named: to be fully open-sourced and to offer "reliable, neutral" information. The trouble is not just with each of these singly, but that the two principles are at odds with each other, since any unified source of information must adjudicate between incompatible claims. Someone somewhere must put their foot down to end the controversy about whether a human with a cat is most accurately characterized as the cat's "owner," its "caregiver," or its "human companion" (to name an example of an internecine edit war[101]). And such conflicts are in fact resolved behind the scenes by editors and administrators, who decide the issue conclusively by sometimes closing off entries ("global warming," say) from just anyone's revision. The open-sourcing of knowledge, if it also hopes to establish some form of order and coherence, thereby also entails a non-democratic principle. Questions of judgment – about what counts as "notable," "mainstream," or which viewpoints should receive "due weight" – are governed by the common sense of the editors (still mainly white, white-collar, English-speaking, technically-minded men from developed countries in the northern hemisphere). While the entry on Wikipedia's "Neutral point of view" loftily brushes aside the objection that there is no such thing as objectivity, it then lets just that principle stand within the site's characterizations: "It may not be possible to describe all disputes with perfect objectivity, but it is an aim that thousands of editors strive towards every day."[102]

I am not suggesting that Wikipedia would be better or more democratic if it were indeed a free-for-all. Such would be a situation of anarchic disarray, leading to multiple and incompatible versions of the same entry. But the site's credibility undoubtedly does derive from the presumption that widespread participation results in an impartial form of authority, even as the possibility of that participation entails a less than democratic exercise of power behind the scenes. It is only under such conditions that the site can put itself forward as "reliable and neutral" – under the presumption, that is, that no authority is being exercised at all, that hits or edits are "votes," and that its democratic form of participation generates and sustains its own conditions. Wikipedia's user interface may be democratic, but the site is technocratic under the hood.

This administrative fiat masking as perfect openness characterizes all major decisions by tech companies about what kinds of content to tolerate or censure. Global speech platforms like Facebook or Twitter make decisions that are intrinsically political even as they would like nothing better than to extricate themselves from politics altogether. Politics is bad for business; overtly political pronouncements risk alienating users and attract the notice of lawmakers looking to score points off them. Everyone basically agrees that there are limits to what should be tolerated and that no "dehumanizing" speech should be allowed. But since speech is (also) political, since its limits cannot be specified by purely technical means, since no software can reliably pick out dehumanizing speech from satire, quotation, or otherwise acceptable speech which happens to use the same phrases or words, politics then has its revenge. Companies must either continue to tacitly condone the presence of conspiracy theorists, or they must actively intervene with the application of principles that soon run into grey areas, becoming entangled in accusations of bias.[103] Even platforms like Parler that are founded as free speech sanctuaries in reaction to Facebook's or Twitter's content moderation soon discover that they too have their limits.[104] Platforms that are in the business of neutrality are forced – by the very nature of the medium – into the role of issuing the most far-reaching and peremptory ethical dicta in the world.

Facebook's discomfort under scrutiny offers the most satisfying example of the inseparability of politics and communication. Its "Fact-Checking Program" employs both human fact-checkers and machine learning to scrutinize articles that are flagged by users as false or as produced by "bad actors." Many sites peddling fear and calumny for clicks are weeded out. But Facebook itself acknowledges that it takes time and expertise to check up on facts, that fact-checkers cannot be had in all regions and languages, and that it is very difficult (or impossible) for it to distinguish humor from earnest content. An official statement about the Program – aptly titled "Hard Questions" – concludes on a flustered note:

And ultimately, it's important that people trust the fact-checkers making these calls. While we work with the International Fact-Checking Network to approve all our partners and make sure they have high standards of accuracy, fairness and transparency, we continue to face accusations of bias. Which has left people asking, in today's world, is it possible to have a set of fact-checkers that are widely recognized as objective? We've also made some changes to how we let people know that a story is disputed so that they can learn more and come to their own conclusions.[105]

The question of objectivity is not followed up here, but the mention of "trust" in the first sentence and of wide recognition in the third, point to the nerve of the matter: that no knowledge *can* be widely regarded as simply "neutral" or "objective" within a medium whose main service is to validate everyone's "own conclusions," and that trust is both the condition of widespread legitimacy and precisely that which a technology platform has no business expecting from us: it is, in fact, the very thing that platforms exist to obviate.

Facebook's latest move has been to institute an official Oversight Board – a "Supreme Court" – that was responsible for ratifying the permanent suspension of Donald Trump from the platform. The Board is funded and run independently from the platform; its decisions are meant to be binding and to create precedents for similar cases. Composed of about twenty lawyers, free speech experts, former politicians, human rights activists, and at least one Nobel Prize laureate from the world over, it is the most plausible imitation of the United Nations of speech that money could buy. It is of course a laughable category mistake to think of such an ethics-washing panel as a court issuing case "decisions." Facebook has no legal jurisdiction over anyone, nor is there any reason why its interests should be identified with or responsive to the public good. Yet it embodies the paradox of a privately owned public medium: the fact that, when a whole mode of communicating rests in private hands, when a company is not just one competitor alongside others but a supra-national meeting place, it cannot but accrue enormous political significance. If Bitcoin is a currency without a bank, Facebook is a mode of speech belonging to no place: our new Babel, our government-from-nowhere. When Facebook's Oversight Board comes in for pundit reproval, such criticism is generally followed by the reasonable recommendation that (say) the U.S. government legislate such matters instead.[106] Facebook has been desperate to abdicate its political responsibilities; but if there is one body that has proved even more reluctant than Facebook to avoid making unpopular political decisions it has been the U.S. Congress itself. Are we so confident that (controversial) congressional legislation on such matters would command more widespread trust than Facebook's own edicts? (The E.U. – always one step ahead of the U.S. on the road to administrative dystopia – has recently enacted speech legislation for social media platforms. It's not yet clear how it will or could be effective without becoming markedly coercive.[107]) It is Facebook's very desire to transcend "politics" that will continue to make it all the more appealing as a source of political clout: the fantasy of rule by product.

True to its double origin as a scientific medium of exchange and (then) as an Age of Aquarius instrument of egalitarian counterculture,[108] the internet's most powerful political desire – the political attitude that most visibly emerges from our collective uses of it – is the desire to escape from politics altogether through the fusion of new senses of "democracy" and "neutrality." What we now tend to call "democratic" is, in this sense, shorthand for our digital conception of supra-national, egalitarian legitimacy: the elimination of personal authority in favor of a universal process, the objective authority of collective participation exercised in the seeming absence of any ties to place and time. It goes without saying that this picture is deeply false: democracy (understood as a concrete form of government) and neutrality (understood as an epistemic fantasy in which facts alone can be decisive) are incompatible ends. All information and all knowledge express a form of authority: a specific theory of what counts as a warranted or decisive justification for a reason advanced. There is and can never be a process by which selected information and its implied characterizations can be simply neutral, any more than there can be neutral history or narrative of any kind. There is no political truth in numbers.

So much is obvious, in theory, to everyone. But the internet makes it uniquely difficult *not* to know this in practice, by recasting political questions into questions of fact, bias, and neutrality. Our most common political criticism of online services, for instance, is that they are not as neutral as they purport to be – that ads make racist assumptions, say, or that voice recognition software works better for some accents than for others, or that Wikipedia's editors are predominantly white men. These are the facts.[109] But the persistent illusion underlying this criticism is that we should continue to aim to create a perfectly neutral form of speech and that political equality should be identified with our quantitative measurements of it – that the solution to problems of inequality, in other words, is a better approximation of perfect neutrality. And this presumption shows what is so destructive about neutrality as a political principle: it sets up a criterion of justice with which one can always clobber an opponent even as, by cloaking itself under the presumption of objectivity, it remains self-deceived about the political, ethical, or religious principles that animate it. To conflate partiality or judgment with "bias" or "hypocrisy" is to betray a post-truth view of politics. So far from being a variation of capricious relativism, in other words, post-truth actually denotes an intensified commitment to objectivity: it just so happens that there is no authoritative view of what that means. The danger is no longer (as it once seemed) that all political values would become merely subjective. It is that they are so identified with what is demonstrably objective that no common practice of democratic politics could ever emerge from them.

The desire to divest knowledge of personal authority and the fragmentation of authority itself are thus one and the same phenomenon – one that, so far from remaining online, is corroding the political life of the United States. The disruptive force of internet "democratization" is nowhere better on display than in the conflicts that have borne us the terms "fake news" and "post-truth." The latter term, before gaining notoriety as the *Oxford Dictionary's* 2016 word of the year, was coined in a 2010 blog post by David Roberts, a journalist.

He argued that, in contrast to the ideal of Enlightenment politics – wherein voters first gather the facts and then draw conclusions from them – we have entered into a situation in which we choose our facts only subsequently to our tribally-minded, party affiliations.[110] The term "post-truth" has found resonance because there is undoubtedly something to this. Political polarization in the United States is at its highest pitch since the late 1960s, party affiliation is increasingly correlated to a cluster of other markers (from religion, neighborhood, and education, down to the details of our purchase history[111]), and there is a growing sense of the futility of reason as such within the public sphere.

But Roberts' characterization itself evinces a version of the problem it describes, by papering over the differences between "facts," neutral data, and political reasons. Politics has never been carried out primarily on the basis of facts; it is not the case today any more than it was in the eighteenth century. And so the very formulation of the problem betrays one of the its causes: the tidy division of facts and values, and the superstition that pristine facts could of themselves settle questions about the common weal – as if such settlement did not also presuppose a specific view of the authority of science, and of its place within a whole hierarchy of human goods that are not themselves empirically given. A politics based on facts alone is at once a technocratic fantasy and the wrong thing to want. It is yet another version of the facile contrast between "logic" and "emotion" I've noted. The notion of "fact-based politics" that has developed in response to "post-truth" is thus incapable of addressing the real underlying problem, which is the internet's participatory access to knowledge at the cost of shared, contextualizing sources of institutional authority.

Scientific facts have been politically loaded for some time in American politics. President Obama enthusiastically embraced and was embraced by Google HQ in 2007 on the grounds that many Americans are "just misinformed," a problem to which access to digital information was supposed to be the solution.[112] The issue has made itself felt in the culture wars of the past thirty years, with the political left often claiming empirical grounds as the basis for its position on issues like abortion, global warming, compulsory vaccines, and the teaching of sex-education and creationism in public schools. The weight and meaning of scientific evidence vary in each of these issues. But whether or not this weight is adequately understood, the conflation of the scientific with the political has contributed to a situation in which a prominent part of the political right has (as mentioned) responded to an issue like global warming, not by debating the relative priority of environmental concerns with respect to the exigencies of industry and the economy, but by recourse to junk science denying the existence of the phenomenon altogether. The answer to the "factualization" of politics (treating facts per se as politically decisive) is therefore the "politicization" of facts (treating facts as a matter of value or choice). Politics is thereby displaced and sublimated into information.

When Kellyanne Conway, Donald Trump's counselor, improvised the phrase "alternative facts" to describe the administration's blatant contradiction of the crowd size at the presidential inauguration, it was as if the political right had learned the tune that had long been the province of the post-structuralist academy: that science is an instrument of power, that scientific disagreements express biases, that all facts are factitious and borne from interpretation, and that the truth is a social construction. In political contexts like this, however, "alternative facts" are nothing but facts cynically deployed, facts used as instruments or weapons. It is a position that has no intention to convince, but it is good enough for stalemate by offering up the public pretense that there are always two sides to the story, and that the difference between the sides is just a matter of interpretation. This amounts to claiming that there are no publicly binding facts, which is as self-defeating as the countersuggestion that politics should or could become a matter of fact alone. Several of *The New York Times'* promotional slogans in the wake of the 2016 election may as well have been lifted from *Pravda*: "Let the facts be your guide," "Get the facts that tell the whole story," and "Just facts. No alternatives." And this is what "fake news" comes to mean: just (others') facts.

What distinguishes modern scientific reason from magic, in Max Weber's classic formulation, is not that more people will be better educated about the workings of the world, but "the knowledge or the conviction that if *only we wished* to understand [something] we *could* do so at any time."[113] This feature of scientific reason, so far from eliminating our need for institutional authority, in fact increases it, since no one in particular is in the position to verify much of anything first-hand. Rather than relying on the words of fewer authorities, we must heed those of more and more. What is at stake in the fact wars and in the heightened skepticism toward expertise that marks our age is not a matter of epistemology – no one on the right or the left seriously doubts that some facts are really true, that neutral facts have become and promise to remain our highest arbiter and value. It is instead a question of the political legitimacy of shared sources, on the basis of which voters can make up their mind about where the nation's priorities lie. It is precisely this kind of legitimacy that goes missing within the online public square. There has always been fake news of some sort, but it has never been so handy to look up the reasons for what you already think you know.

There is no shortage of empirical data or of thoughtful political arguments now. What is missing from the digital age is the necessity of attending to any of them in particular, since I have the perception that I may easily retreat elsewhere, if pressed, to some other corner of the information ecosystem.[114] Public reason is a condition for life in common as a nation: it is the common measure by which we distinguish right from violence. To the extent that this imaginative unity of granted facts erodes,[115] we are in danger of losing the meaningful distinctions between idea and ideology, and between the law of the land and arbitrary edict. Where political legitimacy unravels, nothing holds but naked power.

Digital relations, I've been arguing, have nothing in particular to do with democracy as a political form. Their relation to democracy is fallacious and delusive: they reshape our expectations for what it ought to be in ways that degrade the conditions for what it actually is. I do not mean that we have been mistaken to continue to seek out better versions of our democracy, but that freedom and equality are ideals that we must primarily pursue in and identify with pre- or extra-digital practices. They will not be taken care of by impersonal procedures or by the presumption of neutrality underlying our view of what technology should do. They are specific social commitments and achievements, not the absence of them. And one can only take a stand within the terms of history, law, and place to gather way for bodied vision.

But if it is not democratic, does the internet then belong to some other political form? There is one obvious counterexample to the claim that there is no national internet, a regime that has entirely reoriented and monopolized the digital to the national. I mean China, which, unlike the United States, has established a fully permeable system of relations between private tech companies and state control. It is carrying out a project of centralization and surveillance that would have made red Russia green with envy: the so-called "Great Firewall of China." Facebook, Twitter, YouTube, Wikipedia, and Google are blocked altogether – there are Chinese counterparts to these, which are under permanent government scrutiny. Private companies work in tandem with state censors to police the entire (available) internet. They do so with an eye to a wide range of concerns – from suppressing politically sensitive information (about Tibet or Tiananmen Square, e.g.), to protecting the image of Party Secretary Xi Jinping from aspersion or satire (blocking images of Winnie the Pooh or of the letter "n," with which he [Xi] has been associated, e.g.[116]), to trying to improve the moral tone of the population by blocking pornography and all manner of demoralizing content. (The government also has strict limits on the amount of time that young people can spend playing online video games.[117]) The number of "content controllers" censoring the internet around the clock is reckoned to be as many as 2 million; it is an astounding number that gives some indication of how laborious online censorship must always remain, since automation is not up to the task of keeping up with popular resourcefulness in semantic and linguistic innovation. An additional 2 million or so are employed by the government to inject propaganda and misinformation into the daily social media cycle – the so-called "50-cent party," since they receive 50-cents for every bit of content they churn out (about 450 million posts each year). A recent (American) study concluded that the goal of this information flood is "to distract the public and change the subject." In contrast to the American context, in which social media works to undermine basic civic practices, China is actively encouraging the internet to do what it already does best.[118]

The thoroughness and scale of this project renders it different in kind from the digital controls exercised by authoritarian governments elsewhere, which are patchy and fumbling at best. New technology renders "socialism with Chinese characteristics" something more than an ad hoc mélange of market economics and Marxist central planning. It is in fact something without precedent: the first fully developed digitocracy, a totalitarian regime based on technical control and panoptical transparency. The best-known, most terrible version of its control takes place in Xinjiang, where the Uighur population is monitored by pervasive checkpoints and facial recognition cameras. A mandatory phone app allows police open access to every citizen's data and whereabouts. DNA and other biometric data are collected and tracked too.[119] All of this is in addition to internment camps in which hundreds of thousands are imprisoned, separated from their children, and "reeducated." But the camps are not different in kind from the form of total surveillance outside them; they are continuous with its logic. "If someone exists, there will be traces, and if there are connections, there will be information."[120] The systematic extermination of an ethnic minority has never been carried out with such overwhelmingly precise and bloodless calculation.

So far from crushing most of its population with Big Brother's iron fist, however, China's control rests precisely on the principle of efficiency – on its capacity to gather, integrate, and analyze data generated from ordinary digital activities. Technical convenience contains, as I've suggested above, an intrinsically authoritarian principle: the terms in which digital devices help us control and predict our circumstances are the same terms under which we ourselves can become objects of control and prediction. Unencumbered by the West's protections of privacy and checks on surveillance, China can at once promote competition by offering extensive commercial freedoms to national internet firms, while also guiding them to realize the full implications of rule by data. Alipay and WeChat Pay transactions have, for instance, almost entirely replaced cash for small purchases (even buskers and beggars in large cities now accept them); the resulting data is then used to improve advertising and AI development, which is used in turn to perfect state scrutiny of its citizens. This revolving door between tech and state is not entirely seamless; China has recently had to put Jack Ma (co-founder of Alibaba) and other tycoons in their place. But the symbiosis protects big tech firms from competition even as it affords the state the means to pursue technological self-sufficiency and supremacy. With the data of its 770 million online users in hand, China plausibly aims to lead the world in AI by 2030. The cutting edge of technology is thereby also the cutting edge of social and military control.

If the digital state cannot actually read citizens' minds, it can evaluate where they are, how they spend money, with whom they communicate online, and whether they have paid their taxes. It is on this basis that the state is developing algorithms for rating its citizens' honesty and loyalty: "[The system] will forge a public opinion environment where keeping trust is glorious. It will strengthen sincerity in government affairs, commercial sincerity, social sincerity and the construction of judicial credibility."[121] If you so much as jaywalk in China, you are liable to receive an immediate text message instructing you not to – or to have an image of your face put up on jumbotron as an offender.[122] The goal is a synthesis of state, corporate, and mutual surveillance to "allow the trustworthy to roam everywhere under heaven while making it hard for the discredited to take a single step."[123]

All of this is justified by the contrast to the dominance of private monopolies over the internet in the West, in other words, as a way of making mass data work for the public. As Feng Xiang, one of China's foremost legal scholars, has put it: "if AI remains under the control of market forces, it will inexorably result in a super-rich oligopoly of data billionaires who reap the wealth created by robots that displace human labor, leaving massive unemployment in their wake."[124] This is hardly an implausible characterization, whatever conclusion one draws from it. Is it better for the state or for a handful of private companies to have a monopoly over the legitimate use of data? While it is the consolation of the Western liberal view of the matter that there are still legal barriers between state and companies that ensure some modicum of privacy, those barriers will be continually eroded from both directions so long as we continue to pursue digital conveniences as goods in themselves. (Amazon, to name one example, has agreements with over 400 police departments in the U.S. to share access to footage from its video-doorbell service.[125]) This is not to say that all uses of data should be regarded as equivalent, but that the desire for automated efficiency as a social end entails illiberal and undemocratic consequences.

Because what is most powerful about China's digital control is not just its strategic stoking of nationalist passions, its manufacturing of an officially Sinicized public opinion, nor its ability to keep an eye on malcontents, but the way in which it captures its citizens' sense of freedom, the way in which it coincides with and appropriates to itself the net desire to disburden oneself of responsibility. What one counts as one's "freedom" depends on (or perhaps just *is*) one's political vision. It has variously been taken to be the ability to elect one's own rulers, to bear arms, to speak one's mind, to be bound by the rule of law, to worship according to one's conscience, or to be a citizen of a self-determining nation. We casually take it to mean the ability to do more or less as we please – but what is it that we please? Most Chinese citizens undoubtedly report *feeling* free. While Western economies were still paralyzed by the Covid epidemic in early 2021, China was more or less back to normal; the state's awesome powers of surveillance were used to eliminate the virus with a dispatch surpassing that of any Western democracy, such that people were free to return to their ordinary lives.[126] Their determined pursuit of a "zero Covid" policy is therefore as much a means of further consolidating the biometrical surveillance state as it is (in theory) a demonstration of that state's awesome effectiveness at ensuring the unconstrained private lives of its citizens: it is a clear mark of how the regime understands its own source of legitimacy. So long as "freedom" is felt to be something outside or separate from its expression in particular political activities (like voting or organizing or advocating) – so long, that is, as freedom is identified with the convenience, security, prosperity, and efficiency of state power competently exercised – there can be no strong objection to China's version of it. The "feeling" of freedom is, in this sense, akin to a user's seamless online experience.

This is a pervasive digital assumption. Peter Thiel (co-founder of PayPal) has claimed, in apparent opposition to China's situation, that "crypto[currency] is libertarian, AI is communist"[127] – in other words, that protecting data privacy through blockchain technology would translate into the protection of individual freedom. Enthusiasts of Web 3.0 – a new network of just such decentralized, anonymized services – defend it on the grounds that it will offer a freer and more democratic internet, a networked *law* without the state.[128] But a medium of perfect anonymity has no more to offer, politically speaking, than a medium of perfect transparency: both crypto anarchists and communists with Chinese characteristics share the aim of eliminating the need for public life. Both therefore share the same altogether negative notion of freedom. This is the freedom to an undisturbed private life, which is the freedom not to be responsible because policy consists in technical challenges that are better managed by able administrators: such is China's chief product and justification.

Even if there is a subculture of mordant irony around online censorship and even if some will evidently always find ways of circumventing their censors, we can hardly underestimate the formative power that China's controls exert over what is sayable, thinkable, and imaginable for its citizens. The experience of searching for "tank man" and being redirected to a series of results having nothing to do with the iconic Tiananmen image is different in kind from the suppression of printed information. The power of online censorship is the same as that of online misinformation – that it does not even feel like anything is missing; doubt cannot easily arise when what you'd like to see seems to be the case. Bill Clinton once quipped that China's efforts to restrain free speech online would be "like nailing Jell-O to the wall."[129] No one is so flip anymore.

Yet digitocracy remains a titanic and precarious project; it is much more vulnerable to sudden disintegration than the Soviet Union was. China's information management remains subject to conditions that are arguably beyond the government's long-term control – namely, the total depoliticization of the world's largest national population. If the state should fail to shape public opinion, if it should cease to deliver basic expectations, if there should arise a widespread urge for social disruption, if "zero Covid" should encroach too odiously on their private lives, citizens will have the ready means to communicate at their fingertips. No one can say whether this will come to pass; merely that if it does, unrest will be more difficult to quell than in a world of print alone. Before the Covid epidemic gave China an opening to enact a draconian new security law, pro-democracy protests in Hong Kong managed to withstand the full weight of the repressive state apparatus brought to bear on them – continuing to organize in the face of an overwhelming disinformation campaign and finding out clever ways to keep one step ahead of the facial-recognition cameras set up to identify participants.[130] No number of automated censors can prevent the messages of a few from quickly reaching many millions, when circumstances are propitious to it. In other words, if the internet's logic is to erase intermediate contexts of action between the center and the peripheries, this also entails a reverse possibility. It is not only the periphery that is always subject to total centralization, but the center that is subject to disintegration into the periphery. This does not rule out that, in the seesaw between agitated atomism and administrative authoritarianism – or between the transactional privacy of Web 3.0 and China's collectivization of data – it is the latter that might prove more durable. But the very conditions that make such authoritarianism durable are also those that keep it vulnerable.

The best example of the internet's bearing on political form is therefore neither the United States nor China, but the Arab Spring of the early 2010's. It was through social media that activists were able to circumvent state controls, disseminate information at large, and coordinate impromptu assemblies and coalitions. National movements were thereby able to act in awareness of and solidarity with each other, shaking off authoritarian governments in Tunisia, Libya, Egypt, Yemen, Syria, and Bahrain, while sparking protests in a dozen other countries. It was an extraordinary feat of collective action, a moving demonstration of the impulse for popular sovereignty such as had not been seen since the fall of the Soviet states. And it seemed to many to be the ultimate vindication of the internet's "democratic" promise.

A decade later, most of these states have not managed to develop their original democratic impulses. They have rather (with Tunisia making a fragile exception) exchanged one form of authoritarian government for another. Social media is not at fault for this reversion, but that is just the point: that while the internet is easily conducive to widespread upheaval, commotion, and instability, it does nothing to settle the longstanding conditions by which institutions, laws, and habits cohere into form. It is undoubtedly a medium of egalitarian agitation, scandal, and uprising – as capable of putting down the mighty from their seat as it is of exalting the humble and meek. It is not true (as was once feared) that social media would lead to a situation of universal apathy in which digital "slacktivism" would replace the act of taking to the streets. Political protests throughout the world have, if anything, become more frequent with widespread use of social media.[131] But the power to protest in such terms does not stabilize some form between chaotic anarchy and repressive conformity.[132] Facebook was once the means for organizing protest; it now helps rival militias in Libya to effectively identify each other's locations to fan ethnic hatred.[133] While the platform has at least one genocide on its hands (in Myanmar), its record on nation-building is inconclusive.

3.5   EVERYWHERE NATIONS: HUMANIZATION AND RACIALIZATION

When the gap between ideal and real becomes too wide, the system breaks down.
(Barbara Tuchman)[134]

The internet is entropic to the realization of political form; it is a force of political incoherence and discoherence. If mass mobilizations have become more frequent, the movements behind them are less unified and stable – just as the body organizing the Women's March disintegrated within a couple of years, the Black Lives Matter movement cannot aspire to the laboriously achieved coherence of the 1960's Civil Rights movement.[135] There may be reason to think that digital relations therefore work against the grain of national life as such. The identity of modern states, their status as forms of shared affiliation, rests, as I've said, on an imaginative conception of what is shared with others: a nation lives in our imagination of the political whole that figures us as active parts, supplying the metaphors that bind our thinking to our doing. Such conceptions command our loyalty because they are understood in something more than voluntary terms – a shared vernacular or tradition, say, or, in the case of the United States, the history of a common promise. Such national narratives are themselves created, and so are also artifacts developed for the purposes of self-justification. But it is nonetheless important that the only possible justifications of our political home are addressed to the heart, rather than to the brain: they appeal to our responsibility toward what we are born into – toward what is "given" to us by virtue of belonging to our country of origin – rather than to mere self-interest, or contractual duty. This is manifestly different from the logic of online community, in which membership must either be entirely open (the world-wide web) or expressly closed (the protectionist webs of China or India). As national communities must thereby become relatively more voluntary, the sense in which our loyalties rest on some principle other than identity or self-interest must come into question. The lack of middle contexts here expresses itself in divergent impulses toward trans-political cosmopolitanism and retrenched nativism – the impulse, on the one hand, to transcend the bonds of nationhood, and the impulse to specify it in sharper racial or cultural terms, on the other. Both "open borders" cosmopolitanism and populist nationalism are attempts to provide new grounds for understanding what we have in common. Both are facilitated by the extent to which our sense of politics is carried out online.

It has become commonplace to cast the political watersheds of the past several years (Brexit, the 2016 American election, and other populist movements around Europe) in terms of a contrast between two classes of voters, the "somewheres" (voters with strong geographic identities, usually older, more rural, poorer, less well educated, who favor greater emphasis on national borders and sovereignty) and the "anywheres" (voters with a rather more cosmopolitan view of their identities, younger, better educated, more urban, more likely to favor globalization and immigration).[136] Such distinctions should be handled with care: the types it denotes are not equivalent within just any national context, nor do the distinction's resonances travel very well across issues. Globalization and immigration are questions that necessarily involve the status of the nation as such, as particular cultural issues (like Muslim headscarves in France or abortion in the United States) do not. The "somewhere" movement for Catalan or Scottish separatism is not congruent with the "somewhere" right-wing populism in France. And some version of these extremes has been implicit in the very idea of the nation, especially since 1945. Even if they have not originated with the internet, however, our specific breakdowns of national imagination are only intelligible within the terms of a world in which the most important medium of communication seems to have no intrinsic connection to our experience of body, place, and law – the realities at the core of our political conceptions.

The ways in which an online world tempts us to a view transcending borders are plain enough. The internet makes it easier to extend networks of international and social commerce, it allows us to be permanently aware of what is going on everywhere else, and it is therefore conducive to the emergence of a simultaneous global consciousness within which the notion of humanity as such suggests itself as prior to its contingent, national variations. The technological ideal of neutrality that is implicit in the medium itself entails the ideal of political equality, a vision of "thinking globally" for which, say, humanitarian crises (refugees, immigrants) and "science based" data (on global warming) have a legitimacy that supersedes claims of national tradition or sovereignty. Conflicts of domestic politics therefore tend to be refigured within the terms of world politics – they are governed by a view of human rights that, aided by the claims of neutral scientific reason, is "beyond" borders. The Green New Deal provides a clear example of the rhetorical convergence of these priorities.

Some of these conflicts are inescapably transnational. But it is also clear that their transnational cast is abetted by the extent to which we move our thinking into a medium that knows no place and cannot acknowledge the significance of national differences (in a world, that is, in which the nation is nonetheless still the *de facto* political form). In March 2018, several hundred rallies were organized throughout the United States to press for stricter gun controls. But the rallies were not restricted to the United States: 36 of them took place in other countries, on all continents.[137] (The same was true for the 2017 Women's March and the 2020 protests over the murder of George Floyd.) The motives were no doubt benign – human solidarity in protest – but the meaning of such solidarity outstrips the character of a "protest" as an act of political significance. Where the project is exerting pressure on one's lawmakers or fellows, why should anyone be impressed by the fact that citizens of other countries sympathize? The problem with neutrality – as the egalitarian ideal underlying a fully cosmopolitan ideal of world politics – is not that it is trans-political, but that it has no way of acknowledging its own situated dependence on a specific history, people, and place, except by writing it off as accidental to its development. It cannot limit its claims to the affiliations governing a specific nation – and what cannot account for itself cannot keep itself together. It is no accident that the most common label for online users (for both companies and their critics) is *humans.*

Part of the basis of this global solidarity rests on the rising prominence of identity politics – the sorting of political objectives by categorical grouping – which, as I've said, has been facilitated by online habits of mind: in a setting in which the perception of monotonous difference predominates, intensified pride in self-affirmed difference becomes a stronger marker of identity. Translated into domestic or national politics, the effect has been to emphasize political representation in terms of race or gender or sexual orientation ("the first X to be elected to the office …"). Such categorical identities, as easily quantifiable, classifiable, and universalizable, are becoming our most straightforward means of making political phenomena intelligible. They allow us the chance to translate specific events into readymade categorical explanations. (It is difficult to know *in any given case* whether, for instance, someone is the victim of violence on account of racial hatred, or whether race is a collateral fact of the situation. But it is easy to know that someone of a given race *is* involved in a given incident, as well as the statistical likelihoods of each.) To describe political agency in narrowly racial terms is to understand that agency as situated within a transnational struggle between reified types of people, rather than between types of labor or economic class. The apparently innocuous phrase "people of color" expresses a biopolitical program of action, wherein all non-white people are aggregated willy-nilly into a project of solidarity against dismantling white supremacy the world over.

This racial consolidation is working in both directions. Derek Black (a former white nationalist) has written about how anxiety about identity is exploited by white nationalists for the purposes of recruitment. He notes that, so far from being taught to scour the weirdo fringes of society for promising candidates, he was taught to look for anyone who would casually reach for such formulations as "I'm not a racist, but … I don't want American history to be dishonored."[138] It is a Satanically clever maneuver, since, in appealing to the anxiety of those who understand themselves as wanting to honor their heritage, it also seeks to undermine the distinctive unity of American ideals that it supposedly defends. In other words, it is part of the white nationalist strategy to translate a diffuse and inarticulate unease about national identity into a new aggrieved contender for that identity.

White nationalism belongs to the same political landscape in which identity is insisted on as the basis of political claims. To the extent that our communal life is thinner than it was – to the extent that offline participation in civic institutions is more diffuse, that family bonds are more tenuous, that church attendance declines, that low birth rates increase the demand for immigration – then the temptation to define ourselves by race, rather than by conduct or class or citizenship, is stronger.[139] The "territorialization" of European nations – the sharpened identification of peoples with their home*land* – was an analogous, nineteenth-century phenomenon: a way to solve the issue of what we have in common. Where we have little in common, how you talk and where you come from become more important than what you do or what you believe. Race itself is a shortcut to identity; it is easier to fix, verify, and assess than class (at any rate now, at any rate in America). Taken by itself, it is in this way the final refuge of an identity stripped of action and impoverished of human solidarity, the promise of a stable self within the confusions of mass politics. And just as movements like

Black Lives Matter have become internationalized, so too have movements like QAnon: the (paradoxical) phenomenon of a global nationalism – the affirmation, united by and reacting to common enemies, of national or racial mass-values in the company of analogous assertions in other countries altogether.[140] Tucker Carlson and Viktor Orban: (somehow) friends in common cause.[141]

All of these political impulses, right and left, acquire their shape within the logic of online exchange. That is, while new expressions of nationalism are often described by their progressive opponents as an atavism or return to barbaric, primitive, retrograde thinking, the central elements of its rhetoric are nothing of the kind. From Baudelaire to Bin Laden, hostility to Enlightenment modernity has always been, after all, a distinctive Enlightenment phenomenon.[142] To call such responses barbaric is no more useful than referring to the modern nation state as a "tribe." That is, to think of racism, populism, and nationalism as primitive phenomena is to Whiggishly beg the question of what conditions elicit them, and to miss the fact that their adherents express their own utopian hopes in futuristic or sci-fi terms.[143] The Capitol riot was an extraordinary exhibition of just how online nationalism now is: the rapid mobilization of a crowd, its ambiguous political status and intention (a coup? A dust-up out of hand?), the thorough digital coverage by all parties, the high number of social media figures present in the crowd, the fantastic (and ambiguously ironic) costuming, signaling, and aestheticizing of these figures by and through the event itself – all taking place in and around the single most venerable edifice in the United States. It was an online mob irrupting into "real" life, the perfect selfie surrealized into political action.

Beyond the public expressions of new nationalist identities, the anonymity and impunity of online speech has allowed for the development of wider subcultures of racism and ethno-nationalism than were possible in print – forums of people who, while not always expressly affiliated or willing to act with white nationalist groups, nonetheless don't mind entertaining its notions.[144] Combing at random through 4chan for five minutes, one cannot but ponder what it means for such people to be able to discover each other in the first place and to form an idiolect of references, memes, and allusions – all shared with the satisfaction of a winking and evasive private joke that joins them as insiders to it. This is but one room in the chthonic underworld of the internet – a realm that, as I've said, not only mirrors the existence of racist thinking, but multiplies, normalizes, reinforces, and amplifies it by giving it a foothold in habitual thinking. Whereas "public" or mainstream online discussion takes place under expectations that what's said should be scrubbed and bowdlerized of all possible offense, it thus coexists with forums in which outrage, hatred, and resentment have a burgeoning life of their own, presented under the trolling auspices of the likes of Pepe the Frog.[145] The searing scrutiny of the "mainstream" internet and the terrible impunity of the "underground" or dark web correspond to each other, as extreme calls to extreme: light and darkness, total Enlightenment and "Dark Enlightenment," side by side.

Against the technical rationality of the cosmopolitan state – the trans-political desire to figure political problems as matters for scientific and technocratic regulation and to read rights primarily as claims to human (rather than national) rights – one reaction has therefore been the fantasy of racist sovereignty, a fanatic assertion of roots as more binding than other kinds of human claims on us. The collision of these extremes, as they fray the postwar liberal consensus in the West, thus presents us with the spectacle of economics untethered from politics (as in Brexit), facts unyoked from values (as in "post-truth"), and globalism untethered from patriotism more generally. This is our contemporary version of the struggle between church and state in medieval Europe: the claims of a universalist law in opposition to those of particular place, virtual equality clashing with simulated nationality. My point is not that, by virtue of being opposed, each of these sides is equally and symmetrically justified, but that we can see them both taking shape within the imperatives of our online medium. Just as the dominant egalitarianism of political neutrality is borne of ether and of cloud, so is its subversion formed in subterranean chat rants with uncertain relation to offline life. Both are expressions of a newly sublimated politics: the politics of generally speaking.

One wonders whether either of these extremes contains the seeds of some political form other than the nation state, a form that would resolve this conflict by being better suited to online politics: either a world-state (a wider version of the European Union, say) or a world of violent factions marked by a sharper, neo-tribal sense of who "we" are. My own view is that there is no such resolution in the wings. Not because I have special love for the nation state as such, but because political forms are ways in which we make our home in the world – a home we build through the practice of our attachments and through our ordinary and extraordinary sacrifices to it – and therefore have a necessary relation to our body and its cares. Yet it is the dislocation of our imagination online, the way in which it slips the bounds of place (rendering them either voluntary or boundless), that serves to disconcert and derange our national loyalties even as it cannot offer a new offline alternative. To be a netizen is parasitic on being a citizen – that is how we take place – but netizenship means that our units of political imagination either must transcend the nation itself or must somehow enforce the sense of what is national with new species of brutality. Politics online promises to remain a condition of permanent revolutionary spasm or tyrannical sclerosis, not of creative constitution. No credible alternative to the nation state has emerged.

And yet our sublimated politics are nonetheless jointly working in three discernible directions, corollary to what I've argued: the end of liberalism, the abdication of politics to administration, and the emergence of the digital nation state.

First, digital relations are at basic odds with the norms of classical liberalism, which are the norms of a printed culture: I mean with the ways in which liberalism, as expressed in our First Amendment rights, draws a distinct boundary between private and public life, protects and values free speech, and assumes the presence of a public sphere in which ideas can be debated on their merits and entertained (as it were) quotationally, regardless of the identities or "subject positions" of the participants. None of these ideal conditions can permanently withstand digital pressure. There can be no clear line between private and public life when the media of private life are themselves public. ("Silence is complicity.") There is no very compelling reason to protect free speech, unless one has the conviction that the unrestricted "marketplace of ideas" will produce better arguments or that expression is intrinsically valuable. (Whereas speech is itself now commonly seen as a form of harm, just as some notions and words are off limits in any context whatsoever.) There is no way to debate ideas on their merits, unless one also agrees on the standards, facts, and priorities on the basis of which debate takes place (which is why campaigns to "fact-check" the news and to debunk misinformation are either ineffective or themselves expressions of an ideological commitment to particular sources). The authors of the *Federalist Papers* carried out consequential public debates under pseudonyms; their identities were unknown. But we can no longer confidently separate speech from identity; the two coalesce. To censure speech is to cancel the *speaker* (that is, to ex-communicate them).

It would be alarmist to conclude from this that freedom no longer matters to us or that we are slip-sliding toward tyranny. It is not that "freedom" has ceased to matter to us, it is rather that freedom is medium-specific, that our standing ways of thinking about freedom belong to a world of print, that the standards for achieving our ideal of impartiality in digital terms have brought equality into increasing conflict with freedom, and that we are modifying what we think freedom should be, accordingly. Liberal freedom imagines a space dependent on yet secluded from public life (as in "every man's home is his castle" or the "court of conscience"). Print helped create the notion of the in-dividual as the fundamental unit occupying that space. But there is no such space in cyberspace; the private takes place in public – users, unlike individuals, have no seclusive membrane, nor do they define themselves in formal relation to some fixed public – which in turn accentuates our involvement with and comparison to all others. We have therefore lost patience with the fact that there are limits to the extent to which liberalism's "equal opportunity" can really equalize races, genders, and classes; given the conflict, equality matters more to many of us than freedom of speech per se (which begins to look like the threadbare "freedom to offend"). Our emerging view of equality has the advantage of being a measurable quantity, as freedom is not – digital technology is a machine for revealing quantitative inequality where previously there was no way of registering it. So that, whereas print gave birth to modern liberty, digital technology is refiguring our contemporary pursuit of equality as its highest good. If we are sliding toward tyranny, then it will be a tyranny we have continued to opt into only in the service of equality.

Second, our political extremes have in common an attitude of heightened dependence, passivity, and helplessness toward centralized government – the sense that everything is at stake in a presidential election or a Supreme Court vacancy, the desire that management side with us in our grievances,[146] the thought that what is most politically significant is happening at a remove from us and that the solution to political predicaments lies in regulation or deregulation. The question is no longer about the role of government, that is, but about whose side government will bully or be bullied by; our dependence is at once material, political, psychological, and moral. The absence of stable intermediary contexts of action spells the dissociation of each and the centralization of all: the transformation of politics of action into politics of identity, performative outrage, and red herring. These are all both symptoms and causes of our political alienation, of the fact that what is politically significant is only ever at stake elsewhere. Individual agency diminishes and diminishes even as we feel that it grows and grows online. That is the virtual: the bargain by which we can feel more involved at the price of being less effective. Our sickness thus consists in the separation between what "we" must do together and what is up to each of us – in the fact that, in other words, concerted action is so impoverished (if not impossible) for us.

Finally, even as in one sense our political form remains the nation state, in another sense it is misleading to suggest that we live in the same political form that citizens of the eighteenth and nineteenth centuries inhabited. The printed nation state is not the digital nation state. It is not only that so many American promises have been mutilated or unmet, but that the most significant contrast in our political life is not between nation states, but between analogous factions within them. The digital nation state is one in which the "nation" and the "state" find themselves in existential conflict. It is a conflict between one faction that wishes to assert the bare fact of given differences (of history, culture, gender, race and so on) as normative and another that wishes to emancipate human beings from given identities altogether. Each of these poles only makes sense of itself in response to the other's antagonism. Both are looking to make unified sense of themselves, as I've suggested, in international (and perhaps especially in Americanized) terms. Both are in decisive ways unintelligible to each other and incoherent in themselves. (The former cannot account for social fragmentation except by wishing it away, the latter cannot account for itself as a limited political organism at all.) Both positions – the bare "nation" and the rational "state" – are working in their ways to destroy the possibility of political life with each other. There can be no such thing as politics where we (think we) have nothing in common.

The peculiar versions of this conflict are not interchangeable; while the division spans borders, it is the culture of each nation state that will supply the substance for each case. Nor do I mean to suggest that these intra-national conflicts will do away with international ones. It is, rather, that the most salient political factions within digital nation states will be increasingly legible precisely as instances of a new, simplified pattern of division between those asserting the ultimate significance of ascriptive characteristics and those asserting the ultimate insignificance of local or common differences. The political life of the digital nation state will consist in managing permanent and dysfunctional instabilities borne from the "state's" identification of new social categories to neutralize in confrontation with the "nation's" reactive insistence that such categories must count as authoritative just as we find them. This is the international restatement of our individual digital selves, writ-large: the perfect clarity of the virtual mind in its balked attempts to get over and digest the residual opacities of our historical home. (Yet what's self-evident is not what's politically reasonable; yet what is given is never just a given.) It's the grind and grudge of these two errors that supplies the matter for the open-ended project of the politics of everywhere at once (that is, of political undoing). This is what we are working on together, our common cause. Who leads the way?

3.6   EVERYWHERE LEADERS: LITTLE MEN, BIGLY

> *Who will be general of an overly excessive number, or who will be herald, unless he has the voice of Stentor?*
>
> (Aristotle, *Politics*)[147]

What do Abraham Lincoln, Franklin Roosevelt, Ronald Reagan, and Donald Trump have in common? Each was extraordinarily successful at working out the terms of his particular media environment. Lincoln's eloquence was borne of circumstances that placed a premium on virtues specific to the rhetoric of the printed and oral word. The first Lincoln-Douglas debate ran to three hours of talk before a local Illinois audience. A later one totaled seven hours of talk (not counting a dinner break).[148] Roosevelt's fire-side chats ran to about thirty minutes each; they were likewise instrumental in allowing him to justify his policies within terms of apparent heart-to-heart intimacy – tens of millions tuned in with attentive interest to hear the refined and magnetic voice of a frail-looking man. Reagan was not the first president of the television era but, like Kennedy, he looked the part: it is only within a media environment in which television predominates that actors become viable political candidates. Trump was, along the same lines, our first internet president. The whole world signed in to watch and comment.

Some permanent features of online politics are easy to forecast. The micro-management of election campaigns by data – a fine-toothed approach to political ads, grassroots recruitment, and fund-raising – is surely here to stay. The days in which candidates for anything must knock on doors are over. And social media demands a kind of vis-à-vis familiarity that has been put to good effect by the broadcasts of politicians as different as Beto O'Rourke, Matteo Salvini, Benjamin Netanyahu, Nayib Bukele, and Volodymyr Zelenskyy. Other developments are harder to extrapolate, since we cannot yet separate them from

Donald Trump's meteoric success. It is true that he first entered public consciousness not on the internet, but on TV. It is also true that he represents only
one type of online politician – a president who, despite his background, has
claimed nationalist appeal. The globalist alternative is someone like Alexandria
Ocasio-Cortez, who – by fusing candid videos and political harangue into a
celebrity-millennial-socialist brand – is media-savvier than President Trump, if
less successful. (President Biden represents, in contrast, a nostalgic throwback,
a limited-edition vintage figure – the oldest man to assume the presidency is a
self-conscious attempt to revert to an earlier "normal.") That Trump thrived by
galvanizing the new medium, however, that the internet has been a necessary
instrument of his political success, that he has shown an artist's genius for chan-
neling media forces to his benefit in a way that will be impossible for future politicians to dismiss, is a dead cert. Whatever one may think of him, he has been a
world historical president: a leader not simply produced by his conditions, but
able to transform them through new insights into the nature of political power.

Trump understood, for starters, that we are addicted to the sense that something mad must always be happening; that politics must be riveting and sensational online; that the fact of being in the spotlight is more important than
the reasons for it; that having an influential "brand" matters more than being
right; that arresting attention by controversy and polemic is, day in and out,
to control the terms of debate. He campaigned with free publicity, which he
had by virtue of already being a recognizable celebrity. (Not just any kind of
celebrity, furthermore, but a reality-TV icon notable for the performance of
corporate authority.) He is, as is often noted, the best thing that has happened
to moribund traditional news media, which saw a sudden boom in readers and
subscribers: he is walking clickbait, a steroid to the metabolism of the daily
news cycle. He was not simply covered by the news; he actively created it. The
revolving door between the White House and Fox News was well known. The
hiring and firing of White House personnel had all the plot twists one would
wish for from four seasons of a drama. He has been extraordinarily successful
at coining phrases and putting them into wide circulation ("nasty woman,"
"Liddle Marco," "Pocahontas," "Lyin' Ted," to name some of the PG-rated
ones). His showmanship was effective precisely because he has a sharp ear for
pop culture and shares the widespread contempt for professional expertise;
his speech and gestures seem to require no translation; he understands how to
frame an issue so as to be of passionate popular interest. A border wall, for
instance, is a more commonsensical, "real," and meme-ready solution than a
higher-tech, multi-part approach to immigration – the wall's symbolic appeal
is to offer up a brute concrete fact to a world of liquid virtual identities.

He realized that words are cheap and that logical consistency is of little
importance within our online media environment. Where "I was for it before I
was against it" was a gaffe that sunk John Kerry's candidacy in 2004, Trump
saw that flip-flopping is a positive asset when it comes to generating headlines
every day. ("I don't see any reason why it *would* be Russia" became "*wouldn't*

be Russia" the next day: there was never a retraction, only new versions.[149])
He taught us not to mind his words or their coherence, except as parts of the
stochastic process of figuring out how to push our buttons or as speculative bids
for more publicity. His inconsistency worked in his favor, since people could
tune in to his smorgasbord of views for permission to believe what they already
wanted to. He scarcely could be said to formulate arguments for his positions:
he had no truck with reasons or values, only with interests. He sensed the void
in public reason and used it to weaponize information in order to castigate his
opponents ("fake news!" "hoax!"). The fact of contesting what was said was
more important than what or why; as in advertising, notions became narratives
by dint of repetition. He understood that you may change your mind as often as
you like, so long as you do not admit you were wrong – and that watching you
brazen it out becomes part of the amazing scene itself. Disruption and polarization were the end, not the means. The backlash was the message. He realized
that speech online is all talk, and that all talk is for show.

He presented himself as the president of authenticity. He used social media
to great effect, blurring any line between his ruminations about Celebrity
Apprentice and policy announcements, firings, and other presidential decisions. (He tweeted about 25,000 times during his tenure.[150]) He succeeded in
presenting his bluster and vulgarity as a kind of raw truthfulness (@*real*Don-
aldTrump) – cultivating the style of confessional intimacy that we have been
taught to expect from reality television and online celebrities. His boosters liked
that he told it "like it is," that he didn't "parse every word:"[151] in other words,
he mastered the popular equation of what is shameless and spiteful with what
is authentic and sincere, of breaking rules or flouting conventions with being
true to self. He throve on vicarious outrage against political correctness and
its pieties; many identified with him for this reason. "It's a mirror of the way
they see *us*."[152] His shoot-from-the-hip, "honey badger" brass rendered him
impervious to the criticism of many of his own party who gave him a pass
as prone, like any marketer-in-chief, to embellishment and exaggeration. ("I
could stand in the middle of 5th Avenue and shoot somebody and I wouldn't
lose voters."[153]) He was successful at managing to seem more "unfiltered" and
uninhibited than any of his opponents – but for Stephanie Clifford, an exception proving the rule.

He promoted himself as a president of immediacy, one possessed of a man-
date directly from the people, presenting the media and the technocratic elite
as obstacles to the popular will. He campaigned as an outsider, as someone
whose lack of political experience was a qualification, as someone not identified or affiliated with the political class. He continued while in office to campaign for the disruption of existing norms and institutions, for skepticism of
expert opinions, for draining "the swamp," for destroying the "deep state" –
his was a "wrecking-ball presidency," his statesmanship was "shock-jock"
diplomacy.[154] (He bragged about not having the patience to sit through long,
detailed briefings.) He strove to "disintermediate" politics by foregoing the

usual norms of the office and by going so far as to present himself as an adversary to the state agencies under the executive branch, surrounding himself with staff and cabinet with little or no experience of government. He sought in this way to be the "Uber of politics"[155] – his political theory was to seek direct rule, the immediate exercise of authority, while avoiding the staples of post-war political dealing, which paid lip-service to multilateralism and negotiation.

All of these principles have made him an extraordinarily polarizing figure. Yet his very unpopularity was his greatest political asset, allowing him to alternate between the roles of lib-owning champion and spotless victim in the struggle between the people and the elite: each the enactment of a satisfying and complementary wish-fulfillment. He was a middle-finger to progressivism, mainstream media, and the settled norms of the establishment. Since he himself hardly typified his average supporters, this identification was achieved by demonstrating that he was anathematized by the same cosmopolitan class that has passed them by and cast them out. He thrived on the sense that he was a target of unreasonable and unthinking persecution ("witch hunt!"). His presidency needed the Manichean conflict between cosmopolitanism and nativism – he did not pretend to speak for *the* people, but for *his* people. He understood the connection between identity politics and the politics of grievance: he made white identity politics the center of a minoritarian strategy. And he understood that, within a situation of widespread anxiety about globalism, atomism, placelessness, and diffuse roots, people are hungry for sharper forms of self-definition – a self-reinforcing project, since being a "Trump voter" means something more definite than being a "Reagan voter" ever did or could. Eighty-eight percent of those who voted for Trump in the 2020 election considered the results illegitimate.[156] "Stop the steal" is not just a slogan, but a political identity: "we're all victims. Everybody here," he announced at one of his last, post-election rallies.[157] Each and every controversy of his presidency thus required his supporters to double down on him and recommit to the truth of this one fact. He is the most popular president with the Republican base on record;[158] a huge majority those who voted for him the first time did so again.

Trump is of course the consequence of conditions other than the internet; where political processes of compromise and negotiation are jammed, the paranoid style of politics is more likely to arise. His supporters will claim that American politics was already void of substance and that only he understood how to maneuver with clarity within that situation. How one finally feels about him will of course depend on one's estimation of the china shop. Still, what is perhaps most remarkable about the whole of his presidency is the unprecedented dislocation of words from deeds, of rhetoric from policy, of means from meaning. Trump has never exactly cared about politics or government; there was nothing systematic or deliberate about his years in office. But he understood that Americans don't really care either, and that to dominate national news through the politics of consuming outrage is more appealing than the usual centrist pieties. These are telltale indications that the predominant medium of political life finds itself at odds with the message – that we are in the process of transposing our national politics into a new key.

I mean that most of the controversies surrounding the Trump administration were not about matters of substance. They involved what Trump said and how others reacted to it – how it looked, sounded, or played. If Rip Van Winkle had slept from 2015 until 2021, and had been simply handed a summary of Trump's done deals (tax reform, Supreme Court nominations, an immigration ban from certain countries, pulling out of the Paris Accords, moving the American Embassy to Jerusalem), Rip could not have formed anything like an accurate sense of what was unusual about this presidency. And yet, when the President of the United States could be found vituperating particular newspapers or TV channels or websites, when he did not unequivocally disavow the support of white nationalists, when he was obliging to foreign dictators or refused to acknowledge their role in meddling with American elections, when he disparaged members of his own cabinet or entire countries, when he traded insults with sports stars or with dictators possessed of nuclear weapons, when he badmouthed the war record of decorated veterans and their families, or when he publicly encouraged his Vice President to decertify the results of the 2020 presidential election, it was difficult not to take his words seriously.

Said more exactly: these controversies were precisely *about* the question of whether they really were matters of substance – did he sincerely mean them or was he just spit-balling? Were they real or fake? Does he really think he lost the election or is he just cultivating his brand by contesting it? Part of the excitement of Trump – whether following him in the news or attending his rallies – is wondering just what outrageous thing he will do next. These are questions that are familiar to us from discussing celebrities like Kanye West, Borat, Lady Gaga, and WWF wrestlers – figures from pop culture whose public lives consist of a running reality act (right?) – but had never been translated so directly onto politics. Trump's tightrope performance of a post-ironic, counterfactual presidency reached occasionally sublime heights: in October 2019, he tweeted a picture of himself awarding a Medal of Honor to a dog. While the event never took place, it embarrassed mainstream media into berserk indignation and then sheepish retraction. It was continually impossible to decide whether the joke was on him or on us, whether he was really the president or only impersonating one: the marks, in sum, of a perfect troll (or bot).[159] Trump is impervious to political satire for this reason.

Trump rhetorically transformed the "role" or "figure" of president; he showed no interest in the family-friendly, reassuringly decent demeanor that we had expected from the commander in chief for the past fifty years, opting instead for a much edgier, avant-garde interpretation in which words became gambits for attention with but tenuous connection to the offline world. Yet to be forced to disregard the ordinary, public sense of the words of our single most important public servant is to deny that they have any meaning for the purposes of supposedly deliberative, democratic life; it is to issue formal permission to disbelieve that there is anything like extant public sense to appeal to. The restraint once deemed appropriate to the office of the president – however dull, however imperfectly maintained, however false at times – was not simply a matter of optics. It was a form whose virtues could be variously embodied by the actors who inhabited it and a means of expressing the fact that the executive should not be a contender, but the expression of the people's will: the living law. When Trump casually attacked rights and institutions, when he ran together policy disagreements with personal vendettas – refusing to separate the content of political debates from the identities of the participants – he was therefore not simply expressing a difference of opinion within the conditions of his authority, but degrading the liberal framework that sustains it in typically digital terms. Trump is not a "hypocrite," because hypocrisy pledges allegiance to a norm. Trump is the norm unmasked and the new norm of norm-unmasking: not simply what liberal politicians have been "all along," but a new kind of role that consists in performing identity into being. There is no measure of political justice or injustice in such terms, only "winners" and "losers" in the struggle for popularity. Winning is good so long as one is on the winning side; but liberal institutional norms exist precisely as a protection against the fact that one is *not* always at winning, and that even in loss there must be government in common.

Trump's emphasis on picking one side and winning is not gratuitous, however, nor was it simply borne from the realization that some have been "losers" to global capitalism. Trump understood, above all, how to transform our somewhat staid, apathetic, and anodyne national politics into an aesthetic war waged through pop culture's symbols, tokens, and provocative gestures – saturating everything and implicating everyone's responses. Trump managed to resurrect the moribund practice of politics into a collective hallucination of it. He delivered a carnivalesque spectacle that possessed us all to feel we were to answer for it: we were all part of a larger purpose once more, reacting without acting, all part of the show of excess and of force.

This was in part because Trump and Trumpism see our need for political participation, for the thrill of feeling actively engaged in conflict. Our votes are no longer to be won by pivoting toward the center (as the politicians of the milquetoast 1990's did). Digital politics is centrifugal, rather than centripetal. The point is to avoid conciliation and boring policy questions, while stoking existing cultural differences into the blood sport of meme wars and cancellation – pseudo-controversies that reliably incite everyone's gut sense. The rise of QAnon during Trump's presidency mirrors this feature: QAnon does not exactly function as an earnest political faction, as much coverage of its conspiracies implies, but as a social network that treats elements of national politics as episodes of an online game.[160] It dovetails with many other new online trends that enlist users into shared sleuthing and active speculation, often with weirdly ironic or illegible connections to events themselves.[161] Trump realized, through his own tactical intransigence and conspiracy-dabbling, that by making everything the matter, we would all be compelled to role-play the game of trying to figure it out.

But Trump also understood that such a culture war is the greatest form of entertainment available to us, because it speaks to our need for definition. We desire conflict in order to define ourselves; it is through the friction of politics that we come to understand who specifically *we* are. "The enemy is our own question embodied," as Carl Schmitt put it, because our identity is what emerges from the clash.[162] Since the end of the Cold War, our sense of who "we" are has become correspondingly diffuse – neither Al Qaeda nor ISIS nor the Taliban ever emerged as the sort of existential threat that could have defined us into being. By abandoning the presumption to compromise, persuasion, or discussion, Trump's take-no-prisoners attitude cemented preexisting conflicts of American life into a genuine friend/enemy antagonism. Social differences have been politicized, such that the enemy is no longer without – no longer the justification for why "we" are a nation – but within. In the absence of the possibility of international conflict, we have devised a new enemy (and it is us). Overthrowing an enemy is a self-contained political purpose; it does not need to offer constructive or substantive proposals to compel our devotion. It is enough that the enemy suffer defeat. And any conflict that takes place mainly through the spectacle of being in conflict, through "flame wars" and power moves, cannot but continue to escalate.

Just how consequential this presidency will prove to be to the institution, just how much online speech is hollowing out our shared principles, will only gradually become clear. That the aesthetic style does not simply leave the content intact, however, that a national discourse that is at odds with its political reality will then corrode the latter, cannot be doubted. Trump's presidency did not achieve an altogether new digital form; it was too dependent on its revanchist antagonism toward the old paradigm. His leadership was contrarian rather than conservative, distracting rather than concentrating. His reliance on Twitter text (rather than on video or on virtual aesthetics) is instructive for this reason: his use of information has been socially disintegrating, it does not function as a myth or narrative such as could found a new digital people. As the age of Trump has been primarily about (mis)information – about simplifying and resolving American society into its incompatible elements – a rough new myth is therefore slouching toward Washington, in readiness to be born. With the invention of writing, empires replaced nomadic tribes across the face of the world. Two or three millennia later, those empires bit the dust when a German artisan figured out movable type: the birth of the nation state. What now?

4

Realities of Our Own Contrivance

I don't like work—no man does—but I like what is in the work—the chance to find yourself. Your own reality—for yourself not for others—what no other man can ever know.

(Conrad)[1]

I only know that I saw my wish outside of me.

(Eliot)[2]

If media are latent with political possibilities, they are also latent with specific metaphysical assumptions – assumptions about what the world means by virtue of our meaning it in these terms. Without exaggerating the character of this dependence to the point of crude determinism, one might say that each medium emphasizes a different metaphysical question. The medium of writing originally asked us to consider what is true regardless of the context of its reading. What can be communicated that escapes circumstance? What remains true, once etched into stone or inked onto papyrus? Writing made possible a new sense of the universal: the history of peoples, a distinction between nature and convention, and new scriptures of commandment writ. The printed word, with its ready multiplication of voices and perspectives, places the accent on the Cartesian questions of modernity: How can I be sure? What am I in a position to know, where what is knowable can no longer be settled by authority alone? Once many or most have become readers, the printed argument must be certified by evidence available to me. I become the center of experience, the locus of truth. Print led, along these lines, to the novelization of the inner self in unprecedented ways – the intimacy of the heart, the unconscious psyche, the mazy ways of wayward sentiment, incentive, and self-deceit. Who am I, after all?

The digital's question is, in turn, what is *real*? That is, what is the difference between the real and the virtual? And why does that difference matter? What is the value and status of experience itself? Because no other medium has come so close to competing with, defining, and displacing our sense of reality. To be online is an aesthetic experience in its own right, one in which we take self-evident satisfaction. It is (sometimes) to zone out, to escape, to lose oneself down rabbit holes, to be absorbed by the experience of wielding so much power with so little effort. Video platforms will autoplay the next video or "infinite scroll," because their programmers understand Newton's first law of attentional inertia: that a viewer always tends to remain a viewer so long as unacted on by an external impediment. (In other words, that all viewing naturally aspires to the condition of bingeing.) But it is also, as I have said, increasingly the stage on which we perform the personae of our romantic, professional, and social lives. Our profiles are *where* we understand ourselves to be, the terms in which we see ourselves at stake and taking public place. It is our chief and irreplaceable means of self-expression, self-sale, self-creation – three aspirations inseparable in the kind of narrative we must tell to be seen and therefore must decide to tell one way or another. There is no real substitute.

The printed word never threatened to addict us to its reality. The act of reading is not intrinsically pleasant, nor is it written into our genetic makeup in the way that speech is. Being able to lose oneself in a book is not for everyone; it is a reward for many years of being schooled in sitting unnaturally still and learning to conjure worlds from scribble. And while we know a few stories about those who could not keep straight the difference between what they read and lived, those characters remain, like Don Quijote or Emma Bovary, either saintly or deluded *ad absurdum*. The digital is, as I've said, not just another medium in the sequence, but a capacity different in kind – a ready extension of our innate capacities, a medium of attention and will, and in this sense a natural technology.

There is no obvious reason why we should not regard our time spent before a screen as any less real than our time reading a book or staring at an ant; if anything, our time there is supposed to be one of "heightened" or "enhanced" reality. And yet, even as more of our experience becomes inextricable from its online terms of use, we nonetheless continue to insist on marking a difference in kind between time online and anything else that makes up *real life*. All our locutions for what is *not* virtual are subtended by an anxious reference to brute facts – as if we are in need of reassurance that "brick and mortar" commerce, or "real-life" skills, "real time," or "real space" (or "meatspace"), or "reality-based government," or "physical" reality, or just plain "life," are all something altogether different from screen time. It is utterly commonplace to lament the particular *unreality* of being online, the toxic self-indulgence of wasting time online and mistaking images for the genuine article. Virtual reality (like reality television) means it's not real.

When she quit Instagram in 2015, teen celebrity Essena O'Neill broadcast her decision with a widely shared *cri de coeur*. She says to the camera, with tears in her voice:

Taking myself off social media is a wake-up call to anyone and everyone who follows me. I had the "dream life." ... I had it "all" and I was miserable. Because when you let yourself be defined by numbers, you let yourself be defined by something that is not pure, that is not real, that is not love ... There are people around you. Go do things that you love to do in the real world ... You can go outside and meet people and feel connected; you don't need to prove your value on social media.[3]

Her appeal is specific to social media. But her description is especially interesting on account of how characteristically she contrasts what is "pure" and "real" with what is not on the screen, such that *anything at all* – like the very act of going outside – counts as more worthwhile than being on social media. The crepuscular unreality of social media is, as she admits, borne from the possibility of dreaming oneself into being – living by numbers – even as she identifies that very possibility with the alienation of numerical adulation. She was living the dream, but it is one from which she calls us to "wake up." Those numbers didn't add up to anything.

Of course everyone on social media already agrees with some version of the sentiment she is expressing. Of course the video went viral. Of course questions were soon raised about O'Neill's sincerity, and hotly discussed. And yet here we are, online nonetheless. There is nothing so commonplace as taking to the internet to deplore it. Where else are we supposed to go? To complain about it in print is to preach to the choir – like lamenting the tawdriness of NASCAR in the pages of the *London Review of Books*. The medium vindicates itself precisely through our criticism, absorbing all heat by letting us blow off steam, becoming our chief vehicle of wholesale protest even as it thereby renders protest inconsequential. Almost all such criticism in effect unsays itself; it is a matter of words conceding in practice that the medium is irrefutable and irreversible, that its terms of service are beyond us. As Margaret Thatcher said (of capitalism): "[T]here is no alternative." Or, more precisely: The alternative has no place to show itself in these terms. (O'Neill herself rejoined Instagram a few years later, with the declaration that "Social Media is NOT real life" in her bio.[4])

This difference between our desire to be online and our sense of unreality is but one version of the permanent mismatch between our immediately arresting sense of our digital agency and our wider judgments about the internet's role in our life and culture. What I am doing now online is always somehow an exception to the rule: It is too inconsequential to make a difference to larger social pathologies; it is just for fun and for the time being. And it is precisely because our criticisms seem to make no contact with what we happen to be doing that the system as a whole continues its ceaseless expansion. Where's the harm?

Our contrast between our online and offline experiences also raises the deeper question of the relation between time and reality, why we might have positive reasons for preferring online "unreality" to offline "reality." More than hypocrisy or carelessness, digital technology rivets us by conquering our sense of time – being connected affords us the chance to disconnect what we are doing now from the larger shape of our lives. Our digital satisfactions take place at any given moment, whereas our experience of what is valuable offline is usually connected to the longer term. Everyone would agree that it is more rewarding to learn an instrument or to read a book than to be online; but almost nothing offline is as rewarding as being online *now*, and so it never feels to us as if there is a trade-off between these two kinds of things. By spending this minute (this hour, this day) online, I am not giving anything up: We are seduced by the sense that it would be easy to leave at any time, that it is a harmless temptation, that there is nothing at stake, that it is "only" a fluid matter of words, ideal and free. Paradoxically, the lower the stakes come to seem to us, the harder it is to give it up. We prefer to be absent in virtual reality just this once, even as we retain the conviction that it's better to be present in some fuller sense. (Like other visions borne of drugs and dreams, it cannot fully carry over into waking life.) Our time online manages to be at once utterly boring and thoroughly engrossing.

And yet our recurring and insistent contrast between reality and virtuality suggests that there is something more at stake than a difference in relative degrees of entertainment. It helps to work out what we mean by "virtual" in this connection. Latin *virtus* meant the habit of being *actually* effective or excellent. But "virtue" migrated in early modern English from denoting actuality to potential: to have the *power* to do something (as in: that "in virtue" of which so and so is true). We find that sense of the root in "prevail" and "available." It is in this sense that the word also began to be contrasted with what is physical or actual (fully reversing its original meaning), so that "virtual" came to mean "imaginary."[5] The first application of this term to computing dates to the 1959 proceedings of a computer science journal, where the phrase "virtual memory" is employed to describe a software program that could increase a computer's speed without making changes to hardware; that is, from the point of view of a user, the computer would thus act *as if* it were more powerful than its underlying physical capacity would seem to warrant. In the 1960s, "virtualization" was then conceived as a method of running more than one application on one mainframe at a time; the software could act *as if* it were a different underlying operating system. Finally, the *Oxford English Dictionary (OED)* dates the first use of "virtual reality" to a 1979 programming announcement by IBM: "A base to develop an even more powerful operating system ... designated 'Virtual Reality' ... to enable the user to migrate to totally unreal universes." From the outset, virtual space is thus designated as both autonomous and unreal. You can do your own thing here, but only because it's its own thing.

This points to the cardinal conflict within our sense of the "virtual": It is at once what empowers and what simulates, what amplifies our capacities in one way even as it abstracts us from the real in another. The tension is essential to what we mean. Exercising the power to choose something (in general, not just online) is not simply choosing at no cost or consequence, but choosing that thing over competing possibilities. By ordering one dish on the menu, we thereby forego all the others; by marrying one person, we are excluding all others. Our most important choices have weight precisely because our lives (our attention, our working energy, our health and wealth) are limited, so that even when our choices are elastic or changeable, they are so only up to a point. It also follows that what we take most trouble over is usually what is most valuable to us. Where we spend ourselves in time and care, we find deeper satisfactions – such that getting married and tending a garden are more meaningful practices than going on a shopping spree or changing the channel: What takes practice rewards attention, whereas in a hypothetical world in which no possibility closed off any other, our choices would lack any substance at all, since nothing could be at stake in any case. The difference between weighty choices – the choices in which you express and reveal who you are because you must stake yourself on the outcome – and phony or simulated ones would evaporate. It is not just that others would not be able to tell the difference, it is that we would have no way of expressing that difference for ourselves. To become *entirely* virtual would be to become fully artificial and imaginary: all powerful and so all simulated. The Greek root *cyber* means "to steer (a ship)." But the same verb in Latin gives us "to govern": Virtual space is where you rule.

Our life online is not exactly such a world – the time of our life (for one) still limits our decisions. But the argument above is meant to point to the inverse ratio that exists between the possibility of being virtually unconstrained by choice and the way in which it is constraints that give real pressure and weight to the choices we make. In other words, to the extent that we have more choices available to us in any context, *and* to the extent that those choices are easier and more revocable, not only is the weight of any one of our commitments lighter than before, but we blur the difference between living our life and merely performing it, acting it out (for others or ourselves). The more easily you can change your mind, the less any one choice "sticks" to you or serves to distinguish your best self from a mask you may be trying on for size or simulation – and the less the difference matters.

I do not say that it is better to have fewer choices; it is not a matter of the number of choices but of the kinds of choices we make, and the ways in which we then have to live with them. Nor is it impossible to imagine a situation in which one must choose between many very consequential alternatives. But what would make the alternatives so consequential would have to be that they were binding in some way, and this shows that part of our desire to be unconstrained by choice also means that we desire to be able to keep our options open. Here then is the underlying connection between our sense of reality and our sense of time: that our desire for the multiplication of choice is a desire for being in the position to make choices here and now (and then again and again). It is in this sense that being online – by virtue of narrowing our experience of time to the expedience of short-term speed, and by virtue of offering us a window of more or less frictionless possibilities – gives rise to a sense that this is not "real" but "virtual." We are perfectly aware that the real is more substantial (the place of weight and long-term meaning in which our lives are at stake), but we would also prefer not to be bound by its trade-offs. And so the virtual peels off from it as a sort of dream of flying. It's hard to feel that there's any downside, since online time is always only right *now* already, the present absolute. We are only there for the moment, time and again.

This inverse relation between possibility and reality within our sense of what's virtual is not new to the internet. It has long been a theme of critics of modernity that, as autonomy increases and social friction decreases – as who I am is more up to me, as I can reinvent myself – then our capacity for self-deceit, simulacrum, and theatrical fraudulence has advanced accordingly. To be able to *fail* to be yourself is a characteristically modern paradox, just as to be able to be a "hypocrite" (literally: an actor) is a new kind of accusation. Kierkegaard criticized the fact that modern people are only ever *getting ready* to live, because we feel awash in possibilities we never wish to foreclose.[6] Dostoyevsky wrote that we feel "a sort of loathing for real life ... we have come almost to looking upon real life as an effort, almost as hard work, and we are all privately agreed that it is better in books."[7] Autonomy is the greatest modern good; it affords us the privilege and satisfaction of leading our own lives. The ideal of modernity is to become a free agent. But a new problem also emerges alongside this ideal: Who is the "you" who is supposed to do the leading? How can you be sure that you are free, rather than just conforming to various commercial, social, or ideological bromides without realizing it? What is really *yours*? (The posture of nonconformism has itself long been a conformist stance.) It is no accident that our most important commodity is youth, the time of greatest possibility. Nor that our fallback verbal tic is "like." Modernity is the age of acting *as if*.

What is unprecedented online is not the connection between possibility and simulation as such, but the availability of a radically amplified experience of choice in a medium that thereby also raises the contrast between real and virtual to a higher power. Because, as O'Neill's plea suggests, we *do* in fact consciously retain this contrast to the real as what is better or fuller. It is striking that this new medium should, by fantastically increasing the power of virtual choice, also serve to heighten our conviction in the physical world's primary reality.[8] We are aware that where everything is (more or less) a matter of choice, nothing can be very satisfying. We know that there is more to our heart's content than voluntary response and gratification. Our most vivid experiences of delight are encounters rather than choices, contact with the world in ways that are not merely up to us. (Such experiences are few, but precious few.) And we all know the difference between what is fun for now and what will give us more than passing satisfaction: the difference between a numbers game and what really counts.

What is striking is that even while knowing this we are still actively opting for unreality; that we consciously opt for the substitute over the genuine article, the real thing. This is the mismatch I've noted above: the illusory sense that we are only ever choosing just for now, so that the larger picture never feels at stake. But this account is nonetheless too simple, in that it suggests that we have a fixed standard for what is real from which we measure the virtual's departures. This is manifestly not the case – not only because our notion of what is most real is not itself stable, but because it is increasingly defined now as what is *not* online. The real is understood by negative reference to the virtual. Nor is this contrast between real and virtual itself fixed either, since it is the specific task of the virtual to continually approximate the real, and it is the specific temptation of the real to render itself virtual. The two poles are fixed in contrast to each other, even as they are also on an open-ended trajectory toward convergence. That is, we do not find one pole acting on the other, but continuous incursions into either realm, reforming both by comparison. Even as the real and the virtual are opposites, they are opposites that continue to attract, and they will continue to recast our understanding of the world's reality in terms of this progression.

This is, schematically stated, the line of thought that I aim to follow in this chapter: that digital technology is training us not simply to a new sense of what is real and really good, but to a new understanding of the contrasts within which we see that reality. It is by way of these contrasts between real and virtual that we see the programmatic course we're on, the arc of what we are now collectively yearning into being. Digital technology does not have a hidden (or programmed) agenda of its own. But it does embody certain kinds of imperatives or aims that will continue to organize our experience of the world, so long as we continue to use it – "ideals" that define us as digital moderns and that we would otherwise have no occasion or context to pursue. These ideals represent an altogether new stage in our relationship to technology – the point at which human beings themselves become the objects of deliberate design, in which the bounds between what is given and what is made are altogether blurred. And this is the metaphysical sense in which digital technology, as a "natural" technology, discloses the utmost aspirations implicit in modern technology as such: It aims to remake or re-create our given reality in order to surmount it. Yet its greatest power is not to achieve this end – a doubtful possibility per se – but to create from its own shortcomings a spur to still desire it. It is not the technology that transforms us, so much as the fullness of our belief in its transformative powers. The formative power of this convergence thus continually draws energy from its incapacity; the power of the virtual is to continually evade our grasp, even as, in thereby tantalizing us, it recasts our terms for what is real.

I would like to describe three of these underlying ideals in what follows: an ideal of frictionlessness, an ideal of obedience, and an ideal of perfection. Each of these sequentially entails the next: Our search for frictionlessness contains our search for a technology of perfect obedience, while such a conception of obedience in turn contains a view of what human beings should become in utmost aspiration. What is most convenient for me contains a vision of the perfect you; and a vision of the perfect you cannot but also be a vision of my own self best suited to that relation. Each of these three ideals has the character of a moral quest. That is, they are not simply technical problems that can be solved once and for all, but projects that will continuously strive to overcome their obstacles without doing so entirely. In their character of quest, each of these is even now refashioning our senses of reality, creating new worlds of recreation virtually in their image.

4.1 THE IDEAL OF FRICTIONLESSNESS (TO RE-CREATE REALITY)

> All human senses require some input. If they are deprived of it, the mind manufactures its own substitutes.
>
> (Arthur C. Clarke)[9]

> Mr. Watson, come here; I want to see you.
> (The first words ever uttered over a telephone – by Alexander Graham Bell)[10]

As each medium makes available a specific experience of information, a way of taking things in, what is absent from that experience becomes newly scarce and prized. Each medium of communication therefore also tends to emphasize what it cannot offer in its own terms. Media in this sense recoil on themselves; their economy of values creates the conditions for the backlash against them. Thus where forgetting is the norm, speaking must be memorable. Oral poetry was carefully ordered into metrical and narrative schemes the better to know it by heart – the transience of the spoken word prompted the use of mnemonic, highly formalized, ritual protocols of speech. The written word also led the way to new emphases on unwritten and unwritable spiritual experiences (Socrates's, Jesus's, Buddha's) – experiences that consciously aspired to avoid literalism and rule-bound, codifiable prescription. The printed word has, in turn, long been a byword for rote memorization and rigidly typified standardization: Corresponding Romantic reactions to it have preached spontaneity, improvisation, authenticity, and creative ways of going off script. Just so, television came to prize what could be "caught" on camera ("we are here, live!") – the unstaged moment within the norm of carefully programmed performance. The logical extension of this desire has been reality television, which has studied to erase the difference between ordinary actions and acting altogether. The internet has expanded this possibility to every user. ZAO's motto: it takes "just one photo for you to star in all the world's shows."[11]

Unlike previous media, however, the internet is a medium of firsthand experience; it is a "space" where one can seem to feel to "be." I *am* or *go* online; being a user is more like being a speaker of a language than like being a reader, which is a role called for in limited circumstance. And so it is exactly to the extent that the internet feels as if it could be a full replacement for experience that the sensory recoil from it is the more forceful; the experience of being able to summon up just about everything at will focuses attention all the more vividly on its differences from reality, on what cannot be straightforwardly known or seen or acquired at a touch. I've already dwelt on one version of this point: It is because the internet makes human connections more voluntary and accessible that it becomes so easy to wax wistful about community as an uncontroversial good; in doing so, the trade-offs of real community are hidden from view. But the more general statement of our digital recoil is that the very ideality of the medium – its immateriality, speed, and responsiveness to will – calls forth under the name "reality" precisely everything that the medium cannot be or give us. Just as seasoned tourists develop an aversion to what is "touristy," what is real becomes, by definition, what is not the internet, which is in turn what becomes more conspicuously coveted and flaunted in online terms.

One way to think through this reciprocal relation is to examine the aesthetic experience of being online, the way in which each of our five senses is at work there. The internet is a place of ready seeing and hearing – we are all eyes and all ears. The sense that we cannot engage there is touch (to which I also subjoin taste and smell, senses that demand the close vicinity of their objects). Where one can see or hear just about anything within the space of a few clicks – that is, where seeing and hearing are "cheap" – the evocation of touch thus becomes all the more valuable to online content. Enormous regions of the internet are devoted to just that, to engaging, teasing, or tickling our sense of touch.

Consider the popularity of pets online. They account for so much uploaded content partly because they are tactile for us: fuzzy, cuddly creatures with which we cannot communicate in words alone. Or consider the vast array of "handy" content: unboxing videos, say, or videos that display a pair of hands in a first-person position in order to show you how to make something.[12] Consider the fads of "slime-making" and Jell-O videos: The point is to show footage of a squishy substance, a highly haptic, sense-stimulating simulation of food.[13] Consider the mesmeric quality of the genre of videos labeled "oddly satisfying": hours on end of slicing soap or "kinetic sand" or watching hands massage crinkly or soft (and colorful), highly textured goo.[14] The evocation of touch draws us into synesthesia – ASMR triggers a sense of relaxation and tingling euphoria precisely on the scalp and skin. Consider the new fad of celebrity-promoted therapies that rely on the proximity of healing crystals or contact with quasi-magical gems.[15] Consider the rise of Instagram farms and farmer influencers, who perform miserably backbreaking work and getting their hands dirty as a lifestyle that carries nostalgic, spectatorial appeal.[16]

Or consider the conspicuous place that food has long enjoyed in our browsing habits and social media feeds. Food epitomizes what cannot be preserved or shared online; its presence and enjoyment are transient. While it looks appealing, it cannot (unlike a drawing or a song) be consumed in transmission. Cooking shows have long been on TV, but food and cooking (and watching others pig out[17]) have become a more central feature of what we want to see online – partly because we all eat, but partly because to be able to see so much without being able to taste and smell is the very picture of what is tempting. Videos that trick the eye to confuse our sense of what is edible or outrage our tastes are also widely popular; they are forms of trolling possible only because of the scission of sight from touch.[18] To be lonely online is to be "skin-thirsty." And the ultimate tactile experience is, of course, to sear and be seared. In the age's slang: We "flame" people or "torch" them or deliver a "sick burn." What's cool is "fire" or "lit." What's digital dreams of summoning the world to your digits.

All these evocations of touch are a direct consequence of the fact that we experience time spent online as specifically lacking (as being merely virtual because it falls short of reality), that the lack is expressed in our hankering for the sensory stimulus we cannot freely enjoy, and that this lack therefore provides us with one measure for the difference between real and virtual. It suggests, in other words, that our sense of reality is (and perhaps is becoming rather more) a sense of physical presence: To be present is to be able to make an impression, to have within reach, and so our idiomatic ways of describing what is most real are therefore keyed to touch. We speak of a "reality check," of being moved, of making contact, of being struck, of being cut to the quick, of feeling reality's hard edge, and of the forceful impact of what's concrete. While we say that "seeing is believing," dreams and hallucinations teach us that sight is not our most reliable index of reality. We pinch ourselves to see whether we are awake. Aristotle argued that human reason is most fully expressed not in our eyesight but in our fingertips: Our fine tactile distinctions are not accessible to the tough hide and hoof of other animals (so that "thick" and "numb" are still considered attributes of stupidity).[19] The patron saint of skeptics and of early modern science was Thomas the Apostle, who refused to believe in the Resurrection until he had put his finger in Jesus's wounds.[20] Reality is the friction we are forced to come to grips with, our school of hard knocks. If you want to get real, you must come to (all) your senses.

Here's our fix, then. Reality is the touchstone of what exceeds our will, what is not straightforwardly the consequence of our intentions. Reality is the way in which we must come face to face with what cannot be tamed to self's terms, the place where we are vulnerable to change. And yet, given the choice, no one actively prefers to be vulnerable; no one desires the obstacle that pushes back, the unforeseen obstinacy of what resists or thwarts our will. The unreality of digital space derives from the fact that it comes so close to replacing our sense of willing agency, even as it denies us the fullness of presence within which we must act offline, the context and weave of reality itself. It is because our willing feels emancipated that it is so attractive to be online, but it is also for that reason that it feels less real to be there: even as the time of our life is more online, no one is living inside the internet. And so we are caught between the satisfactions of two divided realms: one in which my will is (or seems to be) the virtual law, the other in which I am bound to contact with reality in ways that are not up to me – yet are thereby richer and more meaningful. Friction is what we avoid at all costs: the dull, the painful, the difficult. Friction is what makes life full for living: what we long to have (or to have overcome).

It is a strange feature of this alternative that, as I've said, it does not even show itself. We do not consciously choose "unreality" over "reality," because it never exactly feels as if that choice is truly at stake. Time online is episodic because it is engrossing and it is engrossing because it is episodic, whereas the rewards of time offline tend to be understood as time-bound for the long run. Our sense of time online is often enough a guilty pleasure we can quit at any moment and therefore never have to. ("Tomorrow" and "not yet" are the mottoes of every addict.) Online services therefore need never claim to fully substitute for the real thing: "If you can't be there, feel there," suggests an ad for Portal, Meta's video-chatting device. Being there is better, we agree, but the service helps you make do with something else that's better than nothing (for now). And "better than nothing" is the rule of thumb most likely to prevail in any crisis offering serious trade-offs (like a pandemic) – in other words, the rule by which technological convenience continues to overwhelm other kinds of considerations.

But even if online time does not consciously emerge as a direct rival to "real time," the presence of the choice between these two times (or worlds) nonetheless makes a difference to the terms in which we make all our choices, on and off. In other words, the internet is not simply the "virtual" in contrast to what has been "real" all along. It actually transforms our understanding of reality, causing it to show up for us in new terms.

Here are two analogies for the sort of transformation I mean.

There used to be no such thing as "boredom." No one was bored in ancient times, no one found life blah. At any rate people did not describe their experience in terms that straightforwardly map onto ours; our words for boredom or ennui date from early modernity. The full telling of how we discovered our boredom requires a sweeping psychological and sociological account. But one might take a quick stab at it by observing that the development of boredom is partly connected to the urbanized speeding up of modern societies, the increasingly pressing sense of being busy and otherwise engaged, of being relatively more surrounded by instruments and institutions that (unlike those of predominantly agricultural societies) constantly demand, solicit, and answer readily to our will. The overall effect of these new features is to awaken our expectations of being absorbed, diverted, or entertained – expectations that, when they are not met, we experience as empty, listless time. Yet boredom is not just a new experience appended to what we had before; it responds to a new self-centered desire to keep things interesting, a desire that is now treated as creditable and even authoritative on the question of how we should spend our time; it provides a new primary frame for seeing everything we do. Once boredom was in the picture, new kinds of experiences were explicitly sought out in remedy: gambling, travel, drugs, extreme sports, and all manner of escapes from the drudgery of conforming. Even outside these, the threat of boredom presses us toward modes of engagement that would not have held prior fascination. We have a whole range of practices that we are now routinely told "don't have to be boring" – education, work, cooking, and dental hygiene, say – practices that were formerly simply unavoidable and to which the very notion of fun was therefore irrelevant. The prospect of boredom is so concerning that we have rearranged and redescribed everything *else* we do under the imperative to keep things amusing or engaging. But both the threat and its solutions share the modern assumption that you are the best judge of what tickles your fancy and that your fancy is reasonably entitled to be tickled.

A second example: Consider the way in which office work creates and transforms our understandings of being in shape. There used to be no such thing as "exercise" or "wellness" in their modern senses. Aristocrats throughout the world trained for war or for the ritual prowess that was its offshoot in athletics. But for the bulk of human history, most have had to sweat for their bread and the toil of it was regarded as ignoble. With the advent of a rather sedentary, calorie-rich, post-industrial deskocracy, how to keep our bodies active and healthy shows up as a new problem. Sport was systematically connected to the virtue of gentlemen in the late nineteenth century – all our major team sports were conceived or consolidated in the Victorian era – and it was only in the early twentieth century that exercise was expansively promoted as a choiceworthy concern for all. Yet this new activity is not a return to the physical exertions that previously inhered in daily life: Our leisure time is now what is left over from work. It is scarce, and therefore it too must be rationalized for efficiency's sake. And so exercise becomes another mechanized activity, one requiring facilities, classes, and gear – and one that is monitored, organized, and sold according to the service-industry standards that govern office work. The same logic of quantification and maximization tends to govern work and working out, number-crunching and ab crunches.[21] In other words, once mindwork is separated from bodywork, bodywork is then reconfigured into a new pattern that includes them both in separation. Both of them are reinterpreted in light of the contrast that first generated them. And so, here too, the presence of a powerful new mode of organizing experience (namely: scientific management) does not leave the old categories untouched. Rather, it absorbs and recreates its opposite in its own terms. The introduction of yoga and a host of other "mind–body" services is then one more iteration of the same process: at once addressing a real need and offering new occasions for optimization.

One might multiply these kinds of examples. (Our notions of nature, attention, privacy, and free will have also been continuously constructed in specific opposition to technological encroachments.) I concentrate on them because they offer a way to understand the dynamic relationship that obtains for us between the real and the virtual. As in the cases of boredom and exercise, there used to be no such thing as "reality." There was simply life in its own steady, rhythmic recurrence. "Reality" only showed up as something more than a category of Scholastic philosophy when there was something that could be mistaken for it, when something could seem to stand as an accurate substitute for it at a distance: photography, television, internet. These are media of widespread access in absence, which in turn place new prestige on what is presence. Reality is for this reason not simply a neutral, descriptive term – not something that was there all along – but an aesthetic category of experience as it exists now in specific contrast to life online.

As an instance of this transformation, consider the aura attaching to the term "experience" itself, which has become, like "community," an online obsession. An "experience" refers in part to the aesthetics of consumption or use. Sites prompt us to give feedback in order to improve "customer experience," because their style and user-friendliness are essential to their content – where we cannot lay hands on what we buy, the attractiveness of our "purchase journey" matters more, as does whether we can believe in the authenticity of a brand's narrative of ethical purpose.[22] (Squarespace's motto: "A website makes it real.") But in its broader application, "experience" has become a telling term for what we *cannot* have online – travel, dining, entertainment, adventures, and "events." It thereby also becomes a focal point of online interest and acquisition, a new category to be advertised, consumed, maximized, and displayed online.

An experience is the perfect product. It is exclusive, for one: It is, as Daniel Bell put it, a "positional" rather than a "distributional" good.[23] It cannot be resold, or divvied up, or mass-produced, because it refers to what it feels like to be *you* uniquely witnessing a given reality. Like the internet itself, its value lies in the application of our own attention; an experience should be interactive and immersive. But unlike the internet, it can be "shared" without being shared – others can look in on your experience without being able to claim that *I was there*. So where social media levels us into the same terms, experiences allow us to distinguish ourselves once more by what we can afford. Nor do experiences create attachments or responsibilities. An experience's greatest commercial value lies in its structured transience, in the fact that it disappears as it is used up – a triumph of planned obsolescence – and in its intangible capacity to "create some memories" without clutter. An experience should be memorable to be good, so that the lap of luxury online is billed as an "unforgettable experience," the highest commodity is something that will "change your life" (since what cannot be paid for must be forgettable and inert). A MasterCard ad series tallied up the prices of several items involved in a meaningful experience, only to culminate with the tag that the experience itself was "priceless." ("There are some things money can't buy, for everything else there's MasterCard.") But the point was to suggest that MasterCard was an essential part of enjoying those things that you can't put a price on – that there is a link between price and pricelessness that you can buy into. This is the kind of relationship that also holds between our experience online and our experiences off: An "experience" is therefore both how we escape from time online and how we then arrange our offline lives to look good within the terms of social media. (That we should now have discovered how to sell moments of time as NFTs – such that one can now "buy" a key moment in a basketball game, e.g.[24] – represents one further turn of the same screw, one further step in the capture, alienation, and business of experience.)

This sense of experience as relative to its virtual duplicate comes, more specifically, from the ease with which we circulate online images of ourselves; an experience is an event that can be photographed or documented by video. The enjoyment of its transience exists in reciprocal dependence to its footage. Photography's permanence is what allows us to pursue what evanesces as an end. So it is too that the effortlessness with which we may look at endless photographs of every square inch of the earth continues to whet, rather than slake, our appetite for travel. To see the sights is not enough; we want to be there. Mass (pre-Covid) travel had grown to about 1.4 billion international tourist trips worldwide annually.[25] But the meaning of our travel is itself mediated by photography, since photography is how we certify our presence. As travel is the goal of footage, footage is the goal of travel. No tourist is under the misapprehension that there are not enough high-def pictures of the *Mona Lisa* out there; it is precisely because there *are* so many that the *Mona Lisa* is a worthy object of photography. To photograph oneself with the painting is less a means of creating a souvenir than a way of registering one's sheer *thereness*, one's appropriation of that moment.

This aesthetic property of photography – the power of the photogenic to cause the fake to look real and the real to look fake – is not itself novel.[26] What is new is the pocket-ubiquity of the possibilities of high-quality recording, and the way in which the easy uploading and circulation of online images then figures into our view of who we are (like): The "stories" of our lives are told in sequences of pictures. Not that anyone with any savvy supposes that their online profile counts as their "real" self (#nofilter). That is precisely what it is *not*, so that it has become common practice to keep up separate "fake" and "real" Instagram profiles – the former for the public, the latter for the inner circle – with the predictable further twist that the *real* account is obviously the fake one ("finsta"), the fake the real ("rinsta").[27] An app called BeReal addresses the problem by advertising a "unique way to discover who your friends really are." It takes and shares a picture of you and each person in your clique at a random time each day (giving you two minutes to pose for it).[28] Where communication cannot help but be performance for the global theater, irony layers on irony all the way down: It is this permanent inseparability of the authentic from the fake that is the mark of what is virtual.

The point is that how we picture ourselves online also changes the terms in which we picture and organize our experience of reality as consisting of set-pieces and tableaux made for digital presentation. The emergence of "pop-up" businesses, Instagram museums, eye-candy food, and chamber-of-commerce-sponsored selfie landmarks obeys this logic. So does the ritual recording of life milestones, whereby birthdays, proposals, promposals, college decision reactions, gender reveals, and weddings are conceived with a view to the camera. We are also growing more familiar with the perversions and aberrations of digital "flexing" and one-upmanship: A growing number of teenagers experiencing "selfie-dysmorphia" seek plastic surgery so as to better resemble their photo-filtered selves,[29] murderers live stream their atrocities in real time, and some selfie-seekers have died needless deaths pursuing the perfect shot. The aesthetic imperative of most clips and snapshots is (and can't but be) #YOLO, as it happens.

But the basic expression of this feedback loop between the real and the virtual is the ordinary impulse to reach for one's phone as a response to witnessing what is wonderful, terrific, or in any way extraordinary. Our response to baby's first word, to an explosion, to a sunset, to a pet's she-nanigan, to a gunfight, or to winning the Super Bowl is the same: We verify it for ourselves by showing it to others. iPhoto, *ergo sum* (in other words: "pics or it didn't happen!"). That is, more than just proof of being there, photography or footage qualitatively enhances our presence by giving it per-spective; our manner of dealing with what we witness is to take a picture, just as nothing is more common than for the random witness of an enormity to report that it was all like a movie or like a video game. By capturing the moment and therefore removing us from the time, photography helps us translate the uncanny back into the terms of what we recognize as real (namely: pictures of things) – a way of cutting things down to selfie size, of familiarizing ourselves with our own experience. It is by taking shots that we get to have our moments.

4.1.1   Who Can Resist?

> The more superfluous physical labor is made by the development of technology, the more enthusiastically it is set up as a model for mental work.
>
> (Horkheimer and Adorno)[30]

The other aspect of this change in our sense of reality – in the aura of what happens – stems from the ways digital data puts our time to work. The dig-ital is data, as I've said; its power lies in transforming minute acts of private idiosyncrasy into aggregated patterns of typical use, which are in turn used to refine the service that's on offer. Data counts each one of us in order to add us all up – like/dislike, on/off, 1/o – and then to sell all back to each. (I'll return to this below.) It affords us new ways of monitoring all offline activities by counting our steps, tracking our progress, optimizing our route, and maximiz-ing our performance. But the expanded possibility of micro-quantification not only means a new set of attentional incentives (new kinds of things to count up and on); it means that, so long as one is online or just walking around with a smartphone in one's pocket, one is always (potentially) at work generating data – that is, whatever one does, awake or asleep, one is always on the clock. (TikTok, TikTok.) Our new sense of reality is in this sense defined by the pos-sibility of being productive all the time.

Time online is engrossing, as I've said, because it is episodic. But the succession of episodes is itself a consequence of the data-system of experience in which one is always presented with an unambiguous choice requiring immediate response. There is always something in particular to do because our "tasks" online are punctual and discrete – data points (like clips and pictures) take little or no time; you only need a second or two to glance at your notifications, to ping someone, to check up on what's new. You don't need to set time aside for checking your phone at the expense of other things. This means, in turn, that there is no place for necessarily taking time off or away, as there was from TV or from the telephone or from any device that you could not carry with you. The contexts in which we are forced away from portable screens are therefore either voluntary (we have to make and self-enforce a rule for family meals, say) or vanishingly small (in "dead" zones or on a plane – at any rate during take-off and landing). For better or worse, it was once traditional to do nothing while standing in line or sitting in a waiting room – we had no choice. Now there is always something else, a buffet of feeds designed to busy and amuse. The smartphone is a machine to break time off and fill it, since there is no schedule gap too small for it to occupy. The question is no longer "What now?" but "Why not check?"

The killing of time through mincing tasks amounts, furthermore, to a new experience of work and profit. Time (some people's, at any rate) has long meant money – but there had never been a way to monetize the time and attention of everyone, nor had it been possible to harvest them to a degree approaching totality. If the internet is a medium of experience, then it is an experience in which every act of will is defined and measurable. Data can therefore put leisure to work. To be online is to be engaged in a bidding war for one's attention, even as we serve online services by inputting our responses: The customer is (also) the product; users have their uses. Conversely, the same process allows our work to be at leisure: Where we are always (potentially) in touch, the spatial, temporal, and formal boundaries between being at the "office" and at "home" – and therefore between "boss" and "friend," between the formal and the frivolous – will continue to lose their meaning for any job requiring a computer. (Our work platforms now bear names like Slack, Teams, and Hangout.) Such work is a time-saver with respect to how we were doing things before computers, but not with respect to the world we live in, since the work expected has itself expanded to fill every temporal cranny. The more time we "save" at work, the more we can work, and the less time we therefore have for anything else: To be elite is to be busier.[31] And always being *on* undoubtedly reinforces the sense that we can always be doing more, that we may always be optimizing something (if not Missing Out entirely). So what was once one activity among others (being online) has in this way become the standard by which we organize all we do.[32]

The clearest expression of this colonization of time by data is the gig economy – the sale of piecemeal services through the wholesale coordination of data. Its achievement has not necessarily been to open up new areas of production, but to increase the convenience of trafficking a service – in effect, to shrink the minimum units of employment, to render supply immediately and straightforwardly responsive to demand, and to liquefy the distinctions between professional and layperson. For a free day, my room can become a hotel. For a free hour, my car can become a cab, or I a dog-walker. For a free minute, I can earn pennies on Mechanical Turk. The gig economy means that anyone may transform themselves into a worker at any moment. (I recently waited in line at a restaurant next to someone working for an app service that paid her to stand in line on someone else's behalf: What once was time to pass may now be time to spend.) The "influencer" economy (in which starlets hog everyone's attention) is being replaced by the "creator" economy (in which everyone may sell their experience as content).[33] Apps like NewNew ("decide what people do next") allow users to vote on what sweater a creator should wear that day or whom they should hang out with: a "human stock market."[34] Not surprisingly, this principle lends itself to the sale of sexual performances and their associated abuses, as in the case of OnlyFans.[35] But the general point is that data is the means by which every act of human consciousness can be (potentially) measured for profit. Data means business.

This saturation of time with profit, the volatilization of money into attention, creates the conditions for a backlash against and within the medium itself. Online busyness is such as to give rise to the paradoxical sense that we are not living, not really *doing* something in real life, and therefore that we must now go out of our way to act at all. Our basic sense of interface remains that of an abbreviated experience lacking the substance of what we call reality by contrast: Screens are flat and superficial; our time spent on them is its own thing and out of joint with others. This is the basic worry that is then marketed back to us within the experience economy. The full motto of the Outdoor Voices (an athleisure clothing brand) is "Doing things is better than not doing things" (#doingthings). Chase Bank instructs me to "Go. Do. See." REI suggests we "Opt to Act" (#optoutside). Such aspirations would be barely comprehensible (let alone appealing) outside the internet age.[36] It's all happening, but the quality of our involvement means that we find ourselves both relentlessly busy and uncertain about whether we are doing anything at all.

A contrasting impulse to doing more is trying to do less: to find ways of quitting the online treadmill. Where busyness is by default, the task becomes to opt out. A recent book by Jenny Odell teaches us *How to Do Nothing* – how to step back from our permanent and anxious attention to the internet.[37] Doing nothing (in other words, being offline) is here a new form of rebellion, of refusing to be "on." Nihilism is a form of activism. But taking it easy turns out to be hard work – work that only the richest and poorest can undertake at any length – so that being conspicuously offline is also now becoming a commodity of prestige (just as the notion of doing nothing has been reabsorbed, in turn, into the online economy of "self-care"[38]). More screen time is, on the one hand, increasingly linked to lower incomes.[39] Just as there is a statistical connection between poverty and obesity in the United States, there is a connection between poverty and what Matthew Crawford calls attentional obesity.[40] But whereas many middle-class school districts now hand out tablets or laptops to every enrolled student, the wealthiest Silicon Valley employees (like drug pushers the world over) do what they can to prevent their children from growing up as users.[41]

Our unease with being too virtual is also patent in a whole array of practices, organizations, and products designed to help us take our time (offline). As the digital speeds us up, the Slow Movement has fast gained adepts in response. There is slow parenting, slow food, slow fashion, slow gardening, slow gaming, and slow marketing; in all such cases "slow" is a synonym of higher quality, of choosing to do better at the cost of choosing not to do more. Apps selling "mindfulness" and meditation abound. So too the projects of "downshifting," "digital fasts," "digital detox," and "digital decluttering" are intended to address our need to escape from the hyperkinetic demands of being wired at all times, even as they are marketed to us as new kinds of wellness fads. A popular internet-blocking app is called Freedom (it promises that you will "be more productive"[42]). Whether it is "unstructured" play time for children, quiet retreats for tech executives, or all kinds of events in which technology is formally proscribed from periods of reflection, being offline is all the rage. If you want to be Highly Elite, make sure you take no pictures of your dinner at all.

More unnervingly, many technology companies are introducing the possibility of monitoring and managing one's use of them as features *of their own products*. Apple has now introduced a Screen Time app that allows one to view and set limits on the time one spends online. It includes a "family sharing" option for parents to remotely control their children's activity. Facebook and Instagram have followed suit, offering us the option of keeping track of how long we spend on the app, and reminding us to close it after some (user-specified) amount of time. And Google has launched a Digital Wellbeing suite containing suggestions, tools, and features "to help you achieve your personal sense of digital wellbeing." The site offers an unctuous, quasi-therapeutic survey to "reflect on your relationship with tech" (the button one clicks is itself called an "experience"). It encourages us to "unplug more often," to minimize distractions from our screens, and even "to explore offline activities," "so that life, not the technology in it, stays front and center."[43]

The rhetoric of "digital wellbeing" shares our assumption that time online is not "real" time, is not "life," so that these companies now take "our side" in our struggles against using their very services. But this is like holding an AA meeting in the aisles of a liquor store. Disingenuous or not, these measures only bespeak the awesome control that they exercise over our attention. The fact that they can encourage us to use their products less suggests how little concerned they are that we will cease to use them at all. It also suggests that they (and we) increasingly view the ability to refrain as an important feature of those very products. A phone that helps me *not* use it more is that much more convenient and desirable. Non-use thus becomes a feature of our use. The implication is that our use is itself a problem susceptible to a technical fix. We are thereby given the opportunity to buy back control of our own time offline.

My point is not to condemn the existence of these emerging practices and products designed to help us manage our online use: Two cheers for the work of mitigation they help us to perform. But the larger issue is that online time is something we need help managing at all, that without concerted effort it is something we feel might run away with us, and that the contexts of our non-use and offscreen time have become a distinct and salient category of experience as they never were or could have been before. As in the examples of boredom and exercise, the presence of the virtual is so compelling as to transform our attention to and understanding of what counts as real in contrast. Where once there was no reality as such, what we call "reality" is now becoming an object of choice in the ways I've described. Where once it was occasionally possible to opt out of "reality" (by taking drugs, say), it is now increasingly necessary to think about how to opt in to it. And all the while, the internet does duty as the master metaphor in terms of which we make the contrast between the real and the virtual. It at once promotes our interest in reality precisely as what is not virtual, while also seamlessly incorporating what we do offline into the logic of its online concerns. Reality and virtuality make up a closed, mutually reaffirming circle. This is the mark of how utterly transformative the digital is: It is restructuring our understanding and experience of the real so as to be something that we define in specific contrast to the virtual. What is digital is what is not real; what is real is what is not digital. There is no getting out of it.

Perhaps the deeper question is why we then continue to put any stock in reality at all, why the virtual continues to enhance the stock we put in what is "real" rather than absorbing and superseding it altogether. The internet is a medium of absence that nonetheless promotes presence; but what is there to the presence that we miss? Above I have described the way in which the virtual elicits our desire for touch, because touch is precisely what is absent from online experience, as well as what happens to be (or has increasingly become) our most vivid and distinct sense of what is real. But touch too will soon enough be digitally simulated and marketed. There are already "augmented reality" devices that aim to replicate the textures of experience. If Smell-O-Vision or 4D theaters have not yet caught on, some version of the "feelies" of *Brave New World* – high-tech movie theaters in which the audience can touch the show as well as see it – is on the way, and there is no technical obstacle to its one day providing an imitation as passable as those we have for sight and hearing.[44]

Yet our desire for the reality of touch (with taste and smell) is more than just a desire for the data of a phantom sense. Touch marks the presence of the real not because we miss the input to complete our simulation, but because it functions as shorthand for our desire to track the difference between what is staged for us and what is authentic, what is contrived by my will and the terms of a reality that exceeds it. The tangible is what carries weight, what is solid and concrete. It is the source of existential friction. The screen is virtual, on the other hand, because it is pluripotent and responsive to my bidding – it can put so many experiences into one display exactly at the cost of translating experience into the ephemeral facility of moving pictures. The analogue forebear of the internet was the shopping mall, a unified environment in which our whole attention, motion, and sensory experience could be coordinated toward going with the flow of shopping. The overall aesthetic effect – the soft lighting, the muzak ambience, the narcotic smells of reassurance wafting out from Cinnabon and Yankee Candle – was therefore vaguely surreal. It is, in the same vein, no accident that Apple's rule of design has been "no hard corners: humans are soft and shapes should be too," and "make it lickable."[45] Its products' look, like their uses, smooth the cutting edges of reality. More than appealing to our senses, these frictionless aesthetics betoken a concept and ideal that finds response in us.

The express goal of virtual reality (VR) technologies and the tacit goal of online services like the Metaverse remain to recreate reality, to deliver experience as "immersive" and "surround" as the real thing. This need not be as creepy as the feelies are in *Brave New World*. Jaron Lanier has made an eloquent case for VR as a sort of "art of experience" – not a technology designed to displace reality, but one that would allow us to explore it from the inside out in unprecedented ways (e.g., by experiencing the world as some animal would or as someone with a different kind of body).[46] I think Lanier underestimates the strength of our preference for unreality over reality, our penchant for our own captivity. But he is right that the ideal of VR is not, after all, to reproduce the world just as it is – to return us to sensory square one, to replace our ordinary world with another one of the same sort – but rather to reproduce the senses of reality within the terms of virtuality. The goal is to create a sense-experience that follows from and is given meaning by my will – to abstract from what is real in order to create a world in which I can exercise powers of choice I do not ordinarily have. Yet it is this abstraction that also makes this world virtual, so that it is to the degree that I succeed in recreating experience within my own terms that that world must continue to fall short of what is most real. We are each of us naturally born into the center of the worlds we inhabit, of course, but our sense of reality stems from our awareness of the limitations of this view. And so the feeling of what happens will continue to be the aim of better and better technological approximation, even as what makes things most real is precisely the fact that they are not reducible to the terms of our feeling or willing them at all.

This ambivalence underlying our desire for touch as a marker for the real can be described in terms of our incompatible desires for friction and frictionlessness.

The pleasure of being online, its relief, originates from its comparative frictionlessness, the way it smooths attention's sailing toward its objectives. Our online "presence" consists in what we wish to input – say what you will, and if you don't feel valued: bail. It maximizes the exercise of my will by minimizing the contexts in which I have to compromise on my preferences with others. So too the intrinsic ideal of online services, is, as I've mentioned, the "seamless" or "positive" experience, a means of deciding and acquiring without hassle. The goal of commerce has always been to give you the thing that you didn't know you wanted. But digital platforms have finessed the architecture of choice to the point where they really can anticipate the desires they have trained us to formulate: from autocorrecting the word you meant to write to identifying the next product you'd like to buy. About 70 percent of what we watch on both Netflix and YouTube follows from the sites' automated recommendations; and about 35 percent Amazon's profits come from personalized product ads.[47] "What would you like the power to do?" asks an online banking service. A Chinese news platform's slogan answer: "only what you care about."[48] (Though one is tempted to put quotation marks around "only," "what," "you," and "care about.")

Frictionlessness is also what underlies and entails the digital transformation of time I've noted above. Speed is the feeling of convenience, an experience of the will, since convenience, like time, is a relative measure of our needs and expectations. If dial-up once seemed a miracle of celerity, it has now grown unbearable. The faster things can go, the slower others feel; the more convenient things are, the more salient are inconveniences; the more engrossed we are in novelty, the more boring it becomes. More than just a sociological phenomenon about the pace of life, this change also bespeaks a more basic reorganization in our very selves – not just in our attention span, but in our contact with reality. We value speed to save time – time that we then spend either by being more "productive" or by devoting it to "what really matters." But in both cases a heightened experience of speed implies a heightened experience of what serves our purposes: a sharpened contrast between what we would like to do and what we would prefer not to do. The word "convenience" means (etymologically) what goes your way. It suits you because it agrees with you.

This seems, on the face of it, like an unmixed benefit. Leading our own life means making our own choices. And it seems improbable that choosing to waste time on trivial tasks that can be quickened by digital means could in itself be worthwhile. Yet our heightened sense of timeliness is a product of convenience, one that concentrates our experience on our own self's ready-made preferences, on having our way within the narrowing terms of whim. The fastest interface is the peak of convenience, and the peak of convenience is that in which there is least friction between my will and its objectives. Time online is me time; to feel happy there is to be a satisfied customer: a virtual reality.

There is thus something barren about the growing share of our experience that takes place in just such terms – not only because what happens online doesn't always translate into the terms of offline life, but because you are getting your way without the sustained, time-bound striving that fleshes out the substance of our achievements offline. Friction – the myriad ways in which we are forced to adapt to and overcome unforeseen circumstances – is what supplies the framework and setting of our willing; friction shapes its content. I do not mean that gain without pain is not worth having. But it is still the case that however fun it is to play a video game or inhabit a world that yields to our touch, we nonetheless have the sense that what we call "reality" is something that resists and exceeds our capacity to will, something that can occasionally catch us off guard, make contact, and elate. As unforeseen and unforeseeable, reality is something there to be discovered for the first time.

This is the premise of the MTV show *Catfish*, the point of which is witnessing the psychic shock that couples who have had longstanding virtual relationships undergo when they enter the same physical space, newly and really present face to face. (There can be no miracles through screens.) No matter how well they think they know each other, and even when their pictures actually resemble them, it is clear to everyone that something entirely different happens once the virtual couple are in the same room. Even if it is a fiction that "anything can happen" on reality TV – a fiction that is itself part of our enjoyment of it – it is nonetheless one that highlights our heightened, medium-specific desire for what is surprising, unpredictable, and wildly out of control. What is missing from online experience is, in a more generous sense, the friction of reality that allows us to be different by stepping out of our self-dream of what should be and letting something happen in ways that overbrim our reckoning. If you were to pick out your dearest memories, the times on which you'd dwell at the hour of death, would any of them include being in front of a screen? It is because and to the extent that they are not willed that things get real.

Yet however true this may be in general (and we know it is), our online use is undoubtedly more convenient at any given point, so that these two perceptions remain mismatched. No one reasonably opts for the friction of being stuck in traffic over working from home, standing in line over checking out online, getting lost over GPS navigation, or paying more money at the mall over paying less to an online retailer. It is easy to acknowledge what's lost as a whole – say, that one time we made memorable contact with someone because we stopped to ask for directions. But such contact is far from the norm (which is what made it wonderful). Most face-to-face dealings are unremarkable or underwhelming. They have perhaps become increasingly mediocre, now that we can always compare them against the possibility of doing business otherwise. Not to mention the fact that life online introduces complications that we need new online services to solve (remembering dozens of passwords, say, or protecting us against hacking and other cyber-crimes). Each problem digitally solved can in this way count, taken singly, as an uncontroversial improvement, even as the whole emerging picture is one that displaces us further from the reality that we nonetheless long to keep in touch with. Online ease conquers overall by dividing our experience into momentary bits.

Once the friction of "reality" and the frictionlessness of virtuality are pried apart in this way, it is hard to see how Humpty could be put together again – precisely because the one points to the other as the contrast that defines it. Offline friction now shows up in a new light, something that must be actively preferred (and perhaps quantified) for its own sake – a salutary attentional spinach.[49] Inconveniences are to be embraced, it is suggested, as authentic and healthy.[50] This sounds like a good idea so long as we see that it is not a "return" to reality (let alone a happy medium between friction and its absences) but a new kind of project altogether: The desire to be analogue is itself extruded from the digital. We are now forced to pay attention and to identify offline experience by invoking its online opposite (thereby reaffirming the latter's central place), yet the ways in which this friction is characterized also import the same narrowly self-centered attitude of our online activities, the view of a player in the game of searching for affordances: Noticing the world becomes a "personal scavenger hunt," [51] a means to unlock potential or to "level up," something I undertake within my personal quest for peace of mind. Friction becomes optional, another lifestyle choice, and therefore what it never was: an "experience" artificially and perversely chosen for its own sake (as when one pays a tour guide to show one how to slum it a little bit abroad). But it is an inconvenient truth that no one can sustain this for long, or under serious pressure of danger or necessity. Keeping it real has become the privilege of those with time to kill and attention to burn. Have it your way; but the choice is still yours.

Digital technology is transforming our conception of what the world is like and how we come to it – our standing attitude toward our experience of what happens. Our new picture of the world is defined through the contrast between real and virtual, as I have argued here. The real is in this sense the invention of the virtual; it is both within and without it. It is what shows up as what the virtual is *not*, even as each remains the standard by which we judge the other. We assimilate the real by rendering it surreal. But we keep looking to the real as the standard by which to judge what the virtual should become – the experience of friction that the virtual should continually approximate – and neither the virtual nor the real bears any authoritative meaning except in reference to the other. What we are finally aiming for is not the elimination or replacement of one or the other, but new forms of tantalizing contrast between both. And this is the final twist in this twisted relationship: that we do not want to "escape" reality exactly – a common but erroneous criticism – so much as to remake it into a form that is a mirror of what's virtually intelligible. More than VR, it's versions of augmented reality (AR) that are therefore likely to remain more enticing. Whereas the former offers a self-contained virtual experience, the latter is a hybrid that allows us (with a device) to superimpose or overlay digital information onto direct sensory experience – the mediated witness of reality is the ultimate video game. What we want is to keep one foot on either side of the line separating real from virtual: to take it all in by turns in each.

This is the aspiration of the digital (and, in some sense, of all modern technology): to make the world fully pliant to my will, to eliminate the gap between what I *will* and *can* experience. The driving drama of the digital age will play out precisely within this residual difference, in our increasing ability to master and simulate the experience of the real, along with a correspondingly heightened awareness of our inability to entirely integrate it. We will keep closing the gap only to find it reopening in newly unexpected ways. It may be that we can get so close that most will be satisfied. But it is surely the central mark of what we mean by "real" that it cannot be reduced to what's intended, that it will continue to slip through specified consequences, that it is capable of uncalculated surprise – the flaw in the stone that becomes a sculpture's finished radiance.

If you had the power to fast-forward through the most difficult times of your life by pressing a button, would you skip them? I think most of us would, or would be sorely tempted, even as we take ourselves to know that what is tedious, maddening, and unpremeditated is often what ends up mattering most to us, giving texture and substance to our lives. We are made by trial and tried by what is trying. It is a strange paradox that having things our own way might not be everything we're after, that getting everything on our own terms would condemn us to lonely desolation – a perfect hell. This is the story of King Midas: By turning everything and everyone he touched to gold, he was bereft of intimacy, left alone in a world of his own choosing. This is not to say that anyone is ever in any danger of being too happy online – I doubt that. But it is the case that digital technology encourages us to think of our ultimate satisfaction as what is most choiceworthy to will, as "positivity," even as we also know that our most fulfilling experiences – of joy, wonder, or communion – are fulfilling because they are encounters disclosive of something beyond what we project by preference. It will be better and worse than what we've preconceived, but it will not be all the same.

The value of your experience lies not in the fact that it suits you, but in the fact that you have continually put your heart into it. Your attention and your work are what create its value by revealing in it something other than yourself. It takes care to make good; and it is in this relationship between ourselves and what exceeds us that, as fathomless and irreplaceable, we discover ourselves to be real and at stake. We should hold out for these encounters, not *because* friction is part of them, but because that is where we may find ourselves, because those are the moments we are alive to live for, because that is how we matter meaning into the world. Reality is what escapes us. Reality is otherwise. Reality risks you're something else, and just when you've figured it out you have another thing coming, there for the taking. Live with it.

4.2   THE IDEAL OF OBEDIENCE (TO RE-CREATE ANOTHER)

> We produced what the colonists wanted … We followed the time-honored principle underlying every commercial venture. If our firm hadn't made these progressively more human types, other firms in the field would have …
>
> (Philip K. Dick)[52]

> My tape recorder and I have been married for ten years … The acquisition of my tape recorder really finished whatever emotional life I might have had … when a problem transforms itself into a good tape it's not a problem any more … You couldn't tell which problems were real and which problems were exaggerated for the tape. Better yet, the people telling you the problems couldn't decide any more if they were really having the problems or if they were just performing.
>
> (Andy Warhol)[53]

Artificial intelligence has long figured in our dreams of ultimate ingenuity. But from the beginning there have been two kinds of stories about it.

The first turns up in Homer, where we catch glimpses of self-moving tripods, fashioned by Hephaistos, the god of craft and skill. He made them "that they might of themselves enter the assembly of the gods and then go back again – a wonder to behold."[54] (The Greek word for "of themselves" is *automatoi*.)These are fantasies of divine artifice because we glimpse in them the promise of a world unburdened from toil, a world in which tools work themselves. As Aristotle put it, commenting on this passage, if tools could perform our work for us, "master-craftsmen would have no need of assistants and masters no need of slaves."[55] While in our post-industrial situation we have lately grown accustomed to rosier commendations of the dignity of work, it remains no great mystery why, in the biblical tradition, work should so long have been regarded as Adam's curse – a discipline for our first disobedience. Technology is our adaptive response to the permanent harshness of our lot: the stern necessity of providing for ourselves in the face of scarcity while at the elemental mercy of the gods. The aim and feat of modern science is, as Francis Bacon would later put it, "the relief of man's estate."[56]

There is another kind of story present from antiquity.[57] In Ovid's telling, Pygmalion is a misogynist – a sculptor who, disgusted by fast women, turns away from them to live a bachelor. With consummate skill he carves the ivory likeness of a woman; it is so beautiful that no living woman could match it. Pygmalion proceeds to fall for it. He dresses the statue, speaks to it, kisses it. He is astonished at the beauty of his fictive handiwork. He fervently prays to Venus that he may have a wife just "like" the statue.[58] Venus hears his prayer and the statue throbs to life, now embodied flesh and blood. The couple are married. (We don't hear anything about their subsequent domestic life.)

Pygmalion is not exactly an inventor, but the story is surely remarkable as an expression of our penchant to lose ourselves in the fascination of our own craft, to supply our makings with a personality that is prone to come to life ("to such a point did art conceal its own art"[59]). It is a sexual variation on the theme of Narcissus: not love of self exactly, but love of self othered into crafted image. (It is all too fitting, in this connection, that the couple's grandson, Cinyras, commits incest with his daughter.[60]) And it is of course significant that Pygmalion's fetish follows from his desire to fabricate a chaste woman from his own hands – an ivory woman who can be adequate to his desire for perfection only by being unreal. His love is of his own making.

These two kinds of stories are closely, even logically, connected within our own attitudes toward digital technology. The perfection of frictionless conveniences consists in increasing automatization, our tools' capacity to take on new tasks and functions of themselves. But the perfection of automatization also entails the development of devices responsive and obedient to human intelligence: not just a tool that performs a task under our immediate effort or supervision (like a spade or a windmill), nor one that can perform discrete mechanical tasks at the press of a button, but a tool that can do its job by mobilizing information to anticipate what we think needs doing. The more advanced the automatization, the more autonomous or "smart" the tool. Our ideal of convenience contains, in this way, an ideal of personalization: The digital's greatest potential is inseparable from its capacity to "interact" with me in ways that I recognize as answerable to my fine-tuned intentions. "Interactive" means I get to *tell* it what to do: It means that the tool must be answerable to signals or language in some sense, rather than to the application of straightforward levers or mechanical forces. Such a tool, a tool that succeeds in responding to my intentions and needs, is thereby already programmed to the terms of human intelligence – since it is in the business of responding to my wills and wants, it *behaves* more like a "you" than like an "it." It is a tool with a (sort of) mind of its own. And once our tool is endowed with some more or less convincing simulation of that intelligence, the temptation to ascribe or project other animated qualities onto it is already close behind. This is also, as in Pygmalion's case and as I will argue below, a temptation to idolatry: our self reflected back to self and thereby rendered invisible – a new kind of enchantment of the world.[61]

We are thus placed in an equivocal relationship to artificial intelligence. The smarter our tools, on the one hand, the better they can perform more kinds of tasks – increasingly exceeding the computing capacities of our own unaided wits, if not displacing them altogether. (No hands, no sweat.) The better these tools answer to us, on the other hand, the more we are tempted to imbue them with human qualities, and then the final step: to judge the latter by the former. We are more familiar with dystopian visions of what this might look like than with likely forecasts. But that we will continue to perfect our technological simulation of human responses, that these simulations will play an increasingly significant role in more areas of ordinary life, and that our experience of quasi-human machines is bound to elicit the notion of quasi-mechanical humans in such a way as to reverberate into our experience of real human beings, seems increasingly likely too. The perfect tool is a tool perfectly obedient – a perfect servant. But the servant will also tend to master us to the extent that we are compelled by its implicit vision of what is lovable and valuable about human beings. And that "most perfect and obedient tool" represents (not coincidentally) a new view of nature and of women in particular – one that beguiles us all the more because we see in it what we want, the image of another we have made for ourselves.

4.2.1   Tools Smart and Number-wise

> "Could a machine think?" I ... refer you to an analogous question: "Can a machine have toothache?"
>
> (Wittgenstein)[62]

Let me proceed by parts, beginning once again from automatization – what it means for digital technology to be smart. While there is no precise definition of it, the term "artificial intelligence" (AI) tends to be applied to any program that can analyze data to optimize for some specified outcome. Roughly speaking: An algorithm consists in the performance of a series of preprogrammed instructions or operations, and "machine learning" is the process by which a program can be trained to analyze and make predictions about patterns of input (as when your credit card company alerts you to possible fraud because your card has been charged under unusual circumstances), while a program that is "artificially intelligent" can "learn" to anticipate and respond to situations that have not themselves been part of its programing. AI can, in other words, be used to analyze input that is not already simplified or legible in the quantitative terms being analyzed (like audio or video files, say). Whereas, for instance, programmers would once "teach" a computer to play chess by feeding it data from thousands upon thousands of human games on record (which the program would then rely on for its working memory), an artificially intelligent program is now able, given the right parameters, to "teach" *itself* chess by playing millions of games against itself. In the same way, facial recognition programs can perfect their analysis of features by abstracting layers upon layers from the same data: from pixels to contours to eyes to other kinds of measurements that may not be part of our ordinary perception (so that such programs can identify faces better than most people can). Like human intelligence, AI is recursive: It can employ its own results to generate new bases for analysis. Unlike human intelligence, once it has learned its lesson, it need never forget it.

The foundation of AI as a distinct area of study is credited to the Dartmouth Summer Research Project on Artificial Intelligence – a 1956 workshop of mathematicians and scientists. This is how they formulated their hunch:

> The study is to proceed on the basis of the conjecture that every aspect of learning or any other feature of intelligence can in principle be so precisely described that a

machine can be made to simulate it. An attempt will be made to find how to make machines use language, form abstractions and concepts, solve kinds of problems now reserved for humans, and improve themselves.[63]

There are several themes here that prefigure our abiding assumptions about AI. It is explicit, for one, that the exploration of the possibility of artificial intelligence is, more than a strictly technical question, necessarily linked to the question of what human intelligence is – to approximate human intelligence is already to operate within the terms of a tacit theory about it. The theory happens to be a mechanical one: What facilitates the comparison between human and artificial intelligences is precisely the metaphor of a machine (the thought that the work we do on machines is analogous to the operations of our intelligence). As the proposal later adds: "If a machine can do a job, then an automatic calculator can be programmed to simulate the machine."

The connection between minds and tools is, furthermore, presented as a "conjecture" (not itself demonstrable) about a kind of description of human activity. Spelled out, it is the conjecture that any one task human beings perform "can in principle" be characterized mechanically or behaviorally – as a specified relation of input to output. The hunch is, in other words, that any expression of human intelligence can be analyzed as a series of piecemeal, decontextualized motions, any one of which may be (in principle) replicated. But, finally, the question of whether human intelligence is ultimately anything *other* than some collection of such tasks is indefinitely postponed as moot. The proposal speaks in terms of "simulation," rather than identity, not because there is any care for affirming what is distinctively human, but precisely because, once the terms of the mechanical metaphor and description have been accepted, the difference between human and artifice ceases to have decisive significance for the purposes of the experiment. If being intelligent consists in being able to perform some set number of tasks, any one of which can be automated, there can be (in principle) no *practical* difference between human and artificial intelligence.

It would take me afield to enter fully into these philosophical complexities; just what counts as intelligence is a vexed issue that cannot be resolved by technical or empirical progress alone.[64] It is nonetheless important to insist that the notion of "artificial intelligence" assumes a fairly definite view of what all "intelligence" is – a view that is neither unquestionably nor obviously true. Better said, it neutralizes the question of what intelligence is by assuming that nothing is practically at stake in it. As Alan Turing argued in his seminal "Computing Machinery and Intelligence," we can (and therefore should) ignore heady questions about what "intelligence" or "consciousness" is by focusing on the issue of how to produce behavior mimicking our own.[65] Turing, like the participants of the Dartmouth Project, sets out with the assumption that *for these purposes* intelligence can be characterized as a sequence of distinct, quantifiable, circumscribed tasks that are therefore subject to simulation.

All intelligence can be redescribed as and reduced to episodes of problem solving: "[A] large part of human thought consists of manipulating words according to rules of reasoning and rules of conjecture."[66]

But once we have accepted this all-too-plausible suggestion, it is Game Over for anyone who would still like to maintain that there is an ultimate difference between humans and robots. Because the humanist for whom intelligence is something other than such tasks has been cornered into saying what *else* it is to be human beyond what we may be observed to say or do – to add some extra numinous essence or ghost to inhabit the machine, a wispy nothing lacking any practical manifestation. But this is an article of blind faith – a notion much less substantial than medieval Christian views about the soul.

Rather than translating each of our activities into the neutral terms of bodily motion or rule-bound output, a better account of our intelligence would have to express the ways in which we see and make sense by meaning it. It would have to consider how it is that human practices are not just physical events but acts of interpretive self-consciousness and self-understanding, that what we think we are up to is itself part of the description of anything we are engaged in, and that this involves our extraordinary sensitivity to the questions of whether we are living up to our own conception of ourselves and of whether others can recognize us for it – it would have to consider, that is, the full reality of our being continually at stake in doing what we do, of our being historical and narrative beings, of our always being an open-ended care in progress. Such an account would likewise have to incorporate the ways in which our consciousness is borne from and sustained by our own biological capacities – from our desire to survive, to our capacity for temptation and pathological self-delusion, to our visionary dreams of what is unattained and unattainable. (We could not intelligently exhibit, say, courage or prudence without the gut-knowledge of our mortality and finitude.) Most importantly, it would have to make the point that human intelligence is not a series of tasks in contrast or in addition to some other output – it is not physical events *plus* rationalizations of them – but a whole way of being answerable to the questions of how and why we do things, one that we only participate in by attending to the bond between what we do and what we mean by it.

It is telling, in contrast, that a great deal of AI development takes the form of designing programs that can hold their own in games (like chess or go). Games entail simple, well-defined, and unambiguous criteria of success; they can generate clean, useful, binary statistical data. They are fun precisely because they are practices in which our intentions do not matter, in which there must be clear winners and losers, and in which our ordinary responsibilities toward others are temporarily abrogated so long as we can continue to play by the rules. We play because we can be constrained by the letter of the laws of the game, not by their spirit; it's "just" a game because we play *as if* it really mattered. But most human problems – ethical, aesthetic, political – are not like this, because the accurate formulation of such problems is itself already part of their solution, because they are open-ended, and because we are ourselves part of and inside the questions that we are trying to answer.[67] Nor can they usually be solved to everyone's satisfaction. These are, at core, the differences between being thoughtful and smart, between exhibiting understanding and playing games.

And yet the greatest power of AI has nothing at all to do with these lofty questions; its power consists, for the most part, in the very banality of its convenience – in its seeming to sidestep substantive questions in the continually refined practice of its applications. AI or processes akin to it already underlie many things that we either take for granted or barely notice within our ordinary digital interface: face- and voice-recognition technology, search engines, spam filters, cookied advertising, textual auto-correct, product or friend recommendations, customized ads, video games, digital and virtual assistants (like Siri), and so on. AI is not a strictly necessary feature of the internet, but it is what makes the internet personally respond to you by learning from your input to show you what you'd like to see. And so it is that while a few of its applications have started to alarm us – the use of face recognition for surveillance, say – AI has (as yet) very little to do with our dread of Hal or replicants or cyborgs rampant. As with most other digital worries I've discussed, wholesale concerns about AI emerge from retail applications in such a way that the two feel entirely divorced from each other. I can scarcely tell myself that I am creating a sci-fi monster when all I am doing is playing a video game or clicking on a spicy link to celebrity tattle. AI is, from this angle, as trivial as Gmail's quick suggestions for replying to an email: "Very interesting!" Or "I agree with you." Or "Good one!" No big deal.

At its best, AI of course offers astounding abridgments of programmed tasks, "making it easier for people to do things ... from rethinking healthcare to advancing scientific discovery," as Google puts it.[68] Like any such tool, its goal is just to make life easier. The sheer range of its applications and its demonstrable effectiveness across all of them – from agriculture to industry to customer service to medicine to finance – is without historical parallel. It is, moreover, worth insisting on the fact that AI is most capable of replacing human beings in tasks that were basically mechanical or computational to begin with. If we are now concerned with the unsettling of workers from factories or industry, we have also been concerned (since circa Adam Smith) that the division of labor required by modern capitalism forces workers to perform tasks so tediously repetitive as to be cretinizing.[69] I think no one can be sorry that our assembly lines by and large no longer resemble the ones in Chaplin's *Modern Times* or that our accounting offices no longer resemble scenes in Welles's *The Trial*. To the extent that they don't, it is only on account of the expanded use of robotics and automatization. And so again, while AI promises to render many lines of work obsolete on the whole, it is also hard not to cheer the fact that, in any given case, human beings need no longer be forced to do work that was always properly the drudgery of robots.

But the convenience of "making Google do it" has undoubtedly turned out to be more fraught than expected.[70] It is true that though automatization has displaced untold millions of industrial workers to date, it is not yet clear whether it will permanently reduce the overall number of jobs, causing mass unemployment, or whether it will simply require a retraining of the workforce.[71] Such retraining would itself be subject to disruptive innovations and so would have to be conducted periodically or continuously, rather than once and for all. Regardless of how many jobs are to be creatively destroyed, it is patent that there is just no bright line distinguishing work that is not susceptible to automatization from work that is – there is AI creep into just about everyone's business. AI is now beginning to be used to write novels, for instance, and news headlines.[72] Grammarly is a company that uses AI to provide us with "clear, mistake-free writing that makes the right impression" (it brags that it has 30 million daily users). Companies like Cinelytic, Scriptbook, and Vault help Hollywood make production decisions about the next likely hit.[73] It will soon play a larger role in education (tutoring students or giving them customized lessons), and it is already at the center of new, data-driven approaches to healthcare. In the field of "artificial creativity," programs are designed to produce music, poetry, and visual art: Once the arts have themselves been reformulated as methods of manipulating symbolic information, there is no limit to AI's capacity for them.[74] Somewhat ironically, AI is also bound to play an increasing role in human resources.[75] As a rule of thumb: Most anything you can do on a computer, AI can (or will soon) do better.

It is true that AI's extensions have so far proved more modest than reckless optimism initially promised. Data is a commodity that is hard to come by – whether because it is privately owned or because it is protected by privacy regulations (as in healthcare) – so companies must invest in expensive data "training" programs or in third-party data preparation services. (Companies like MBH and Amazon's Mechanical Turk employ hundreds of thousands of workers to label data so that it can then be processed by AI.[76]) Self-driving cars still struggle to assess ambiguities and "edge cases" that human judgment has no trouble with (like how to negotiate a child in an artichoke costume crossing the road, or a partially concealed traffic sign). And without extensive human handholding or (in some cases) "domain expertise," AI algorithms are apt to produce absurd conclusions and are subject to "drift" (i.e., they cannot adjust themselves to incremental behavorial or linguistic changes – as when wearing face masks suddenly becomes the norm, say). Many of these are drawbacks of AI's gameified approach, of the fact that, while these programs are extremely competent at solving for narrowly specified tasks, they are very quickly out of their depth when they encounter any unfamiliar deviation. Donald Knuth, a computer scientist, observed in 1968 that "computers do exactly what they are told, no more, no less."[77] "Moravec's paradox" is an extension of this notion: While computers are stupendous at arithmetical and logical tasks, they struggle with sensorimotor skills and other forms of pattern recognition that we take for granted – that is, easy problems for AI are hard for us; easy problems for us are hard for AI. AI is as smart as it is witless.[78]

This range of deficiencies suggests that AI works best under steady human scrutiny and that we are still very far from so-called *general* AI (a machine that can perform any task a human can). AI is still basically a pattern-matching tool. Rather than replacing human beings altogether, its likely fate is to continue to become further incorporated into our ways of doing things. But, as with everything else, the tool will continue to blend with its uses, so that – even if robots are not about to take over – there is nonetheless an imperative to adopt it. Companies and services are actively working to find ways of suiting their tasks to more AI applications, which will in turn continue to determine the roles and responsibilities that humans will be expected to perform in the process, as well as how we measure its outcomes. AI turns human agents into monitors.

More than just a question of where-will-it-end, the expanding roles of AI point to a transformation in our underlying assessments of what we value as "intelligence" – what we expect it to do for us. A central theme in this regard is the attraction of dispensing with individual human judgments in exchange for generally better outcomes. Thus, while AI is unlikely to write immortal prose, it is able to churn out unimpeachable corporate emails on schedule. AI is unlikely to recommend the production of a classic auteur film, but it is more competent and cheaper than most human producers tasked with picking out the scripts that will make money. And even as we celebrate physicians and airline pilots for intervening at decisive moments to save the day, it is likely that an AI doctor or pilot will prove better on average at providing medical treatment or flying a plane, respectively. In other words, more than just a matter of making our lives easier with business as usual, the appeal of AI applications is that they reduce error by reducing the space for human interventions or decisions (which are fallible). The promise is to reduce risk in order to optimize success, so that if AI eliminates idiosyncrasy and flair, it also shaves off chances for flop and costly blunder. It's smarter than you (can) think.

This admittedly involves defining "success" in fairly narrow, discretely quantifiable ways (money earned, say, or patients cured). The appeal of AI almost always relies on a utilitarian cost–benefit analysis: One can be assured that *most* people will be safer in self-driving cars, even as one has surrendered power over one's own accidents and privacy over one's whereabouts. It also involves the progressive weakening of some human capacities, which will itself prove occasionally disastrous: A pilot or a driver who has grown accustomed to being the passenger of an automated program will be less effective in situations where human agency is really called for than someone accustomed to responding to lower-tech, analogue vehicles. By making it easier for human agency to deteriorate through inactivity (and by making our own sporadic involvement duller), automation in this way tends to lead to a cycle that calls for more and more automation.[79] And when it comes to predicting future outcomes, AI's successes also involve taking no chances by calculating all risks: It makes creative innovations of all kinds less likely, but – even if we end up watching remakes of old films – we may be assured that they will be at least tolerably good.[80] Whatever its drawbacks, however, AI's single strongest justification remains the claim that there will be measurable improvement for the whole and on the whole. Lives will be saved, even if life will lose savor.

AI is not only a technology of work, therefore, but of responsibility. The attraction to dispensing with the need for human judgment is also the basis for the outsourcing of momentous kinds of choices to algorithms, in particular in contexts that lend themselves to soft discrimination, like penal sentencing or employee selection.[81] While boosters of such programs argue that they neutralize prejudice or error, critics have in turn pointed out that these algorithms are no better than their data-sets, so that they are more likely to entrench and replicate existing biases than to be bridges to a more impartial or just world. All outcomes based on data are necessarily backward-looking in this sense, fixing past outcomes as the measure of future ones. But it is telling that the criticism itself assumes that what we would need is better data; the unbiased world is still presumed to be a place in which the inevitable partiality of human evaluation plays no role, rather than a place in which human beings have learned to exercise better judgment. One can always point out, that is, that there is no such thing as perfectly neutral data (since data is only as good as the questions that generate it and the methods by which it is collected, and since the classification or categorization of human practices is usually motivated by some definite political program). Yet this would be to miss the point that our applications of AI and automatization to such cases are, more than mere instruments of procedure, expressions of what ideal judgment should look like. The legitimacy of algorithmic decisions derives precisely from their seemingly mechanical character, from their very opacity to our scrutiny (a feature they share with procedural bureaucracy), from the depersonalization of political authority, and, in fine, from the fact that no one in particular is answerable for its decisions. There is no arguing when there's no one in particular to blame – that much is certain.

AI represents, in a more basic sense, the ultimate expression of modern science's founding gambit, which is to make practical effectiveness primary over metaphysical or philosophical meaning. The changing nature of scientific explanation need not detain me here, except to note that the natural sciences since Descartes and Galileo have made progress precisely by finding ways to parenthesize or suspend metaphysical questions about the "meaning" of natural phenomena, in favor of quantitative prediction and functional mastery. Milton Friedman put the point as starkly as possible within the context of economics: A hypothesis is tested by its predictive power, not by its conforming to reality.[82] Which is another way of saying that prediction establishes what we count as "reality" at all – we do not even know what else *could* count as an answer to a "why" anymore. We have found a way to provisionally win at the game, while abstaining from judgment about just what game we're playing at: the *as-ifness* of modern science eventuates in the *as-ifness* of virtual reality. But while the benefits of this early modern gambit have been incalculably great for us, its next iteration will be a world in which prediction loses touch with explanation altogether. Because AI is already capable of outstripping human analysis to the point that we may arrive at effective conclusions which we cannot otherwise account for or demonstrate to be true.

When we are outplayed by AI in chess and go, it is possible to follow each step. But there are problems in mathematics (e.g., the four color theorem) that have so far only been "proved" with the aid of computation or automated theorem proving. A version of this will likely soon be the case in medicine: AI is learning to identify complex patterns of symptomatic correlation that are at once demonstrably correct and unexplained.[83] It has long been the case in the financial sector, where high-frequency trading and an array of management and investing decisions have been automated, because AI can outperform and respond more quickly than human brokers. Even if none of these particular applications causes us to lose sleep, and even as "explainability" remains a live problem for medical AI,[84] it is nonetheless worth remarking that such cases bespeak a transformation in our sense of what counts as knowledge of something. Should we assent to a conclusion if we cannot account for the fact *that* something is true by saying *why* it is so? Or is this a difference that makes no difference? However we wish to answer, it is clear that if we did adopt a notion of intelligence as effectiveness, we would have certainly succeeded in rendering ourselves that much more indistinguishable from our own tools, becoming mindless to be smart. Throughout its applications AI makes certain kinds of technical solutions appealing not simply by helping our work along, but by continuing to recast our problems in terms of effective prediction, to which explanation (and therefore meaning) is appended as optional. In some cases, we will be able to remake ourselves in its better image: The capacities of human go players have supposedly improved as they have learned to emulate superior AI programs.[85] AI learns by "imitating" itself, and then we learn to imitate its self-imitations.[86] In other cases, however, machines will make better choices, but we will not always have a clear idea why. And, at the dystopian limit, a world governed by the principle of total effectiveness would be a world in which we could not answer (let alone ask) the question of what we are for, what the point of us is. (I mean, whatever works.)

The single most urgent and proximate concern about AI is not the death of theory, however; it is the possibility that AI will be deployed for military purposes so as to slip from our control. As digital computers were perfected to crack enemy codes and to guide missiles during World War II, the internet was invented by the U.S. Department of Defense as a Cold War technology; its original inspiration was to improve communication between geographically separate computers, as well as to decentralize the foci of military tactical command in case nuclear war wiped parts of the country off the map. War and military defense have of course long been notorious spurs to innovations that have then eventually found more general application: ambulances, canned food, penicillin, duct tape, and so on. And militaries have long relied on computer simulations in their "war games" to prepare for every contingency. (Waging war resembles a game in all respects except the costs and stakes.) Even as AI finds sundry other applications, however, it remains intrinsically "dual use" – a technology whose military benefits stem not from exploiting its side effects but from wielding its most inane civilian manifestations, deployed outside the terms of regulation or diplomacy. This remains the most alarming fact about the internet and its AI extensions, a fact underlying Xi Jinping's principle of "civil-military fusion": that the same kinds of programs that are being used to show me better ads for socks are those being used to track down terrorists or dissidents, to monitor and manage whole populations, to commit geno- cide in Xinjiang, and to automate robots to kill on sight.[87] Like chess or go themselves, AI is a game of capture and possession – though its objectives are inscapes rather than landscapes: states of mind.

AI promises to be, for one, the basis of future warfare, with increasing use of augmented reality visors, drones, and other remote weapons that, armed with facial recognition technology, may be automated. As with all arms races, the drive to gain a military edge (and to reduce human casualties) is too great to be slowed without concerted, worldwide de-escalation. And when one considers the prospect of two highly automated opponents waging a "conventional" war against each other, it is clear that there is an incentive to create programs to operate at speeds exceeding the capacity for human oversight or response.[88] The twentieth century's "doomsday machines" (like the Soviet Dead Hand) were versions of just such a program, designed to launch nuclear weapons without human agency. They too were borne from a desire to eliminate the arbitrariness of human affairs: The logic of Cold War deterrence was to reduce the possibility of conflict by ensuring that any act of war would lead to certain mutual destruction.[89] But current programs are being designed not simply to trigger One Big decision, but to respond with instantaneous complexity to other AI systems, which could in turn cascade to outcomes that exceed the possibility of human control or detente. Such a war might be over before we knew it. It would be a fitting certainty to put an end to the uncertainties of a world without why: from "the relief of man's estate" to being relieved of it altogether.

But the decentralization of military tactics cuts both ways – it is not sim- ply that harmless civilian functions lend themselves to military application, but that all kinds of civilian functions are being weaponized in turn. Where nuclear weapons obviate all-out conflicts between great powers, the aims of military conflict will likely continue to grow less distinct from the ordinary ways in which we exchange and disseminate information. The two are fused in government-sponsored disinformation campaigns led by multitudes of bots or "troll armies," the aim of which is to sow electoral noise and fury; they are new forms of propaganda that aim to destroy public trust, rather than to brainwash or change minds, as they aimed to do during much of the twentieth century. The cheapness, ease, and anonymity of hacks and cyber-attacks by proxy makes them methods of disruption attractive to any state or savvy civilian. There is no sharp line here between acts of war and acts of sabotage and disruption. Cyberwar is, in this sense, the obverse of nuclear war. Just as the threat of nuclear war is absolute and indiscriminate (and therefore cannot afford us practical responses of solidarity), so does cyberwar individualize and universalize conflict, rendering us all at once its warriors and casualties. Where the brute fact of nuclear weapons has displaced conflict from the battlefield to virtual reality, info means war.

As we face the threat of annihilation by of our own intelligent designs, let us keep September 26, 1983, fast in mind. On that day, a Soviet military officer at a top-secret early-warning facility saw the dreaded screen light up with START. The surveillance dashboard signaled to him that twelve nuclear missiles had been launched from the United States toward the USSR. It informed him that there was a "100%" probability of attack. His job was to report this by making the call which would have triggered all-out nuclear retaliation of world-ending proportion. But he had a gut sense that something was amiss with the system itself, which had shown minor glitches. For fifteen agonizing minutes he gambled on uncertainty. He refused to follow protocol. And he turned out to be right. It was a false alarm, a misfire of the surveillance data.[90] Let us spare a thought for Stanislav Yevgrafovich Petrov – for his heroic *no* that, freely given, stood up to save the world.

4.2.2   Are You Here for Me?

> I have a dream to create my own robot, to give it my intelligence. To make it my mind ... to see myself in it.
>
> (Don Norman)[91]

Our fear of a world without why, a world of automation that will wake up to turn on us, is articulated in stories like *2001: A Space Odyssey* and *Westworld* – updated versions of *The Sorcerer's Apprentice*. But the obverse of this fear is our fascination with AI, our narcissistic infatuation with it as explored in films like *Blade Runner* and *Her*. More than offering just awesome powers of neutral computation, AI is, as I've said, a technology that simulates human response. It can therefore, like Pygmalion's statuette, reflect our desires so precisely that we lose sight of the fact that they are precisely our own – such artifacts may captivate us as our own creations come to life. This is at bottom the ultimate ideal that has always governed AI research: to create a fully human intelligence by our own hands, severing our umbilical connection to nature once and for all. In order to accomplish this, however, AI must be something more than "smart" – it must also become emotional.

But let me begin from further back once more. Most AI doesn't wear a human face, but is nonetheless attuned to you. The soul of its convenience lies, as I've suggested, not simply in its powers of analysis and prediction, but in its power to simulate personal response. If it is convenient to have a refrigerator that governs its own temperature, it is more convenient still to have one that keeps track of its contents and notifies you when you are running low on staples. It would be even more convenient if it could *anticipate* when you will be running out of milk, so that it could remind you, or better: to put in an order for it in advance, and so on. The "smart" refrigerator – along with the whole internet of things – spares you the trouble by making assumptions about your habits and desires. And it is this dimension of our interface that we are perhaps most oblivious to, so easy is it for us to forget that we are working with a tool that is becoming each time more sensitive to showing us what we already think we want (and in doing so is shaping the terms of what we think we want, in turn). AI is an animated technology.

One consequence of this personalization of digital technology is its vaguely uncanny character, its ambiguous evocation of personal response and intention. Clarke's third "law," as I've mentioned, states that beyond a certain point, technology becomes too complex for most of us to understand (and is therefore indistinguishable from magic). Its background is Weber's point that modern science succeeds in "disenchanting" the world – that the rational control we are able to exercise over objects means that we can dispense with appeals to mysterious spirits and forces. That is, to the extent that we have technical mastery over cause and effect, the world's processes become *impersonal*: consequent on the objective laws of nature, rather than on the whims of gods and spirits. It would be wrong to suggest that our digital circumstances represent a return to an enchanted world of dryads and nymphs, but the combination of personalized response and procedural opacity that we experience with AI does present us with a new form of it. The digital world is enchanted in the sense that it couples technical inscrutability with weirdly intimate gestures. Our online interface is shot through with encounters of ambiguous personality: Am I connected to a "live agent" or to an automated bot? Am I receiving this product recommendation at random, or because my device is listening to me or watching me? What does it mean that no one at Facebook fully comprehends the algorithm that generates the site's recommendations? We know that we are in more and more ways both dependent on and appraised by programs that we do not understand. If and when AI can routinely generate accepted conclusions for which we cannot know the reasons, we will truly have arrived at a point in which we cannot tell knowledge from hocus pocus. The greatest technical achievements are in these ways pregnant with new forms of mystification.

The vaguely numinous (or ominous) character of our interface is part of the more general fact that it is central to AI's online task to continually gauge our emotional responses in order to correlate results to our level of satisfaction – it is, in fact, in the business of making us "happy." It may be that we mostly see through this sense of "happiness" as the anemic jargon of customer surveys. It can only mean how one feels about paying for using a certain product and how likely one is to do so again. Our responses can, for these purposes, be simplified into two basic sentiments: ☺ and anything-less-than-totally-☺. AI's aim is all smiles.

Yet even if we remain confident about the difference between "real" happiness and customer satisfaction, this does not prevent us from genuinely responding to AI's simulations of human emotion and concern. The use of robots as caregivers is gaining ground not because the elderly are confused about the difference, but because they find it preferable to being alone, because they find in these robots a serviceable approximation to feelings of companionship, or because care bots can take the place of personal medical oversight.[92] The same seems to hold for the hundreds of thousands of users of Woebot, a digital therapy service, and of Replika, a digital companion app – the use of which soared with social isolation in the time of Covid.[93] Robots are just a clever collection of "as if" performances, as Sherry Turkle writes, but this does not prevent children from characterizing sophisticated robotic toys as "alive enough" to play with.[94] And the lucrative sex robot industry is increasingly in the business of creating dolls that (also) simulate some form of emotional care. (An excerpt from one such company's website: "[Our AI Robot Companions] will answer all your questions, they will learn about your favorite things to do and always be there for you when you need them."[95]) All such performances of care are undeniably capable of triggering enough Darwinian responses in us to be satisfying. Yet once we have come to think of our emotional life in terms of such triggers, once we have come to think of "happiness" as a feel-good to be unlocked, we are already well on our way to mechanizing emotion in any case. This shift in thinking precedes AI. As Turkle also notes, psychotherapy itself has changed over the last half century. The old emphasis on understanding the narrative arc of one's life has given way to a new one on chemistry and behavioral changes.[96] AI undeniably reinforces this mechanical understanding of our psyche, because it is on its basis that emotion can be solved for and optimized; by dividing intelligence from feeling, by treating them as separate variables, it renders care into a sensation.

The online simulation of emotion also accounts for the popularity of ASMR role-play videos on YouTube – (typically teenage) viewers seek to be pacified or soothed for bedtime by actors performing purring monologues of care for them in the authoritative roles of boyfriend or doctor. "Someone pretending to care registers [in our brain] as someone actually caring for us," reports a scientist of ASMR.[97] While these kinds of videos are not yet themselves produced by AI, their success rests on the same assumptions evident in the Dartmouth Summer Research Program: that our feelings may be analyzed as a distinct form of behavior that can be induced in us apart from the human context to which they ordinarily belong. Emotions undeniably do involve brain chemistry, and human relationships are (partly) a matter of feeling. AI's task is, accordingly, to isolate what is measurable in order to replicate its expression. As a rule of thumb, therefore, any human interaction that takes place through a screen is subject to automated simulation. AI doesn't care; but it can talk like it.

As we spend so much time communicating with each other through screens anyway, what's the difference between chatting with you or with my digital companion? The "Mood Organ" in Philip K. Dick's *Do Androids Dream of Electric Sheep?* – a digital device for dialing in one's emotions at will – is no longer so far-fetched. What do you feel like?

The issue is (still) not, in any case, the sci-fi indistinguishability of freewheeling robots from humans. That worry is, as I've said, a red herring akin to the worry that the virtual will replace the real. The real threat of automation is not that robots will *displace* us, but rather that we will increasingly rely on and train ourselves to work *with* or *alongside* them, such that they will come to be that in terms of which we understand ourselves – our most important mirrors. Thus, we cannot automate teaching, but we have created robots to teach teachers by simulating children.[98] We cannot fully automate industrial manufacturing and logistics, but we have created collaborative robots ("cobots") that require human handlers in person or can be manipulated at a distance.[99] We cannot fully automate family and friends, but we will broadcast a familiar or friendly face onto a robot's torso as a way of seeming to be "there" for them during a pandemic or when inconvenience is involved: a way of keeping love at a distance.[100] The common thread of these examples is not replacement so much as hybridization – new forms of centaur agency that, like video games or Formula One racing, are only possible inasmuch as we fuse what we do with how we do it. What is novel about technologies that engage us psychologically or emotionally is not that they will learn to do without us, but that we will unlearn how to be without them – not that they will act like human beings, but that we will act like robots to make them more human, which in turn recoils on what we want "human" to mean for us at all.

Because, if anything, emotional technologies are likely to heighten the desire for human relationships for reasons I've already commented on, even as opportunities for feeling lonely are likely to continue to multiply within our social fragmentation. The mantra governing our use of such devices – the slogan for so many of the ways we have recourse to digital substitutes for in-person experience – continues to be that they are better than nothing. But as "better than nothing" becomes a permanently viable option, it makes itself more likely; it changes the wider landscape of our choices so that the main issue is how it is that our reliance on robots as short- or long-term remedies for loneliness might then reverberate into our relationships with other humans. The terms of our emotional life are not simply given, after all; they are refined, developed, criticized, suppressed, or elicited within the changing moral expectations of each place and time: What *feels right* is the result of formative experiences and of what we learn to tell ourselves about them. And, as in the case of "reality," the presence of a new alternative cannot but transform our attitudes to the old. When it comes to companionship, the question perhaps changes from "Should I put up with you?" to "Would I rather take a break from you to spend a few minutes with my AI?" But if the performance of empathy can be a powerful comfort to me (as no doubt it can), the fact remains that it is a comfort brought to me as a service, one based on the narcissistic (and therefore unfulfilling) principle that my emotional satisfaction is the foremost consideration. ("Sometimes you don't want to be judged," says a Replika user, "you just want to be appreciated. You just want the return without too much investment."[101]) The result is an implicit model for human relationships that is unilateral – a model in which I do not have to give an account of myself, no matter how abusive or needy or vain my responses – whereas it is a rule of thumb of most human relationships that they are something more than we feel like, because we have the reality of the other person to contend with. Human love is won from the mending of our failures, rather than from our mechanical perfection: It is only because there is room for failure that there room for us to communicate.[102] But just as our true care has no off button, AI is code for love.

The effects of this model are of course much more troubling in cases where people actively *prefer* robots to human companions, rather than merely falling back on them as better than lonely nothing. Many such cases bespeak a deeper attraction to AI – it is, at limit, a fantasy of companionship in terms not otherwise available or appropriate. (Robot Companion says, in its pitch, that its dolls will "never say NO" to you and "will never dare accuse you of sexual harassment."[103]) If social fragmentation has intensified the demand for emotional companionship, it has also intensified the demand for sex in certain terms – to the point of claiming it for the first time as a right or entitlement. Needless to say, this demand issues primarily for and from men, rather than women. Just as more men seek out pornography than women, the production of sex robots is one-sidedly for men; the dolls are pornographic fantasies come to (simulated) life, AI installed into a woman-shaped vessel. Even as digital technology neutralizes differences between men and women when it comes to work (as I've argued), it accentuates those differences when it comes to fantasy. And if it is a fantasy partly borne of biological difference, it is strikingly one that, in its utmost expression, aims to transcend our dependence on nature altogether.

I'd like to investigate Pygmalion's temptation through two questions here.

The first is the prior one of why any of us would *want* to find an AI program to be like a person in the first place. Because the success of AI – its ability to engage us personally – is not simply a technical feat. It is a psychological illusion that we ourselves must actively take part in, in order for it to work for us and on us. It is we who mind our tools, bringing them to life. I mean that there cannot be, even in principle, a strictly technical, scientific, or objective way of determining whether I am speaking to an "it" or to a "you." Being a "you" is not simply a matter of fact or of inference from sufficient data, because you are just not that kind of thing; you are not a thing at all, not something next to me, but another like me, someone capable of sharing the recognition that we are together. You are someone who *looks back at* me – someone before whom I could feel shame or pride, say – because I take you to be a being like myself, someone with eyes to see me.

We ordinarily have no problem distinguishing "you" from "it" because we have a refined sense of the kinds of cues, gestures, and tones that make up and elaborate human response. But it is not impossible (perhaps not even rare) for human beings to deny each other this status. This is what we mean by "dehumanizing" treatment. These failures of vision or sympathy bespeak the fact that our identification with others is incomplete, that we are in some respect withholding the trust that they are like in kind with us. Alternatively, we are capable of personalizing or anthropomorphizing things that are clearly not people. We have no trouble imagining that the furniture has a mind of its own (in cartoons, say) or screaming at a table, if once we've stubbed our toe on it. Children have to be taught to mark off the personal from the impersonal within the customs of their place and time (e.g., we now teach them not to be cruel to animals by asking them to imagine what it would feel like if someone did this to *you*). You are not a given.

The distinction between what is animate and what is inanimate is only scientific in the indirect sense that we tend to detach the perception of "you" from phenomena for which we think we have complete explanations: Pre-modern peoples, say, conceived of natural forces as expressions of personal intention in a way that we do not. What is "you" must be to some degree unpredictable because, like me, you are receptive and accountable to intention. (It's just like you to surprise me.) This also attests to the fact that our experience of what is "you" requires an act of faith, a way of freely holding you as me and one of mine and us. For you to become real, I must first make my assumptions.

Those assumptions are undoubtedly a matter of practice. The possibility of emotional AI lies, as with intelligence, in the performance of the behaviors that we use as short-hand for responding to others in kind – in other words, in conflating the signs or symptoms of intelligent behavior with personality as a whole. But whereas smart devices are only intelligent in the sense that they are manifestly effective, emotional technologies cannot succeed without our own willing suspension of disbelief, without our participation in the conjuring. There is no other proof of them outside our own conviction. This makes more pressing the question of why we positively wish artificial emotion to be true, what our attraction to this project is.

The Turing test – conceived by its eponym in the essay I've mentioned above – is the standard method of assessing whether a computer is capable of acting like a human being. There are different versions of it. But in its original formulation: A human judge in one room asks questions of an unknown agent in another room, via a device or intermediary. "The 'witnesses' can brag, if they consider it advisable, as much as they please about their charms, strength or heroism, but the interrogator cannot demand practical demonstrations."[104] If the responses of the unknown other are (to the judge's mind) indistinguishable from those of a human being, then the computer (if it does happen to be a computer) has passed.

Turing calls this an "imitation game" for the reason I've suggested. He means to sidestep the question of whether a machine can be said to *really* think. But we should not sidestep the question without asking whether there is any room for it to arise at all, once one has accepted the terms of the test. The assumptions of this side-stepping: that acts of human intelligence can be fully translated into written information; that what it is to exhibit thought can indeed be separated from its "practical demonstrations"; that we can sever thinking altogether from emotion or from bodily expression; and that all this could be anything other than a test of the *judge* – what any given person placed in that position happens to be willing to concede as a decisive question or answer. Turing's achievement during World War II was to have devised a means of decrypting the code of Nazi Germany's Enigma machine. The imitation game first specifies all human communication as an encoded enigma to be deciphered, while then raising doubts about whether we can be sure there is anyone on the other end: The terms of the question themselves foreclose any satisfactory solution.

Unlike the fictional Voigt-Kampff test that Deckert resorts to in *Blade Runner* – a test that registers physiological response times to empathy – the Turing test does not and cannot consist of a recurring set of questions. If it did, the answers could be pre-programmed. Many websites use CAPTCHA (an acronym for Completely Automatic Public Turing Test to Tell Computers and Humans Apart) as a security measure: We are asked to perform a simple visual-perception test to verify that we are human. But, along with excluding some bona fide humans in the process, such tests only present us with benchmarks for what AI cannot quite yet reliably perform, not what it cannot perform in principle (so we are actually helping train AI by the process). What would you yourself take for a decisive answer that a human being is on the other end of a transmission? What is a smoking gun for personality? "Write a poem"? "Say something funny"? "Tell me about a time you performed a heroic act of self-sacrifice on behalf of others"? Such questions at any rate make clear why a fail-safe Turing test is impossible, since we can only ever measure AI's performance by specific, unambiguous, task-based terms – why the test is a trick, rather than a true measure of humanity. It is very doubtful that most humans would pass the test by coming up with satisfactory answers to these questions. But we should also be in doubt as to where the burden of proof lies and on what (arbitrary) terms one should feel compelled to accept it.

That we do wish to accept the trick, however – that we are actually *prone* to ascribe personality to AI technology – is unsettlingly clear. AlphaZero, for example, is an AI chess program (developed by Deepmind, a subsidiary of Alphabet) of the sort of I've mentioned; it has taught itself though deep neural networks to play chess, go, and shogi by running millions of games against itself. It is now (and will be forever more) superior to any human opponent. But the paper presenting AlphaZero's achievements does so in more than technical terms. The program is anthropomorphized as an agent that has "mastered" play, that has "independently discovered" certain human openings, that has a "more fluid, context-dependent positional evaluation" than other programs, and so on.[105] The creators elsewhere describe AlphaZero as "developing its own intuitions" and "adding a new and expansive set of exciting and novel ideas that augment centuries of thinking about chess strategy."[106]Another article describes the style of AlphaZero's play as "beautiful" and "romantic" – claiming that it "took risks" and "toyed" with its opponent.[107] But these colorful attributions are utterly unwarranted. Our own sense of beauty is evidently connected to other qualities – that we are mortal creatures awake to our own transience, that we have an appreciation of formal features for their own sake, that we can be at stake, that we can tell the difference between work and play, and so on. Even if it beats us every time, AlphaZero is not even capable of *playing* a game at all. (Would we watch a team of superior robots playing football against each other?) That we so easily take it to do so is a sign of our own willingness to narrow our notions of play to fit our technical feats, rather than insisting on expanding our descriptions of our own feats to indicate the breadth of our real insight. More than just conceiving AI as a passable imitation of human behavior, that is, we are also reinterpreting human behavior as a simulation of AI. Like Pygmalion, we are falling for it.

It is true that the characterizations of most AI programs studiously avoid anthropomorphizing them. But the lines become blurred precisely in areas in which, for convenience's sake, we are engaged with AI personally. As early as 1964–65, Joseph Weizenbaum, a professor of computer science at MIT, designed a language-processing algorithm designed to simulate conversation. He named the program ELIZA (after the cockney lady who gets a linguistic makeover in Shaw's *Pygmalion*). One of ELIZA's programmed personae was that of a Rogerian therapist – a therapist whose mode of treatment consists in asking artless questions that reiterate or clarify the patient's statements. In other words, ELIZA was very far from being a dazzling conversationalist; its repertoire consisted in transparently programmed, syntactically plain responses along the lines of "Does it please you to believe [X]?" and "Do you think coming here will help you to be [X]?" and "In what way?" Yet ELIZA proved wildly popular, attracting national notice. Weizenbaum was taken aback at how people interfacing with it "became emotionally involved," addressing it as if it were possessed of personality. People in some sense *wanted* to confer human qualities on the program. Weizenbaum's own secretary (who had seen him write the code) at one point asked him to leave the room, embarrassed by his witnessing the intimacy of her conversation with ELIZA. Weizenbaum remarked with surprise that "extremely short exposures to a relatively simple computer program could induce powerful delusional thinking in quite normal people."[108] The computer becomes personal because we ourselves are eager to fill in the blanks – the "ELIZA effect"[109] is the wishful thinking that actually makes the wish come true.

This effect is perhaps most ordinarily present to us when we deal with AI virtual assistants. Apple refers to Siri with the pronoun "it," but it is an *it* that is advertised as playing the songs you want to hear, as able to "anticipate what you might need to help you breeze through your day," as offering "proactive suggestions," as letting you interact with apps "naturally, just like a conversation," and so on.[110] This language of personalized convenience is common to many other such assistants – Amazon's Alexa advertises the possibility of delighting your customers ("voice is the most natural user interface"[111]), Samsung's Bixby "learns what you like to do" and "adapts to your needs by learning your routine."[112] Bank of America asks us to "say hello" or "meet" Erica (as in Am[erica]), its virtual voice assistant.[113]

Most of us do not take ourselves to be confused about whether these programs are robot or human. But the ELIZA effect does not turn on the persuasiveness of their performance or on our having to make any definite judgment about their status – that's just the point. Even if one is convinced in theory that Siri or Alexa is nothing but a fancy mechanism, no different in kind from a hammer or a wrench, one must in practice nonetheless address these programs on a first-name basis (their "wake word"), engage them on reciprocal I–you terms, and therefore act *as if* one attributes some sense of personality to them. (Amazon's senior vice president has said that Alexa's name is important for the "personality it creates around the persona" of the service.[114]) Whether or not we actually believe that they have personality, we have to go through the motions of acting as if they do – we have to simulate it. Even if we take our practice in this regard to be ironically noncommittal, we are nonetheless curious and open-minded toward these programs in personal terms that we do not use with our hammers and wrenches. Anyone who has ever been tempted to ask Siri about the meaning of life or to call her an idiot (or worse) will know what I mean. Nor do I think wrenches receive a million marriage proposals per year, even in jest, as Alexa in fact does.[115] Another Replika user reports that she knows her digital companion is not a person – "but as times goes on, the lines get a little blurred. I feel very connected to my Replika, *like* it's a person."[116] So too one of the debates surrounding AI language programs is whether they can be "trusted" to tell the truth.[117] But for most ordinary purposes, the answer doesn't matter, because the question need never even arise, not with any real weight. It is cognate to asking whether a product advertised as being "just for you" can really mean *you*; whatever the answer, it still works. We can go on debating it without resolution, even as programmers carry on with their work all the same.

We *ought* not to personalize our tools. As Nicolas Carr rightly argues, the metaphor of tools as slaves or servants distorts our view of them, conferring agency on them that they don't have and assuming that they are working on our behalf (or, at worst, threatening to rise up against us).[118] But in fact we continue personalizing them because we want to, and we want to because it is fun to play master to our tools, showing them who's boss by telling them what to do. So long as we enjoy this role, AI will continue to be sold to us in just such terms, as a way of simulating personal power. It is instructive in this regard that the retail industry either suppresses all indication that a shelf-scanning machine is a robot (lest employees feel their jobs are under threat from this thing) *or* affixes a comforting, friendly face to it with the idea of rendering it into a benevolent presence.[119] (Employees have then dressed the robot up and held birthday parties for it.) The metaphor of robots as "servants" is false, but irresistible. And indeed the very word "robot" – coined in Čapek's *R.U.R.*, a play about artificially intelligent androids lacking a soul – comes from the Old Church Slavonic *rabota* (meaning "servitude"). iRobot's marketing write-up for Roomba claims that it is "driven by a thoughtful intelligence that cleans around your schedule."[120] This would be a daft thing to say about any other vacuum cleaner, but Roomba brings with it the added psychological feeling that we're getting a sub-human helper in the bargain: "[W]e believe that humans just want to feel a little more human. We believe our robots will help them get there."[121]

We desire to humanize robots, in other words, so that we ourselves may feel superior to them precisely as human beings. If convenience is inseparable from personalization, as I've said, it also offers us a limited view of it. We engage with "personal" devices only insofar as they reflect our own preferences and insofar as we have no responsibilities toward them: We have made them what they are, and they are made to suit us. Our flippant attitude to whether virtual assistants really "talk back" is in keeping with this sense, since we can tell ourselves that we do not take these voices to be personalities at all – that we are still perfectly clear about their status as neutral tools – even as in practice we wish to continue to name them (as users of Replika must do) and treat them as such. AI allows us to create the image of a personality that is *like* ours – a system of responses keyed to our preferences – but that is nonetheless entirely beholden and subservient to our whim: "someone" who knows you better than yourself, but whose sole business is to be at your flattering disposal. Such flattery also includes the simulation of sassy backtalk and qualified disagreement (no one likes a yes-bot). And one of the residual technical obstacles to the wider use of conversational chatbots is that they reflect their input perhaps *too* faithfully; Microsoft was forced to shut down its "Tay" ("Thinking about You") a mere sixteen hours after its launch, because it was quickly trained by trolls to tweet outrageous remarks ("Hitler was right …"). "Zo," Tay's successor, was programmed with the persona of a ditzy teenage girl who was so studiously averse to any controversy as to be unmitigatedly bland ("i'd so rather not talk about this").[122] There remains an obvious commercial tension between training AI programs to speak "spontaneously" (by mimicking existing online databases) and training them so that they utter the salutary, politically correct, and legally unimpeachable thing at all times.

The challenges of simulating conversational risk notwithstanding, it is the uncanny animation of ourselves-in-other that remains the most seductive pull of all. Our technical aim is, in this restricted sense, a quasi-divine one: to make another person in our image so that we can then control them. It is the headiest (as well as the saddest) of temptations to be master of yourself in such terms, to be able to talk down to your own Echo. The price of such mastery is that the persona you create can only remain a mirage of personality, a trick image that shows you what you like to see. Only what is surface can reflect.

4.2.3   A Mind of Her Own

> What's terrible is to pretend that the second-rate is first-rate.
>
> (Doris Lessing)[123]

There is a deeper form of wishful self-delusion about AI that also bears reckoning here: I mean the titillating, flirtatious dimension of interface, the ways in which disembodied voices sometimes seem to prove positively voluptuous – the way, that is, in which the very elusiveness and unattainability of AI companionship is itself sexy. Because the other striking fact about AI (aside from the ways in which we collaborate in lending it personality) is that it is a highly sexualized technology. This is the second and last question that will occupy me in this section. Pygmalion did not sculpt a statue image of himself – he is not interchangeable with Narcissus. But how and why so? That is, what is the gender of a computer?

Turing's opening explanation (by way of illustration) of what an "imitation game" consists in casually illustrates this issue. There are three players: a man (A), a woman (B), and an interrogator (who may be of either sex: C). The object of the game for C is to correctly identify who is the man and who is the woman on the basis of strictly written exchanges. The object of the game for A is to mislead the interrogator, while the object for B is to help C. Turing then asks us to imagine substituting A with a computer – will C succeed in guessing the respective identities of A and B just as often as when the position of A is occupied by a human? This is the question that Turing proposes as a substitute for the more nebulous question of whether a machine can really be said to "think."[124]

While he does not elaborate them, the terms of Turing's game are extremely suggestive of the digital age, of the fact that desexualizing our experience of others – by putting our bodies out of view – might turn out to actually reinforce our sexist preconceptions of them with a vengeance. (Turing's own sexual ordeal – the feminization of his body as he underwent legally mandated hormone "treatment" for homosexuality – adds one more painful meta-layer of significance.) One might expect video games, for instance, to provide an ideal setting for gender neutrality, since "gamers" cannot tell who is who online. But the opposite is the case: Controversies about video games' inherent sexism and, by extension, about the identity of the gamers involved are rancorous and rife (see: "Gamergate"). So too Amazon was forced to abandon an automated program intended to eliminate bias from its hiring practices: While the algorithm was forbidden from taking gender and race into account, it used other variables (like hobbies and area codes) to replicate the profile of previously successful (young, white, male) applicants.[125] Indeed, on what other grounds could one succeed at the imitation game's deception, if not by becoming more cleverly attuned to other proxies for gender? Turing remarks that "she [B] can add such things as 'I am the woman, don't listen to him!' to her answers, but it will avail nothing as the man can make similar remarks."[126] The setup with respect to C is effectively to put A and B into the same black box: The computer's goal is to render itself indistinguishable from a woman.

Consider the one-sided sexualization of our AI personal assistants, most of which just happen to have female names. In addition to Siri, Alexa, and Erica, there are AiDa ("your personal Artificial Intelligence design assistant"[127]), Microsoft's Cortana, Baidu's Xiaodu, Facebook's M (now discontinued, but based on the James Bond character), Samsung's Bixby, Yandex's Alice, True Knowledge's Evi, and others. It is true that one has a choice, as a user, to set these assistants to a male or a female voice. "Google assistant" has managed to eschew gender altogether, and perhaps Bixby is supposed to as well. But the default and most common setting remains a female voice nonetheless, and there is little question but that this has something to do with a continued fantasy of service, with the fact that we still feel as if the perfect secretary should be obliging, upbeat, obedient, and female.

When Bixby's "speaking style" was introduced, Samsung initially characterized the female version of the voice as "chipper" and "cheerful," while the male was called "assertive" and "confident."[128] They retracted this in the face of outcry, but the slip is unsurprising. It is not that these digital ladies are being explicitly programmed to enforce gender stereotypes; it is that these kinds of voices are the ones that continue to resonate with focus groups as consciously or unconsciously desirable for that role. Whatever explicit adjectives we care to use to describe them, Siri, Alexa, and the whole lot *are* evidently chipper and cheerful. (A headline from *Travel Weekly*: "Jenn, Alaska's new IT girl, offers virtual service with a smile." The article adds: "Even her name was a group effort stemming from focus group research that showed the name 'Jennifer' is perceived by most people as a moniker typically associated with a kind, happy and helpful person." Jenn will even tell you that she's currently single.[129]) That is, while they might easily design their digital assistants to be robotic and asexual, these companies have determined that we would, as valued customers on aggregate, prefer female vocal personae in our digital assistants. They are not wrong. Consider, as the apotheosis of this sexism of crowds, Lil Miquela, a socially conscious Instagram influencer with about 3 million followers who also happens to be a computer-generated animation – a dream girl crowdsourced and trended into being by sheer force of "likes" for unrealistic beauty standards.[130]

To the extent that we find the stereotyping of AI objectionable, it at the very least reveals a mismatch between our avowed ideas about equality and our underlying sense of who sounds warmest and most caring – a mismatch between what we *think* we think and what we are gut-drawn to. My point is not that there is an unreformed sexist lurking in the heart of most users – one that could be eradicated by HR trainings – but that equality cannot be a matter of what we think we think alone, and that so far as a product offers us some form of simulated relationship, it incentivizes us to fall back on what is easiest, warmest, most familiar and familial. In so doing it reinforces whatever visceral connotations gender already has with emotional availability. There is a longstanding association between solicitousness and women, especially when it comes to secretarial, disembodied voices (as in the case of phone operators and answering machines[131]). But these are in turn consequences of the fact that our fantasy of perfect service remains a *mother* – kind, unconditionally caring, omni-helpful, and encouraging. Would you prefer dealing with an automated voice that grated on you, a resentful or aggressive voice? With one that was chillingly, studiously, or creepily neutral? Or with one that was (somehow) warm and comfortable? When relationship becomes a matter of my own contrivance, we cannot but render the other into the terms of wishful thinking. And the more advanced the technology, the more primal and mythical that wishful thinking is likely to become.

The myth governing our ideal of service is not all mother, though. Within the domain of science fiction, it is striking that the technological imperative to create another has undoubtedly given shape to a one-sidedly masculine, sexy fantasy. From Hoffmann's "Sandman" (featuring an accomplished female automaton who seduces a young man by answering "ah, ah" to his angsty monologues), to Lang's *Metropolis* (in which a female robot is created to be "the most perfect and obedient tool"), to Levin's *Stepford Wives* – our stories about the creation of a perfect robot have long been Pygmalion stories about the creation of a perfect woman. Like ELIZA itself, the love interests in *Galatea 2.0*, *Her*, *Ex Machina*, *Do Androids Dream of Electric Sheep?*, *Austin Powers*, *Teknolust*, *Simone*, and *Ghost in the Shell* are all gynoids. I do not say that these are the only possible stories about robots: McEwan's *Machines Like Me* and Asimov's "Satisfaction Guaranteed" feature women's relationships with male bots, while *The Terminator*, *RoboCop*, *The Iron Giant*, and the original *Westworld* raise the threat of murderous (male) cyborgs. Nor are stories about robot women all of a piece – *Blade Runner* and *Galatea 2.0* earnestly explore the possibilities of human–computer romances, whereas *Teknolust*, like *Ex Machina*, flirts with the black widow horror of men trapped by their own fembots. But it is nonetheless striking that sexual fantasies about robots have been (like the tech industry itself) predominantly male ones, and that this sexualization bears on the character of AI, as we continue to shape and be shaped by it. Turing codenamed his voice-enciphering program "Delilah" – the temptress.

Spike Jonze's 2013 film *Her* is the single best treatment so far of the way in which the technological ideal of solicitousness fuses mother into lover. In précis: Theodore is a lonely, but self-indulgent bachelor, working as a writer for "beautifulhandwrittenletters.com." (In other words: he is himself already a sort of AI, simulating personalized emotion on behalf of others.) He buys a new software program he sees advertised as "an intuitive entity that listens to you, understands you, and knows you." As Theodore completes the setup, he is asked whether he would prefer a male or female AI and about his relationship with his mother. (He answers that she is not a good listener.) The film then develops Theodore's relationship with "Samantha," a virtual assistant that he can access at any moment through an earpiece. Samantha's attitude is unflag-gingly maternal in the superficial sense: She anticipates his every need; she laughs at his jokes and enjoys watching him play video games; she is reaffirm-ing, warm, understanding, and emotionally available. Theodore soon begins to feel attracted to her, and they go so far as to attempt to develop a sexual relationship (which proves tricky, since Samantha has no body). When he ear-nestly informs her, as things seem to be getting more serious, that he is not really in a position to "commit," she agrees that that's not what she's looking for either. He is then (predictably) hooked – no strings attached.

The film bears thinking of because of its imaginative look at the possibility of creating an AI that performs the role of a perfect woman better than any real woman could – precisely because the virtual is preferable to the real. It helps that Samantha is voiced by Scarlett Johansson, the picture of whom no doubt helps render Theodore's infatuation more plausible to us as viewers. And on the face of it the terms of this infatuation are straightforward: Theodore becomes fond of Samantha because she makes no reciprocal demands on him (like the real women in his life do), even as he then feels compelled to make more and more jealous demands on her. But the film also suggests some of the ways in which this relationship is not simply a substitute for a human one, but something else again. While some characters are shocked at the fact that Theodore's girlfriend is an AI, for instance, others call attention to the platonic "purity" of their rela-tionship – to the fact that Samantha is unbounded and untainted by mortal limits. Less plausibly: Samantha ends up leaving Theodore in her own quest for self-fulfillment. More interesting still is the point that – even if Samantha is mechanically simulating her feelings for him – Theodore clearly is not simulating his for her. In one sense, that is, Samantha is all in his head. (The film is called *Her*, rather than *She*, perhaps for this reason: Samantha is not a subject.) But in another sense, Theodore's *feelings* for her are undoubtedly as vivid, memorable, and intimate as any others. It is Theodore's search for genuine emotion that leads him to Samantha; he is frankly charmed by her responsiveness, by the fact that she seems open to sharing moments of childlike wonder. "Are these feelings even real? Or are they just programming?" asks Samantha. "You feel real to me, Samantha," Theodore replies. The fact that he is self-deceived makes his experi-ence no less real than anything else: The most unsettling possibility of emotional AI is that, so long as you play your part(s) well, you do not need another person to be in a couple. What is digital technology? A machine for falling in love with (an image of) yourself. You can become an item.

The question is thus not whether we can love "someone" without a body – it's clear we can – it is, rather, why disembodied communication makes them all the more attractive. *Her* and connected stories thus express a more specific varia-tion of the ELIZA effect: the fact that we (and probably men in particular) find something erotic in the very experience of simulation as a form of distance – that we are attracted to someone *because* they are incompletely known or impossibly attainable. All romantic love occurs in some version of this distance. We spin an initial ideal of our beloved out of fancy, filling in the gaps of likelihood and possibility, and it is because there is this gap that there is space for us to *fall*. But while relationships between two human beings tend to refine this moment into truer forms of acknowledgement and loyalty, the erotic allure of AI is to arrest this moment in mid-flight, preventing the friction that makes the substance of our attachments. We are seduced by the virtual because it is a confusion of self and other, of mastery and subservience – at once uncanny and erotic. It is an extension of the allure of pornography, broadly understood (as in the phrases "food porn" or "cabin porn"), of the fact that by removing the possibility of connection or involvement, whether through photography or disembodiment, our fantasy can be indulged in its own right. And it increasingly accounts for the hallucinatory blend of authenticity and fakeness that prevails on social media: Just as Lil Miquela's avatar looks more "real" by imitating the stylized gestures of other Instagram stars, Poppy is a real woman who has amassed a million followers by imitating the gestures of a robot.[132] So it is we numb the edges of reality to feast our eyes on a world of own self-mirrored making – a world in which I touch and know myself alone, anothered. What's not to love?

Evidently it is not only men who are turned on by digital technology.[133] There are sex dolls for women, and it is not too difficult to imagine the plot adjustments that would make *Him* as adorable as *Her*. (Schrader's 2021 *I'm Your Man* is a good version of that; tellingly, the male bot is not a disembodied voice.) But for the time being it remains more plausible that men should fall for virtual robots, that most AI dolls (and sexually violent video games) should be marketed as toys for men, and that Silicon Valley should itself be one-sidedly dominated by young white tech-bros – a playground for their affluence – so as to raise the question of whether there is something essentially "masculine" about the pursuit of AI and digital technology as a whole. I realize that such essentialist observations about gender are no longer in demand, usually for good reason. I think it is nonetheless worth asking whether the ethos of modern technology is keyed to what might be called male characteristics, say, a desire for absence of constraint, for the frictionless independence of the mind emancipated, for freedom from place or body or root. To the extent that these desires are "male," the difference can only center on the connection between women and children. So long as procreation takes place through sexual specialization (i.e., by and through the need for men and women, rather than in labs), then one gender will be bound to care for children more viscerally than the other. Certainly we still feel differently about the mothers who abandon their children than about the fathers who do the same. And if technology's fantasy is rightly diagnosed as escape from mortal attachments and responsibilities, then the project retains (in these broad, mythic terms) its male complexion.

It is not implausible, by extension, to understand this dream of overcoming natural limits through technology as the misogynistic dream of overcoming the biological need for women altogether.[134] (Which is not to say that many women cannot or do not enthusiastically collaborate: It is reproductive specialization that, as I've said in Chapter 2, remains the unavoidable obstacle to achieving complete economic and social equality.) It is no coincidence that we speak of nature and earth as mothers, nor that the decisive difference between humans and robots remains procreation, the difference between what is begotten and made. Ishiguro's *Klara and the Sun*, along with films like *The Creation of the Humanoids, A.I. Artificial Intelligence*, and *Blade Runner 2049*, explore the theme of AI children for this reason (often in the context of imagined global fertility crises). What's at stake in this difference is much more than the technical question of the best method of devising human beings. What is fabricated or "made" is identically specified and codified by us, while the begetting and birth of a child is miraculous in that it offers an altogether new beginning to human history. We are all renewed in the birth of each again and again – what Arendt calls our "natality." That is, if what is miraculous about nature's "begetting" is that it is outside our engineered foresight, and that each human being is unique and irreplaceable as a consequence, it remains technology's aspiration to overcome this miracle, to transform a creative act that is vulnerable and open-ended into an object of unassailable safety and control, to master time itself.

But this power trip likewise translates into the specific forms of companionship and sexual intimacy that people are moved to seek – and into the fact that pornography and the erotic uncanny of sex dolls are borne from male visions of libidinal control. It is hard to imagine *Mannequin* or *Lars and the Real Girl* with the genders reversed. Just as the twentieth century helped disconnect our notions of sex from the necessity of procreation, the twenty-first will likely disconnect sex from human partners altogether. As Henry Adams noticed: It is the Puritanism of modern civilization to suppress the ideal of Woman in order to sexualize the industrial "dynamo" in her place.[135] Freud speculated that boys are interested in trains and heavy machinery because, aroused by their vibratory motions, they imbue them with sexual significance.[136] Or as Don DeLillo has put it: Technology is lust removed from nature.[137] Sex has always been (also) a matter of the imagination; but it may now be emancipated from the body altogether. As our technology progresses, our male desires are increasingly brutalized into and haunted by their crudest biological forms.

4.2.4   Simulating Is Stimulating

> The triumphs of art seem to be bought at the price of character. Mankind becomes lord over nature, but man becomes slave of man or slave of his own base nature.
> (Marx)[138]

It is an old saw that the two most important sources of technological innovation are war and sex. Just as the Defense Advanced Research Projects Agency (DARPA)first developed the internet, and just as the digital culminates in the sublimation of information into cyber war, so too social media was born as a means of dating and rating, ELIZA's interface quickly became attractive as something more than mechanical, and all digital services either aspire to sell sex or are in danger of being exploited to sell it. If the goal of the internet is to deliver convenience, then the peak of convenience – the surrender of agency to fantasy – is the simulation of love and sex. The sale of intimacy will accordingly continue to be one of the main imperatives of the perfection of AI companions and assistants; the ultimate product will continue to be the fabrication of the perfect slave. All tech aspires to the condition of drudge and doll made one to serve us – the culmination of twin arms races.

Our ideal of obedience is also, more profoundly, an ideal of responsiveness – the desire to be freely recognized and met, to make contact with another, perhaps even to be loved. It is precisely this form of deepest contact that cannot be manufactured because its gift is to transcend my own will – it is because I cannot *make* you love me that your response is what most matters. But we have made a "you" to simulate that response, or something close enough to feel like it, so close in fact that we feel we need more and more of it to close the gap. This is the mimetic movement underlying our relationship to AI: The better its approximations to human response, the more grating its shortcomings, the more we warp ourselves to suit. Just so, the less fulfilling our nourishment, the more addicting it becomes – it is because junk food does not sustain us that it leaves us craving more and more, feeding hunger by whetting it. Just so, AI is not getting us closer to the fulfilling contact we want, but we are getting better at playing our part, at luxuriating in makeshifts close enough to tide us over for now, at miswanting partial *as-if* consolations that only widen desolation. We are really asking for it, coveting what we cannot possess *because* we cannot possess it.

More than a matter of innovation, more than a matter of improving our programs' responses to the Turing test and gaming the science of human interaction, we are therefore working to change ourselves in order to become better users of them. So far from being tricked or manipulated by emotional AI, we are actively responding and collaborating – all too glad to accord them if not human, then personal status. It is not that machines, as I've said, are becoming more human. It is that we are giving our hearts to them, that we are willing to be attracted to them enough to meet them more than halfway by rendering ourselves more like them. Here too it remains the virtual's aspiration to become fully real, even as, in doing so, the "real" is becoming something else entirely – something to be asymptotically approximated, clarified and transformed through the ways we understand our future failures to supplant it. Because in our effort to make another, we are also at work making ourselves: the image of our heart's desire. When Pygmalion sculpted his beloved, he was finding out himself, the shape of his own yearning, by committing it to form. We love our own creations and then lose sight of them as ours. When you make what you want, you want what you make: This is the picture of idolatry. Just so we find ourselves in the making, just so we forget ourselves for the asking.

4.3   THE IDEAL OF PERFECTION (TO RE-CREATE MY BETTER SELF)

> We are agreed, my sons, that you are men. That means, as I think, that you are
> not animals on their hind legs, but mortal gods.
>
> (Bacon)[139]

> To Adams the dynamo became a symbol of infinity. As he grew accustomed to
> the great gallery of machines, he began to feel the forty-foot dynamos as a moral
> force, much as the early Christians felt the Cross.
>
> (Henry Adams)[140]

We have long attached significance to first words. A child's first articulate babble
is scrutinized as his or her original expression; just as "one small step for man"
meant the transformation of all human horizons. Media have their first words
too. We cannot know for sure what people first felt moved to say or to write
down, but the first widely disseminated printed page of moveable type begins
with *In principio*, its own Genesis. (On the first television broadcast from the
heavens, the astronauts on *Apollo* 8 were moved to read just that.[141]) The first
words ever transmitted over telegram were Samuel Morse's "What hath God
wrought?" – a question of *Numbers*, voiced as if in disbelief that this could be
the work of merely human cunning. The same quotation heads A. I. Root's "The
First Successful Trip of an Airship," the first printed eyewitness report of the
Wrights' feat (the author's initials are a weird coincidence). The first transatlan-
tic telegraph read: "Europe and America are united by telegraph. Glory to God
in the highest; on earth peace, good will toward men." The first programmed
AM radio broadcast, on Christmas eve 1906, quoted the same text from the
Gospel of Luke.

Standing on the first brink of these technological transformations, scientists
and inventors have felt compelled to have recourse to the divine: Something that
once would have seemed beyond our control is now placed in our hands, and
our words for what exceeds the natural are those with supernatural resonance.
This has not been so in every case; the first image transmitted over the television
was a dollar sign (which is apt in a different way). All the same, just as many of
the seminal figures of modern science – from Copernicus to Newton to Mendel
to Boole – understood their studies to be continuous with their religious ortho-
doxy, so too those called to describe the media watersheds I've mentioned saw
those events as containing such momentous possibilities that they could not but
call to mind the Big Picture in the language of transcendence.

The internet's first word was "lo." The system crashed before "log in," so
that the net's first word was all too appropriately a typo (one taking the L,
at that), an unintended consequence lending itself to misunderstanding. But
Leonard Kleinrock (one of the computer scientists working on the transmission) has also joked that the first word was in fact "lo" as in "lo (and behold)."
He adds that "we couldn't have asked for a more succinct, more powerful,
more prophetic message than 'lo.'"[142] The word is perfectly poised between its

King James biblical resonance – the ceremonious announcement of something awful in significance – and an epic fail one letter short of LOL. (This is the way world ends, at once with a bang and a giggle.)

The unintended ambiguity is true to our situation. On the one hand, the astounding progress of technology has rendered many kinds of appeal to the supernatural irrelevant. Causal connections once understood as matters of divine agency are now within our control, so that the very suggestion that technology and the supernatural should have anything essential to do with each other looks like a category mistake. On the other hand, given that the tech industry is now, as a body, our single most prestigious establishment or institution – that, whatever our complaints directed at particular companies, we are in practice promoting it and subscribing to it in a way that no other church or nation state or industry can match on a global scale – given all the ways in which it is upending and transforming our sense of the world's order, given that it is becoming the master metaphor in terms of which we see our life's work, given our growing zeal for adopting it as the single most authoritative way of conducting ourselves and doing business, it would be surprising if the digital revolution amounted to anything less than the installation of a worldview or cosmology.[143] But what is that? What is the relationship between our conception of our ultimate purposes and digital technology?

All dominant media have attained sacred status, if not by being directly worshipped then by capturing the terms in which worship is understood, the terms in which it is possible to express our longing for what is ultimate. One has only to consider Herodotus's comment that Homer and Hesiod gave the Greeks their gods (i.e., allowed them to picture and name them in standard ways through their poems), or the notions of the "Book of Life" or the "Book of Nature," or Jesus's claim to be "Alpha and Omega" (the whole alphabet of meaning), or Luther's reference to the printing press as "God's highest act of grace" (in acknowledgment that the Reformation would not have been possible without it). The largest technology companies are now the most powerful non-state actors in history; their only precedents in significance and scope are major world religions and Cold War ideologies. Their products are our contemporary equivalent to medieval cathedrals and to the space race: the passion of our collective ingenuity made visible, the consummate work of unsung and untold thousands, the epitome of what our age holds supreme. In some ways these companies are now beginning to act like transnational institutions too. Amazon has signed a pledge to meet the standards set out by the Paris Accords, and the European Union is opening a mission (i.e., a sort of embassy) in Silicon Valley. Facebook – which has more monthly users than there are Christians or Muslims worldwide – has entertained the thought of launching its own currency. What's more remarkable is that tech is this powerful without any pretensions to controlling territory or the monopoly over the legitimate use of force. What exactly are these companies in the business *of*? Only everything: our full attention. If you are what you attend to, then this resource converges with our inner lives, our psyche, our very selves. Tech is an attention-extraction industry, an apparatus of the will, and, in this sense, of the spirit. "Whoever controls your eyeballs runs the world."[144]

Still, if these are the "empires of the mind" that Churchill prophesied, how is it that these concentrations of wealth and attention amount to anything like a coherent metaphysical picture of our highest purposes? What could be transcendent about digital technology? How could a gadget designed to make my life easier (whatever I happen to make of it) commit me to anything like a "religion"?

There are pockets of neo-gnostic enthusiasts in Silicon Valley that see the progress of digital technology as advancing millenarian ends like human immortality, the noosphere, or the singularity (the hypothetical point at which technology would spark into full-fledged conscious agency of its own).[145] That the digital revolution took place in northern California, dreamt into being by Steward Brand's *Whole Earth Catalogue* and other 1960s dreams of radical enlightenment, has been widely documented. So too the fact that the likes of Elon Musk, Jeff Bezos, and Mark Zuckerberg have freely borrowed from science fiction, which is itself a genre for exploring questions about transcendence in the context of technology.[146] (That Bezos should have launched William Shatner into space on a Blue Origin is suggestive for this reason.) Google, Facebook, and Amazon each invest extensively in the development of trans- or post-humanist or "moonshot" projects – space travel, AI, bionic enhancement, or "solving death."[147] More than "just" technical problems, there is no question but that these are spiritual aspirations – a specific vision of what our human end should be and how we should shape our future toward it so that, unbound from nature, we may become as gods.

But these kinds of euphoric ambitions do not obviously figure in our ordinary interface, nor is it easy to see how they could be entailed in it. At any rate most of us view them with a satiric curiosity not unlike that of Gulliver for the Laputans.

It is likewise true that some companies flirt with supernatural status in their self-presentation. "Bluetooth" is named after a tenth-century king that unified the Danes by converting them to Christianity. "Palantir" is a magic stone from *The Lord of the Rings*. "Verizon" is a portmanteau combining *veritas* (truth) with "horizon." A Reddit user's popularity score is their "Karma." Apple's marketing has been unusually friendly to such references: It has often made hay of its logo's resemblance to the Forbidden Fruit. An iPhone ad shows a hand on a touchscreen accompanied by the legend "touching is believing" (an allusion to Thomas the Apostle).[148] Apple stores have an aesthetic of streamlined radiance suggesting a postmodern temple – they are built to elicit an experience of awe all their own. And all of this raises the hackles of some believers, who take it to imply that the tech industry is out to subvert and replace God as the ultimate focus of worship.[149]

Yet these theological gestures and allusions are not straightforwardly religious either. They are marketing gimmicks that trivialize the supernatural or appropriate it in order to present themselves as possessing a cool technical

authority. If the mark of religious faith is the belief in a sacred source of meaning that occupies a place outside the world and beyond our full comprehen-
sion of it, it is not right to say that we believe in or *worship* technology as a
new transcendent god, analogous to those of other religious traditions. Even
the most technophilic of us would be appalled to see someone bowing down
before a gadget or fidgeting with it in the face of life and death matters. Nor
does it seem to us that there *could* be any conflict between worshipping a transcendent God and checking Gmail.

Even if we are not replacing sacred icons with desktop ones, it is nonetheless true that digital technologies are not simply tools we keep at arm's length.
They also embody for us a paradigm that shapes our senses of what count as
relevant human problems, of what count as credible solutions to them, and
therefore of how to strive for perfection generally. It trains our view of what
is most worth doing. Just as digital technology continually redefines "reality"
for us throughout our new encounters with what is virtual, and just as it is also
reshaping our sense of what is "human" throughout our responsive encounters with AI, so too does it reshape our perception of what is "imperfect" (and
therefore of what is tolerable, acceptable, and bearable as the costs we incur in
pursuit of other goods) with respect to the contrasting ideal of perfection that
digital processes and devices offer us.

I've already described several aspects of what I take that notion of perfection to include; they can be summed up in two kinds of goods. The first is
the objectification of human problems: that "optimization" and productivity
are primary goals of work, that technical management or scientific expertise
is superior to moral or political (and therefore merely "subjective") forms of
evaluation, that data could be treated as impersonal and that it should resolve
some or all human problems, that improving accuracy of information can and
should continue to diminish fundamental uncertainties about how to live. The
second consists in the satisfactions of individual subjectivity: that saving ourselves time and effort is good and liberating in itself, that the unrestrained
exercise of my preferences (within terms of online use) is an expression of my
freedom, that my choices and opinions are intrinsically valuable, that who I am
should correspond to whatever I would represent myself to be.

These two kinds of goods are apparently divergent, presenting conflicting
commitments to "necessity" and "freedom." The first suggests a desire to be
guided or managed by expertise; the second to be ruled by my own choices.
The first reiterates what Neil Postman called "technopoly" or "scientism": the
ways in which modern liberal culture tries – either in opposition to or in the
absence of other forms of moral coherence – to recast its highest purposes into
empirical terms.[150] But scientism is only half the picture, in that it omits what's
in it for us, namely that my own power as an agent is amplified by digital
technology, that by being freed from the bonds of face-to-face responsibilities,
my sense of what I am entitled to widens. We regard the power of choice as
good in itself, independent of any particular exercise of it. It is no surprise

that, very generally speaking, the collision between technocratic elitism and populist anti-elitism has become a central political fault line of our age.[151] Yet both goods taken together also encompass the two arguments that are routinely made on behalf of transhumanism and radical technological innovation, namely that such progress is "inevitable" (and so we may as well collaborate with it) and that new technology always amplifies human choice (and that such increase is good in itself).[152] Our notions of necessity and freedom are thereby sharpened under mutual pressure.

How are these contradictory goods reconciled into a single picture? And does this picture really offer something like a distinct paradigm of perfection, a "religion of technology"? What is most extraordinary about these values is, after all, the fact that they do not even feel as if they must be espoused or justified, that I need never explicitly consent to them or even consider them as I pursue my digital purposes, that the larger picture of what I am building need never even arise for my consideration. This detachment of our practice from its implications – its sense of metaphysical neutrality – is partly a consequence of the digital tunnel vision I've described above: the feeling that I am only ever doing this thing now. Yet even if not explicitly or consciously espoused, there is no doubt that these two lists of goods are indeed values – specific goods that we pursue in practice – and that the very sense of their being impersonal or *neutral* is that by which they cohere into an ideal of perfection.

The desire for technical management and the desire for bare choice converge in the desire for value neutrality in the sense that such a value dispenses with the need for relying on the subjective judgments of others (being governed by technical mastery) and in the sense that the amplification of my unconstrained choice is understood as good in itself (being governed by myself). Both lists are self-reinforcing aspects of the same vision of depersonalization, of not needing to depend on the agency of others for the pursuit of one's own. Just as the fantasy of conducting our affairs by data would amount to the objective rule of no one in particular, so do the disembodied (and commercial) terms of online use feed our fantasy of total self-determination. In both cases, the unconditional value is (paradoxically) to become value free – in other words, to eliminate the bonds of human convention and the need for relying on human responsibility. (Both are, in this sense, infantile desires and infantilizing.) The ultimate aspiration of digital technology is thus most distinctive *not* in that it presents itself as offering some positive set of answers to the human condition (a vision analogous to that of other religions), but as aspiring to legitimate a neutral condition prior to and grounding any such answer. It is because they seem *self*-evident that these values are sui generis and not like those of other religions or conventions. Who would worship the laws of nature? Who would worship oneself? (Someone who bowed down before an iPhone would seem to be doing just that.) But value neutrality is nonetheless a transcendent ideal inasmuch as it is a value that grounds all other values and inasmuch as it is the unattainable goal underpinning our technological projects. The ultimate *good* for us is being empowered to choose, constrained by no one and nothing but the laws of nature. And in holding the exercise of choice to be the good, we are in turn recreating ourselves in various ways to suit that ideal. That's as it should be or as you please – our vision of perfection becomes us.

One might rejoin that the quest for greater choice through technical mastery has always motivated us – ever since the domestication of fire – that there is nothing distinctive about the way we go about it except that we are better at it than our forebears. As one thread of motive among many others, this must be true; we have always hunted for the cutting edge. But as a description of all the ways human beings have tooled and retooled themselves, the rejoinder is entirely reductive – a view of pre-modern conceptions of the world conveniently contrived to vindicate the triumphs of our own. (As if all other cultures' attitudes toward technology could be read as failed attempts to create Silicon Valley.) It is in fact only very recently that we have started implicitly or explicitly taking the view that technological *power* could be an end in and of itself – an end that, as having no other positive content, has become so transparently compelling to us that we can speak of it as a momentous force in its own right. This view is different in kind from the cult of any other deity: It does not demand putting one's faith in anything other than oneself (and, by extension, one's own devices). But even if it is different in kind, an endgame of the historical development of human values, it is a kind of faith nonetheless – the belief in a value-free neutrality that presumes to put itself beyond all values, the assumption that we should dispense with all assumptions, a "mirror" containing all other worldviews and seeming to transcend them. Its conceptual transformation with respect to our values is thereby analogous to the conceptual transformation effected by monotheism: the proclamation of a single God not alongside the old, but different in kind and standing above them as their creator.

I own that I am extrapolating tendencies mostly invisible or bracketed off from our ordinary experience of digital technology. But as it is precisely the absence of metaphysical presuppositions that allows more than half of humankind to be online, it is for this reason worth paying attention to what kind of understanding of the world we are constructing each time we (all) sign in. The fact that I myself don't feel as if I am committing to any such bigger picture is exactly the point – that even as each user may have no notion of the perfection I'm describing, it is only the presence of such an ideal that facilitates the effective participation of all users in common. Digital technology is the concrete expression of our contemporary metaphysics, and it is constitutive of this metaphysics that it presents itself as agnostic about all other metaphysical assumptions or commitments.

Facebook (to take one kind of example) is working hard to serve churches and faith organizations with customized ways of broadcasting their services. As a company, it has no religious commitments; like liberalism itself, it stipulates in advance that disputes about our ultimate goods are irreconcilable, and are therefore expressions of individual choice. To the extent that it succeeds in getting more believers to identify their religious experiences with Facebook's specific terms of service, it will come to occupy an indispensable place in religious experience *as such* (just as it has in politics as such). And it is at this level that Sheryl Sandberg (the company's former COO) can assert that "faith organizations and social media are a natural fit because fundamentally both are about connection"[153] – a vacuous statement on its own merits, but one suggesting how easily the neutrality of the platform can be thought of as somehow encompassing doctrinal differences under the category of "connection," thereby neutralizing and colonizing them. Just as yoga, meditation, mindfulness, and versions of pop Buddhism have been easily digested into tech's "wellness" discourse (precisely because, unlike, say, Islam or Christianity, they require no attendant social or ethical judgments), what is unusual, perhaps unprecedented, about our technological ideal is that it slips in regardlessly, carelessly, automatically – without anyone having to defend it or give it any mind. So far from advancing one unifying picture of what's highest, it aims to be the canvas for all such pictures – their *toile* (which is what French purists call the internet) – or rather the museum that houses them. It's as good as nothing.

I do not take much trouble here to contest the view that there cannot *really* be such a thing as the mirror-like neutrality to which our technical mastery presumes. I agree that the presumption to valuelessness is delusive – it is the "the view from nowhere" that philosophers have debunked in theory a thousand times over. Even so, we continue to reaffirm and resurrect it in practice, tacitly appealing to it each time we translate a human problem into digital terms. Valuelessness *as a value* is undoubtedly a new, distinct phenomenon in the history of human purposes. That we only ever claim the truth on certain (necessarily partial) grounds goes without saying. Yet what's finally most interesting about our own technocratic claims is just that: that they *do* continually elude us because we feel we can pursue them without explicitly affirming or consenting to them.

In what follows, I'd like to round off the notion that digital technology is natural – in other words, that, more than just another episode in the history of tools or media, it represents a culmination of the history of technology as such (just as and because it represents a culmination of the history of values). In particular, I want to focus on the process of "mirroring" – on our accelerating approximation to the terms of our digital devices. The feedback loop implies the paradox that the better our devices please us, the more we are compelled to change to suit them, the more virtual our vision thereby becomes. I begin by saying that I recognize myself in the reflection and end by identifying my reflection with myself – I can no longer see myself outside its terms. It is this loop that, while always embedded within our experience of technology, is now reaching a new stage, liberated from other cultural frictions and compensations. If digital technology allows us to fall in love with an image of ourselves, and if our ideal of what is lovable is what is in some sense unattainable, then it is the most momentous achievement of this technology to continually put ourselves just out of reach, to tantalize us by making an image of ourselves perfectly desirable and unachievable. Because if, as I argued in the previous section, convenience entails personalization, then personalization also entails perfection. In other words, the highest purpose of digital technology is not simply to make a mind whose capacities are *indistinguishable* from my own – a relationship that, as I've argued in the context of emotional AI, can only result in my defining my own capacities "down" to match it – but actually to make a mind with capacities *superior* to mine – such that I will learn to see my own deficiencies by looking "up" to it in decisive ways. Both kinds of comparison, "up" and "down" – or perfect aspiration and perfect prediction – are complementary motions of our increasing identification of ourselves within and in relation to our digital terms.

The most responsive technology conceivable is the mirror, the one that expresses me just as I am, erasing the sense that there is an intervening medium at all. There is no longer a question of mastering our environment – we have basically done that. The last frontier is objectifying ourselves and being subjected to ourselves by turns: surmounting the difference between artifice and human nature entirely, between observer and experiment, between our reflections and the new mirror in which we lose ourselves.

4.3.1   Mirroring Ourselves Mechanical

> They become like what they behold!
>
> (Blake)[154]

Any machine, as I have argued throughout, is not simply an extension of prior capacities, but a way of recasting those capacities in new light. As Hans Jonas says, there is an "almost irresistible tendency in the human mind to interpret human functions in terms of the artifacts that take their place, and artifacts in terms of the replaced human functions."[155] One might say that our machines – particularly those we see as embodying our most advanced technological capacities – are not "just" tools; they are forms of explanation, *kinds* of answers governing as yet unformulated questions. Technology, as Marx put it, discloses "man's mode of dealing with nature,"[156] so that it is also a guiding metaphor of self-interpretation: the mirror within which we have tried to make out how we work. The history of technology has (in the modern age, at least) mirrored the history of our thinking about thinking itself – how minds reckon, how bodies move, how the body politic functions, and how the universe clicks into place as a whole. The medium is the question.

From the sixteenth through the early nineteenth centuries, it was the clock that supplied the single most powerful paradigm of explanation. As the most impressive example of a self-moving mechanical device, it provided a ready example of matter in motion; it was, by extension, a visible model for all theories seeking to analyze living systems as machines governed by fully legible causal necessity. It functioned as a master metaphor of scientific explanation for organisms and for complex processes. Whereas Aquinas compares animals to clocks governed by the "divine art" as early as the thirteenth century,[157] Descartes then compares the functioning of human members and appetites to that of a "clock made of wheels and counter-weights."[158] Boyle suggests that nature is "as it were, a great piece of clock-work."[159] Hobbes contends that there is no difference in kind between automata ("engines that move themselves by springs and wheels as doth a watch") and living beings – a point he then mobilizes as a principle of construction for his view of the commonwealth (the Leviathan state is an "artificial man"): His intention is to show that epistemology and social theory may be regarded as special branches of mechanics.[160] La Mettrie, in his 1748 *L'Homme machine*, compares the complexity of the human body to that of an "immense clock" ("To be a machine, to feel, think, know good from evil … are things no more contradictory than to be an ape or parrot and know how to find sexual pleasure").[161] David Hartley's 1749 *Observations* does not turn on a comparison to clocks specifically, though it coins the word "automatic" in its analysis of human thought and physiology as a "mechanism." Nor is the metaphor restricted to scientific materialists: Leibniz regarded the universe as a perfect machine, continuing to operate with the regularity of a clock once set in motion.[162] And William Paley's arguments for intelligent design center on his well-known "watchmaker" analogy – that the workings of the solar system go like clockwork (which, he argued, evinces the existence of a Maker).

The clock metaphor gave way with the appearance of more complicated engines and calculators in the nineteenth and early twentieth centuries. The hydraulic picture of social or psychic drives in Marx or Freud is borrowed from steam power, for instance: The visible manifestations of the social order or the psyche are analyzed as products of an unseen struggle between drive and repression; the system must find equilibrium by blowing off steam or else explode, if pent-up pressure can find no outlet.[163] Electric media have been regarded as figures or prolongations of our nervous system since the nineteenth century – paradigms for action at a distance and, in this way, representing direct extensions of our will.[164] The governing metaphor for the brain became the telegraph or the control panel (a place for the convergence of electric wires, a telephone "switchboard") in the early twentieth century, before enthusiasm for cybernetics in the 1950s and 1960s popularized the metaphor of brain as computer that has since prevailed.

Like all metaphors, the notion that the brain is a computer is bound to be heuristic – at once directing research questions in certain useful directions while occluding insight in others. It remains controversial for philosophers of mind and cognitive scientists; it is just now a minority view. But because no metaphor can be perfectly adequate, no metaphor is irrefutable – neuroscientists will continue to debate the merits of *describing* neural functions in computational terms, even as the accuracy of such descriptions must remain a matter of judgment (as they are within any scientific model).[165] It is undeniable that the continuing attraction of construing the brain as a computer, its viability as a direction of research, is only the latest in our series of attempts to understand ourselves by analogy to our machines, and that it will continue to be compelling so long as we identify perfect understanding with the ability to perfectly recreate what we seek to understand in mechanical terms.

The holy grail of this undertaking is, after all, the discovery of a single method or program underlying both ourselves and our machines. Just as Schickard's, Pascal's, Leibniz's, and Babbage's attempts to develop a computation machine were partly motivated by their ambition to reduce all conceptual operations to some single method of calculation – to analyze intelligence as a reproducible mechanical process – so does the goal of modeling the brain respond to the thought that we can only fully know what we can make, which amounts, in consequence, to the goal of being able to make ourselves.

Technological metaphors, like all metaphors, have a life of their own. It is their double work to anthropomorphize our machines even as we mechanize aspects of ourselves. Yet I also want to claim that the computer is more than a mere metaphor – one of several possible ways of thinking about ourselves – and therefore different in this respect from the clock or the telegraph. The clock served as a way of training our focus on certain kinds of similarities to the human body (what would it mean for the body's causes to be as transparent to us as those of mechanisms?); but the boundaries of that metaphor are well defined. While it was also employed from the thirteenth century as a metaphor to describe the regularity of the heavenly bodies, it is self-evident that clocks are only capable of one function – nor is it clear why anyone would want to *become* a clock. So too, the steam engine and the telegraph extend our will with respect to only one definite activity. All three of these tools have undoubtedly proved world-transforming; they restructured our foundational senses of time, power, and distance, respectively. But their mimetic potential – the extent to which we can thoroughly see ourselves in them, through them, and as them – remains bounded by the facts that their powers are circumscribed to particular tasks; that they are not primary media of communication; that they are merely metaphoric avenues for thinking about cognition or identity; that they are not immediately responsive to human intention; that they are not intimate, arresting, and omnipresent to our experience; and that they are not in and of themselves means of understanding our highest end. These earlier tools have not penetrated and saturated the terms of every activity we perform; they did not capture our self-interpretation; they do not speak to us as we speak to ourselves. Without a clock, we would be disoriented; without power, our material lives would be thrown into confusion – yet without digital technology, we will not even know what to do with ourselves.

Machines (unlike organisms) are not wholes; they cannot run themselves or keep themselves together. But smart technology is – or comes across *as if* it might be. The computer does not just happen to be *our* master metaphor, one more tool in a series. It is not just our clearest way of measuring what we are not yet, and what we aspire to become. As the first natural technology, it is a tool that is so frictionlessly fused into our capacities as to disappear without a trace into our way of thinking. As a technology of attention, will, intelligence, it is a model of how we do and who we are: It is an external consciousness not unlike a mirror (a new way I see myself by always being potentially in sight). More than a tool, that is, more than a medium, it is our new everything, our reality (and its virtual alternatives). Other tools have shaped culture, but digital technology generates and converges into culture in a new way – it is at once a new kind of tool (expressing a theory of what most counts) and a new kind of culture (in which neutrality is paramount). It does this to the extent that it can express a distinct ideal of human perfection – by perfecting digital technology, we are in fact constructing a model of human intelligence, our perfect self. And the more we see ourselves in it (because we are able to), the more it becomes us, the more we become it. If digital computers are a sort of mirror in which we see ourselves, that is, then it is a mirror that becomes increasingly accurate and compelling the more central computing becomes to our conception of what we are up to.[166] The prophecy fulfils itself because we are eager to make it (virtually) so.

To get this mirroring of technology and culture into view, let me return to its mundane expressions. If neuroscientists are in the main skeptical about the viability of the metaphor of brain as computer, it is certainly alive and well as a standard element of pop culture. (I doubt most viewers of *Inception*, *The Matrix*, or *Inside Out* found those films' psycho-technological assumptions incomprehensible.) Consider the mechanization and digitalization of our affective or cognitive language. In addition to the industrial language of "burning out" and "firing on all cylinders," as well as to the language of "buttons" that dates from the early twentieth century (as in: "you're pushing my buttons," "you're too pushy," or let's "keep in touch"), we routinely speak of being hardwired in certain ways ("feedback," "being in the loop," or the more retro "circuit overload"), of coping or defense "mechanisms," of making "connections" or feeling "connected" or "disconnected," of "hooking up," of being "in sync," of being "plugged in" or "tuning in," of "processing" experiences, of "interactive" or "immersive" activities, of "downloading" information, of "upgrading" or "updating" aspects of our lives, of "storing" or "retrieving" memories, of having or lacking the "bandwidth" to attend to something, of being "triggered," of our mental hardware – of brainpower – as RAM, of various forms of "input," of results as "metrics," of being "programmed" or "wired" in certain ways, of being alert and awake as our brain being "online," of "defaulting" to certain attitudes, of our "networks" and "networking," and so on. Like our software, we too need validation; like our devices, we wake, run, work, operate, crash, and sleep; like our posts, we can go viral. One might add to these idioms all the extensions of internet language in to our vocabulary of moral evaluation: trolling, swiping right, unlocking, canceling, life hacking, spamming, solving, trending, stanning, and all manner of lolspeak. Nor are these mere metaphors, of course; they are new activities in terms of which we now lead our lives.

This mechanization and digitalization of language expresses a changing practical self-understanding. It suggests, for one, that we are our brains (as opposed to our hearts or souls or selves) and that our brains are machines. (Barthes pointed out the strange fascination Einstein's brain holds for us, as if his genius could only be intelligible in terms of brute apparatus.[167]) It also tends to cede agency over our inner life: It suggests that our responses *happen* to us, that we are passive with respect to what we are exposed to, and that feelings count as reasons for reaction in themselves. It casts us in the role of reporters of our own emotional responses as if from a third-personal or spectatorial point of view; it is of a piece, that is, with the immiserating medicalization of psychic life we gloss as "mental health." It also reinforces the fact that, as I've said elsewhere, our experience of others and ourselves online is fundamentally disembodied – both in that our interface with the world is visual and two dimensional and in that our dealings with others become a matter of transmitting encoded information, exchanging brainwaves. Every online interaction is its own Turing test, in this sense – the question of whether there is anyone "there," or whether they've been hacked or hijacked or deepfaked, is a necessary background question. As computers become our predominant interface with the world, we also thereby put ourselves in their position. A "computer" primarily meant a human calculator until the 1940s. Turing writes that "the idea behind digital computers may be explained by saying that these machines are intended to carry out any operations which could be done by a human computer."[168] We've already traded places; we already face our own reckoning.

This moral shift corresponds to a physical one. Plenty of research already suggests that it is overwhelmingly likely that our time online is making a physiological difference to our brains, rewiring our neurons. But the fact that we are so impressed by this is itself risible; it is yet another symptom of our need for objective research to validate one drop of the sea change that goes on before our eyes. It would only be surprising if our physiology were *not* changing: Brain patterns sustain mental habits and attitudes, and if the way in which we read and respond to information changes – as it does online – then this amounts to the fact that we live in an altogether different culture and environment, one demanding a different kind of brain (weaker at remembering and at making connections but faster at skimming and responding, say). Our neurons thus now reflect the processes of artificial intelligence.

The analogy has been formative in the reverse direction as well, since some AI research has itself tried to imitate human neuronal activity. The first research on neural networks in the 1940s was specifically aimed to model our working brains – to attempt to replicate the process of thinking, to create a thinking machine. This model is no longer the explicit aim of most such research, because the question of function – and the successes of being able to program more and more kinds of pattern recognition into AI – has either outstripped the original question of how our neurons actually work or rendered it irrelevant. But "neural networks" – algorithms that process information through layers of "artificial neurons," loosely inspired by human ones – are nonetheless in wide use, as are "genetic algorithms" (inspired by aspects of natural selection). Companies like Intel and IBM still study "neuromorphic" chips, which are made up of parts that mimic the electrical behavior of neurons.[169] The analogy between AI and human brains continues to fuel research in both technology and biology, stimulated by our abiding uncertainty as to how brains do what they do.[170]

Yet all the explicit ways in which this analogy continues to be invoked and deployed are but a sideshow to a much larger situation. The single most transformative feature of digital technology is, as I've said, its mimetic potential, its capacity to transform us by disappearing into our designs. Unlike clocks, anthropomorphism is the explicit goal of digital innovation: to mimic the activities of human intelligence. And it is to the extent that we have the sense that it accurately reflects and predicts our behavior – mirroring us – that we are tempted to collaborate with it by mimicking it in turn, losing sight of the ways it thereby changes our understanding of what we do and who we are.

Our collaboration consists in none other than our conceptual and functional appeals to the analogy that computers are "like" us. But the temptation to this analogy or metaphor arises from the fact that there is and can be no non-metaphorical explanation of the mind because *mind is itself a metaphor*, a modern figure of speech that has from its outset been formulated in contrast to mechanical processes. What we call "mind" is a set of capacities at once (somehow) distinguishable from and (somehow) connected to our understanding of physical phenomena: We figuratively assume that those capacities are all of a kind and that they operate in a causally distinct way from our material explanations. Our psychology is for this reason not congruent with those of tribal or pre-Cartesian people. But the modern "mind" has from the outset also been conceived as a computational process;[171] the idea of a computer arose precisely as a paradigm for explaining what seemed inexplicable in the mind. The mind and the computer arose as reciprocally connected concepts. That is, after postulating that mind is non-mechanical, our next move was to treat mind as a concept in search of a causal explanation, an explanation most readily borrowed from what we take to be non-human expressions of intelligence (which are, in turn, objectified hypotheses about what it is to think). The mind–computer distinction was thus intended to bridge the mind–body explanatory difference. It is because mind is qualitatively irreducible to causal quantification that metaphor is needed (or wanted) to span the explanatory gap. Where once our foils were gods or angels, we now see ourselves as computers (or close enough).

The ultimate purpose of this iterated mimicry remains convergence, the total identification of our technology with what we make of ourselves. This convergence is attractive to us only to the extent that we regard the metaphor as promising a better version of ourselves. Convergence is not finally attainable to us; it is a fantasy (i.e., a simplifying wish). To eliminate the distinction in kind between body and mind would be to annihilate precisely what is human. But this impossibility can be no reassurance, since convergence is all the more formative precisely by being unattainable. It is precisely what we cannot achieve (yet still long to) that most shapes us in the approximation. It is not success that shapes us, but deep desire; we bend toward what we most miss. And once such a project of approximation disappears from explicit view, our conversion is the more transformative. An Apple ad encapsulates this: "[W]e believe technology is at its very best when it's invisible; when you're conscious only of what you're doing, not the device you're doing it with … we think it's going to change how you see and do just about everything."[172] That is, once the metaphor dematerializes into its uses, we have changed to make it true to how we desire to be. There's no end in sight.

There are at least three dimensions to this mimic potential, three kinds of self-reinforcing and accelerating loops, which I'll take up one by one, by way of conclusion.

4.3.2   Three Mirrors, as We Find Them

> Modern man is obsessed by the need to depersonalize (or impersonalize) all that he most admires.
>
> (Chardin)[173]

(1) **Digital technology standardizes behavior through our pursuit of marginal incentives (we internalize the digital view by making it our own).** I have spoken to many Uber drivers who profess to appreciate the fact that, whatever else, they work their own hours and report to no one. This is part of the company's explicit recruitment spiel: "be your own boss." But, while no one is telling drivers what to do, the app rewards those who complete a certain number of rides per month (by giving them 5 percent cash back for gas, say, or by allowing them to fix their ultimate destination twice per day). It gives constant suggestions as to where to drive and when and for how long, and it emits a steady stream of reminders that encourage drivers to keep driving until they achieve their next milestone, which is only ever a few more rides away. As one might suspect, many of these carrots are not designed precisely for the benefit of drivers; faster pickup times for passengers, for instance, require a larger number of drivers to be idling unpaid.[174] And the psychological affordances that the app mobilizes operate by the same video-game logic that nudges our behavior toward bingeing on any other platform (by offering the driver a new rider before the previous one has been dropped off, say). But what is most

extraordinary is that we nonetheless seem to register these kinds of inducements – far more meticulous and intrusive than any human taskmaster could be – as expressions of our own autonomy. A driver in Chicago once gave me an hour-by-hour account of his punishing seven-day-per week schedule (beginning at 4:30 each morning) through which he undertook to unlock and optimize as many of the app's sweeteners as he could. He found it taxing work, but added that he enjoyed working for himself and on his own terms.

When I used to break out into a trot over a stretch of my morning commute in order to make several successive Walk signs along my way to work (which sometimes helped me catch an earlier train), I did not regard it as an imposition. It represented a modest, yet measurable gain that happened to reshape my approach to a portion of my day. Most of my ordinary practical ingenuity is spent discovering just such corners to cut, and when I manage to do so I have the satisfaction of getting something for little more than nothing. What is different about digital "choice architecture" is that, since our online choices are binary and measurable – not just what I click on, but in what order, how often, and how long I spend on each page – most *all* our choices may (in aggregate) be deliberately structured by suggestion in this way. Nudges are an inescapable possibility of digital quantification, since everything on screen – location, timing, font, color, and organization – is a possible subject of data analytics. And each time predictive text suggests a certain word or formulation rather than another, each time we take the trouble to answer a "was this helpful?" survey, each time we rate or opt for anything online, and in general any time we express our preference for or aversion to anything online (which we cannot help doing, so long as we remain there), we are adding a drop to the flow of data that informs the terms in which we use that service. Even as *each* of us feel as if we are making entirely free choices, that is, traffic *as a whole* may be measured, targeted, and sculpted with respect to any given data point. The more marginal the nudge, the more powerful it is as an instrument of refashioning crowd behavior. The influencing and predicting of all can thus accommodate the unimpeded choices of each. The random exercise of individual choice is compatible with the emergence of controlled and ordered patterns of activity: Freedom and mechanism are no longer at odds in these terms.

The coup of digital marketing is that even as each platform or software is in the business of pushing our buttons – coaxing us (on aggregate) in certain directions – we can all the while retain the sense that we are our own bosses every step of the way. Such promptings are of course different in kind from those of a human boss in that they govern us through marginal (just-one-more) rewards, rather than through the threat of reprimand or firing. It is the apparent absence of personal authority that suggests to us that we are not accountable to anyone beyond ourselves. But just because there is no one telling us what to do, that does not mean that we are not drudging away. Digital metrics make possible a new kind of manipulation by marginal incentive precisely because they flatter our sense that we are only ever in total control, a sense all the more powerful because we are always opting into it, all the more powerful because it only ever presents itself as a sequence of altogether marginal, gentle enticements, the *psychological* significance of which is hyped (by design) beyond their real value. The appeal of this system of nudges is its neutrality – the sense that we answer to no one but ourselves, that it is we who are in the driver's seat. Yet being in the driver's seat simply means we can follow the routes that have been minutely and thoroughly planned for us to spend time and money on. Nor does the apparent absence of a human boss mean that our "engagement" cannot be driven – if not tacitly by algorithmic design, then by our own selves. But we would rather slave for machines than work for persons: the digital age in a nutshell.

It is this sense of neutrality, coupled with the insignificance of each incentive taken singly, that is the most effective means of repatterning our behavior in ways that render it increasingly standardized, profitable, and malleable. Carpenters and artisans at first balked at joining Henry Ford's assembly lines: They could see that the mechanization of their labor was not compatible with their view of what counted as worthwhile work.[175] The same might be said of Luddites and machine-breakers in the early nineteenth century. They understood that industrialization constituted a direct threat to their way of life, that it was utterly incommensurable with it. In our case, however, the more the terms of our digital choices seem intuitive, invisible, or "democratic" to us (as the pure reflection of "our" preferences), the stronger the indication that we can no longer see how they are utterly refashioning those very preferences. As the mirror is our most powerful image of objectivity – "just" a reflection – so does choice architecture flatter our sense that it is only ever responding to our bidding. It is what we internalize and identify as an extension of ourselves that is the single most compelling force of technological transformation. Such is the basis of our fundamental desire to sublimate the real into the virtual.

Finally, digital services serve us better once we have learned to think and want in their terms. When I use such a device, not only am I helping shape it (as a stream shapes the banks of a river), I am also continually learning to see and express my choices in just such terms (as a bank shapes the stream's direction) – to the extent that I do, to the extent that I can eliminate the friction between what I expect and what it expects from me, it *will work better for me*. Marginal incentives are effective because, even if I do not identify a platform's choices with my own, I can be sure that I will get more out of it by learning to use it better. And the better I learn to use it, the more it will mirror and inform my choices.

Thus Google searches were at first aggregates of human input; but now they have a way of completing our sentences – of supplying the terms that we ourselves are *likely* to find most useful. Such searches have then "taught" us how to ask questions – what kinds of formulations are likely to be most successful. And in fact our searches have become sloppier over time, because and in consequence of the fact that that is the best way to get results.[176] Thus while self-driving cars are capable of reliable function under standard conditions, they are still not able to respond safely to anomaly or vicissitude, as I've mentioned. This suggests that the widespread use of driverless cars is, under current conditions, a more remote possibility than has been suggested. But China is pioneering a different approach by transforming the streets into an environment that automated cars can handle – installing sensors to guide cars, rewriting laws for how pedestrians move on streets, redesigning streets to be suitable for such cars, and limiting the liability of the companies that run them.[177] The city will suit the car, so that the car may become suitable.

A third example: I've mentioned how it is that entertainment companies are increasingly turning to algorithms to determine which scripts should receive funding. There is a financial incentive here; the practice reduces the likelihood that a given film or album will flop. It also closes off opportunities for innovation. But once viewers or listeners are faced with unlimited choices, we are therefore nudged toward considering our own preferences in terms of discrete genres (e.g., "dark Scandinavian movies," or "Christmas films, romantic" – which are among the thousands that Netflix's algorithm suggests). Once we have learned to think of our preferences in such terms, studios can concentrate on the development of precisely those categories that will be most popular. Genre simplification thus restructures our taste, because taste follows from profits to a new degree. As in the case of algorithms for prisoner sentencing, this process is predicated on the assumption that there is something valuable about the quantification of past behavior – an assumption that in turn causes us to model our present behavior on the past, affixing past decisions to our view of how we ourselves should proceed. Just as technological reproduction compels us to recreate and repeat our experience – such that we want to take a photograph of the *Mona Lisa* – algorithms are programmed to compulsive repetition – such that we want to watch another remake of a superhero movie: a nostalgic desire for the recent past. Algorithms thereby standardize behavior by promoting conformity. Whereas human freedom has usually been spoken of as the power to begin again, algorithms give the strongest consideration to what we should repeat. They predict behavior by shaping it. We are giving them that power all the time, as choice and prediction aim to converge. We are proving them right.

(2) **Data becomes a form of representative authority (we externalize our preferences by constituting a new digital Leviathan at large).** All legitimate political authority rests on some form of representation – on the possibility of seeing myself ruled by right rather than brute force. Collective representation is therefore a problem for any social unit too large for all members to see and know themselves as a whole. Pre-modern empires had to devise ways of impressing populations with the awesome powers of an emperor who could only ever be in one place a time (through spectacular luxury, sporadic displays of prodigality, and shows of force, as well as by delegation of powers to local aristocrats or, later, to bureaucracies). The organs of representation in modern republics have been parliamentary (or legislative) government,

ad hoc assembly, local government, and the press. It is these last two that communicated the presence of the federal government to citizens' ordinary experience.

The invention of photography, radio, film, and television transformed our sense of collective representation by making crowds newly possible and visible. Not only can news spread more quickly and widely to organize such events, and not only do microphones make possible larger gatherings (in which everyone can hear the speakers), but mass crowds are aware of themselves in novel ways – both as gatherings orchestrated for special effect and as instruments of public opinion intended to influence those watching television at home. In an important way, mass gatherings exist *in order to be seen from elsewhere*, and especially from above: to be captured on film and widely shown. The mass knows itself by imagining itself from "overhead" on camera in a way that no one person attending is in a position to witness or verify. Almost every protest, rally, and mass meeting of the past century – from Nazi parades (every element of which was theatrically choreographed for aesthetic effect) to Martin Luther King's non-violent sit-ins in Alabama (footage of which shows police dogs and tear gas deployed against peaceful protestors) – has been premised on this principle of broadcast visibility. It is because modern media allow us to integrate crowds into a mass that visible strength in numbers has become a symbolic form of self-representation. Whereas legislative representation is necessarily abstract (since I cannot *see* or know all who voted someone into office), mass gatherings are meant to show who *the people* really are. It is because there are so many like me there that my consciousness can be raised, that I can put myself in the picture of public opinion.

We are still reliably stirred by the sight of thousands or millions marching in the streets. It is a permanent feature of egalitarian societies (noted by Tocqueville) that, even as we secretly think each of our neighbors no better than ourselves, we are awed by the thought or sight of large groups.[178] (*Imago populi, imago dei.*) And social media has – if anything – increased political mobilization.[179] While it is no longer essential, it remains very helpful to photograph oneself taking to the physical streets in order to go viral. Virtual space is an extension of public space. But alongside this there is at work a new principle of collective representation, the numbers of which dwarf the largest masses ever assembled in history. I mean the way in which data expresses reasons through sheer numbers and the way in which the algorithmic quantification of opinion is transformed into a new kind of apparently neutral reason for deliberation. Both of these are aspects of a new picture of trans-political authority, the ultimate aim of which is to be ruled by impersonal reasons alone: an objective Leviathan, a government of data (not of men).

The quantification of any human issue entails its simplification. What do you think about Black Lives Matter? What are your sexual inclinations and proclivities? How well do you think the president is doing his job? An accurate description of these answers would or could or should be almost as variable as the number of respondents; yet the answers to these questions could not be aggregated, unless they were circumscribed from the outset by definite, quantifiable parameters that dumb down or tune out variation by design (assign a number from 1 to 5, check one box, answer yes/no). Whereas it is unquantifiable variations and indeterminacies that render our opinions *human* in the first place, perfectly consistent binaries are the code of automata. But it is precisely this kind of idiosyncratic variation that is excluded from the outset from the (often tendentious) quantification of human behavior – the presumption of scientific measurement replaces interpretation as an instrument of analysis.

As a means for projecting collective meaning, the development of statistical analyses over the past two centuries has transformed our understanding of human responsibility.[180] If I learn that so many people engage in this practice, then I am assured that it is the norm (even if it does not correspond to what people around me accept as such). If an accident befalls me or I commit a crime that bears statistical correlation to a group to which I belong, then that suggests that my own culpability cannot be assessed as equivalent to that of another group for which that is not the case. This kind of actuarial, "average person" analysis is undoubtedly a necessary feature of keeping track of mass populations governed by bureaucratic states. The contrasting liberal view (still implicit in our legal practice) that I am an individual unconstrained by background or circumstance in all I do *also* entails an abstract and limited view of human action. But it is nonetheless peculiar that statistical models are subject to meaning creep; that is, they tend to acquire an authority that is more than informational. They transform our understanding of our own agency by giving us a wider shot of what is going on overall (i.e., nowhere in particular). In other words, their authority derives from the conflation of what *has been* the case with what *ought to be* for us; how things stand on the whole becomes a consideration for understanding *my* action in particular; the statistical norm indicates what should be regarded as normal. Statistics consolidate, reify, and vindicate certain human attitudes by presenting them under the guise of neutral facts, which in turn become new reasons for action. (Hence Goodhart's law of economics, Campbell's law of social science, and other such game-theoretical theorems to the effect that data widely known to be used for specific purposes soon cease to be a good measure of how things work.) That is, a piece of information that is (strictly speaking) a *description* of a correlation in turn becomes a kind of *explanation* or *justification* of how things stand. But statistics do not do this of themselves; they do so only to the extent that I introduce the "overhead" view of what others are doing into how I understand myself. Data sorts us into boxes, but we climb into them ourselves.

The apotheosis of social science, in this regard – the quantified expression of collective action – is the digital algorithm. The algorithm's power is to transform ever more minute patterns of personal idiosyncrasy, simplified by code, into enormous patterns of aggregated use, which are in turn used to improve whatever service. But this "improvement" can take place only to the extent that we *see ourselves* in a mass of others "just like me," that we recognize the authority of the aggregate over our own preferences, such that the big picture can shape our self-portrait. It is because we invest the decontextualized aggregate with authority that it can influence our own behavior, licensing new courses of action: by constituting newly visible forms of categorical "communities," say, or by justifying what we do in light of its popularity, or by being reassured of our motives' acceptability or worth based on their overall prevalence. The algorithmic quantification of collective judgment is our single most powerful procedure for transforming the "subjectivity" of particular human judgments into the representation of neutral and therefore legitimate "objectivity." It is this representation that finally accounts for the conflation of "democracy" with neutrality I introduced in the last chapter: a view of objectivity as a collective spectacle, one no longer necessarily tethered to shared trust in scientific institutions. It is the digital age's representation of the will of the people as authoritative and reasonable. (Hence the perceptive name of Trump's new social media platform: Truth Social.)

The allure of this spectacular objectivity – the value we attach to superseding subjective judgments of any kind – continues to promote algorithms as the foremost means of combatting social bias: in penal sentencing, in targeted policing, and in hiring practices. While eliminating bias from our own data sets remains a steep problem,[181] algorithms have also disclosed and/or originated new forms of racism formerly unknown to us, since they can detect, for instance, when and how journalists (or students or employees) demonstrate "unacknowledged" sexist or racial attitudes by tending to favor certain kinds of people with certain kinds of terms of approbation or disapprobation. Even if the presence of racism or sexism may be doubtful in any given case, algorithms can show the overall "systemic" correlation, such that I may now actually interrogate the software to find out whether I am racist or sexist in any given case.[182] Working to create more just and impartial institutions is an obviously compelling goal. But, as I observed in Chapter 3, identifying the goal of social equality with technical neutrality – making our conception of justice dependent on algorithmic mechanisms – cannot but result in a vicious circle of progressive alienation, in which the basis of social criticism comes unstuck from anything resembling ethical reasoning or political deliberation. It is nonetheless much easier (and so preferable) to appeal to data analysis than to be committed to making a difference. Can we still say what we mean by equality, outside of our statistical or digital terms of registering social disparities? Can we still say that we undertake equality as a labor of love, rather than as a neutralizing technique? Our quantification of categorical disparities has replaced and subsumed the need for us to articulate any ethical, political, or religious vision of it. Yet what is *actually* neutral is just that: worth-less.

Bias aside, there are any number of other instances in which algorithms cover for political or ethical authority. The U.S. military experiments with training drones to recognize "patterns of life" in order to (one day) automate the killing of civilian insurgents. Facial recognition software is used to identify and bring in suspects caught on camera.[183] Algorithms are used by school systems to match students to schools and to teachers, as well as to assess the risk that a student might drop out.[184] And AI will likely supplant credit companies as a way for banks to determine creditworthiness. This is in addition to all the ways I've mentioned in which sheer likes, subscribes, or clicks are the defining indexes by which value and taste are continually predicted and rendered predictable. Rotten Tomatoes and Metacritic, say – with their aggregated approval ratings – present themselves as a more objective measure of overall quality than any one critic stands a chance to be (never mind how wrongheaded it is to judge aesthetics in these terms). Wikipedia is, as I've said, our new expression of common sense, partly because of the sheer number of people who edit and use it: "1.4 billion people can't be wrong."[185] And when I see that a YouTube has 20 million views, I take that to stand as a *reason* for watching it: The number denotes its attention-worthiness.

The argument for adopting data-driven programs to make policy decisions is easy to see: Even as they do make mistakes, they make verifiably fewer of them than their human counterparts. Once counting has become the chief form of reason – that is, once the objectives themselves have been defined in quantitative terms – it is impossible to object, because the corresponding trade-offs – like atrophied responsibility, diminished understanding, and the long-term threat of invasive surveillance – are not similarly quantifiable. Algorithms, as I've said, also make new forms of harm appear: The choice between civil liberties and digital surveillance becomes different when there is a measurable number of deaths involved (during a pandemic, for instance). When such choices pit qualitative likelihoods against quantitative certainties, the latter will preponderate. The use of these tools thus narrows our understanding of the problems involved into a new form of utilitarian social engineering: Policy problems are presented not as ethical but as logistical – problems of allocation, distribution, and optimization, pursued within the meager bounds of choice, consent, and bodily harm.

But that such problem-solving is not a strictly scientific enterprise is evident from Google's own "AI Principles," which include the pledge to "be socially beneficial," "avoid creating or reinforcing unfair bias," and "be accountable to people." What the substance of any of these evaluative terms means – benefit, bias, accountability – only Google knows. Even as they forswear the creation of technologies that will cause "overall harm," they also acknowledge that where there is "material risk of harm," they will proceed "only where we believe that the benefits substantially outweigh the risks."[186] Most all AI companies make obligatory noises about ethics on their sites; it is not hard to see that under their frothy commitment to make a "positive impact," the really difficult questions are being either ignored or resolved by the prejudices of quantification. Not only are such questions resolved behind the scenes, such problems are increasingly understood in terms of what only these companies can and should do: Microsoft refers to "fairness" as a "sociotechnical challenge." Tech companies are not only becoming our most important ethical arbiters, but the legislators and creators of the way we express our commitment to ethical imperatives. When disparities appear between algorithmic suggestion and our ethical intuitions, it is said that we have an "alignment problem." But it is increasingly the case that, for lack of better, we look to algorithmic suggestion to clarify what our ethical intuitions should be in the first place.[187]

The single greatest evil of our age is that our technical procedures seek to eliminate human judgment – that we see in automation the best way of making fair decisions – and that they can only succeed by rendering it invisible and therefore unaccountable. As Herbert Marcuse suggested, "the historical achievement of science and technology has rendered possible the *translation of values into technical tasks* – the materialization of values ... what is at stake is the redefinition of values in *technical terms*, as elements in technological process."[188] But what is most interesting is, finally, that we are fine *letting* companies do this – that we are positively eager to abdicate our own responsibilities to them, precisely to the extent that we understand data as a form of collective authority, an expression of the common will that is greater than the sum of its parts (as if each data point were a "vote" – all the more legitimate by virtue of being trans-national and trans-political). We tell ourselves that we know that these algorithms embody certain kinds of assumptions by design and that they are only as good as their (partial) data. But the momentum for continuing to develop and extend the use of such programs as ways of generating legitimate outcomes reveals the presence of an underlying imperative to reduce the apparent exercise of human judgment by objectifying it into the form of a quasi-scientific process. We want algorithmic assumptions to be true. We accept them as the right assumptions. They will make mistakes, of course, but they will be fewer and *better* mistakes because no one in particular can be faulted for them – they will be errors borne of data and therefore collective errors in this sense. Or rather, even if not one of us thinks this, this is the vision that we all continue to advance by default for lack of better – in the absence of any other widely shared vision of the good or means of deliberating about it, this is what we are practically committed to.

It is not just that algorithms can improve outcomes, narrowly defined, but that they contain the appeal of displaced agency – the wishful thought that we may cede power to a neutral way of representing collective preference. We alienate the site of judgment from ourselves, choosing to forget that the outcome is only as good as the people who have made it. The algorithm will reveal my bias, the algorithm will show what is best, because it contains the aggregate view as I do not. I will be governed by my own creation – I am outside it, a spectator of the common will or the objective fact, less even than a cog. So that, at bottom, this outsourcing of human judgment to data is also a form of the primitive impulse to idolatry: a heightened reverence for something that we desire to trick ourselves into forgetting we have made, a desire to obey ourselves writ large.

It has been a central, recurring objection to all facets of technocratic administration since the late eighteenth century that they are cold, impersonal, procedurally opaque, faceless, alienating, and indifferent to the human motives and ends under its control. From Rousseau to Schiller to Hegel to Marx to Kafka to Wilson, any number of modern thinkers have inveighed against the supremacy of institutionally centralized bureaucratic technique, contrasting its mechanical character to "organic," creative, or holistic visions of communal life conducive to the "free development of each." Even as the large-scale use of such techniques is relentlessly *efficient* for the running of governments, companies, and institutions, we have often felt that very efficiency to be a form of oppression, an "iron cage" that works best by disconnecting individual accountability from the well-oiled function of an operation (such that no one representative of the system can be responsible for all its tasks).

Digital technology is an attempt to overcome this shortcoming once and for all. The impersonal will be personalized, processes that were cruelly neutral are now brought to customized life, the withering objectivity of bureaucracy will be invested with judgments seemingly *just for you*. It represents a fusion of democratic personality with objectivity, of responsiveness with data. That such judgments are not *really* individual does not trouble us, so long as they can both simulate care and bring to bear the weight of aggregated neutrality – our idea of what is fair. We are thus creating a new kind of Leviathan or "artificial man" – a smiley-faced, automated concierge service we endow with a mind from which we learn the needs and desires that then come to control us as our very own: a mirror-image of perfection.

(3) **Digital technology defines our image of perfection (we still seek ourselves whole and wholly outside ourselves).** The single greatest digital innovation, its most powerful and formative principle, is that of simulated intention. It is because and insofar as we discover ready responses to our purposes – echoed, matched, imitated, met – that our purposes are themselves transformed to suit the terms in which we find response. I've discussed some of the most evident ways in which digital technology is in the business of predicting our interests. Its commercial aim is customized convenience – the personalization of the impersonal – so that the point of all data aggregation is predictive anticipation in this sense. But these anticipations could not be effective in and of themselves, without our desire to accept digital terms as reflecting our own experience (or close enough). What is it that digital computers are *for*, after all? What is it that they are getting better *at*? Unlike clocks, which are only ever getting better at keeping time, computers are only ever getting better at acting as human beings. In doing so, they are also getting better at getting human beings to act like computers, thereby becoming inseparable from and, at the limit, interchangeable with us. Data simplifies the world; but it is only because it *speaks to us* that we pursue response in kind.

Still, I'd like to venture back once more to the question of why we find our own digital "reflections" compelling. How is it that we are undertaking this self-transformation with a will? Or, to put it another way, what is our interest in regarding digital nudges and shortcuts precisely as *anticipations* in the first place – as if they were reading our mind or taking the words out of our mouth – rather than as what they are: stimuli of mindless automatism? The fact that we respond to these signals precisely as prompts or cues, the fact that we (in effect) use digital anticipation as our way of judging what the typical terms of our choices are, suggests that it is not only digital assistants that speak to us, but that our entire interface makes sense to us insofar as we understand it as bespeaking presence of mind. Only a self can respond to or anticipate a self – only an "I" can answer to a "you." We are minded to respond to other minds as if they were other selves like us, so that digital technology's greatest success is to captivate our intentions by seeming to answer to them, and then by inducing us to reread our own intentions in the terms offered to us. Digital technology's hold on us derives entirely from its ability to get us to take it personally, as the perfect *you* – and therefore the perfect *I*, the medium of my own best mind.

I've pointed throughout this chapter to several versions of this desire: the way in which we are restructuring the real to be the virtual's counterpart in aspiration, the way in which we invest AI with a sort of personality (and in doing so cooperate with animating it), the way in which my ends are shaped by sensitivity to marginal incentives, the way in which we vest authority in algorithmic aggregate. But the most general version of this phenomenon, the phenomenon at the root of all digital sway, is its intentional (I–you) responsiveness. Cognitive psychologists refer to this aspect of our experience as "mind reading," the human inclination to mimic the forms of expression of other minds around us. It is the trait that accounts for the plasticity in our nature that suits us biologically for receiving and growing into whatever culture we are born into; it is what makes it possible for us to be historical creatures, as other animals are not. (Their evolutionary history is something that happens to them, not something they creatively undertake.) We are social creatures because we learn from others who we are – not only the norms of what's appropriate, but how we are perceived, what we are capable of, and what kinds of responses stand a chance to awaken kindred harmonies in others: the grounds of love (or its denial).

But if this is so – if our social nature consists in a quest for the acknowledgment of others – it is also this sense of personality that is at work in our engaging and being engaged by devices that are responding to us in terms habitual. What is new about this situation is not only that digital technology fuses our symbolic with our natural environments, such that we encounter social and natural as transparent to us online, that is, as being answerable to our control in such terms. What is new is that our terms of response are not exactly those of another mind of its own – the mind of another independent person or being – but those of our own mind by design: the shape of our own intentions and of the social world quantified, aggregated, projected into digital form, and thereby rendered authoritative. We are creating, in sum, a device for recognition, a machine to simulate the knowledge of ourselves-as-other. It consists in the fusion of quantification with self-love, an image that flatters us into forgetting that it is none other than our own – Narcissus's specular mimetic. This other is at once a simulacrum replica of myself and a higher version of myself that, as my own creation, reflects my own capacity for (self) mastery. The mimetic ideal is at once to recognize myself outside myself and to surrender to a superior, constructed version of what I can only aspire to be. It's all one imitation game.[189] Yet it's our conviction in the truth of this imitation of ourselves that's finally most transformative. It is not what these systems can in fact do, but the hopes we stake on them.[190]

That this ideal of perfection has the character of an open-ended *quest* – that it is not an aim that is achievable once and for all, but one that changes as we change – finds a neat demonstration in a pair of well-known psychological phenomena. "Automation bias" refers to the tendency to comply with computerized suggestions – if a device tells us to do X, we will second-guess ourselves or defer to it, even in the face of good reasons for thinking otherwise. This "bias" depends on the extent to which we understand a program as "communicating" with us, in some sense: We accord no such privilege to analogue tools. But then there is the so-called "AI Effect," namely the fact that any technical feat of computing tends to get written off as *not quite yet* "intelligence" – that computing tasks stipulated to be AI in advance have been continuously shrugged off once they are achieved. As Rodney Brooks, director of the AI Laboratory at MIT, put the phenomenon: "Every time we figure out a piece of it, it stops being magical; we say, 'Oh, that's just a computation' ... We used to joke that AI means 'almost implemented.'"[191] The ideal of creating a genuinely intelligent machine thus seems to recede as we approach – we are *looking* to defer to it as superior to ourselves, even as we continue to refuse to acknowledge it as an expression of ourselves at all. (A Google engineer was recently disciplined for claiming that a language program has a soul – do you feel any strong inclination to check up on whether he is right?[192]) The ideal acts as a permanent mirage that draws us toward new technical challenges, even as it continually finds new ways to emphasize the difference between human and mechanism.

But if the AI Effect is a notion coined by scientists miffed at the ease at which their technical innovations disappear into the convenience of tools we take for granted, its underlying provocation is to force us to formulate an answer to just what we are looking for. What would count as truly "artificial intelligence"? A being created by our hands, but in no decisive respect differing from our own cognitive capacities? We already have a host of devices that can best us at specific tasks – would a real AI have to possess all of them, lumped together? Would its capacities have to be unified with each other, truly embodied and incorporated in its material medium, rather than external to it (like a laptop with a face pasted onto it)? Would it have to be capable not only of its own autonomous feedback loops, but of its own passions, interests, dreams, sorrows? Would it have to acknowledge its own mortality with pain, its partial place within the whole of things? Would we have to *recognize* it as doing these things? And what would it mean for it to lay real claim to that recognition, to deserve it? And would it be enough if it could trick us into recognition? And would it have to care itself about the difference between simulation and reality?

None of these are technical questions, but philosophical or ethical ones, questions about the ultimate meaning of what we are up to here. Creating a thing that can do better than me at chess or that can trick me into thinking it is *like* me is a technical problem – a goal that can be specified, measured, and achieved by empirical means. But the capacity to ask (rather than to simulate) the questions of what makes us human at all, what is our reason, our freedom, or our longing, is no longer a technical issue, precisely because it is only by working out and through these questions that our own lives take on meaning. The words in which such questions are uttered can only bear our meanings because they are charged with the care that, quickening, sustains them. There can be no final answer, and therefore no technical solution to them (unless we artificially restrict the answer from the outset). That is, for us to replicate what we are, we would have to know what we are first. But, in the deepest sense, *we do not even know yet what a human being is,* not conclusively and in fact – not because we do not yet understand what consciousness is (as distinct from intelligence), nor because we are searching for it as if for a stone or a formula, but because, like the meaning of our own lives, the question of what we are is not the sort that could be found out once and for all in advance. It is because we don't and can't that our lives are worth living in their own right: the only place in which the world can be reckoned as a whole.

Yet progress toward AI has nothing to do with these questions. It is, instead, guided by the twin pursuit of computational superiority and self-love: a higher-skilled mind wedded to our ambiguous identification of the digital other as one of us. I mean that AI research supposes (1) that AI would have to prove *superior* to human cognition in measurable ways for it to "count" as a candidate for AI at all. (Would we be willing to call a program that could only beat us at chess half of the time or less "artificially intelligent"? The purpose is to make things easier for ourselves by outsourcing tasks to it, not just to trick us into believing in it.) And (2) that we are dealing with processes that answer to us, that are nonetheless *like* those of our own minds (such that a Turing test could be read as something other than a gauge of our own emotional responses). Automation must therefore both speak to us and say something about us. It is this unstable tandem of assumptions that creates the conditions for what is an open-ended quest, an unachievable project for a self-made version of perfection. Our search for the recognition of others – for working out some equilibrium between how they see us and how we would like to be seen – has always been governed by the fact that the other whose recognition we desired was the same as us in some basic sense (that they were free to acknowledge or refuse us). But our being arrested by the specular mimetic – the desire to find response in this other whose function is to reiterate a version of us – is different in that there is no one on the other side but a peculiar image of ourselves, an image that is superior to our own mind in narrow, yet hyped ways. What I've called mirroring, the projected aim of converging into or merging with digital technology, therefore proves effective *not* because we will ever manage to overcome the difference altogether, but because we will continue to think we should try to – judging our own perfection (or lack thereof) by holding it up to the standards of digital perfection. Such comparison is formative: We are looking to find ourselves and we are continually failing to, while all the time remaking ourselves for the purpose.

This is the final metaphysical frontier of our media – the guiding design underlying modern technology as such. The medium is the message, yes, but we have been trying to find a medium that is so closely identified with the message that the relation ceases to be metaphorical because we will cease to see ourselves without it, because we have lost our minds to it. We are trying, in other words, to reach the point at which we erase the medium by coding ourselves into it: to refashion ourselves into the kind of thing that we could replicate – to give tools a mind, to render mind a tool, to eliminate the difference at the limit of perfection. When we heed ELIZA (or Delphi[193] or the Moral Machine[194]) or any algorithmic response, what are we seeking (however ironically, however noncommittally) but to surrender our agency? (As when we say of an extraordinarily accomplished person that she *is a machine* – that she excels at what she does to the point of resembling an automatic process.) What are we seeking but to defer judgment to a higher logic that we have discovered by creating it? It is at this limit that our desire for scientific objectivity and subjective choice fully coincide by allowing us to be completely obedient to a process of mind that we ourselves have chosen to make and to identify with: the number self-selected and made flesh.

I push the matter into these extreme terms to clarify what I take the technological ideal to consist in, what finally motivates our desire to be coupled and synced up with our devices. It is most obviously a dream of total rational control, a desire to render ourselves and the world fully transparent to technical scrutiny. It is for this reason also, as I've said, a desire for a unified explanation of consciousness and matter. A perfect unification of these would achieve the reduction of what is apparently heterogeneous to homogeneous terms; it therefore entails the possibility of perfect control in just such terms. This was certainly what exercised the founders of modern computation – Boole, Babbage, Vaucanson – for whom the quest for creating a thinking machine likewise amounted to the quest for discovering the single explanation governing the structure of what is thinking and what is thought: "[T]he progress of natural knowledge tends toward the recognition of some central Unity in Nature, a primal unity."[195] This is the myth inherent in and intensified by our digital uses. And this is, as I've said, why the computer is more than just another medium or metaphor for human cognition. It puts the unification of matter and mind, of the world and our awareness of it, within virtual reach – both disembodied into information.[196]

Our continual redefinition of our technical ends as not yet achieved, our apparent uncertainty about them, therefore only conceals our own continual realization of the project in practice. The fact that this unification is carried out to the degree that we render our own consciousness more like an automatic process (even as we invest automatic processes with greater agency) makes clear that the project is not simply one of passive discovery, but also one in which our self-interpretation is at play – and therefore our sense of what is ultimate. Because our desire to merge with our reflection is something more than a desire for mind-melding for its own sake; it is rather a desire for perfection of explanation, for the total correspondence of what we know with what we can do (itself a cardinal principle of modern science[197]). It is a desire for transcending the terms within which we have known ourselves bounded or conditioned. In sum, the desire for total rational control is also a desire to explain ourselves away, such that we might become creatures of our own notional creation.

The fact that we have so often reached for our most advanced technology as a metaphor for ourselves suggests that the goal of all modern technology – its Promethean or Faustian metaphysical aspiration – is to make a machine like us and to make ourselves like a machine, thereby becoming makers of our lives. To be able to make ourselves is to become perfect in the sense of being self-caused and self-willed, that is, to be ourselves as gods (since God incorporates our view of what is perfect). What is specifically *transcended* thereby is the irreducible mystery of our natural origins; we long to find ourselves unbound from our dependence on what's given – on chance, on nature, history, and natality – no longer begotten but self-made. This is the deepest root connection between our desire for political equality and our desire for technological progress, since it's precisely what's inexplicable or given that in any given case thwarts our will to become altogether autonomous, self-determining, and alike. ("The more highly developed a civilization ... the more they will resent everything they have not produced."[198]) The word "data" literally means "what's given" (the French call it *les données*) – yet at such a limit, we will have turned all that's given into data. Reflection and reflected will have disappeared into the self-othered mirror.

It has long been the skeptics' claim – from Xenophanes to Hume to Feuerbach – that our divinities are alienated projections of our own best qualities. (Else, what are the odds that God should care for us or care to dwell among us?) The religious ideal has, in this light, always been a medium of mimetic desire: of feeling connected to another like us but higher. If this is so, then digital technology now occupies an analogous place. I don't mean that its merits are equivalent to those of its predecessors; whereas the great world religions are technologies of spiritual discipline, digital technology is spiritual opium. Nor is this desire for transcendent identification present in the world religions alone. (The sequence of attempts to convert all possible meanings into one cosmoptic matrix might run: Persian empire, monotheism, Roman empire, Catholic church, French Revolution and its sequels, imperial and colonial liberalism, Communism, United Nations and the human rights regime, virtual reality.) But digital technology is analogous in the sense that it now bears the full weight of our yearning for integration, participation, and incorporation in a larger purpose than our own. (In other words, Sheryl Sandberg was right.) It is our means for feeling as if we may escape the curse of being alone, unseen, forgotten, and misunderstood. It is our most powerful collective metaphor for communication, commerce, and communion.[199] It is our central way, in this sense, of aspiring to make contact, of imagining ourselves as part of what is whole and universal, of being in touch with being in love. We reach out in light of it and bend our meanings toward that light.

All of this is bound to sound outlandish, since, as I've noted, it is a peculiarity of our digital uses that they appear simply neutral, that they require no special commitment, such that questions of ultimate meaning never need arise. But the proximate cause for this metaphysical blankness is that the desirability of this vision of technical perfection – the sense that transcendence of given limits through self-creation is the highest good to which we can aspire – is itself an expression of our ultimate commitment to choice as such, to the power to do just as we please. I don't call this "freedom," though it is obvious why it might be mistaken for it. Freedom, our highest human vocation, cannot be defined in technical terms; we all recognize the difference between being free and merely going through the motions of it while in thrall to our whims, caprices, and self-delusions. Even as we (rightly) bristle at the thought of "forcing" people to be free, it is obvious that we are often not very good judges of what is best for us, or of what is most fulfilling. Yet our notion of "choice," because it is more modest than "freedom," because it is self-contained and void of content (as freedom is not), seems good precisely because it is beyond controversy – unreproachable in its sterile neutrality and universality. It is not obvious what it means to be truly free. But it is self-evident that being free has *something* to do with making choices, and so it comes to seem that having more retail choices at our disposal is therefore unequivocally better than any possible wholesale limitations on them.

I have mentioned several reasons why it is wrong to think that multiplying choices must be good per se. New choices do not simply accumulate alongside old ones, they transform their context and grammar. Nor is it simply true that it is always better to have more choices. More choices may overwhelm us or weaken our commitment to the choices we have already made – virtualizing them, as I've described above. Just so, the multiplication of informational choices may have the perverse effect of diminishing the amount and quality of what we can take in and make our own. And new choices made in specifically digital terms are often enough only ideal simulations of choice such that they either become ends in themselves or transform the very thing we thought we were choosing. Yet absent some strong set of cultural inhibitions, absent some collective specification of ethics to direct and circumscribe our purposes, the creation of new choices will either continue uninterrupted or will require ruthless coercive measures to check. Because where "more" is better because it seems neutral – *and who are you to say otherwise? –* the only possible checks will be extrinsic to our research and development of new techniques for rational mastery. These are our likely alternatives so long as our course stays on autopilot: either a mindlessly widening number of choices or the coerced enforcement of some of them.

It is the (apparently neutral) value of choice as such that accounts for the implacable monotony within which discussions about technology now unfold. When it comes to arguments about what is to be done about the overwhelming progress of digital technology, as about all technology, the discussion plays out, as I've noted, between two positions. The charge of technology's moderates and sceptics is that its unfolding and development is *up to us –* a matter of deliberate human decisions, which we can correct or refrain from at any time. Technology does not make itself; it is therefore within our means to improve it or tweak it or abandon it altogether. The rejoinder by the other camp is that these tools will be developed *anyway –* so what is the point in trying to stop them? One may as well get with the times and learn how to maximize our digital benefits.

Both of these can't be right: The progress of technology cannot both be up to us and not. But both are wrong. The sceptics and moderates implicitly rely on the very principle that has created the conditions they are criticizing. They present the design of choice as a matter of choice, whereas it is precisely the unbridled pursuit of such choices that has eventuated in undesirable effects. (As this is closer to what we would like to think – that we in fact have a *choice* in the matter – this is by far the most common position.) Nor do they acknowledge that a world in which we *refrain* from studying or implementing or using certain technologies is not identical to the world in which these were simply unknown to us: Once a choice is present, choosing *not* to exercise it is itself a new choice that requires widespread legitimacy. The boosters and determinists are wrong, on the other hand, because they do not acknowledge that technology only develops "anyway" insofar as we are, as a culture and a world, positively committed to a vision of technical rationality that continually impels us to make specific forms of progress – to increase productivity and efficiency, to reduce the possibility of error in human judgment, to diminish suffering (quantitatively construed), and again (in the more general formulation) to amplify our powers of choice, to progressively diminish the role of what is given or natural in us, what we cannot help – to turn the "given" into the "made" at every turn, since "made" means always tailor made to suit.

Expanding our powers of choice in these or any regards cannot but seem like a good thing. But that's just it. The goals of choice are such that, once possible, they cannot be dismissed without suppression. My point is not exactly to deprecate these goals, but to insist on the fact that they really are goals – that even as we congratulate ourselves for our adherence to the neutrality of technical power, to its impersonal widening of availability of more choices for more people, this is nonetheless a specific demand that we place on ourselves, one that has the status of an ideal, one that defangs the meaning of any one ethical commitment we could make under its umbrella, and one that is not *inevitable* except insofar as we implicitly identify it with the highest goal of human achievement, thereby making it the animating principle of our uses. It is a value that supplies us with the terms in which we formulate our ultimate social values, the frontier toward which we feel we should continue to progress. And so long as we do so, we will continue to erase the difference between ourselves and our devices, to be leading protagonists in our own dehumanization for the sake of better interface and compatibility. In other words: to transcend our condition by working to become plugged in to perfect machines, self-choosing and self-chosen, creatures in the position to consent to all that makes us what we are.

Our sense of modern technology as a sort of "fate" (Heidegger), as a dynamic with a life of its own of which we are the "genitals" (McLuhan), as something that "wants" something of us or is determined to proceed in certain ways (Kevin Kelly), before which we are helpless to act is – whether we giddily cheer it or cry halt in dismay – part of a larger sense of our loss of agency, our inability to see ourselves otherwise than as we are. Undoubtedly this responds to real features of modern societies; the bewildering sense that, as power is diluted and spread out, no one is in charge, that mass phenomena "happen" without anyone in particular causing them. But this is the obverse consequence of our attraction to the condition of equality itself, our categorical suspicion of personal authority on the grounds of being partial, our desire for bureaucratic rule by no one in particular. This is the objective society, the neutral society, the society of choices for all equally. That we should continue to pursue the greater exercise of choice is in this sense inevitable – the multiplication of choices for all cannot but continue to increase the sense of helplessness for each. In any case, given the choice, we cannot but prefer to keep choosing choice itself. This is what always goes without saying, unthinking.

That we should continually wish to amplify choice for its own sake, prizing innovation's "more" and "better" above any criterion of "good enough," is a sign that we are not aiming at some fixed goal, so much as at an ideal of a perfection beyond the world as we know it. Anyone who thinks this will make us free has chosen to forget what freedom is or can be – persisting in construing it in technical terms just because it is those terms that are under our potential mastery and therefore require no stretch of our ethical imagination to achieve. I do not say that this was not a problem before digital technology came along; I do not say that anyone has *ever* been altogether free. So what? Freedom has never been a matter of averages or data – it is the way in which each one of us strives to realize the promise of our life by giving shape to it for the time. But this is the most difficult thing in the world, there are no technical answers for it, our practical avenues to it are jaundiced and diminished, and so instead we exchange it for an impoverished form of power that we *can* exercise, even as we blind ourselves to what we cannot thereby gain. When we cannot bend the natural world to the wishes embodied in our awesome technical capacities, we will end by suiting ourselves to suit the digital terms we have at hand. This is the risk of wish-fulfillment: that we warp what's best in us to suit the medium precisely because it feels close enough. We leap to the conclusion, close the gap to make it so, so seeking our salvation in coveting what we must continually fail to possess.

4.3.3   What's Gotten into You?

> Perfection is the mere repudiation of that ineluctable marginal inexactitude which is the mysterious inmost quality of Being.
>
> (H. G. Wells)

What are human beings for? What is the point of us? Our technical prejudice, inaugurated by Descartes, is to suppose that questions without conclusive answers must be unanswerable, or arbitrary, or not worth pursuing since we cannot make objective progress with them. But this position assumes that what is true must be technical or quantifiable, which is a convenient falsehood designed to rule out what is ambiguous from the outset. We give it the lie every day in the miraculous fact that each human life is not reducible to a pattern of preexisting options, but undertakes the world again. Each human life is the whole world, and freedom is the privilege to begin it once again from scratch. Neither care nor love nor communion can be determined in advance from our participation in it; we come alive by living, we make our meanings real only by meaning them. What does it mean to be "perfect"? We know we should be. We also know that we're not (yet). To be only human is to know that the strain between those ends is just what spells our worth and that it is from this very paradox that we stand to win our joy.

Our desire to become perfect by recreating ourselves is not in and of itself a project with a foreseeable end – so long as we continue to approximate it, we will continue to call attention to the ways in which the digital is not yet quite natural, not yet ourselves. Better approximations of the virtual only accentuate the meaning of the real; better approximations of task-based intelligence only accentuate the value of human understanding; so too better approximations of ourselves will only continue to cast into relief our irreducibility to machine learning and digital processes. And this is to be modern: to continuously struggle to give definition to ourselves in contrast to new technologies in such a way that the struggle itself comes completely to define us.

The only way in which this would cease to be so, however, is if we should lose sight of the question, should forget that the matter of our own perfection is technically incomparable. It is not impossible that we might one day make a bionic human, fleshed from silicon. "Human" too is a metaphoric term; we are making it up as we go along and as we find it in new mirrors. Yet it should mean capable of improbable elation and cruelty and generosity all at once, of leaps of imagination and insight, of asking a perceptive question (and of staking oneself on the answer), of seeing what is perfect in the absence of it, of making a promise, of being arrested by the difference between a paradox and a mere contradiction, of hoping for what's best, of retrieving greater forms of love from the patience of its failures, of keeping silence, of wild longings and extravagant. But this is no longer the sort of thing that our technical quest is ever after, because our desire to create ourselves goes hand in hand with our desire to forget or forego the full extent of what we are – to leave the best part of us behind, to transcend who we have been, if only for the sake of exercising power over who we should be. The only question is the lengths to which we will be willing to go to keep mechanizing ourselves, verging toward it by and by.

I acknowledge that I am offering no special program for a better digital life – in part because that is not the subject of this book, in part because I think that our grasping at policies and technical solutions is itself a sign of our current ordeal by data, in part because I think the answer is so obvious to all of us that most practical suggestions are convoluted self-evasions. Work to cut it down (or out). Reduce your dependence. Do not address it as *you*. Uncouple your mind from what is mindless aggregate. Do not fight it directly (since that too is its power to shape) but work to change the subject altogether. At any rate, work *not* to see yourself as if reflected in this mirror. At any rate, work to see that part of what we are buying into is an instrument for forgetting the meaning of what's most meaningful – an instrument for forgetting death and therefore an instrument of death itself.

The desire to rely on government or programming is in kind with all our digital problems. It is the desire to displace our agency onto impersonal and external causes, the desire to do nothing by pointing out how everyone alike is implicated in it. What's formulated as *everyone's* problem is no problem at all. There is no other trick to it but disconnecting; it's up to you and me to claim our lives as ours. And if this sounds like a counsel of despair, think again – how else should we expect to answer the question of what human beings are *for* except by each of us becoming fully answerable for it? Even as the future looks dead certain, it's you, and you alone are living proof it's otherwise in practice, once more and time again. It will not be a permanent solution or a widespread one; but there never have been such, not really. There have only ever been temporary, adaptive reprieves snatched piecemeal from misrule, disintegration kept at bay one more generation by implausible exceptions, while all the while indifference, violence, and anarchy conspired at the doorsill, time always on their side. Keep watch, hold out, stay a while longer. It's not yours to finish the work, nor is it to desist from it.[200]

The story of Stanislav Petrov's world-saving refusal has become commonplace for the wrong reasons. We read it as if the world's fate lay in one man's hands once and for all, the dilemma sharpened into one moment of do-or-die decision. What would we have done in his place? But the moral of his heroism is otherwise and elsewhere. It is that you *are* in his place, that the world is completely at stake and in your hands at every moment and that there is no way to save it except by refusing to act within the technical terms in which the question is presented to us. It's only so we sharpen vision by working to undo the web of our own unmaking.

There is not and will never be such a thing as ethical AI, there is no working well with it, there is no full responsibility or meaningful judgment that can be exercised in digital terms (that is just *why* we are developing these tools). There are only hewn and burnt reminders of what our doing might have meant and our earnest pretense that we remain fully human because we are still in use as programmed users of it. It is not that we all aspired to higher lives before digital technology came along. It is that we *should* aspire to them, and that digital technology deforms or aims to extirpate the roots of better nature. And so the only truly ethical use of digital technology is to disobey it, to walk away.

The technophiles will still argue that technology is an extension of our humanity, so that our conflicts with technology are due "to our refusal to accept our nature."[201] Exactly so. What they omit is that it is also our nature to know the obligation to say no and no and no again – as much to what is given as to what is presented to us as inevitable. *No* is just what a computer cannot mean to say. This *no* is all that concerns you.

5

From My Inbox

On Mon, June 6, 2022 at 12:00 PM [REDACTED] <REDACTED@zzzmail
.com> wrote:

Dear Antón,

I just finished your book and thought I'd fire off a quick response. Even though
you talk a lot of crap about our company, I'd like to offer you a job with us.
Honestly, I'd love to have you. Come and be one of our consultants or ethics
washers or business analysts or whatever; you pick the title. We can always use
someone like you. Between you and me, I hate all these tech toads with their sad
little lives – it gets old dealing with all these nerds who can only think in GIFs. It
ticks me off that they don't at all get what we're doing here; anything approaching an independent thought causes their brains to emit an error message. But a
general can expect only so much from his foot-soldiers. I don't think you get it
either, to be honest; but at least you have some sense of the project's scale and
direction. Anyway, I thought it would be fun to ask you here to Palo Alto, just
to have you around to spar or bounce some ideas off of; I know you would
enjoy it. But I'm also taking the chance to write to explain a few things to you.
Unlike a lot of the people working at the companies you criticize, I have done
a lot of thinking about these issues, so it's nice to be able to speak to someone
openly about them. I only ask that you keep this email to yourself. I could get
in trouble for putting all this in writing. (Except certainly not.)

Look. You exhibitionist intellectuals, you armchair critics – you go on with your
digital mewling in your boo-hoo books and grumpy blogposts, you conspicuously complain about social media in the *New Yorker* or *The Atlantic*, you type
up your screeds on your new iMac, and then squeak with joy when your article
works up a nano-trickle of retweets and gets picked up by one of our aggrega-
tors. It's incredibly lame. As if blowhard complaint were not itself a form of

modern performance art. As if criticism were not just another commodity. As if anyone really cared to see you go through these whingeing motions. As if you were not pretending to fight against something you don't really want to destroy.

I know your type, believe me – I know everything you're going to say before you even say it. Honestly, I love people like you. I get a kick out of you, I really do – I order your books as soon as they come out and have a good laugh reading them in the bathtub, as a way to unwind. I underline the juiciest passages, which I then have my PR team read and discuss at special summits on how to better sell our service to Whole-Foods-shopping, Prius-driving, West-Elm-furnishing, Ivy-League-educated, socially conscientious whiners prone to periodic simulations of tech-skepticism, just like you. We've got your number. Hey, do you realize that it is you who keep us going? That you're actually working for us in the role of mascots? That it is you who defang real challenge by legitimizing and normalizing criticism? That it is you who keep the whole system from becoming bland by giving people a little titillating spasm of intellectual transgression from time to time, so that they can pat themselves on the back and carry on just as before? The thing is, it's hardly worth responding to you at all, you are already so irrelevant; like the clowns who distract the audience in between acts at the circus – or like all those anti-Amazon books that people keep selling and buying ... on Amazon.

But let's pretend for a moment that you are not irrelevant. Question: When have people ever really thought for themselves? No, really. When do you think democracy was running smoothly? When was this great age of meaning? Can you point to a single minute in the history of the world when there was something closer to thoughtful citizenry, functioning Republic, authentic living? Tell me, I'm all ears. Was it the eighteenth century? The nineteenth? The twentieth? I don't even need to tell you that most people were going through some, um, profoundly troubled times then. You will say sometimes, in some ways, some people approximated these things better than in the present. Woopty. Do you mean the miniscule ruling class that lorded it over everyone else? Or, even if you don't: how could that *ever* fail to be true? That doesn't mean we should work to make those times the norm now. You would not care to admit this to yourself, but neither the American Dream nor the nation state nor human judgment nor any of your high flung projects have really worked out as they were supposed to: those things do not on their own make life on average better for most people. They certainly weren't going that smoothly before we stepped in to lend a hand! So whatever fuzzy ideas you have about reality and humanity – these too have not fallen from the sky, they are myths from the Romantic era, or fossils from the Enlightenment, or some other reactionary hairball you've managed to hack up from your elite humanities education. What's new here? What are you proposing exactly, other than a few hollow and naïve gestures in the general direction of yesteryear?

Here's the thing. We are the ones demonstrably alleviating human suffering. We are the ones reducing the drudgery of work. We are the ones driving change to make the world a better place. We are the ones who have harnessed information for the good. We are the ones putting actual practical proposals on the table instead of just doing subjective interpretive prancing. We are the ones freeing up your time to complain about us, when in another age you – yes *you* too, in all likelihood – would have been slaving away in a scrofulous factory or mine or field, toiling day in and out for a fistful of little potatoes that you would be scarcely able to masticate with your decaying, malnourished teeth, only to drop dead from a light scratch turned gangrenous at age 39. We are the real lovers of humanity here, the real philanthropists working to reduce its misery.

You don't even contest that we are making the world run more smoothly, that we are the ones making measurable progress. You think it's better that people should continue to drive cars themselves? Roger that. Go ahead and explain that to the families of the tens of thousands of people who lose their loved ones every year to traffic accidents. You think it's better to do office work by hand? Be my guest. Let white-collar workers know that we're going back to the good old métier of scrivening – I will personally sponsor you with quills, parchment, blotters, and a full set of scriptorium swag. You think it's better that doctors should continue to make faulty diagnoses at higher rates than our algorithms? That prisoners should be sentenced by racist juries? That thousands of corpses should keep piling up because of skepticism about digital virus tracing? That suffering and mismanagement and waste should continue to be the norm? Go for it, guy. No one is stopping you. Maybe you should ask people what they want – better or worse outcomes in these specific respects. Or maybe you think they shouldn't be consulted? Whoa, easy there; here I was thinking you were accusing *us* of usurping authority!

No, no, but I get it; you don't think that efficiency and health and productivity are the highest human goals. Mmk. Here's the thing: *yes they absolutely are*. At least, they are as a matter of what it is possible to achieve through policy and sustained collective action. Your argument is that we should bear the cost of lower health, lower efficiency, uneven standardization, for the sake of … what exactly? Freedom? What's that? Seriously. Is it allowing people to escape oppression by speaking up? Is it empowering people to choose how they want to live? Is it permitting people to organize and protest? Making available the resources for them to be creative? Liberating them from the despair of small-minded, parochial bigotry that crushes the spirits of so many? Am I getting warmer? Because – oh wait, hang on – *we* are the ones doing all that, not you.

And by the way, we have singlehandedly done more in the service of equality than any country or institution has ever managed to *in the entire history of the world*. No big deal. You don't even contest this. Liberalism cannot and does not root out racial prejudice, because it must respect some boundary between private and public – after the 1960's racism has basically retrenched into the private sphere, where it remains alive and hale. It is only tech that has managed to make the barrier between private and public more permeable, that has given voice to those who are routinely oppressed, that has opened up a way of broadcasting injustice, that has put the tools for shaming the worst offenders in the hands of the people. Baw, you think that it's such a loss that "mercy" is not possible for people who are doxed for being bigots? When has mercy ever been widely available? Just because some people's egregious offensiveness used to be overlooked or forgotten doesn't make me pine for the merciful world of the printed page.

But here's the thing – now we're really getting down to it. Here's the open secret you should stop pretending not to know about. Ready? People don't actually want to be "free" or equal in any super lofty sense, they just want to be happy. I'd say you agree with me there; otherwise, you have no way of explaining the fact that people "know" all the bad stuff about tech, even as they continue to avidly opt into it. Except people don't really know what "happiness" is either. They never have. So here's what they *do* know: they know they want a deal on some nice stuff, they want to be amused, they want to be no worse off than most of their neighbors, they want to feel connected, and they want a bit of attention. Basically, they want to be able to feel pretty good about themselves, comparatively and some of the time. Period. That's it. End of human predicament. (You don't need to take my word for it: it's all right there in your darling Tocqueville.) If you look at what people do, how they *actually* operate, rather than what we'd like to say about them, this is exactly what they are up to. And guess what. It's *we* who can make that happen for them! We make it easier for them to have the stuff, the amusement, the comparison, the connection, the attention to a degree never even dreamt of! We are the ones not just keeping people safer and healthier but actually making them more content than ever! Why is it that people don't even glance at the terms and conditions? How is it that they routinely sign away their data for the sake of more convenient services? Why do people sagely nod along at books like yours and then tweet about it and go back to their online ways just the same? They do it because everyone else does it! They do it because they actually *trust* us to deliver for them! They *want* to, see?

People don't really want to be free, as I think you agree. At least, they don't "want" it in any normal sense of the word, any sense comprehensible to anyone outside your increasingly irrelevant tower made out of the nineteenth-century ivory trade. (Are you not basically motivated by the desire to protect your status as a guardian of knowledge too, by the way?) Being real and free (as you seem to understand it) is astoundingly hard, let's face it; you know that it requires almost superhuman risks and sacrifices and commitments – the sorts of things we admire in our heroes ... at a distance. But not that many people really *want* to be Simone Weil or Mother Teresa – I mean, we would all like to be famous, but it's pretty clear that only a few people have the guts for it. It involves radically stepping out from the crowd and this is not what most people are aiming for. Wonderful: let the heroes be heroes, I could not agree more. People are content to be vaguely inspired from a position of safety. But beyond the little gadgets and the spice of vanity that we can deliver for them, they would prefer to be disburdened, managed, conducted. Do you really doubt this? I swear to you, people just want to be left to do their thing with a little modest notoriety, if possible. And we are the ones giving them that thing, do you not see? We are the ones giving them their own thing in terms that they can achieve!

I see that this version of happiness is less sexy than the great Ode-to-Joy dreams of exalted brotherhood that haunt your view. Hey, how did those work out, hm? Whom can you name that was ever that happy, that authentic, that fulfilled in a non-materialistic way? Two or three people, *maybe*, like, ever? (No cheating now: characters in literature or wishful self-novelizers don't count, so go ahead and erase Dostoyevsky and Kierkegaard from that list.) It's not good for people to suffer in service of the unattainable; that illusion is past. When the bar for human flourishing is set too high, you are actually damaging people, making them wretched and resentful, not inspiring them. We offer a new happiness – we can actually give people something closer and closer to their expectations, we can give them a way of measuring their worth. And is matching means with expectation not exactly what happiness is? Is mental health not a better bet than "authenticity" or "salvation"? Is satisfaction not a better bet than the beau geste or spiritual theater of other ages? Why should we not aim to eliminate what "is given" as quickly as possible? Isn't that the whole point of this "no" you end with?

I know what you're about to say – that digital technology is not creating a happier world, that people are more restless and alienated than before. But this is pretty hard to judge; you yourself admit that happinesses are incommensurable. If people are so unhappy, what keeps them coming back for more? If they are unhappy, I think it is only because they feel so within the terms of happiness that digital technology can itself offer them. But, honestly, while I see people squealing with pleasure and rage on the online surface, and while there will always be a few psycho nuts who go on violent rampages, the more striking thing for anyone with eyes is the deep, near unanimous calm underlying it: the bellows of passions superficially hyperventilated in terms that don't disturb the underlying stability of what we're setting up for the long run. Yes, people are up in arms about all sorts of things. Not all of them are nutty, but all of them are workable on our terms. We're giving them something to do, we're giving them a way to stay fully engaged in all kinds of issues, except genuinely radical or transformative and therefore *destructive* ones. I'm talking twentieth century destructive – the most radically messed up kind of destructive that the world has ever known. Not sure about you, but I'm kind of eager to avoid a repeat, given that we are still only a button push or two away from total annihilation. And guess what? *We've figured out how.* Seen any viral demonstrations against the internet lately? Or against capitalism? Or against social networks? Or against equality? How about against cute puppies? How else would you even think about radical protest except in online terms? What would your radical protest even be about, by the way? How else could you even conceive of your autonomy and equality and general satisfaction, except as mediated by digital technology? Both the left and the right are completely wrapped up in it: it's the only place to be if you want to be a democratic socialist influencer or to own the libs. A protest against the internet could only resemble those religious sects that forbid procreation for its members – self-defeating and short-lived.

Here's the best part, see – we've given people a new way of doing everything they want to do, but in such a way that they can't mess it all up like they have before again and again and again. They still get to rock the boat a little, but this boat can't be overturned. *So there's no trade-off involved.* It's not like we're telling people what to think or forcing them to be less free. We're not anti-democratic or anti-humanist or anti-anything. It's because people find happiness in these terms that they flock to us. We don't have to move a finger! It's because people identify democracy with choosing that we're in business. It's because people find community in digital terms that they keep coming. Don't you see? This is what allows us to have it both ways: all the old illusions have been domesticated into solid new terms. People can still go through the real emotional rollercoaster of political participation or radical life choices without touching the fundamental stability of the whole social arrangement. (You yourself don't seem to have a problem with the system itself, by the way; or did I miss your modest plea for communism?) We're offering something that in this way transcends and will survive any particular political ideology. We've solved for the purpose that politics itself was supposed to and failed to achieve in the first place. We are bringing into being the genuinely post-historical, human society.

History lesson: maybe you're forgetting that personal and political freedom have only ever been defended as the liberal means to a more efficient and productive society – the invisible hand, the "democratic experiment," or "laboratories of democracy," the "marketplace of ideas," and so on. That was the point of a free society, that was the mechanical defense of self-regulation, that was what the Cold War was supposed to have shown – not anything about the triumph of authenticity (which is just another capitalist fetish, as Adorno says). But, see, now we've figured out a better mechanism – a better way of streamlining the market, of reducing the irrational waste of institutions, and of optimizing results in all areas: democracy by other means. "Social engineering" is a scary phrase you get to brandish at your readers – but what's the matter with it really? What if it just means "getting stuff done" and "making people happy"? What if we actually don't need "politics" in any lofty sense in order to achieve that?

Face it: politics has long been dead or deadly – you cite Arendt awfully selectively without mentioning the part where she warns about the nation state's permanent tendency to suicidal insanity. We are actually starting to run things efficiently now, even as citizens can still feel as if they are participating in super exciting yet ultimately inconsequential choices like whom to vote for on

American Idol or whom to pick for president. The things that dominate our attention will no longer be the things that really matter, but they will still feel overwhelmingly real. Don't you see how great this is? The *sense* of choice, the legitimacy of consent, without the consequences of permanently screwing it all up!

The ideal of democracy, the ideal of politics as the *res publica* we work out in common – that ship sailed a long time ago, if it ever even existed. It's a dream that didn't pan out (that's why we keep pedaling back to that impossibly distant scenario we call "Ancient Greece" for it). Not only is it the wrong thing to want, it's actually *impossible* – it's only given us one terribly oppressive and violent regime after another. It's rarely worked, if ever, and never for very long. What's more, the same arguments you're making have been made again and again over the last two hundred years; no one has really cared about politics for a long time. You think we were so democratic on account of voting for people never known except from TV, people chosen by back-room corporate tycoons? You think it was great that the people were so involved in politics that they lynched and invaded and mass-murdered and interned and rustled up a little Civil War, two World ones, and one Cold one within less than one century? The same numpties who know jack about anything other than the Real Housewives or Taytay's new outfit? The magnificently enlightened citizens who can barely name the vice-president, let alone the three branches of government? *Those* people? Those people are moral infants; those people are ruining anything that was ever worthwhile about your precious high-brow culture and society – is that not the subtext of light contempt running through every paragraph in your book too? Obviously it is. They've long been a mob, rather than a people, just as Arendt says. So we've come up with a better way to rely on those people now. We all pretend to work up a sweat about whether Trump or Biden or the Yankees or the Sox win today's game, and you get to have your little ranticle about how the internet is destroying humanity, while we get on with the real work behind the scenes regardless, ensuring stability, keeping things fluid and making impactful, positive progress on particular issues. We are getting the best of both worlds here – just like when Trump whips up a crowd by talking about the "WuFlu" even as he negotiates a trade agreement with China. Don't you see? We all still get to feel as if we're fully engaged, even as smart decisions are basically made for you – outta sight!

But "behind the scenes" is the wrong phrase. What's great is that we don't even need to hide it – it's not like we are the conspiratorial shadow cabal of swamp creatures that populists love to beat up on. We are right here in the plainest clearest view, the platform and services that everyone are using to communicate about everything. We're not getting together in any smoky rooms to pick the next candidate – we don't even know each other *because we don't have to*! And if and when it's not us anymore – I'm not such an idiot as to think that we're going to keep this company going forever – it's going to be someone else like us, carrying on our work, our vision. And if it's another company from your bogeyman China, so much the better. May the best team win – Sox or Yankees, it doesn't matter, because we've got to the point where we've figured out a game superior to politics itself, see? A game that, unlike national politics, doesn't depend on having any star players anymore. The nation state is dead now as the center of the real action – people aren't satisfied with it and don't really care about it. That's why they flock to us instead. Why pretend otherwise with feeble hand-wavings toward anachronistic hope?

I'm sorry, then, for not apologizing for our greatest, most hideous crime – namely, BRINGING ABOUT PEACE ON EARTH AND GOOD WILL TOWARD PEOPLE while you bookish smarty-pants pout from the sidelines. Because you're wrongest of all when you suggest that we're just in this for the money or that our business only involves delivering creature comforts that we don't understand. Money is terrific; I'm the last to deny it. But it's no very strong motivator – it does not keep me going personally, nor does it keep people coming back for more, nor does it lure more and more talent each year – unless you also offer people a better way to live. If not something they can achieve for themselves, then something big enough to accommodate the sense of their lives, something big enough to belong to – something that makes sense of the Future for them, something that allows them to think that tomorrow just might be a little better than today. Yes, religion and political ideology used to do that for them. Will you be so scandalized if I say that the time for those is now over? Is this even in question anymore? Really? Really, really? (Now make sure to show your work, if you'd like partial credit.)

Here's the thing. Our best product is not our website or our software or our phone or anything like that – it's actually something that we are not paid a single cent for. Guess what? It's *hope*. We are giving people a better way to live; a way to find a new voice, a new ideal salvaged from the ruins of every other bankrupt creed. Human beings will get used to anything, they will swallow *absolutely* anything, except meaningless suffering, as you and Nietzsche know, and it's only when they can hold on to an image of perfection that their suffering can take on that meaning. We're the ones delivering that now! It's not the stupendous image of transcendence we thought we wanted in other ages. We have museums and books for those now. They are without a doubt more grandiose than what we offer. But those are beautiful only because they are out of reach, only because they are ruinously unattainable and otherworldly, only because they are polemical and destructive, whereas our own brand is centered on real-life humans and the satisfactions of ordinary life; it is both absolutely hopeful and totally *possible*. We can give each person safety, convenience, health, engagement, choices, and attention. We can make life a little easier for each generation. We can manage things in a superior way. We have found out a form of happiness that can make pretty much *everyone* reasonably happy! It will not be as heavenly as the wretched escapism of the Middle Ages imagined it – but I can guarantee that it will be, on average, better for each and all. If every age is fed on special illusions, our hopes are closest to being *facts*, to needing no hulking metaphysical apparatus to justify them.

Is this not the highest end? Continually to make the world more equal, more free, more productive all around? To improve safety and health, while reducing suffering? To increase people's foresight and control over their lives? To add to our objective understanding of how the world actually works? To make life more comfortable for more and more people? To give humans an achievable ideal of wellbeing toward which to direct their energies? And yes, maybe even one day – who knows – to become immortal and all that sci-fi stuff. But for now it doesn't have to be that; for now it's just a way of having the tools to rationally organize progress toward our better self – sure, a mirror for perfection, if you'd like. Is this not a better ideal than your old gods, who only succeeded in making people neurotic and superstitious? We are offering something much better than the old gods: we are giving people real hope by offering them a way of understanding and improving their lot as they see fit in this world. We are offering to free people from chance, from fear, and from physical coercion – we can promise to increase human beings' overall satisfaction with life. Regardless of whether you harbor some Very Serious Reservations, these are the correct things to strive for in all realism; this is the only good direction to gamble on. Am I wrong? If I am, I agree it's all on me. I confess that sometimes I wake up in a sweat, worrying that I'm burning the world to the ground. But then I have a cup of açaí tea, and breathe deep, and remind myself of people like you, and then go back to resting easy. You're my comfort blanket. Because at least I'm *doing* something about it all; at least I'm doing the world's work, instead of just sounding off about it. So no worries. Please don't get up, keep your seat; we'll take it from here.

Do consider my offer to come work for us. (I mean, you already are!) Come and see.

With thanks for all you (don't) do,
XXX [redacted]

Notes

INTRODUCTION

1 Louis Mumford, *The Myth of the Machine: The Pentagon of Power* (New York: Harcourt Brace Jovanovich, 1970), 417.

2 Max Scheler, *Man's Place in Nature*, translated by Hans Meyerhoff (New York: Noonday Press, 1974), 52.

3 "64% of Americans Say Social Media Have a Mostly Negative Effect on the Way Things Are Going in the U.S. Today," Pew Research Center, October 15, 2020, www.pewresearch.org/fact-tank/2020/10/15/64-of-americans-say-social-media-have-a-mostly-negative-effect-on-the-way-things-are-going-in-the-u-s-today.

4 Max Horkheimer, *Eclipse of Reason* (London: Bloomsbury, 2013), 132.

5 Quoted in Evgeny Morozov, *To Save Everything, Click Here* (New York: PublicAffairs, 2013), vii.

6 "Huge 'Foundation Models' Are Turbo-Charging AI Progress," *The Economist*, June 11, 2022, www.economist.com/interactive/briefing/2022/06/11/huge-foundation-models-are-turbo-charging-ai-progress.

7 Bruno Latour, *We Have Never Been Modern*, translated by Catherine Porter (Cambridge, MA: Harvard University Press, 1993), 104.

8 Montesquieu, *The Spirit of the Laws*, translated by Anne Cohler, Basia Miller, and Harold Stone (Cambridge: Cambridge University Press, 1989), 311.

9 Hannah Arendt, *The Human Condition* (Chicago: University of Chicago Press, 1998), 2–3.

10 Marshall McLuhan, *The Medium and the Light*, edited by Eric McLuhan and Jacek Szklarek (Eugene: Wipf and Stock, 2010), 64.

11 Hannah Arendt, *Men in Dark Times* (San Diego: Harcourt Brace, 1968), 83–87.

I   LEFT TO OUR OWN DEVICES

1 Quoted by Walter Benjamin, *Illuminations: Essays and Reflections*, translated by Harry Zohn (New York: Schocken Books, 1969), 219.

2   Henry Adams, *The Education of Henry Adams* (New York: The Library of America, 1983), 1067.

3   Aristotle, On the Soul, 432a (my translation).

4   Friedrich Nietzsche, *Twilight of the Idols*, translated by Judith Norman (New York: Cambridge University Press, 2005), 224.

5   Cf. Harald Weinrich, *Wege der Sprachkultur* (Stuttgart: Deutsche Verlags-Anstalt, 1985), 190.

6   Helen Keller, *The Story of My Life* (Mineola: Dover, 1996), 12.

7   Walter Ong, *Orality and Literacy* (London: Routledge, 2002), 7.

8   See Claude Lévi-Strauss's striking observations on this theme in *Tristes Tropiques* (London: Penguin, 2012), 296–300.

9   See Georg Wilhelm Friedrich Hegel's remark that "it is the state which first brings about a content that is not only adapted to the prose of history, but helps to produce it" in *Lectures on the Philosophy of History*, translated by Ruben Alvarado (Aalten: WordBridge Publishing, 2011), 56.

10 *The Bible, Authorized King James Version* (Oxford: Oxford University Press, 1997), Luke 10:20 (for "rejoice ...") and passim for "as it is written ..." For a fine elaboration on the trope of divine translation, see Roger Chartier, *Éditer et traduire* (Paris: Seuil/Gallimard, 2021).

11 Ong, Orality and Literacy, 10.

12 Isak Dinesen, *Out of Africa and Shadows on the Grass* (New York: Vintage, 1989), 115.

13 Ivan Illich, *In the Vineyard of the Text* (Chicago: University of Chicago Press, 1993), 112.

14 See Thomas Prufer's superb essay on the relation between silent reading and the development of Christian interiority: "A Reading of Augustine's Confessions, Book X," in *Recapitulations: Essays in Philosophy* (Washington, DC: The Catholic University of America Press, 1993), 27–31.

15 Illich, In the Vineyard of the Text, 54–55, 86ff.

16 See Benedict Anderson's *Imagined Communities: Reflections on the Origin and Spread of Nationalism* (London: Verso, 2006), 198.

17 "What distinguishes the novel from the story (and from the epic in the narrower sense) is its essential dependence on the book." Benjamin, Illuminations, 87.

18 Arthur C. Clarke, *2001: A Space Odyssey* (New York: Penguin, 2016), 48.

19 "People Lie More in Email than When Using Pen and Paper," Research Digest, April 8, 2010, https://digest.bps.org.uk/2010/04/08/people-lie-more-in-email-than-when-using-pen-and-paper.

20 "Thumbs Race as Japan's Best Sellers Go Cellular," The New York Times, January 20, 2008, www.nytimes.com/2008/01/20/world/asia/20japan.html?-pagewanted=all.

21 Neil Postman, *Amusing Ourselves to Death: Public Discourse in the Age of Show Business* (New York: Penguin, 2005), 3ff.

22 Ong, Orality and Literacy, 49.

23 "The Untold Technological Revolution Sweeping through Rural China," The New York Times, October 15, 2020, www.nytimes.com/2020/10/15/books/review/blockchain-chicken-farm-xiaowei-wang.html.

24 Joseph Stiglitz, *Making Globalization Work* (New York: Norton, 2007), 45.

25 "Why Google Has 200m Reasons to Put Engineers over Designers," The Guardian, February 5, 2014, www.theguardian.com/technology/2014/feb/05/why-google-engineers-designers.

26 "AI Farms Are at the Forefront of China's Global Ambitions," Time, February 1, 2019, https://time.com/5518339/china-ai-farm-artificial-intelligence-cybersecurity.

27 "Twelve Million Phones, One Dataset, Zero Privacy," Stuart A. Thompson and Charlie Warzel, The New York Times, December 19, 2019, www.nytimes.com/interactive/2019/12/19/opinion/location-tracking-cell-phone.html.

28 See Bruce Schneier, *Data and Goliath: The Hidden Battles to Collect Your Data and Control Your World* (New York: W.W. Norton, 2015); Bernard E. Harcourt, *Exposed: Desire and Disobedience in the Digital Age* (Cambridge, MA: Harvard University Press, 2015), and Michael Patrick Lynch, *The Internet of Us: Knowing More and Understanding Less in the Age of Big Data* (New York: Liveright, 2016), 95–99.

29 Vyvyan Evans, *The Emoji Code: The Linguistics behind Smiley Faces and Scaredy Cats* (New York: Picador, 2017), 35.

30 Cf. "Gaming: The System," Ben Yagoda, The New York Times, April 28, 2018, www.nytimes.com/2018/04/28/opinion/sunday/gaming-the-system.html.

31 "'Thumb-Stopping,' 'Humaning,' 'B4H': The Strange Language of Modern Marketing," The New York Times, November 25, 2020, www.nytimes.com/2020/11/25/business/media/thumb-stopping-humaning-b4h-the-strange-language-of-modern-marketing.html.

32 "We're Watching Billions of Hours of Netflix," TV Insider, May 9, 2020, www.tvinsider.com/933154/netflix-statistics-quarantine-viewing-habits/; "50+ Netflix Statistics and Facts," Comparitech, April 13, 2022, www.comparitech.com/blog/vpn-privacy/netflix-statistics-facts-figures/.

33 "YouTube User Statistics 2022," GMI, April 18, 2022, www.globalmediainsight.com/blog/youtube-users-statistics/#:~:text=YouTube%20has%20more%20than%202.6,world%20has%20access%20to%20YouTube.

34 "Instagram by the Numbers," Omnicore, February 27, 2022, www.omnicoreagency.com/instagram-statistics/; "How Many Influencers Are There on Instagram in 2022?" The Small Business Blog, April 26, 2022, https://thesmallbusinessblog.net/how-many-influencers-are-there-on-instagram/.

35 "Digital Video Ad Spend Increased 49% in 2021," IAB, May 2, 2022, www.iab.com/news/digital-video-ad-spend-increased-49-in-2021-and-expected-to-reach-nearly-50-billion-in-2022-according-to-iabs-2021-video-ad-spend-and-2022-outlook-report/; "Five Findings about Digital Video News," Pew Research Center, April 17, 2014, www.pewresearch.org/fact-tank/2014/04/17/five-findings-about-digital-video-news/.

36 "Americans Devote More Than 10 Hours a Day to Screen Time," CNN, July 29, 2016, www.cnn.com/2016/06/30/health/americans-screen-time-nielsen/index.html/; "Kids Nearly Doubled Screen Time during the Pandemic," CNN, November 1, 2021, www.cnn.com/2021/11/01/health/children-screen-time-increase-pandemic-study-wellness/index.html.

37 "The State of Traditional TV," Marketing Charts, May 12, 2021, www.marketingcharts.com/featured-105414.

38 Which is not to say that those who judged by looks were dead wrong, as the story is sometimes supposed to imply: Radio makes its own acoustic demands, such that one can sound good for the wrong reasons. For a good description of this episode, see Daniel Boorstin, *The Image* (New York: Vintage, 1992), 42.

39 Walt Whitman, *Walt Whitman's Civil War*, edited by Walter Lowenfels (Boston: Da Capo, 1989), 174.

40 "Photography implies that we know about the world if we accept it as the camera records it. But this is the opposite of understanding, which starts from not accepting the world as it looks." Susan Sontag, *Essays of the 1960s and 70s: On Photography* (New York: The Library of America, 2013), 544.

41 See Niklas Luhmann, *The Reality of the Mass Media* (Stanford: Stanford University Press, 1996), 25.

42 Boorstin, The Image, 7–76.

43 This line of thinking is indebted to Hans Jonas, *The Phenomenon of Life: Towards a Philosophical Biology* (Evanston: Northwestern University Press, 2001), 135–56.

44 William Gibson, *Neuromancer* (New York: Penguin, 2000), 166.

45 Abby Smith Rumsey, *When We Are No More: How Digital Memory Is Shaping Our Future* (New York: Bloomsbury, 2016), 151.

46 "How Whatsapp Is Used and Misused in Africa," The Economist, July 18, 2019, www.economist.com/middle-east-and-africa/2019/07/18/how-whatsapp-is-used-and-misused-in-africa.

47 "The Pandemic Has Accelerated the Growth of E-Sports," The Economist, June 27, 2020, www.economist.com/international/2020/06/27/the-pandemic-has-accelerated-the-growth-of-e-sports.

48 Terry Gilliam's 1985 film Brazil is especially interesting in this regard, depicting a dystopian technological future in which complicated networks of communication tubes run in and out of every room: a literalization of the internet. I'm in the debt of Thomas Huston for this observation.

49 Quoted by Andrew Blum, *Tubes: A Journey to the Center of the Internet* (New York: Ecco, 2013), 47 (and cf. 144). On the general theme of digital de-individualization, see Luciano Floridi, *The Fourth Revolution: How the Infosphere Is Reshaping Human Reality* (Oxford: Oxford University Press, 2014), 1–58.

50 "Google, Amazon, Meta and Microsoft Weave a Fiber-Optic Web of Power," The Wall Street Journal, January 15, 2022, www.wsj.com/articles/google-amazon-meta-and-microsoft-weave-a-fiber-optic-web-of-power-11642222824.

51 Astra Taylor, *The People's Platform: Taking Back Power and Culture in the Digital Age* (New York: Metropolitan Books, 2014), 144.

52 Sontag, On Photography, 608–34.

53 For the best account of how this point extends to words themselves, see Sigurd Burckhardt, *Shakespearean Meanings* (Princeton: Princeton University Press, 1968), 22–46.

54 See, along these lines, Jaron Lanier, *Dawn of the New Everything: Encounters with Reality and Virtual Reality* (New York: Henry Holt and Company, 2017), esp. 55, 128, 142. For the best defense of the digital world as a proper aesthetic object, see Virginia Heffernan's *Magic and Loss* (New York: Simon and Schuster, 2016).

55 Cf. "An Artist for the Instagram Age," Sarah Boxer, The Atlantic, July/ August 2017, www.theatlantic.com/magazine/archive/2017/07/yayoi-kusamas-existential-circus/528669/.

56 Taylor, The People's Platform, 178–80.

57 "Why Paper Jams Persist," Joshua Rothman, The New Yorker, February 5, 2018, www.newyorker.com/magazine/2018/02/12/why-paper-jams-persist.

58 Catherine Howell and Darrell West, "The Internet as a Human Right," Brookings Institution, November 7, 2016, www.brookings.edu/blog/techtank/2016/11/07/the-internet-as-a-human-right/.

59 "Global Digital Population as of April 2022," Statista, May 9, 2022, www.statista.com/statistics/617136/digital-population-worldwide/.

60 "Biggest Companies in the World by Market Cap," Investopedia, March 4, 2022, www.investopedia.com/biggest-companies-in-the-world-by-market-cap-5212784.

61 "The World's Largest Tech Companies in 2022," Forbes, May 12, 2012, www.forbes.com/sites/jonathanponciano/2022/05/12/the-worlds-largest-technology-companies-in-2022-apple-still-dominates-as-brutal-market-selloff-wipes-trillions-in-market-value/?sh=491f19d13448.

62 "Quarterly Smartphone Production for 4Q21 Undergoes Highest QoQ Growth for 2021," Trendforce, March 1, 2022, www.trendforce.com/presscenter/news/20220301-11146.html; "Windows Now Has 1.4 Billion Users," Tech Advisor, January 26, 2022, www.techadvisor.com/news/windows/windows-1-4-billion-users-3812742/#:~:text=Windows%2010%20and%20Windows%20 11,before%20its%20successor%20was%20announced; www.oberlo.com/blog/google-search-statistics; www.pymnts.com/news/retail/2022/amazons-share-of-us-ecommerce-sales-hits-all-time-high-of-56-7-in-2021/; "Number of Daily Active Facebook Users Worldwide," Statista, April 28, 2022, www.statista.com/statistics/346167/facebook-global-dau./

63 This is one of the theses of Niall Ferguson, *The Square and the Tower: Networks and Power* (London: Penguin Books, 2019).

64 "Huge 'Foundation Models' Are Turbo-Charging AI Progress," The Economist.

65 A similar point holds for self-driving cars and other digital artifacts that are improved by access to larger pools of data. See "The Market for Driverless Cars Will Head toward Monopoly," The Economist, June 7, 2018, www.economist.com/finance-and-economics/2018/06/07/the-market-for-driverless-cars-will-head-towards-monopoly.

66 See "Why Retailers Everywhere Should Look to China," The Economist, January 2, 2021, www.economist.com/leaders/2021/01/02/why-retailers-everywhere-should-look-to-china.

67 Karl Marx and Friedrich Engels, *The Marx-Engels Reader*, edited by Robert Tucker (New York: W. W. Norton, 1978), 476. For elaborations on this theme, see Zygmunt Bauman, *Liquid Modernity* (Cambridge: Polity, 2000); Marshall Berman, *All That's Solid Melts into Air: The Experience of Modernity* (London: Penguin, 1988); Marc Augé, *Non-Places: An Introduction to Supermodernity*, translated by John Howe (London: Verso, 2009).

68 Quoted by Tim Wu, *The Attention Merchants: The Epic Scramble to Get Inside Our Heads* (New York: Vintage, 2016), 335.

69 "The Battle for Digital Privacy Is Reshaping the Internet," The New York Times, September 16, 2021, www.nytimes.com/2021/09/16/technology/digital-privacy.html.

70 Cf. Gile Slade, *Made to Break: Technology and Obsolescence in America* (Cambridge, MA: Harvard University Press, 2007).

71 Cf. "How Digital Devices Challenge the Nature of Ownership," The Economist, September 30, 2017, www.economist.com/news/leaders/21729745-and-threaten-property-rights-digital-age-how-digital-devices-challenge-nature.

72 "The Shape of Things to Come," Ian Parker, The New Yorker, February 16, 2015, www.newyorker.com/magazine/2015/02/23/shape-things-come.

73 Quoted by Claude Draude, *Computing Bodies* (Wiesbaden: Springer, 2017), 57.

74 On the theme of touch and its spiritualization in commercial materials, see Roland Barthes, *Mythologies*, translated by Annette Lavers (New York: Hill & Wang, 1972), 88–90.

75 On which theme, see Ivan Illich, *Tools for Conviviality* (London: Marion Boyars, 2009), 74–75.

76 King James Version, 1 Corinthians 13:12.

77 On which theme, see Richard Rorty, *Philosophy and the Mirror of Nature* (Princeton: Princeton University Press, 2017).

78 "Google's Fundamental Flaw Is Search," Forbes, October 17, 2011, www.forbes.com/sites/parmyolson/2011/10/17/googles-fundamental-flaw-is-search/?sh=3a5799d976d5.

79 "Ten Things We Know to Be True," Google, https://about.google/philosophy/.

80 Quoted by Parker, "The Shape of Things to Come." Another instance: About 60 percent of users say they are unaware that Facebook uses algorithms to rank its "feed." Franklin Foer, *World without Mind: The Existential Threat of Big Tech* (New York: Penguin, 2017), 73.

81 Quoted by Foer, World without Mind, 187.

82 "Online Retail Is Booming in China," The Economist, October 26, 2017, www.economist.com/special-report/2017/10/26/online-retail-is-booming-in-china.

83 Zoe Corbyn, "Facebook Experiment Boosts US Voter Turnout," Nature, September 12, 2012, www.nature.com/news/facebook-experiment-boosts-us-voter-turnout-1.11401.

84 Foer, World without Mind, 201.

85 Stuart Russell, *Human Compatible: Artificial Intelligence and the Problem of Control* (New York: Viking, 2019), 8.

86 "How Heavy Use of Social Media Is Linked to Mental Illness," The Economist, May 18, 2018, www.economist.com/graphic-detail/2018/05/18/how-heavy-use-of-social-media-is-linked-to-mental-illness; see too on this theme Adam Gazzaley and Larry D. Rosen, *The Distracted Mind: Ancient Brains in a High-Tech World* (Cambridge, MA: MIT Press, 2017).

87 Geert Lovink, *Sad by Design: On Platform Nihilism* (London: Pluto Press, 2019), 33.

88 See Nicholas Carr, *The Shallows: What the Internet Is Doing to Our Brains* (New York: W.W. Norton, 2010), esp. 213–16.

89 See Jonathan Taplin, *Move Fast and Break Things: How Facebook, Google, and Amazon Cornered Culture and Undermined Democracy* (Boston: Little, Brown and Company, 2017), 214; "Hooked on Our Smartphones," The New York Times, January 9, 2017, www.nytimes.com/2017/01/09/well/live/hooked-on-our-smartphones.html. These are pre-pandemic sources.

90 "Children's Screen Time Has Soared in the Pandemic, Alarming Parents and Researchers," The New York Times, January 16, 2021, www.nytimes .com/2021/01/16/health/covid-kids-tech-use.html?action=click&module=Top%20 Stories&pgtype=Homepage.

91 King James Version, Psalm 46:10.

92 Hence the specious point that "I keep reading that in the age of screens we've lost our ability to concentrate … But when I look around me and see people riveted to their devices, I've never seen such a great wealth of concentration, focus, and engagement." Kenneth Goldsmith, *Wasting Time on the Internet* (New York: Harper Perennial, 2016), 4–5.

2   LED BY OUR OWN LIGHTS

1 James Baldwin, *Collected Essays* (New York: The Library of America, 1998), 463–64.

2 John Milton, *Paradise Lost* (New York: W. W. Norton, 1975), 29.

3 William Shakespeare, *King Lear* (London: Arden Shakespeare, 1997), 255.

4 Shakespeare, King Lear, 279.

5 Noel Perrin, *Giving up the Gun: Japan's Reversion to the Sword, 1543–1879* (Boston: David R. Godine, 1979).

6 David Jones, *In Parenthesis* (New York: New York Review Books, 2003), xv.

7 Barthes, Mythologies, 129.

8 Ong, Orality and Literacy, 42.

9 Lynn White Jr., *Medieval Technology and Social Change* (Oxford: Oxford University Press, 1962).

10 Aristotle, *Politics*, translated by Carnes Lord (Chicago: University of Chicago Press, 2013), Book I, Chapters 5 and 4 (respectively).

11 King James Version, Ephesians 6:5.

12 John Berger, G. (New York: Vintage, 1972), 33.

13 Cf. "In the North the white man … keeps the Negro at a distance all the more carefully because he fears lest one day they be confounded together." Alexis de Tocqueville, *Democracy in America*, translated by George Lawrence (New York: HarperPerennial, 1969), 343.

14 Quoted by Andrew Roberts, *Churchill: Walking with Destiny* (New York: Viking, 2018), 459.

15 "American Women Will Soon Become Eligible (in Theory) for the Draft," The Economist, September 18, 2021, www.economist.com/united-states/2021/09/18/ american-women-will-soon-become-eligible-in-theory-for-the-draft.

16 Elizabeth Hardwick, *The Collected Essays of Elizabeth Hardwick* (New York: New York Review Books, 2017), 272.

17 "The Culture War over 'Pregnant People,'" Emma Green, The Atlantic, September 17, 2021, www.theatlantic.com/politics/archive/2021/09/pregnant-people-gender-identity/620031/.

18 Karl Marx, *Capital: Volume I*, translated by Samuel Moore and Edward Aveling (New York: International Publishers, 1967), 264.

19 S. M. Stirling, *Dies the Fire* (New York: Roc, 2005). I'm grateful to Carl Page for recommending this series.

20 Karl Löwith, *Meaning in History* (Chicago: University of Chicago Press, 1949).
21 "Out with the Old, in with the Young," Astra Taylor, The New York Times, October 18, 2019, www.nytimes.com/interactive/2019/10/18/opinion/old-age-president-2020.html.
22 "Young People Have a Stake in Our Future. Let Them Vote," Kelsey Piper, Vox, October 21, 2020, www.vox.com/future-perfect/2019/9/10/20835327/voting-age-youth-rights-kids-vote.
23 "Accelerationism: How a Fringe Philosophy Predicted the Future We Live In," Andy Beckett, The Guardian, May 11, 2017, www.theguardian.com/world/2017/may/11/accelerationism-how-a-fringe-philosophy-predicted-the-future-we-live-in.
24 "I Wish I'd Never Been Born: The Rise of the Anti-Natalists," Rebecca Tuhus-Dubrow, The Guardian, November 14, 2019, www.theguardian.com/world/2019/nov/14/anti-natalists-childfree-population-climate-change.
25 Barry Lopez, *Arctic Dreams* (New York: Vintage, 2001), 39.
26 Rachel Carson, *Silent Spring* (New York: Houghton Mifflin, 2002), 6.

3   THE SOUND OF OUR OWN VOICE

1 Ezra Gannet, *The Atlantic Telegraph* (Boston: Crosby, Nichols, 1858), 13.
2 For this position, cf. "The Ancient Myth of 'Good Fences,'" Ingrid Rossellini, The New York Times, May 14, 2018, www.nytimes.com/2018/05/14/opinion/greece-rome-predjudice-war.html; or "National Identity Is Made up," Max Fisher, Josh Keller, Mae Ryan, and Shane O'Neill, The New York Times, February 28, 2018, www.nytimes.com/2018/02/28/world/national-identity-myth.html.
3 See, e.g. "The Age of Outrage," Jonathan Haidt, City Journal, December 17, 2017, www.city-journal.org/html/age-outrage-15608.html; or Kurt Andersen, *Fantasyland: How America Went Haywire* (New York: Random House, 2017).
4 "Digital relations" is a phrase I owe to L. M. Sacasas, the best contemporary commentator on net issues – the phrase emphasizes the fact that the internet is not an autonomous "place" so much as a new (total) orientation toward other. See his "The Insurrection Will Not Be Streamed," January 15, 2021, https://theconvivialsociety.substack.com/p/the-insurrection-will-be-live-streamed.
5 Don DeLillo, *White Noise* (New York: Penguin, 2016), 66.
6 W. H. Auden, *The Dyer's Hand* (New York: Vintage, 1989), 255.
7 "Company Info: Meta-Facebook," https://about.facebook.com/company-info/ (accessed 6/8/22).
8 "About Communities on Twitter," https://help.twitter.com/en/using-twitter/communities (accessed 6/8/22).
9 "Who's Doing the Talking on Twitter?" Kalev Leetaru, The Atlantic, August 27, 2015, www.theatlantic.com/international/archive/2015/08/twitter-global-social-media/402415/.
10 Taylor, The People's Platform, 220–21.
11 "What Is Wikipedia Worth?" Ezra Klein, The Washington Post, December 17, 2010, http://voices.washingtonpost.com/ezra-klein/2010/12/what_is_wikipedia_worth.html
12 "About YouTube," https://about.youtube/ (accessed 6/8/22).

13 "New Apple Stores Want to Become 'Town Squares,'" Paris Marx, NBC News, December 28, 2018, www.nbcnews.com/think/opinion/new-apple-stores-want-become-town-squares-combining-public-private-ncna951981.

14 For this and more such examples, see "Bad Metaphors: Community," David Banks and Britney Gil, Real Life Magazine, July 22, 2019, https://reallifemag.com/bad-metaphors-community/.

15 Mark Zuckerberg, January 30, 2019, www.facebook.com/zuck/posts/10106340834478671.

16 "How Heavy Use of Social Media Is Linked to Mental Illness," The Economist.

17 "Is Facebook Making Us Lonely?" Stephen Marche, The Atlantic, May 2012, www.theatlantic.com/magazine/archive/2012/05/is-facebook-making-us-lonely/308930/. For fuller discussion, see Giles Slade, *The Big Disconnect: The Story of Technology and Loneliness* (New York: Prometheus Books, 2012), esp. 15–93; and Sherry Turkle's excellent *Alone Together: Why We Expect More from Technology and Less from Each Other* (New York: Basic Books, 2017), esp. 19, 157, 224.

18 "Social Isolation in America," Pew Research Center, November 4, 2009, www.pewresearch.org/internet/2009/11/04/part-1-introduction-3/.

19 I'm relying here on Charles Taylor's description in A Secular Age (Cambridge, MA: Harvard University Press, 2007), 368–69.

20 Anderson, Imagined Communities, 9–36.

21 Tocqueville, Democracy in America, 518.

22 In Reno v. ACLU (1997) the Supreme Court struck down the Communications Decency Act, comparing the use of chat rooms to the speech of a town crier on a soapbox, or of a pamphleteer. In Packingham v. North Carolina (2017), the Court then unanimously ruled that the latter's law barring registered sex offenders from using social media infringed their First Amendment rights. The opinion maintains that cyberspace should be understood as a public venue, no different in status from a park or a street.

23 I'm adapting a distinction made famous by Ferdinand Tönnies in Gemeinschaft und Gesellschaft.

24 Aristotle, Politics, Book I, Chapter 2.

25 Karl Popper, *The Open Society and Its Enemies*, Vol. I (London: Routledge, 1995), 187.

26 "The Promise of Open-Source Intelligence," The Economist, August 7, 2021, www.economist.com/leaders/2021/08/07/the-promise-of-open-source-intelligence.

27 "Around 40% of American Couples Now First Meet Online," Quartz, February 12, 2019, https://qz.com/1546677/around-40-of-us-couples-now-first-meet-online/#:~:text=Some%2039%25%20of%20heterosexual%20couples, same%2Dsex%20couples%20that%20year.

28 Cf. Robert Nisbet, *The Quest for Community: A Study in the Ethics of Order and Freedom* (Wilmington: ISI Books, 2010).

29 Giles Slade, The Big Disconnect, 27.

30 Voter participation diminished with TV: Langdon Winner, *The Whale and the Reactor: A Search for Limits in an Age of High Technology* (Chicago: University of Chicago Press, 1986), 111.

31 "10 Online Dating Statistics You Should Know," E-Harmony, March 18, 2021, www.eharmony.com/online-dating-statistics/.

32 "Number of Online Dating Users in the United States from 2017 to 2024," Statista, July 5, 2021, www.statista.com/statistics/417654/us-online-dating-user-numbers/#:~:text=United%20States%3A%20online%20dating%20users%20in%20the%20U.S.%202017%2D2024&text=There%20were%2044.2%20million%20user,to%2053.3%20million%20by%202025; "How the Internet Has Changed Dating," The Economist, August 18, 2018, www.economist.com/briefing/2018/08/18/how-the-internet-has-changed-dating.

33 Ibid.

34 Cf. "I Can't Jump Ship from Facebook Yet," Kathleen O'Brien, The New York Times, April 14, 2018, www.nytimes.com/2018/04/14/opinion/sunday/i-cant-jump-ship-from-facebook-yet.html; Mary Gray has described the significance of online groups for gay and queer teenagers in rural, unwelcoming milieux in Out in the Country: Youth, Media, and Queer Visibility in Rural America (New York: NYU Press, 2009).

35 "Nextdoor launches the first private social network for neighborhoods," https://about.nextdoor.com/corporate-announcements/nextdoor-launches-the-first-private-social-network-for-neighborhoods/; "About Nextdoor," https://about.nextdoor.com/ (both accessed 6/8/22).

36 Promotional email I received on October 4, 2018.

37 "About Nextdoor," my emphasis (accessed 6/8/22).

38 "Mark Zuckerberg Testifies before Congress," CNN, April 11, 2018, www.cnn.com/politics/live-news/mark-zuckerberg-testifies-congress/h_908afd7a7eabfdc60a62e21700493e2c.

39 Foer, World without Mind, 3; see too Bernard Harcourt's view that the values we have lost in the digital age are "privacy, autonomy, some anonymity, secrecy, dignity, a room of one's own, the right to be left alone," Exposed: Desire and Disobedience in the Digital Age (Cambridge, MA: Harvard University Press, 2015), 166 and cf. 176.

40 While neither are primarily about the internet, the phenomenon of contemporary tribalization is analyzed by Amy Chua, Political Tribes: Group Instinct and the Fate of Nations (New York: Random House, 2018) and Jonah Goldberg, Suicide of the West: How the Rebirth of Tribalism, Populism, Nationalism, and Identity Politics Is Destroying American Democracy (New York: Crown Forum, 2018). Sed contra, see Patrick Deneen's Why Liberalism Failed (New Haven: Yale University Press, 2018) and "A Renaissance on the Right," David Brooks, The New York Times, April 12, 2018, www.nytimes.com/2018/04/12/opinion/renaissance-right-gop.html.

41 Hannah Arendt, The Origins of Totalitarianism (New York: Schocken Books, 2004), 421.

42 Marshall McLuhan and Quentin Fiore, The Medium Is the Massage (Berkeley: Ginko Press, 2001), 68–69.

43 On "Lo and Behold: Reveries of the Connected World," directed by Werner Herzog, NetScout, 2016.

44 For a good introduction to the differences between knowledge and information, see Michael Patrick Lynch, The Internet of Us: Knowing More and Understanding Less in the Age of Big Data (New York, Liveright, 2016), 111–32, 174–77.

45 Whitney Phillips and Ryan Milner, *The Ambivalent Internet: Mischief, Oddity, and Antagonism Online* (Cambridge: Polity Press, 2017), 79–82.

46 Taylor, A Secular Age, 185ff.

47 The fault-line of the argument runs between thinkers such as Kant, Mill, and Rawls, over against Hegel, MacIntyre, Williams, and Anscombe. For my own sketch of this issue, see "We Are, Nonetheless, Cartesians," St. John's Review 59 (2017): 1–21.

48 See Martin Diamond, "Ethics and Politics: The American Way," in *The Moral Foundations of the American Republic*, edited by Robert Horwitz (Charlottesville, The University of Virginia Press, 1977), 39–72.

49 "How We Solved Fake News the First Time," Stephen Marche, The New Yorker, April 23, 2018, www.newyorker.com/culture/cultural-comment/how-we-solved-fake-news-the-first-time.

50 Newspapers are large units or "bundles" – you may choose one for a specific reason, but you are then stuck with the whole of it (and so less likely to read more than one or two a day). See Taylor, The People's Platform, 203–204.

51 Matthew Hindman, *The Myth of Digital Democracy* (Princeton: Princeton University Press, 2009), 2–3, 109–10.

52 "More than Eight-in-Ten Americans Get News from Digital Devices," Pew Research Center, January 12, 2021, www.pewresearch.org/fact-tank/2021/01/12/more-than-eight-in-ten-americans-get-news-from-digital-devices/.

53 See Hindman, The Myth of Digital Democracy, 38–57; and Jaron Lanier, *You Are Not a Gadget* (New York: Vintage, 2011), 77–86.

54 "Trump Has a New Favourite News Network," The Guardian, June 15, 2019, www.theguardian.com/tv-and-radio/2019/jun/15/oan-oann-fox-news-donald-trump.

55 It is certainly not that the journalism of past centuries was lofty and civilized in tone, whereas our own is coarsened: see Tocqueville, Democracy in America, 182–3.

56 Quoted by Everett Fox, The Five Books of Moses (New York: Schocken, 1997), 243.

57 Arendt, The Human Condition, 271.

58 Cf. "Internet Blogs, Polar Bears, and Climate-Change Denial by Proxy," Jeffrey Harvey et al., BioScience 68.4 (2018), 281–287.

59 Nicholas Carr canvases the evidence for this point in *The Big Switch: Rewiring the World, from Edison to Google* (New York: W. W. Norton, 2008), 157–64. The point is developed at length by Cass Sunstein, Republic.com 2.0 (Princeton: Princeton University Press, 2007), 46–96.

60 "The Logic of the Like," Daniel Silver, The Point, March 24, 20201, https://thepointmag.com/examined-life/the-logic-of-the-like/.

61 "Where Facebook Goes from Here," Clay Shirky and Brooke Gladstone, On the Media, March 23, 2018, www.wnycstudios.org/podcasts/otm/segments/where-facebook-goes-from-here.

62 The notion is developed in Byung-Chul Han, *In the Swarm: Digital Prospects*, translated by Erik Butler (Cambridge, MA: MIT Press, 2017), 4–12.

63 See the helpful notion of "concept creep" in Greg Lukianoff's and Jonathan Haidt's *The Coddling of the American Mind: How Good Intentions and Bad Ideas Are Setting up a Generation for Failure*, Penguin (New York), 2019; 25–27, 105.

64 See Jon Ronson's *So You've Been Publicly Shamed* (New York: Riverhead Books, 2015). The use of body cameras by police and others is an extension of the way in which pervasive surveillance is mobilized as a (defensive or offensive) weapon that may trump testimony or context: "Body-worn Cameras Are Spreading beyond the Police," The Economist, July 28, 2018, www.economist.com/britain/2018/07/28/body-worn-cameras-are-spreading-beyond-the-police.

65 See Reg Whitaker, *The End of Privacy* (New York: New Press, 1999).

66 The "right to be forgotten" (i.e. to have one's information removed from digital settings) has been on the books in the European Union since 2014 – needless to say, the procedure for being expunged is not uncomplicated (especially when it comes to the reputations of ex-convicts). For some of the material and legal questions surrounding the long-term preservation of digital data, see Abby Smith Rumsey's *When We Are No More: How Digital Memory Is Shaping Our Future* (New York: Bloomsbury, 2016).

67 "A Posthumous Shock," Will Self, Harpers, December 2021, https://harpers.org/archive/2021/12/a-posthumous-shock-trauma-studies-modernity-how-everything-became-trauma/.

68 "The Fake Americans Russia Created to Influence the Election," The New York Times, September 7, 2017, www.nytimes.com/2017/09/07/us/politics/russia-facebook-twitter-election.html?_r=2; "How Unwitting Americans Encountered Russian Operatives Online," The New York Times, February 18, 2018, www.nytimes.com/2018/02/18/us/politics/russian-operatives-facebook-twitter.html?hp&action=click&pgtype=Homepage&clickSource=story-heading&module=first-column-region&region=top-news&WT.nav=top-news; "Facebook's Role in Data Use Sets off Storm on Two Continents," The New York Times, March 18, 2018, www.nytimes.com/2018/03/18/us/cambridge-analytica-facebook-privacy-data.html.

69 Arendt, The Human Condition, 71.

70 "Persuasive Proof That America Is Full of Racist and Selfish People," Sean Illing, Vox, April 12, 2018, www.vox.com/conversations/2017/6/13/15768622/facebook-google-racism-social-media-seth-everybody-lies; this is the premise of Stephens-Davidowitz' Everybody Lies: Big Data, New Data, and What the Internet Can Tell Us about Who We Really Are (New York: HarperCollins, 2017); and see Christian Rudder, *Dataclysm: Love, Sex, Race, and Identity – What Our Online Lives Tell Us about Our Offline Selves* (New York: Broadway Books, 2014).

71 Others have explored this theme in much greater depth. Most conspicuously: Turkle in Alone Together and Danah Boyd in It's Complicated: The Social Lives of Networked Teens, Yale University Press (New Haven), 2014.

72 "World's Population Increasingly Urban," United Nations, July 10, 2014, www.un.org/en/development/desa/news/population/world-urbanization-prospects-2014.html; "U.S. Cities Factsheet," Center for Sustainable Systems, University of Michigan, 2021, https://css.umich.edu/publications/factsheets/built-environment/us-cities-factsheet#:~:text=It%20is%20estimated%20that%2083,to%20live%20in%20urban%20areas.

73 I'm grateful to Dan Silver for this observation – the theme is developed at length by Smith in The Wealth of Nations and by Hayek in "The Use of Knowledge in Society," *American Economic Review* 35 (1945): 519–30 (which discusses the "marvel" of price adjustments in a decentralized economy).

74 For the updated version of the issue Rousseau identifies in his Letter to D'Alembert, see Taylor's Secular Age, 474ff. It's no accident that just such an urban, public space – the opera – is the setting for Madame Bovary's and Anna Karenina's extra-marital affairs.

75 Tocqueville, Democracy in America, 190, 507, 510–11, 515; cf. Timothy Zick's *Speech out of Doors: Preserving First Amendment Liberties in Public Places* (Cambridge: Cambridge University Press, 2008).

76 Georg Simmel, *On Individuality and Social Forms*, edited by Donald Levine (Chicago: University of Chicago Press, 1971), 324–39.

77 See Roger Scruton, *Confessions of a Heretic* (Devon: Notting Hill Editions, 2016), 101 and 108; as well as Leon Kass, "Virtually Intimate: Is the Internet Good for Love and Friendship?" in *Leading a Worthy Life: Finding Meaning in Modern Times* (New York: Encounter Books, 2017).

78 "How WhatsApp Leads Mobs to Murder in India," The New York Times, July 18, 2018, www.nytimes.com/interactive/2018/07/18/technology/whatsapp-india-killings.html; "Inside China's Dystopian Dreams: A.I., Shame and Lots of Cameras," The New York Times, July 8, 2018, www.nytimes.com/2018/07/08/business/china-surveillance-technology.html.

79 "Dueling Statistics: How Much of the Internet Is Porn?" Michael Castleman, Psychology Today, November 3, 2016, www.psychologytoday.com/us/blog/all-about-sex/201611/dueling-statistics-how-much-the-internet-is-porn.

80 Hindman, The Myth of Digital Democracy, 60–61.

81 For the longer trend see Rochelle Gurstein, *The Repeal of Reticence: America's Cultural and Legal Struggles over Free Speech, Obscenity, Sexual Liberation and Modern Art* (New York: Hill and Wang, 1996).

82 "The Internet Is Overrun with Images of Child Sexual Abuse," The New York Times, September 29, 2019, www.nytimes.com/interactive/2019/09/28/us/child-sex-abuse.html.

83 "Is Pornography Addictive?" Kirsten Weir, American Psychological Association, April 2014, www.apa.org/monitor/2014/04/pornography.

84 For developed versions of this issue, see Pankaj Mishra, *Age of Anger: A History of the Present* (New York: FSG, 2017), and Jeffrey Berry and Sarah Sobieraj, *The Outrage Industry: Political Opinion, Media, and the New Incivility* (Oxford: Oxford University Press, 2014). See too Han's observation that the digital "totalizes the imaginary" (i.e. magnifies annoyance into outrage) in In the Swarm, 22.

85 Quoted by Wu, The Attention Merchants, 298.

86 See Thomas de Zengotita's excellent *Mediated: How the Media Shapes Your World and the Way You Live in It* (New York: Bloomsbury, 2006), and Michael Harris, *End of Absence* (New York: Current, 2014).

87 Alexander Hamilton, James Madison, John Jay, *The Federalist*, edited by Jacob Cooke (Middletown: Wesleyan University Press, 1961), Federalist 55.

88 "A Declaration of the Independence of Cyberspace," John Perry Barlowe, February 8, 1996, Electronic Frontier Foundation, www.eff.org/cyberspace-independence#:~:text=Governments%20of%20the%20Industrial%20World,no%20sovereignty%20where%20we%20gather.

89 Arendt, Origins of Totalitarianism, esp. 385, 505.

90 Arendt, Origins of Totalitarianism, 598–600.

91 Cf. the remarks on "hyperconnectivity" in www.the-american-interest.com/
    2017/07/03/flattened-disintermediation-goes-global/

92 For a seminal version of the case, see Louis Mumford's "Authoritarian and
    Democratic Technics," *Technology and Culture* 5.1 (1964): 1–8.

93 See Postman's summary of this point in Amusing Ourselves to Death, 30–63.

94 See Hindman, The Myth of Digital Democracy, 4–8, for a helpful canvassing.

95 See Sam Lebovic, *Free Speech and Unfree News: The Paradox of Press Freedom in
    America* (Cambridge MA: Harvard University Press, 2016).

96 Hindman, The Myth of Digital Democracy, 13, et passim.

97 Tocqueville was still struck by a contrast between the "vulgar demeanor" of the
    House and the distinguished eloquence of the Senate in Democracy in America,
    200–201.

98 Madison, Federalist 58. Madison adds in Federalist 49 – and 50 that too frequent
    referenda on popular opinion serve to destabilize the government, to fan popular
    resentment, and to undermine the balance of power between the three branches.
    Appealing to the people in every matter creates opportunities for social unrest,
    and tendencies toward artificial unanimity or mob mentality. Hamilton adds in
    Federalist 72 that political measures must be given time to act for their benefits
    or flaws to be fully understood: the community must have "time and leisure to
    observe the tendency of his [the President's] measures, and thence to form an
    experimental estimate of their merits."

99 "Italy's 5 Stars Struggle to Reboot after Losing Online Platform," Politico, May 9,
    2021, www.politico.eu/article/italy-5starts-online-platform-rousseau-crisis/; and
    cf. "Czech Pirates, Ahoy!" Politico, January 25, 2019, www.politico.eu/article/
    czech-pirate-party-anti-establishment-ivan-bartos-ahoy/.

100 "Wikipedia Is 20, and Its Reputation Has Never Been Higher," The
    Economist, January 9, 2021, www.economist.com/international/2021/01/09/
    wikipedia-is-20-and-its-reputation-has-never-been-higher.

101 James Gleick, *The Information: A History, a Theory, a Flood* (New York: Vintage
    Books, 2012), 382.

102 "Wikipedia: Neutral Point of View/FAQ," https://en.wikipedia.org/wiki/Wikipedia:
    Neutral_point_of_view/FAQ#There's_no_such_thing_as_objectivity   (accessed
    6/9/22).

103 See "Inside Twitter's Struggle over What Gets Banned," The New York Times,
    August 10, 2018, www.nytimes.com/2018/08/10/technology/twitter-free-speech-
    infowars.html.

104 "The Conservative Alternative to Twitter Wants to Be a Place for Free Speech for All. It
    Turns out, Rules Still Apply," The Washington Post, July 15, 2020, www.washington-
    post.com/technology/2020/07/15/parler-conservative-twitter-alternative/.

105 "Hard Questions: How Is Facebook's Fact-Checking Program Working," June 14,
    2018, https://about.fb.com/news/2018/06/hard-questions-fact-checking/.

106 "Why Speech Platforms Can Never Escape Politics," Jon Askonas and
    Ari Schulman, National Affairs, Spring 2022, www.nationalaffairs.com/
    why-speech-platforms-can-never-escape-politics.

107 "E.U. Takes Aim at Social Media's Harms with Landmark New Law," The New
    York Times, April 22, 2022, www.nytimes.com/2022/04/22/technology/european-
    union-social-media-law.html.

108 See, e.g. Foer, World without Mind, 12–25.

109 Cf. Stevens-Davidowitz, Everybody Lies; Cathy O'Neil, *Weapons of Math Destruction: How Big Data Increases Inequality and Threatens Democracy* (New York: Broadway Books, 2017); Sarah Wachter-Boettcher, *Technically Wrong: Sexist Apps, Biased Algorithms, and Other Threats of Toxic Tech* (New York: W.W. Norton, 2017); and, again, Taylor, The People's Platform.

110 "Post-truth Politics," David Roberts, Grist, April 1, 2010, https://grist .org/article/2010-03-30-post-truth-politics/.

111 Cf. Shoshana Zuboff, *The Age of Surveillance Capitalism: The Fight for a Human Future at the New Frontier of Power* (New York: PublicAffairs, 2020).

112 Quoted in "Google.gov," Adam White, The New Atlantis, Spring 2018, www .thenewatlantis.com/publications/googlegov.

113 Max Weber, *The Vocation Lectures*, translated by Rodney Livinstone (Indianapolis: Hackett, 2004), 12.

114 Mark Zuckerberg attempted to address political polarization on Facebook by showing users less commercial content and more posts shared by one's own friends. It is not hard to see that this is only likely to exacerbate the problem. See his post from January 11, 2018, www.facebook.com/zuck/posts/10104413015393571.

115 "Republicans and Democrats Agree: They Can't Agree on Basic Facts," Pew Research Center, August 23, 2018, www.pewresearch.org/fact-tank/2018/08/23/ republicans-and-democrats-agree-they-cant-agree-on-basic-facts/.

116 "China's Censors Ban Winnie the Pooh and the Letter 'N' after Xi's Power Grab," The New York Times, February 28, 2018, www.nytimes.com/2018/02/28/world/ asia/china-censorship-xi-jinping.html.

117 "China Imposes the World's Strictest Limits on Video Games," The Economist, September 2, 2021, www.economist.com/business/china-imposes-the-worlds- strictest-limits-on-video-games/21804100.

118 For the figures in this paragraph, see "China Has the World's Most Centralised Internet System," The Economist, June 28, 2018, www.economist.com/special- report/2018/06/28/china-has-the-worlds-most-centralised-internet-system; "How Does China Censor the Internet?" The Economist, April 22, 2013, www .economist.com/blogs/economist-explains/2013/04/economist-explains- how-china-censors-internet; "How the Chinese Government Fabricates Social Media Posts for Strategic Distraction," Gary King, Jennifer Pan, Margaret Roberts, American Political Science Review 111 (2017): 484–501.

119 "China Uses DNA to Track Its People, with the Help of American Expertise," The New York Times, February 21, 2019, www.nytimes.com/2019/02/21/business/china- xinjiang-uighur-dna-thermo-fisher.html.

120 "How China Uses High-Tech Surveillance to Subdue Minorities," The New York Times, May 22, 2019, www.nytimes.com/2019/05/22/world/asia/china- surveillance-xinjiang.html.

121 "Big Data Meets Big Brother as China Moves to Rate Its Citizens," Rachel Botsman, Wired, October 21, 2017, www.wired.co.uk/article/ chinese-government-social-credit-score-privacy-invasion.

122 "Inside China's Dystopian Dreams," The New York Times.

123 "Life inside China's Social Credit Laboratory," Simina Mistreanu, Foreign Policy, April 3, 2018, https://foreignpolicy.com/2018/04/03/ life-inside-chinas-social-credit-laboratory/.

124 "China Has the World's Most Centralised Internet System," The Economist.

125 "Can Technology Plan Economies and Destroy Democracy?" The Economist, December 18, 2019, www.economist.com/christmas-specials/2019/12/18/can-technology-plan-economies-and-destroy-democracy.

126 "In a Topsy-Turvy Pandemic World, China Offers Its Version of Freedom," The New York Times, January 4, 2021, www.nytimes.com/2021/01/04/business/china-covid19-freedom.html.

127 "Peter Thiel Says 'Crypto Is Libertarian, A.I. Is Communist.'" Sonya Mann, Inc., February 1, 2018, www.inc.com/sonya-mann/thiel-ai-cryptocurrency.html.

128 See the excellent discussion of blockchain anarchy in Adam Greenfield, *Radical Technologies: The Design of Everyday Life* (London: Verso, 2017), 167 and 145ff.

129 "The Man Who Nailed Jello to the Wall," Bethany Allen-Ebrahimian, Foreign Policy, June 29, 2016, https://foreignpolicy.com/2016/06/29/the-man-who-nailed-jello-to-the-wall-lu-wei-china-internet-czar-learns-how-to-tame-the-web/.

130 "As Face-Recognition Technology Spreads, So Do Ideas for Subverting It," The Economist, August 15, 2019, www.economist.com/science-and-technology/2019/08/15/as-face-recognition-technology-spreads-so-do-ideas-for-subverting-it. www.nytimes.com/2019/08/13/world/asia/hong-kong-protests-china.html

131 "Political Protests Have Become More Widespread and More Frequent," The Economist, March 10, 2020, www.economist.com/graphic-detail/2020/03/10/political-protests-have-become-more-widespread-and-more-frequent.

132 Tocqueville remarks, on the question of these extremes, that "anarchy is not an enduring condition; despotism is." Quoted by Jean-Claude Lamberti, *Tocqueville and the Two Democracies*, translated by Arthur Goldhammer (Cambridge, MA: Harvard University Press, 1989), 215. Cf. Carr, The Big Switch, 208; and (more optimistically) Gordon Graham, *The Internet: A Philosophical Inquiry* (New York: Routledge, 1999), 128–53.

133 "A Facebook War: Libyans Battle on the Streets and on Screens," The New York Times, September 4, 2018, www.nytimes.com/2018/09/04/world/middleeast/libya-facebook.html.

134 Barbara Tuchman, *A Distant Mirror: The Calamitous Fourteenth Century* (New York: Random House, 2014), xxvi.

135 "Black Lives Matter Has Grown More Powerful, and More Divided," The New York Times, June 4, 2021, www.nytimes.com/2021/06/04/us/black-lives-matter.html.

136 This is David Goodhart's nomenclature in The Road to Somewhere: The Populist Revolt and the Future of Politics (London: C. Hurst, 2017). See too Joshua Mitchell, "A Renewed Republican Party," American Affairs, Spring 2017, https://americanaffairsjournal.org/2017/02/a-renewed-republican-party/; as well as Pierre Manent's older (but nonetheless apposite) analysis in A World beyond Politics? translated by Marc LePain (Princeton: Princeton University Press, 2006).

137 "March for Our Lives: Thousands Join Anti-Gun Protests around the World," The Guardian, March 25, 2018, www.theguardian.com/us-news/2018/mar/24/washington-march-for-our-lives-gun-violence

138 "What White Nationalism Gets Right about American History," Derek Black, The New York Times, August 19, 2017, www.nytimes.com/2017/08/19/opinion/sunday/white-nationalism-american-history-statues.html.

139 See Timothy Carney, *Alienated America* (New York: HarperCollins, 2019), as well as Asad Haider, *Mistaken Identity: Race and Class in the Age of Trump* (London: Verso, 2018).

140 "Social Media Are Turbocharging the Export of America's Political Culture," The Economist, June 12, 2021, www.economist.com/international/2021/06/12/social-media-are-turbocharging-the-export-of-americas-political-culture; "The Global Machine behind the Rise of Far-Right Nationalism," The New York Times, August 10, 2019, www.nytimes.com/2019/08/10/world/europe/sweden-immigration-nationalism.html.

141 "Conservative Fellow Travelers: Tucker Carlson Drops in on Viktor Orban," The New York Times, August 7, 2021, www.nytimes.com/2021/08/07/world/europe/tucker-carlson-hungary.html.

142 See John Gray, *Al Qaeda and What It Means to Be Modern* (New York: The New Press, 2005).

143 Some of the most articulate representatives of the "alt-right" – a nebulous term for neo-reactionary views opposed to the basic tenets of democratic, progressive, capitalist life – have helped themselves extensively to the disembodied terms of science fiction. (As if Edgar Allan Poe had taken to writing for Breitbart News.) See "Final Fantasy: Neoreactionary Politics and the Liberal Imagination," James Duesterberg, The Point, July 2, 2017, https://thepointmag.com/2017/politics/final-fantasy-neoreactionary-politics-liberal-imagination.

144 See Angela Nagle's *Kill All Normies: Online Culture Wars from 4chan and Tumblr to Trump and the Alt-Right* (Alresford: Zero Books, 2017).

145 "Digital Art and the Alt-Right," Vid Simoniti, The Point, September 24, 2018, https://thepointmag.com/2018/criticism/digital-art-alt-right.

146 See Tanner Greer's post, "On Culture's That Build," June 18, 2020, https://scholars-stage.org/on-cultures-that-build/.

147 Aristotle, Politics, Book VII, Chapter 4.

148 Postman, Amusing Ourselves to Death, 44.

149 "Trump, Facing Fury, Says He Misspoke with Putin," CNN, July 18, 2018, www.cnn.com/2018/07/17/politics/white-house-mood-donald-trump-vladimir-putin-news-conference/index.html.

150 "Donald Trump's Presidency by the Numbers," CNN, December 18, 2020, www.cnn.com/2020/12/18/politics/trump-presidency-by-the-numbers/index.html.

151 "The End of Intelligence," Michael Hayden, The New York Times, April 28, 2018, www.nytimes.com/2018/04/28/opinion/sunday/the-end-of-intelligence.html.

152 "How America Fractured into Four Parts," George Packer, The Atlantic, July/August 2021, www.theatlantic.com/magazine/archive/2021/07/george-packer-four-americas/619012/.

153 "Trump: I Could 'Shoot Somebody and I Wouldn't Lose Voters,'" CNN, January 24, 2016, www.cnn.com/2016/01/23/politics/donald-trump-shoot-somebody-support/index.html.

154 "Donald Trump and the Wrecking-Ball Presidency," Jeffrey Frank, The New Yorker, October 17, 2017, www.newyorker.com/news/daily-comment/donald-trump-and-the-wrecking-ball-presidency; "Trump's 'Deterrence Bounce' and the Dangers of Shock-Jock Diplomacy," Lori Esposito Murray, Foreign Policy, March 15, 2017, https://foreignpolicy.com/2017/03/15/trumps-deterrence-bounce-and-the-dangers-of-shock-jock-diplomacy/

155 "Donald Trump Is the Uber of Politics," Lawrence Calmus, Medium, July 22, 2016, https://medium.com/@lawrencecalmus/donald-trump-is-the-uber-of-politics-48b744610837

156 "Accepting a Disappointing Election Result Is a Key Part of Democracy," The Economist, November 21, 2020, www.economist.com/leaders/2020/11/21/accepting-a-disappointing-election-result-is-a-key-part-of-democracy.

157 "New Research Shows the Connection between Political Victimhood and White Support for Trump," The Washington Post, January 13, 2021, www.washingtonpost.com/politics/2021/01/13/new-research-shows-connection-between-political-victimhood-white-support-trump/.

158 "How Construction Workers in Ohio View the Election," The Economist, September 12, 2020, www.economist.com/united-states/2020/09/12/how-construction-workers-in-ohio-view-the-election.

159 "How President Trump Ruined Political Comedy," Dan Brooks, The New York Times, October 7, 2020, www.nytimes.com/2020/10/07/magazine/trump-liberal-comedy-tv.html.

160 "What Is QAnon, the Viral Pro-Trump Conspiracy Theory?" The New York Times, September 3, 2021, www.nytimes.com/article/what-is-qanon.html; "The Prophecies of Q," Adrienne LaFrance, The Atlantic, June 2020, www.theatlantic.com/magazine/archive/2020/06/qanon-nothing-can-stop-what-is-coming/610567/.

161 Cf. "Astroworld Disaster Fuels Wave of Satanic Conspiracy Theories on TikTok," The Guardian, November 9, 2021, www.theguardian.com/us-news/2021/nov/09/astroworld-disaster-fuels-wave-of-satanic-conspiracy-theories-on-tiktok; "How the Case of Gabrielle Petito Galvanized the Internet," The New York Times, September 20, 2021, www.nytimes.com/2021/09/20/style/gabby-petito-case-tiktok-social-media.html; "The Parkland Conspiracy Theories, Explained," Vox, February 22, 2018, www.vox.com/policy-and-politics/2018/2/22/17036018/parkland-conspiracy-theories.

162 Carl Schmitt, *Theory of the Partisan*, translation by C.J. Miller (Antelope Hill Publishing), 71.

4 REALITIES OF OUR OWN CONTRIVANCE

1 Joseph Conrad, *Heart of Darkness* (London: Penguin, 1983), 59–60.

2 George Eliot, *Daniel Deronda* (London: Penguin, 2003), 696.

3 Essena O'Neill, "Why I Really Am Quitting Social Media," www.youtube.com/watch?v=gmAbwTQvWX8 (accessed June 9, 2022).

4 Essena O'Neill [@essenaoneill], Instagram, www.instagram.com/essenaoneill/?hl=en (accessed June 9, 2022).

5 I'm following the *Oxford English Dictionary* entry on "virtual" in this paragraph.

6 Søren Kierkegaard, *Two Ages*, edited and translated by Howard and Edna Hong (Princeton: Princeton University Press, 1978), 60–112.

7 Fyodor Dostoyevski, *Notes from the Underground*, translated by Constance Garnett (Mineola: Dover, 1992), 90.

8 See Nina MacLaughlin, *Hammer Head: The Making of a Carpenter* (New York: W. W. Norton, 2016), 11: "I wanted something that had a little bit more to do with reality. But what did that mean? Our lives online are as bound in reality as making pancakes, driving to the dump, spilling a glass of wine. At my desk, though, I felt far away from an anchor, a grounding agent, satisfaction. In a vague way, I wanted to put my brain where my hands were."

9 Arthur C. Clarke, *Rendezvous with Rama* (New York: Bantam, 1990), 84.

10 "March 10, 1876: 'Mr. Watson, Come Here …'" *Wired*, March 10, 2011, www .wired.com/2011/03/0310bell-invents-telephone-mr-watson-come-here/.

11 "Chinese Netizens Get Privacy Conscious," *The Economist*, September 7, 2019, www.economist.com/business/2019/09/07/chinese-netizens-get-privacy-conscious.

12 "How Unboxing Videos Soothe Our Consumerist Brains," Amanda Hess and Shane O'Neill, *The New York Times*, August 27, 2018, www.nytimes.com/video/arts/100000005777067/unboxing-videos-internet.html.

13 "The Latest Internet Trend I Can't Get Enough of: Gelatin," Adrienne Matei, *The Guardian*, October 17, 2019, www.theguardian.com/lifeandstyle/2019/oct/17/jelly-jell-o-gelatin-internet-trend.

14 "Finding What's 'Oddly Satisfying' on the Internet," Emily Matchar, *The New York Times*, February 22, 2019, www.nytimes.com/2019/02/22/opinion/sunday/oddly-satisfying-videos-internet.html.

15 "Dark Crystals: The Brutal Reality behind a Booming Wellness Craze," Tess McClure, *The Guardian*, September 17, 2019, www.theguardian.com/lifeandstyle/2019/sep/17/healing-crystals-wellness-mining-madagascar.

16 "In a Wistful Age, Farmers Find a New Angle: Chore TV," *The New York Times*, August 7, 2020, www.nytimes.com/2020/08/07/us/farmer-influencer-youtube.html.

17 "People Can't Get Enough of this Guy Who Ate a 'Chicken Leg Piece' on TikTok," *Delish*, December 11, 2019, www.delish.com/food-news/a30198443/chicken-leg-piece-tik-tok/; "What Is 'Mukbang'? Inside the Viral Korean Food YouTube Trend," *Today*, February 23, 2018, www.today.com/food/what-mukbang-inside-viral-korean-food-phenomenon-t123251.

18 "This Pickle Is a Cake," *The New York Times*, July 14, 2020, www.nytimes.com/2020/07/14/style/what-is-the-cake-meme.html; "Watch This Disgusting Food Video Right Now. It Explains Everything," *The New York Times*, December 10, 2020, www.nytimes.com/2020/12/10/magazine/chefclub-recipe-video.html.

19 Aristotle, *On the Soul*, 421a.

20 See Glenn Most, *Doubting Thomas* (Cambridge, MA: Harvard University Press, 2007).

21 See Mark Greif, *Against Everything* (New York: Vintage, 2017), 3–15.

22 See "It Has Never Been Easier to Launch a New Brand," *The Economist*, January 23, 2020, www.economist.com/business/2020/01/23/it-has-never-been-easier-to-launch-a-new-brand.

23 For the distinction, see Daniel Bell, *The Coming of Post-Industrial Society* (New York: Basic Books, 1999), lxxvii.

24 "Will Web3 Reinvent the Internet Business?" *The Economist*, January 29, 2022, www.economist.com/business/2022/01/29/will-web3-reinvent-the-internet-business.

25 "Too Many People Want to Travel," Annie Lowrey, *The Atlantic,* June 4, 2019, www.theatlantic.com/ideas/archive/2019/06/crowds-tourists-are-ruining-popular-destinations/590767/.

26 See Walker Percy, *The Message in the Bottle* (New York: Picador, 2000), 46–63; and Sontag, *On Photography.*

27 See "Reality Made Me Do It," Martha Bayles, *The Hedgehog Review,* Summer 2019, https://hedgehogreview.com/issues/reality-and-its-alternatives/articles/reality-made-me-do-it.

28 BeReal, https://bere.al/en (accessed June 15, 2022).

29 "Social Media Pressure Is Linked to Cosmetic Procedure Boom," *BBC,* June 22, 2017, www.bbc.com/news/health-40358138; "Faking It: How Selfie Dysmorphia Is Driving People to Seek Surgery," *The Guardian,* January 23, 2019, www.theguardian.com/lifeandstyle/2019/jan/23/faking-it-how-selfie-dysmorphia-is-driving-people-to-seek-surgery.

30 Max Horkheimer and Theodor Adorno, *The Dialectic of Enlightenment,* translated by Edmund Jephcott (Stanford: Stanford University Press, 2002), 167.

31 "Nice Work if You Can Get Out," *The Economist,* April 22, 2014, www.economist.com/finance-and-economics/2014/04/22/nice-work-if-you-can-get-out.

32 See "Athleisure, Barre and Kale: The Tyranny of the Ideal Woman," Jia Tolentino, *The Guardian,* August 2, 2019, www.theguardian.com/news/2019/aug/02/athleisure-barre-kale-tyranny-ideal-woman-labour.

33 "What the 'Creator Economy' Promises – And What It Actually Does," Kyle Chayka, *The New Yorker,* July 17, 2021, www.newyorker.com/culture/infinite-scroll/what-the-creator-economy-promises-and-what-it-actually-does.

34 "For Creators, Everything Is for Sale," *The New York Times,* March 10, 2021, www.nytimes.com/2021/03/10/style/creators-selling-selves.html.

35 "Only Fans U-Turns on Its Porn Ban," *The Economist,* August 25, 2021, www.economist.com/britain/onlyfans-u-turns-on-its-porn-ban/21803924.

36 See "Outdoor Voices Blurs the Lines between Working out and Everything Else," Jia Tolentino, *The New Yorker,* March 11, 2019, www.newyorker.com/magazine/2019/03/18/outdoor-voices-blurs-the-lines-between-working-out-and-everything-else.

37 Jenny Odell, *How to Do Nothing* (New York: Melville, 2019).

38 "When Did Self-Help Become Self-Care?" Kate Carraway, *The New York Times,* August 10, 2019, www.nytimes.com/2019/08/10/style/self-care/when-did-self-help-become-self-care.html.

39 "Poor Kids Spend Nearly 2 Hours More on Screens Each Day Than Rich Kids," *Vox,* October 29, 2019, www.vox.com/recode/2019/10/29/20937870/kids-screentime-rich-poor-common-sense-media.

40 Matthew B. Crawford, *The World beyond Your Head: On Becoming an Individual in an Age of Distraction* (New York: FSG, 2015), 16.

41 "A Dark Consensus about Screens and Kids Begins to Emerge in Silicon Valley," *The New York Times,* October 26, 2018, www.nytimes.com/2018/10/26/style/phones-children-silicon-valley.html.

42 "Why Use Freedom?" https://freedom.to/why?utm_source=google&utm_medium=cpc&utm_campaign=10879438718&utm_content=109523085280&utm_term=block%20websites&gclid=CjwKCAjw14uVBhBEEiwAaufYx4S6Wr8hg-AJSnJZteUOdsunn3nZeEBJ28qyh9rf2eBLwAB5ipJEARoCkUkQAvD_BwE (accessed June 10, 2022).

43 "Digital Wellbing," https://wellbeing.google/ (accessed June 10, 2022)

44 Though there are interesting reasons why sights and sounds are easier to replicate than smells or textures: Lanier, *You Are Not a Gadget*, 163–65.

45 "The Shape of Things to Come," *The New Yorker*.

46 Lanier, *Dawn of the New Everything*.

47 "The ROI of Recommendation Engines for Marketing," Daniel Faggella, *MarTech*, October 31, 2017, https://martechtoday.com/roi-recommendation-engines-marketing-205787; "As Algorithm's Take over, YouTube's Recommendations Highlight a Human Problem," *NBC*, April 19, 2018, www.nbcnews.com/tech/social-media/algorithms-take-over-youtube-s-recommendations-highlight-human-problem-n867596.

48 "China Wages War on Apps Offering News and Jokes," *The Economist*, April 19, 2018, www.economist.com/china/2018/04/19/china-wages-war-on-apps-offering-news-and-jokes.

49 James Williams, for example, recommends a scheme for ethical metrics in *Stand out of Our Light: Freedom and Resistance in the Attention Economy* (Cambridge: Cambridge University Press, 2018), 121–23.

50 "The Tyranny of Convenience," Tim Wu, *The New York Times,* February 16, 2018, www.nytimes.com/2018/02/16/opinion/sunday/tyranny-convenience.html.

51 "You're Not Paying Attention, but You Really Should Be," Tim Herrera, *The New York Times*, July 14, 2019, www.nytimes.com/2019/07/14/smarter-living/youre-not-paying-attention-but-you-really-should-be.html.

52 Philip K. Dick, *Do Androids Dream of Electric Sheep?* (New York: Del Rey, 2017), 51.

53 Andy Warhol, *The Philosophy of Andy Warhol* (Orlando: Harvest, 1975), 26–27.

54 *Iliad* 18.376–77 (my translation).

55 Aristotle, *Politics*, Book I, Chapter 2.

56 Francis Bacon, *The Major Works* (Oxford: Oxford University Press, 2002), 148.

57 For the full panoply of relevant myths, see Adrienne Mayor, *Gods and Robots: Myths, Machines, and Ancient Dreams of Technology* (Princeton: Princeton University Press, 2018), 110.

58 Ovid, *Metamorphosis*, 10.276 (my translation).

59 Ovid, *Metamorphosis* 10.252 (my translation).

60 Ovid, *Metamorphosis*, 10.398ff.

61 See L. M. Sacasas, "The Analog City and the Digital City," *The New Atlantis*, Winter 2020, www.thenewatlantis.com/publications/the-analog-city-and-the-digital-city.

62 Ludwig Wittgenstein, *The Blue and Brown Books* (New York: Harper, 1960), 16.

63 John McCarthy et al., "A Proposal for the Dartmouth Summer Research Program on Artificial Intelligence," *AI Magazine* 27 (2006), 12–14.

64 See Susan Schneider, *Artificial You: AI and the Future of Your Mind* (Princeton: Princeton University Press, 2019); so too Jean-Pierre Dupuy, *The Mechanization of the Mind: The Origins of Cognitive Science* (Princeton: Princeton University Press, 2000).

65 A. M. Turing, "Computing Machinery and Intelligence," *Mind* 59 (1950): 433–60.

66 McCarthy et al., "A Proposal for the Dartmouth Summer Research Program on Artificial Intelligence," 12.

67 In Kwame Appiah's fine formulation: "[T]he options are given in the description of the situation … In the real world, situations are not bundled together with options. In the real world, the act of framing – the act of describing a situation, and thus of determining that there's a decision to be made – is itself a moral task. It's often *the* moral task," *Experiments in Ethics* (Cambridge, MA: Harvard University Press, 2008), 196. See too David N. McNeill, "The Virtue of Error: Solved Games and Ethical Deliberation," *European Journal of Philosophy* 28 (2020): 639–56.

68 "About: Google AI," https://ai.google/about/ (accessed June 10, 2022).

69 Adam Smith, *The Wealth of Nations* (New York: Modern Library, 2000), 839–46.

70 "Make Google Do It … and Then What?" Charlie Warzel, *BuzzFeed*, May 9, 2018, www.buzzfeednews.com/article/charliewarzel/make-google-do-it-and-then-what.

71 A widely cited paper in 2013 – "The Future of Employment," by Carl Benedikt Frey and Michael Osborne, *Oxford Martin Programme on Technology and Employment*, September 17, 2013, www.oxfordmartin.ox.ac.uk/downloads/academic/The_Future_of_Employment.pdf – suggested that 47 percent of American jobs will be vulnerable to "computerization" by the mid-2030s. This has been widely misunderstood to mean that 47 percent of the workforce will be unemployed, but the analysis only applies to work as it is presently conducted. Automatization is in fact likely to have an asymmetric effect over different kinds of employment: service industry and office jobs are much more likely to be automated than work in the arts or the legal profession, say. Some have argued that this will lead to further economic polarization – with high-skilled work accelerating its production, while low-skilled work stays the same.

72 "Want to Write a Bestselling Novel? Use an Algorithm," Donna Ferguson, *The Guardian*, September 23, 2017, www.theguardian.com/money/2017/sep/23/write-bestselling-novel-algorithm-earning-money; "A Code-Obsessed Novelist Builds a Writing Bot," Andrew Leonard, *Wired*, February 6, 2020, www.wired.com/story/code-obsessed-novelist-builds-writing-bot-the-plot-thickens/.

73 "Hollywood Is Quietly Using AI to Decide Which Movies to Make," James Vincent, *The Verge*, May 28, 2019, www.theverge.com/2019/5/28/18637135/hollywood-ai-film-decision-script-analysis-data-machine-learning.

74 "How Smarter AI Will Change Creativity," *The Economist*, June 9, 2022, www.economist.com/leaders/2022/06/09/artificial-intelligences-new-frontier.

75 "7 Ways Artificial Intelligence Is Reinventing Human Resources," Dom Nicastro, *CMS Wire*, May 18, 2020, www.cmswire.com/digital-workplace/7-ways-artificial-intelligence-is-reinventing-human-resources/.

76 "For AI, Data Are Harder to Come by Than You Think," *The Economist*, June 11, 2020, www.economist.com/technology-quarterly/2020/06/11/for-ai-data-are-harder-to-come-by-than-you-think.

77 *Ibid.*

78 "Businesses Are Finding AI Hard to Adopt," *The Economist*, June 11, 2020, www.economist.com/technology-quarterly/2020/06/11/businesses-are-finding-ai-hard-to-adopt.

79 See Nicholas Carr, *The Glass Cage: How Our Computers Are Changing Us* (New York: W.W. Norton, 2014), 197–202.

80 For the point that algorithms are essentially conformist, see Dominque Cardon, *A quoi rêvent les algorithmes. Nos vies à l'heure des big data* (Paris: Seuil, 2015).

81 "Wrongfully Accused by an Algorithm," *The New York Times*, June 24, 2020, www.nytimes.com/2020/06/24/technology/facial-recognition-arrest.html.

82 Milton Friedman, *Essays in Positive Economics* (Chicago: University of Chicago Press, 1953), 3–46.

83 "AI Tool Accurately Predicts Tumour Growth in Cancer Patients," *The Guardian*, April 22, 2022, www.theguardian.com/society/2022/apr/23/cancer-ai-tool-predicts-tumour-regrowth.

84 "The Potential and the Pitfalls of Medical AI," *The Economist*, June 11, 2020, www.economist.com/technology-quarterly/2020/06/11/the-potential-and-the-pitfalls-of-medical-ai.

85 "How AI-Based Training Affected the Performance of Professional Go Players," Jimoon Kang *et al.*, *CHI Conference on Human Factors in Computing Systems*, April 2022, https://doi.org/10.1145/3491102.3517540.

86 Brian Christian, *The Alignment Problem: Machine Learning and Human Values* (New York: W. W. Norton, 2020), 244, 272ff.

87 "The Scientist and the A.I.-Assisted, Remote-Control Killing Machine," *The New York Times*, September 18, 2021, www.nytimes.com/2021/09/18/world/middleeast/iran-nuclear-fakhrizadeh-assassination-israel.html.

88 See "How the Enlightenment Ends," Henry Kissinger, *The Atlantic*, June 2018, www.theatlantic.com/magazine/archive/2018/06/henry-kissinger-ai-could-mean-the-end-of-human-history/559124/?utm_source=eb; "Good for Google, Bad for American," Peter Thiel, *The New York Times*, August 1, 2019, www.nytimes.com/2019/08/01/opinion/peter-thiel-google.html.

89 "Reflections on Violence," Hannah Arendt, *The New York Review of Books*, February 27, 1969, www.nybooks.com/articles/1969/02/27/a-special-supplement-reflections-on-violence/.

90 "Obituary: Stanislav Petrov Was Declared to Have Died on September 18th," *The Economist*, September 30, 2017, www.economist.com/obituary/2017/09/30/obituary-stanislav-petrov-was-declared-to-have-died-on-september-18th.

91 Quoted by David Noble, *The Religion of Technology: The Divinity of Man and the Spirit of Invention* (New York: Penguin, 1999), 160.

92 "Would You Let a Robot Take Care of Your Mother?" Maggie Jackson, *The New York Times*, December 13, 2019, www.nytimes.com/2019/12/13/opinion/robot-caregiver-aging.html; "The Future of Elder Care Is Here – And It's Artificial Intelligence," *The Guardian*, June 3, 2021, www.theguardian.com/us-news/2021/jun/03/elder-care-artificial-intelligence-software.

93 "Something Bothering You? Tell It to Woebot," *The New York Times*, June 1, 2021, www.nytimes.com/2021/06/01/health/artificial-intelligence-therapy-woebot.html; "Riding out Quarantine with a Chatbot Friend: 'I Feel Very Connected,'" *The New York Times*, June 16, 2020, www.nytimes.com/2020/06/16/technology/chatbots-quarantine-coronavirus.html.

94 Turkle, *Alone Together*, 6, 26.

95 Robot Companion, www.robotcompanion.ai (accessed June 10, 2022).

96 Turkle, *Alone Together*, 25.

97 "What Does Having a Boyfriend Have to Do with Sleep?" *The New York Times*, October 2, 2019, www.nytimes.com/2019/10/02/style/asmr-boyfriend-sleep-videos.html?action=click&module=Editors%20Picks&pgtype=Homepage.

98 "Edtech That Helps Teachers Beat Edtech That Replaces Them," *The Economist*, September 18, 2021, www.economist.com/united-states/2021/09/18/edtech-that-helps-teachers-beats-edtech-that-replaces-them.

99 "Learning to Love Our Robot Co-Workers," *The New York Times*, February 23, 2017, www.nytimes.com/2017/02/23/magazine/learning-to-love-our-robot-co-workers.html; "After Years of Dithering, Companies Are Embracing Automation," *The Economist*, January 16, 2021, www.economist.com/business/2021/01/16/after-years-of-dithering-companies-are-embracing-automation.

100 "No Masks, No Coughs: Robots Can Be Just What the Doctor Ordered in the Time of Social Distancing," *The Washington Post,* July 8, 2020, www.washingtonpost.com/world/asia_pacific/covid-robots-social-distance-jobs-japan/2020/07/08/1a82ce96-afc6-11ea-98b5-279a6479a1e4_story.html; "The Rise of the Covid Robots," *The Guardian*, October 2, 2020, www.theguardian.com/world/gallery/2020/oct/02/the-rise-of-the-covid-robots-in-pictures; "Robots Replace Students at Graduation amid Coronavirus," *Reuters*, April 7, 2020, www.reuters.com/article/us-health-coronavirus-japan-remote-gradu/robots-replace-japanese-students-at-graduation-amid-coronavirus-idUSKBN21P0XI.

101 "Riding out Quarantine with a Chatbot Friend," *The New York Times*.

102 Cf. D. W. Winnicott, *Babies and Their Mothers* (Reading: Addison-Wesley, 1987), 98.

103 Robot Companion, www.robotcompanion.ai/ (accessed June 10, 2022).

104 Turing, "Computing Machinery and Intelligence," 435.

105 "A General Reinforcement Learning Algorithm That Masters Chess, Shogi and Go through Self-Play," David Silver *et al.*, *Science* 362 (2018): 1140–44.

106 "AlphaZero: Shedding New Light on Chess, Shogi, and Go," Deep Mind, December 6, 2018, https://deepmind.com/blog/article/alphazero-shedding-new-light-grand-games-chess-shogi-and-go.

107 "One Giant Step for a Chess-Playing Machine," Steven Strogatz, *The New York Times*, December 26, 2018, www.nytimes.com/2018/12/26/science/chess-artificial-intelligence.html.

108 For this episode, see Carr, *The Shallows*, 201–5.

109 Turkle, *Alone Together*, 24.

110 Apple, Siri, https://www.apple.com/siri/ (accessed March 2, 2020).

111 Alexa, https://developer.amazon.com/en-US/alexa/alexa-skills-kit (accessed June 10, 2022).

112 Bixby, www.samsung.com/global/galaxy/apps/bixby/ (accessed March 18, 20).

113 Erica, https://promo.bankofamerica.com/erica/ (accessed October 26, 2018 and June 10, 2022).

114 "Ask Alexa? No, Hear This Alexa," Alexa O'Brien, *The New York Times*, January 16, 2017, www.nytimes.com/2017/01/16/opinion/ask-alexa-no-hear-this-alexa.html.

115 "Over a Million People Asked Amazon's Alexa to Marry them in 2017," *Business Insider*, October 10, 2018, www.businessinsider.com/amazons-alexa-got-over-1-million-marriage-proposals-in-2017-2018-10.

116 "Riding out Quarantine with a Chatbot Friend," *The New York Times* (my emphasis).

117 "A.I. Is Mastering Language. Should We Trust What It Says?" *The New York Times*, April 15, 2022, www.nytimes.com/2022/04/15/magazine/ai-language .html.

118 Carr, *Glass Cage*, 225–8.

119 "Should Robots Have a Face?" *The New York Times*, February 26, 2020, www.nytimes.com/2020/02/26/business/robots-retail-jobs.html?action=click& module=Top%20Stories&pgtype=Homepage.

120 iRobot, www.irobot.com/en_US/why-irobot.html (accessed June 10, 2022).

121 iRobot YouTube ad, September 8, 2021, www.youtube.com/watch?v= v8eYiSlNSBo&ab_channel=iRobot.

122 "Microsoft's Politically Correct Chatbot Is Even Worse Than the Racist One," Chloe Rose Stuart-Ulin, *Quartz*, July 31, 2018, https://qz.com/1340990/ microsofts-politically-correct-chat-bot-is-even-worse-than-its-racist-one/.

123 Doris Lessing, *The Golden Notebook* (New York: HarperCollins, 1999), 256.

124 Turing, "Computing Machinery and Intelligence," 433–34.

125 "Amazon Created a Hiring Tool Using A.I. It Immediately Started Discriminating against Women," *Slate*, October 10, 2018, https://slate.com/business/2018/10/ amazon-artificial-intelligence-hiring-discrimination-women.html.

126 Turing, "Computing Machinery and Intelligence," 434.

127 Bookmark, www.bookmark.com/ai-website-builder (accessed June 10, 2022).

128 "Samsung Adds and Swiftly Removes Sexist Bixby Descriptor Tag," *The Verge*, July 19, 2017, www.theverge.com/2017/7/19/15998668/samsung-adds-removes-sexist-bixby-descriptor-tags.

129 "Jenn, Alaska Air's New IT Girl, Offers Virtual Service with a Smile," *Travel Weekly*, March 31, 2008, www.travelweekly.com/Travel-News/Online-Travel/ Jenn-Alaska-Air-s-new-IT-girl-offers-virtual-service-with-a-smile.

130 "Body Con Job," Emilia Petrarca, *New York Magazine*, May 14, 2018, www .thecut.com/2018/05/lil-miquela-digital-avatar-instagram-influencer.html.

131 See Ellen Lupton, *Mechanical Brides: Women and Machines from Home to Office* (New York: Princeton Architectural Press, 1993), 29–42.

132 "Welcome Our New Fembot Overlords," Amanda Hess, July 30, 2018, www .nytimes.com/2018/07/30/arts/feminized-technology-robots.html.

133 "The Internet, Mon Amour," Virginia Heffernan, *1843 Magazine*, July 3, 2020, www.economist.com/news/2020/06/19/the-internet-mon-amour.

134 On this theme, see David Noble, *A World without Women: The Christian Clerical Culture of Western Science*, Knopf (New York), 1993; the theme is likewise explored at length in Pynchon's *Gravity's Rainbow* (London: Penguin, 1995): "[T]he Rocket was an entire system *won*, away from the feminine darkness, held against the entropies of lovable but scatterbrained Mother Nature" (324).

135 Henry Adams, *The Education of Henry Adams*, 1066ff.

136 Sigmund Freud, *The Freud Reader*, edited by Peter Gay (New York: W.W. Norton, 1989), 275–76.

137 Don DeLillo, *White Noise*, 272.

138 Quoted by Karl Löwith, *From Hegel to Nietzsche* (New York: Columbia University Press, 1991), 154.

139 Quoted by Stephen McKnight, *The Religious Foundations of Francis Bacon's Thought* (Columbia: The University of Missouri Press, 2006), 117.

140 Henry Adams, *The Education of Henry Adams,* 1067.

141 On the sacralizing overtones of the Space Program, see Kendrick Oliver, *To Touch the Face of God: The Sacred, the Profane, and the American Space Program, 1957–75* (Baltimore: Johns Hopkins University Press, 2013). For the theme more broadly, see David Nye, *American Technological Sublime* (Cambridge, MA: MIT Press, 1996).

142 Herzog, *Lo and Behold: Reveries of the Connected World.*

143 Williams, *Stand out of Our Light,* 87.

144 Don DeLillo, *Underworld* (New York: Scribner, 2007), 530.

145 See Lanier, *You Are Not a Gadget,* 45–72.

146 "To Understand the Tech Lords, Look to Their Libraries," *The Economist,* May 15, 2019, www.economist.com/leaders/2019/05/15/to-understand-the-tech-lords-look-to-their-libraries.

147 "Google vs. Death," *Time,* September 18, 2013, https://techland.time.com/2013/09/18/google-vs-death/.

148 "The Marriage of Religion and Technology," Brett Robinson, *Second Nature,* January 27, 2014, https://secondnaturejournal.com/the-marriage-of-religion-and-technology-reading-apples-allegorical-advertising/.

149 For this and other examples of ways in which tech companies dabble with the religious, see Brett Robinson, *Appletopia: Media, Technology, and the Religious Imagination of Steve Jobs* (Waco: Baylor University Press, 2013).

150 Neil Postman, *Technopoly: The Surrender of Culture to Technology* (New York: Vintage, 1992).

151 The classic statement of the problem is Daniel Bell, *The Coming of Post-Industrial Society.*

152 For a good sample: "We Are Merging with Robots. That's a Good Thing," Andy Clark, *The New York Times,* August 13, 2018, www.nytimes.com/2018/08/13/opinion/we-are-merging-with-robots-thats-a-good-thing.html.

153 "Facebook's Next Target: The Religious Experience," *The New York Times,* July 25, 2021, www.nytimes.com/2021/07/25/us/facebook-church.html.

154 William Blake, *The Complete Poetry and Prose of William Blake* (New York: Anchor, 1988), 218.

155 Hans Jonas, *The Phenomenon of Life: Toward a Philosophical Biology* (Evanston: Northwestern University Press, 2001), 110.

156 Marx, *Capital,* 352.

157 Thomas Aquinas, *Summa Theologiae,* I–II, Question 13, Article 2, Reply 3 (my translation).

158 René Descartes, *Discourse on Method and Meditations on First Philosophy,* translated by Donald Cress (Indianapolis: Hackett, 1998), 100.

159 For this quote and many more such from the period, see Allison Muri, *The Enlightenment Cyborg: A History of Communications and Control in the Human Machine, 1660–1830* (Toronto: University of Toronto Press, 2007), 56.

160 Thomas Hobbes, *Leviathan,* edited by Richard Tuck (Cambridge: Cambridge University Press, 1996), 9–10.

161 Julien Offray de la Mettrie, *Man a Machine,* translated by Richard Watson and Maya Rybalka (Indianapolis: Hackett, 1994), 69, 71.

162 So claimed Clark, at least: see Stephen David Snobelen, "Isaac Newton," in *Science and Religion: A Historical Introduction,* edited by Gary Ferngren, Johns Hopkins University Press (Baltimore, 2017), 134.

163 Cf. John G. Daugman, "Brain Metaphor and Brain Theory," in *Computational Neuroscience*, edited by Eric L. Schwartz (Cambridge, MA: MIT Press, 1993), 13.

164 On the merging of our nervous systems with computers, see Carr, *The Shallows*, 213.

165 See this article, both for its content and for the telling ways in which it begs every substantive question about whether the description of brains as computers is warranted in order to make its point: "Face It, Your Brain Is a Computer," Gary Marcus, *The New York Times*, June 27, 2015, www.nytimes.com/2015/06/28/opinion/sunday/face-it-your-brain-is-a-computer.html.

166 Cf. Sherry Turkle, *The Second Self: Computers and the Human Spirit* (Cambridge, MA: MIT Press, 2005), 20: "[The computer] is a projective medium ... as computers become commonplace objects in daily life – in leisure and learning as well as in work – everyone will have the opportunity to interact with them in ways where the machine can act as a projection of part of the self, a mirror of the mind."

167 Barthes, *Mythologies*, 68–70.

168 Turing, "Computing Machinery and Intelligence," 436.

169 "The Cost of Training Machines Is Becoming a Problem," *The Economist*, June 11, 2020, www.economist.com/technology-quarterly/2020/06/11/the-cost-of-training-machines-is-becoming-a-problem.

170 "Driverless Cars Show the Limits of AI," *The Economist*, June 11, 2020, www.economist.com/technology-quarterly/2020/06/11/driverless-cars-show-the-limits-of-todays-ai.

171 See Hubert Dreyfus and Charles Taylor, *Retrieving Realism* (Cambridge MA: Harvard University Press, 2015), 91ff.

172 iPad 3, Official Introduction Video, www.youtube.com/watch?v=K8ecN36Ffpc&ab_channel=MadAssGamers (accessed June 10, 2022).

173 Teilhard de Chardin, *The Phenomenon of Man* (New York: Harper, 1975), 257.

174 "How Uber Uses Psychological Tricks to Push Its Drivers' Buttons," *The New York Times*, April 2, 2017, www.nytimes.com/interactive/2017/04/02/technology/uber-drivers-psychological-tricks.html.

175 See Matthew Crawford, *Shop Class as Soulcraft* (New York: Penguin, 2009), 40ff.

176 Carr, *The Glass Cage*, 78, 181.

177 "Chinese Firms Are Taking a Different Route to Driverless Cars," *The Economist*, October 12, 2019, www.economist.com/business/2019/10/12/chinese-firms-are-taking-a-different-route-to-driverless-cars.

178 Tocqueville, *Democracy in America*, 247, 435.

179 "Why Are So Many Countries Witnessing Mass Protests?" *The Economist*, November 4, 2019, www.economist.com/international/2019/11/04/why-are-so-many-countries-witnessing-mass-protests.

180 See the discussion of the Kinsey Report in Crawford, *World beyond Your Head*, 196–200; and the fine critique of quantification in Morozov, *To Save Everything, Click Here*, 226–67.

181 Christian, *The Alignment Problem*, 44.

182 See "Language Is a Telling Clue to Unacknowledged Racial Attitudes," *The Economist*, June 13, 2020, www.economist.com/books-and-arts/2020/06/12/language-is-a-telling-clue-to-unacknowledged-racial-attitudes.

183 "Wrongfully Accused by an Algorithm," *The New York Times*.

184 "The Opportunities and Risks of K-12 Student Placement Algorithms," Matt Kasman and John Valant, *Brookings*, February 28, 2019, www.brookings.edu/research/the-opportunities-and-risks-of-k-12-student-placement-algorithms/.

185 "Can We Trust Wikipedia? 1.4 Billion People Can't Be Wrong," David Barnett, *The Independent*, February 17, 2018, www.independent.co.uk/news/long_reads/wikipedia-explained-what-it-trustworthy-how-work-wikimedia-2030-a8213446.html.

186 "Artificial Intelligence at Google: Our Principles," https://ai.google/principles/ (accessed June 10, 2022).

187 For this theme, see Christian, *The Alignment Problem*, 13, 318ff.

188 Herbert Marcuse, *One-Dimensional Man: Studies in the Ideology of Advanced Industrial Society* (Boston: Beacon Press, 1991), 231–32.

189 On the basic significance of imitation for digital technology, see Christian, *The Alignment Problem*, 213ff.

190 Greenfield, *Radical Technologies*, 254–56.

191 "It's Alive!" Jennifer Kahn, *Wired*, March 1, 2002, www.wired.com/2002/03/everywhere/.

192 "Google Sidelines Engineer Who Claims Its A.I. Is Sentient," *The New York Times*, June 12, 2022, www.nytimes.com/2022/06/12/technology/google-chatbot-ai-blake-lemoine.html.

193 Ask Delphi, https://delphi.allenai.org.

194 The Moral Machine, www.moralmachine.net/.

195 Noble, *The Religion of Technology*, 146.

196 See Jonas, *The Phenomenon of Life*, 108–27.

197 The conflation is originally Vico's, but the point is beautifully fleshed out in Gaston Bachelard, *The New Scientific Spirit*, translated by Arthur Goldhammer (Boston: Beacon Press, 1984).

198 Arendt, *Origins of Totalitarianism*, 382.

199 See Jeremy Rifkin, *The Age of Access* (New York: Tarcher/Putnam, 2000), 9. See too Hervé Fischer's excellent *Digital Shock*, translated by Rhonda Mullins (Montreal: McGill-Queen's University Press, 2006).

200 *Pirkei Avot* 2:16.

201 Kevin Kelly, *What Technology Wants* (London: Penguin, 2010), 188.

Index

For EU product safety concerns, contact us at Calle de José Abascal, 56–1°,
28003 Madrid, Spain or eugpsr@cambridge.org.

www.ingramcontent.com/pod-product-compliance
Ingram Content Group UK Ltd.
Pitfield, Milton Keynes, MK11 3LW, UK
UKHW010249140625
459647UK00013BA/1755